# THE INDIVIDUAL INVESTOR REVOLUTION

Other books by Charles B. Carlson

*Buying Stocks Without a Broker*

*Chuck Carlson's 60-Second Investor: 201 Tips, Tools, and Tactics for the Time-Strapped Investor*

*Free Lunch on Wall Street: Perks, Freebies, and Giveaways for Investors*

*No-Load Stocks: How to Buy Your First Share & Every Share Directly from the Company with No Broker's Fee*

# THE INDIVIDUAL INVESTOR REVOLUTION

by Charles B. Carlson

McGraw-Hill
New York • San Francisco • Washington, D.C. • Auckland
Bogotá • Caracas • Lisbon • London • Madrid • Mexico City
Milan • Montreal • New Delhi • San Juan • Singapore
Sydney • Tokyo • Toronto

*To my mother and father, for whom it is a privilege to be a son;*
*To Denise, for whom it is a privilege to be a friend.*

**McGraw-Hill**

A Division of The *McGraw·Hill* Companies

1 2 3 4 5 6 7 8 9 0   DOC/DOC   9 0 2 1 0 9 8 7

P/N
PART OF ISBN 0-07-012049-8

The sponsoring editor for this book was Susan Barry and the production
supervisor was Tina Cameron. It was set in Times Ten and Garamond Condensed
by Douglas & Gayle Limited.

Printed and bound by Quebecor/Martinsburg.

McGraw-Hill books are available at special quantity discounts to use as
premiums and sales promotions, or for use in corporate training programs.
For more information, please write to Director of Special Sales, McGraw-Hill,
11 West 19th Street, New York, NY 10011. Or contact your local bookstore.

 This book is printed on recycled, acid-free paper containing a minimum of 50% recycled de-inked fiber.

# CONTENTS

# ACKNOWLEDGMENTS

I'd like to thank the readers of *DRIP Investor*, *No-Load Stock Insider*, and *Dow Theory Forecasts* investment newsletters for their insights over the years—insights that have helped to shape this book's contents.

I would also like to thank my literary agent, Wesley Neff, for his assistance in crafting the book's focus and contents. My editor at McGraw-Hill, Susan Barry, also deserves many thanks for her assistance and patience.

I'd like to thank the staff of Horizon Management Services, especially Elberta Miklusak, Juliann Kessey, Mike Proctor, Rob Baron, Chris Vaughn, David Wright, Tanya Habzansky, Michael Gutierrez, Richard Moroney, and Kenneth Pogach, for their support.

Finally, I would be remiss if I did not give special thanks to Avis Beitz. Avis has been my right-hand person on all of my book projects,

# PREFACE

*Webster defines "revolution" as "a complete change." Notice the word "complete." A revolution is not incremental. Revolution is sweeping, altering forever the very landscape from which it springs.*

The financial markets have undergone a revolution in recent years, one centering on the individual investor. Formerly the "have nots" of the investment world, individual investors are seeing a leveling of the playing field, especially when it comes to access to financial markets. Brokers are no longer a necessity for individual investors to access financial markets. Investors can go it alone via no-load mutual funds, direct-purchase programs, and other investments that require no middleman and, in many cases, no sales fees.

On the information front, individual investors now have at their disposal more market intelligence than ever before, intelligence that had been available only to the biggest investors. Best of all, much of this market intelligence is free or very cheap.

One of the factors driving the individual investor revolution has been technology, most notably the Internet. In many ways, investing has become the "killer application" of the Internet, allowing investors—rich or not so rich, living in the U.S. or anywhere in the world—to participate on an even playing field with institutional investors in terms of access and information.

If you need further evidence of individual investors's growing clout, consider what Wall Street institutions are doing to court the individual investor. The 1997 merger between white-shoe investment banking firm Morgan Stanley and the brokerage firm of Dean Witter (formerly owned by that retailer to the middle-class, Sears, Roebuck) was all about the individual investor. The front-page headline in *The Wall Street Journal* announcing the merger between Dean Witter and Morgan Stanley said it all: "Wall Street Wants The 'Little Guy,' and It Will Merge to Get Him." And Wall Street is not the only suitor of individual investors. Corporate America is courting the little guy, too. "They (individual investors) provide an important balance to institutional holders. Besides that, ours is a global consumer brand, and individual investors can relate to that on a personal level," says Mary Healy, an investor relations specialist at McDonald's, a firm that allows individual investors to buy their first share and every share of stock directly from the company, without a broker.

Why do Wall Street and corporate America now find individual investors irresistible? Money, and lots of it. The liberalization of *individual retirement accounts* (IRAs) and the shift from defined benefit plans (in which a centralized entity chooses the investments and promises a specific pension) to defined contribution plans (in which an employee invests his or her pension directly and the return depends on his or her choices) have put trillions of dollars in the control of individual investors. And with money comes power.

Unfortunately, having the power, the access, the information to compete on a level playing field, and *realizing* you have the power, the access, and the information are often two different things. Many individual investors still believe that they are powerless, that they still must invest on Wall Street's terms, not their own.

This book aims to change all that.

*The Individual Investor Revolution* is an attempt to show individual investors that a revolution is, indeed, occurring, one that puts Wall Street and Main Street on equal footing. But having power is not enough; individual investors must use their newfound power and profitability wisely. For that reason, this book provides a blueprint for maximizing the opportunities that face the individual investor. From buying investments without a broker to taking a global approach with your investments, from strategies for squeezing out every bit of return from your portfolio to simple "macro" tools that give you an edge on the competition, from using the Internet to research and track your investments to building a profitable investment portfolio for the 21st century—*The Individual Investor Revolution* represents a step-by-step blueprint for the successful do-it-yourself investor.

*Chuck Carlson*

# INTRODUCTION

*Beware, Wall Street pros—your big secret is out.*

For many years, Wall Street institutions have perpetuated the idea that you, the individual investor, don't have what it takes to go it alone. You don't have the access to the financial markets that the pros have. You don't have the market intelligence. You don't have the connections. You don't have the technology. In short, you can't possibly succeed on Wall Street without the assistance of Wall Street pros, who gladly will share their knowledge, technology, and access to the markets (for a fat fee, of course).

Fortunately, the investment playing field has leveled dramatically for individual investors in recent years. Now you're never going to hear that from Wall Streeters because they benefit by maintaining the "big secret" of investing. Nevertheless, the fact is that you *do* have what it takes to go it alone on Wall Street. You *do* have the access. You *do* have the market intelligence. You *do* have the technology.

This leveling of the investment playing field, in essence, represents a true revolution for the individual investor, a process of financial empowerment and independence that is likely to accelerate in the years ahead.

In the pages before you is a thorough look at the evolving individual investor revolution on Wall Street. Chapter 1 examines the factors fueling the revolution. Chapter 2 provides 10 simple yet powerful rules for doing battle in the individual investor revolution. In Chapters 3 and 4, you'll explore a key part of this revolution—improved access to the markets. As the chapters show, investors who feel comfortable making their own investment decisions now have a plethora of choices for direct investing. You can now buy hundreds of U.S. and international stocks, treasury securities, and mutual funds without a broker in amounts that make sense for your own pocketbook, and, in many cases, paying little or no fees in the process. Thus, even investors with tiny investment funds have potentially the same access as big institutional investors when it comes to buying nearly any investment.

Of course, improved access to the financial markets without the ability to make sound investment decisions would be of little value. Fortunately, investors today have a myriad of research tools at their disposal that a few years ago were available to only the wealthiest investors. Chapter 5 takes a fresh look at the wealth of investment information and intelligence available today to any investor possessing a computer and modem. It also provides strategies for harnessing the power of the Internet, highlighting the best spots in cyberspace for researching stocks, and tracking your portfolio.

Interestingly, this individual investor revolution is occurring against a backdrop of unprecedented market strength. Indeed, in the last three years (1995–1997), the Standard & Poor's 500 has averaged a gain of more than 31 percent annually. That's nearly three times the long-run average annual return of just 11 percent. Although the strong markets have made most of us richer, they've also made us sloppier investors, especially when it comes to "capturing the crumbs" that can help portfolio returns during more difficult market climates. The long-term winners of the individual investor revolution will be those who don't confuse genius with a bull market, who understand that the extraordinary market gains in recent years are blips and not constants, and who realize the importance of fighting for every last bit of portfolio return. Chapters 6 and 7 provide practical and user-friendly strategies and tools for surviving and thriving in the more challenging investment environments I foresee.

It would be unfair to provide the weapons for fighting the individual investor revolution without providing a comprehensive war plan that pulls all the elements together. Chapter 8 accomplishes this task by providing the ultimate individual investor portfolio for the 21st century.

It's an exciting time to be an individual investor, a time of unprecedented opportunities and limitless investment choices. It's also a time of many challenges. Rest assured, the future is not likely to be as generous or forgiving as the recent past. Successful investors will need a plethora of weapons to win the investment battle that lies ahead. Consider these pages your battle plan for fighting and winning the individual investor revolution.

# CHAPTER ONE

# THE GOLDEN AGE
# OF THE INDIVIDUAL INVESTOR

*These are the best of times for individual investors.*

Never before in the history of the financial markets has it been so easy, convenient, and inexpensive for individual investors to participate in the financial markets on their own terms. Never has there been the wealth of free or nearly-free research tools available to small investors. Never has there been the plethora of investment products catering to individual investors. Never has there been so many low-cost and often no-cost ways to educate oneself on the financial markets. Never has there been the ability to join forces with other individual investors to learn, study, and invest directly. Never has the government been so proactive in providing vehicles and policies to allow self-reliant investors to secure their financial futures.

The sad thing is that although many people are taking advantage of the opportunities presented by this golden age, millions more—the worker making minimum wage, the retiree on a small, fixed income, the single mom struggling each month to make ends meet, the youngster who thinks that investing is an "adult thing"—are not. These investing "have nots" either don't believe this "golden age" exists or think it is only for the wealthy and connected. Certainly someone with modest means and modest understanding of the complex machinations of Wall Street doesn't have the ability to participate in the financial markets, to "get in the game," to go toe-to-toe with the Wall Street pros and win.

I'm here to tell you that's simply not the case. Any investor—young or old, rich or not-so rich—can take advantage of this golden age of the individual investor. How?

1

$ Do you have $25? That's all you need to invest in such blue chips as Coca-Cola, Johnson & Johnson, and Intel—and pay nothing in commissions or brokerage fees.

$ Do you make only minimum wage? That minimum-wage job may give you access to the best deal in the investment world— your company's 401(k). As we'll discuss, a 401(k) allows you to invest even a few dollars a month across a variety of investment vehicles. Not only does a 401(k) plan allow those with meager incomes to get in the game, but the plan allows your money to grow tax-deferred. Better still, your employer may match part or all of your contribution, thus providing you with "free" money.

$ Do you have a computer and can you afford about $19 per month? If so, then you can go online and have access to the type of free market research and information available only to market professionals just a few years ago.

$ Do you have earned income but, because of your age, are no longer allowed to contribute to your regular individual retirement account (IRA)? You still might be able to make contributions to the new Roth IRA and see your money grow tax-deferred and withdrawn tax-free.

$ Are you someone who's short on years and dollars but long on investment "want to"? Even if you are still too young to open up an investment account in your own name, means exist for you to participate in this investor golden age via special investment accounts geared toward children and young adults.

Indeed, a revolution is occurring today on Wall Street, one in which Main Street and Wall Street are competing on a level playing field. In fact, one could argue that the playing field is being tilted in favor of the individual investor, and I'll tell you why later in this chapter. But for now, the key point to understand is the following: You can be a successful player in today's financial markets. You can enjoy the benefits of long-term investing, regardless of the size of your investment nest egg. You have the ability to change your financial future, as well as the financial futures of your children and grandchildren.

You *can* be a winner in the individual investor revolution.

## ACCESS AND INFORMATION

In recent years, Wall Street has seen a revolution in two important areas:

$ Low Cost/No Cost Access to Markets: Using a broker is no longer a prerequisite for participating in the markets. Investors now have the ability to go directly to the company (U.S. or foreign), the mutual fund, or the U.S. Treasury to buy their investments. Investors can even trade investments between themselves without ever going through Wall Street and incurring a commission (I explain this "buddy system" in Chapter 3). If they choose, individuals can invest via such user-friendly programs as IRAs and 401(k) plans, which require little in the way of investment minimums and offer a variety of tax advantages. Furthermore, investors can choose the way they interact in the market—telephone, mail, or the Internet—that's best for them. Best of all, this improved access oftentimes comes with a price tag of zero. That's right—free. And if you decide to use a broker, you can do so for as little as $5 per trade.

$ Information: Want to know a company's financial position? Whether corporate insiders are buying the stock? What competitors are saying about the firm? Or perhaps you'd like to bounce your ideas off other like-minded investors. With an Internet connection and a few keystrokes on your computer, you can have at your disposal a powerful arsenal of investment tools to assist your decision-making process. And these tools, in many cases, are free.

An important catalyst for the individual investor revolution has been technology, specifically the Internet. The Internet has altered forever the way investors interact with the financial markets. It has turned the broker into a computer, allowing investors to trade quickly, efficiently, and very cheaply. The Internet, with its plethora of information sources, has also eliminated the need for the broker as an information source.

## Money Means Power

Another major catalyst for the revolution has been money. Individuals, through stock and mutual fund accounts, 401(k)s, and IRAs, control trillions of dollars. *The Wall Street Journal* estimates that in the last 10 years or so, the percentage of households' financial assets in stocks has more than doubled to about 50 percent. In 1997 alone, investors pumped more than $227 billion into stock equity funds. Demographics ensure that the amount of investment dollars at the disposal of individual investors will continue to swell. It's estimated that by the year 2008, individuals aged 45 to 54—the age group that earns the most and saves the most—will see their numbers increase by nearly 10 million. Another investor-heavy age group—55 to 64—will grow by more than 11 million by 2008.

Another reason Wall Street is panting for individual investors, particularly baby boomers, is the trillion-dollar transfer that will take place over the next decade. According to *Fortune* magazine, over $6 trillion in assets will likely be accumulated by parents of baby boomers through 2011. In what form this trillion-dollar transfer takes place has important ramifications for the financial markets. Obviously, a major component of this asset buildup is real estate. The gravy train in real estate prices for the past two decades created major wealth for some individuals. As real estate is liquidated to settle estates, substantial amounts of money will be freed up for stock investing, either directly or via mutual funds. Once you understand the size of the moneybags controlled by individual investors now and how much those bags will grow over the next 15 years, the reasons for Wall Street's infatuation with individual investors become quite clear.

Money means power on Wall Street, which means Wall Street will do whatever it must to capture these dollars. That means adopting investor-friendly ways of doing business. That's why several full-service brokers are doing what was unthinkable a few years ago—offering no-load mutual funds. That's why you see $5 commissions (or zero commissions, in some cases) for online trading. That's why you see big full-service brokers, who've lost an estimated 25 percent of their business in recent years to discount brokers and mutual funds, scooping up discount brokerage firms that cater to individual investors. That's why you see Morgan Stanley, an investment bank whose traditional ways of making money (corporate underwriting, merger and acquisition advising, bond trading) are volatile and susceptible to profit squeezes, merging with Dean Witter, whose business of managing money for individual investors carries with it more stable profit margins. And Wall Street firms are not the only entities pursuing the individual investor. Corporate America is discovering the value of having individual investors on its shareholder roll and is pursing them vigorously, too. That's why you see more than 400 companies, including such blue chips as General Electric, Wal-Mart, McDonald's, Exxon, IBM, Walt Disney, and Compaq Computer, allowing investors to buy shares directly from the companies—the *first* share and every share—without a broker and for little or no fees.

## UNCLE SAM

Yet another catalyst for the individual investor revolution is the U.S. government. The last two decades have seen a dramatic shift toward more individual investor-oriented policies coming from Washington. This shift has increased the attractiveness of a variety of investments, from stocks and bonds to mutual funds and money-market accounts. For example:

$ When Ronald Reagan took office, the top income tax bracket for individuals was 70 percent. Today, the top tax bracket is 39.6 percent. Individuals in the top tax bracket now keep more than 60 cents of every dollar in dividends versus just 30 cents in 1980. Furthermore, the capital-gains tax rate was recently reduced to 20 percent from 28 percent on investments held more than 12 months. And that rate will drop to 18 percent on investments bought after 2000 and held more than five years. Because it's not what you earn but what you keep that truly matters, the drop in income and capital-gains tax rates over the last 20 years has helped fuel a dramatic rise in after-tax investment returns. This rise increases the attractiveness of "getting in the game" for individual investors.

$ Government legislation leading to the development of 401(k) plans and IRAs (Roth, traditional, and Education) has created opportunities for many investors, including those with limited resources, to access the markets to fund their retirement. (More on 401(k) plans and IRAs in Chapter 3.)

Of course, the government's reasons for creating these programs are self-serving. Each time Uncle Sam liberalizes rules concerning retirement investing, he is saying, "I'm helping you help yourself; don't expect my help down the road because my pockets may be empty." Still, there's no denying the important role Uncle Sam has played in placing power in the hands of individual investors.

This power is especially evident in the shift by corporate America to defined-contribution plans (401(k) programs and the like) from defined-benefit plans. For decades, defined-benefit plans—programs in which companies controlled where money was invested on behalf of employees, and individuals were paid a retirement based primarily on years of service and salary levels—were commonplace in corporate America. With such plans, investors had very little, if any, say in the investment process. Your company made all the decisions. Even if you were the second coming of Warren Buffett, you had no way to take advantage of your investment acumen.

That all changed in 1980. Actually, it was the Revenue Act of 1978 that would change retirement investing forever. Tucked away in the Act, in Section 401, paragraph (k) was a passage that would be added to the Internal Revenue Code to equalize the tax benefits provided by profit-sharing plans to rank-and-file workers and higher-paid employees. This simple piece of the legislation led to a major change in how Americans would save for retirement. Today, 401(k) and defined-contribution plans, which permit individuals to direct the investment of their retirement dollars, have become the retirement program of choice for U.S. companies. As of 1997, more than 25 million employees at 267,000 businesses owned roughly $1 *trillion* in 401(k) plans. That's $1 trillion that is being controlled by individuals who decide where the money goes. This is a revolutionary shift in the power structure of the financial markets.

My guess is that future governmental policies will place greater financial control and power in the hands of John Q. Public. For example, a popular panacea for fixing the Social Security problem is to allow the establishment of personal investment accounts. The National Commission on Retirement Policy, a private group of lawmakers, economists, pension experts, and business executives, released a report in 1998 discussing ways to shore up Social Security. Among the recommendations was a proposal to divert into personal investment accounts two percentage points of the 12.4 percent payroll tax levied on workers and their employers to finance Social Security. The change would allow individuals a choice of investment options for the money accumulating in their government-administered accounts, including stock-index funds and treasury securities. My guess is that sometime within the next decade you will not only be deciding where to invest your 401(k) dollars; you'll also be deciding where to invest at least part of your Social Security dollars.

## STRUCTURAL CHANGES

The growing clout of individual investors is responsible for a number of structural changes in the way Wall Street does business. For example, you might notice that stocks are now quoted in sixteenths. This wasn't always the case. For years, stocks were quoted in eighths on the New York Stock Exchange. The practice of using eighths is said to come from a centuries-ago practice when Spanish pieces were the medium of exchange, and those pieces could be broken into as many as eight pieces. However, when was the last time you bought a gallon of milk for $2 1/8? Or a McDonald's value meal for $3 3/8? Think of the hue and cry that would be heard if your corner grocer priced products to the nearest eighth of a dollar instead of quoting prices in decimals. That store would go out of business in a heartbeat.

One reason stocks continued to be priced in eighths was that the powers that be on Wall Street wanted it that way. Wall Street makes its living on the crumbs left behind by investors, and pricing stocks to the nearest eighth produces huge windfalls for broker-dealers. By some estimates, if stocks were priced just a penny or two cheaper, U.S. investors would save billions of dollars a year. Fortunately, change is on the way. The move to sixteenths is the first step on the way to decimal pricing (pricing stocks to the nearest penny), which is likely to occur sometime within the next three years. Why the change? Individual investors, with the help of a more investor-friendly Securities and Exchange Commission, are pushing for change.

Another structural change is the way Wall Street is approaching traditional *initial public offerings* (IPOs). Historically, individual investors have not had much luck getting a piece of Wall Street's hottest initial public offerings. These IPOs are reserved for the underwriter's biggest and best customers, such as mutual funds and other institutional investors. However, in recognition of the growing clout of the individual investor on Wall Street, a number of investment banks are building relationships with retail brokers to distribute shares of stocks they underwrite to the brokerage firms' customers. Charles Schwab has reached agreements with a number of big Wall Street firms to distribute IPO shares to their customers. Other brokers, such as E*Trade, have similar deals.

In an article describing these relationships, *The Wall Street Journal* sums up succinctly the reason behind these deals: "The moves, which were expected, come as securities firms scramble for access to individual investors and the money they are salting away. At the same time, margins for traditional investment-banking business have declined over the years." Now I'm not saying that every John Q. Investor who wants shares in the hottest IPOs only needs to trade through Schwab to get them; Schwab will likely target, at least initially, more sophisticated clients for IPOs. Still, the fact that investment banks are courting retail brokers means that access to IPOs over time is likely to become easier for small investors.

Another structural change that is putting individuals on a more even keel with institutional investors is the access to trading systems that had previously been used solely by big investors. For example, firms such as Garden State Securities (800-713-3186) in New Jersey and PT Discount Brokerage (800-248-5008) in Chicago give individual investors access to Nasdaq's SelectNet system and Reuters Instinet trading system. These trading systems usually feature favorable bid-ask spreads and low commissions for trading Nasdaq stocks and allow individuals to participate in "after-market trading."

One corporate information vehicle that has been closed to individual investors but will likely open in the future is the corporate conference call. It is not uncommon for corporations to hold conference calls with Wall Street analysts to field questions and keep the analysts apprised of new developments. Individuals have not been welcomed at these conference calls, which is too bad because these calls often contain information that moves stock prices.

Pressure exists, however, to allow individuals similar access to corporations. The Motley Fool financial forum on America Online and the Internet has taken the lead in calling for greater access to corporate conference calls by individual investors. Motley Fool also offers a conference call feature on its Web site (http://www.fool.com).

## OVERCOMING ROADBLOCKS

Despite the millions of investors who have joined the individual investor revolution in recent years, the numbers should be even higher. Unfortunately, too many investors stay on the sidelines for a variety of reasons. There's the fear that you'll lose money, the misconception that you need a lot of money to be an investor, and the concern that you don't know enough to invest wisely. By addressing some of these roadblocks, perhaps those of you who still haven't joined the revolution will change your minds.

### You Can Be a Successful Investor

I have a unique perch from which I watch the investment world. On the one hand, I write investment newsletters geared toward individual investors. I hear from literally thousands of investors every year. I know what individual investors are thinking. I know how they're investing. In many cases, I also know their successes and failures. On the other hand, I'm a professional money manager. I co-manage a no-load mutual fund for the Wisconsin-based Strong Fund Family (the Strong Dow 30 Value Fund). I have a CFA (Chartered Financial Analyst) designation and an MBA from the University of Chicago. I know what unique pressures professionals must overcome to invest successfully. Thus, I see both sides of the investment fence. And I know the following is true—You can be a successful investor. Don't be intimidated by the trappings of Wall Street, the jargon of the markets, the air of superiority given off by so-called "experts." I've heard from many individual investors who started with little knowledge and tiny bank accounts who did fine in the financial markets. You can, too.

Now don't expect to hear that from other Wall Street professionals. After all, Wall Street often refers to individual investors as "dumb money." The "smart money," of course, are the geniuses who work on Wall Street. Wall Street's conventional wisdom says that you're better off following the moves of "smart money" investors while doing just the opposite of what the "dumb money" investors—that's you— are doing. I'm sure there was a time when individual investors were dangerously uninformed. Quite frankly, up until the mid-1970s, few good reasons existed to educate oneself. Even if you made your own investment decision, you still had to use a full-service broker and pay top buck to execute a trade.

However, with the advent of discount brokers, no-load mutual funds, and dividend reinvestment/direct-purchase plans, the payoff from becoming a self-reliant investor has grown tremendously. Today, thanks to the plethora of financial newsletters, magazines, books, newspapers, tv and radio shows, and online financial information, it has never been easier or cheaper for individuals to educate themselves on investments. And millions of investors are availing themselves of this educational process. I meet thousands of investors each year via my speaking engagements. What I see are small investors who increasingly understand market risk, who know the importance of diversification, and who are willing to look further ahead than the next week or month in order to achieve decent market returns.

In fact, in many respects the playing field is now tilted *in favor* of individual investors. You don't have to deal with a lot of the issues and pressures that cause professionals, especially mutual-fund managers, to post mediocre results:

$ *You don't have to deal with cash inflows/redemptions.* Mutual-fund managers are constantly dealing with the problem of how to handle cash inflows. Holding too much cash can be death to a fund's performance if the market is rising. Yet if a fund manager has only so many investment ideas, he or she may be forced to put more money into stocks in which he or she otherwise would not choose to invest. Let's also say you're a fund manager who buys small-capitalization stocks. And let's say you're good at your job and your performance is excellent. What happens is that you'll be flooded with new money from investors chasing your performance record. Unfortunately, the stocks your fund could buy when it had $50 million in fund assets may not be the type of stocks you can buy when your fund has $500 million or $1 billion in assets. You might have to broaden your investment universe in order to accommodate money flows. This means that you may be forced to change your investment style. It's not uncommon for many top-performing mutual funds to migrate toward mediocrity as the fund's asset size grows. Another problem for fund mangers is cash outflows. Because most mutual funds don't have a lot of cash in reserve, redemptions by fund holders may force a fund manager to sell stock. You might also be forced to sell shares at the precise time you want to be a buyer rather than a seller. Your hands are tied, however. Individual investors don't have the problems of cash inflows and redemptions. Chances are, you're not receiving millions of dollars every day to put to work in the market. Likewise, only you can trigger redemptions in your portfolio by deciding to sell stock.

$ *Your performance isn't posted every day in the newspaper.* Mutual-fund managers have their performance displayed every day in the newspaper. Having to show the world how you did each day is yet another pressure that fund mangers have to handle, and this pressure may skew investment decisions to an extremely short-term time frame. Individual investors don't have this pressure.

$ *You don't have to deal with bosses, fundholders, and a board of directors.* Pressure makes investors do funny things. The more pressure on a fund manager, the more likely the pressure will cloud decision-making. Individual investors don't have to deal with such pressures.

$ *You don't have to deal with an investment committee.* Many mutual funds and investment companies have committees that pass judgment on recommendations made by analysts.

Committees have become more prevalent as fund companies, stung by the departures of "star" fund managers, have moved toward selling investors on their funds' particular investment approach, not its "star" people. Investment committees can provide consistency to the decision-making process. Committees also lead to watered-down recommendations that are palatable to the whole group. Unfortunately, in the investment world, it's often the renegade investment choice, the one that requires a bit of contrary thinking, the one on which you'll never get 10 people on a committee to sign off, that produces the biggest results. Individual investors don't have to run their best ideas past anyone for approval.

$ *You don't have to worry about short-term performance.* The name of the game in the mutual-fund business is asset accumulation. Because most investors choose funds based on performance, a mutual fund cannot afford to have too many bad quarters. Thus, most managers don't run funds with two- or three-year time horizons in mind. Three months is more like it. Short-term thinking often causes fund managers to chase hot stocks, avoid long-term (but highly profitable) turnaround situations, buy and sell stocks too quickly, or shift styles to catch the latest investing style *du jour*. Individual investors don't have to worry about short-term performance. You can buy undervalued stocks and wait for the value to be realized. You don't have pressure to switch investment styles in order to focus on good short-term performance. You can invest for the long term and avoid incurring transaction costs and tax liabilities.

$ *Your hands aren't tied when it comes to owning an investment.* Robert Stansky, the manager of the $70 billion-plus Fidelity Magellan Fund, can't buy small- and micro-cap stocks (these are stocks with market capitalizations—which are the stock prices multiplied by the number of outstanding shares—of $500 million or less). The fund is too big to invest in small stocks. Thus, Mr. Stansky's universe of investment possibilities is limited. You don't have this problem. Being able to choose any investment across all asset classes enhances your flexibility. Many professionals don't have this luxury.

$ *You can use certain no-cost investment plans that exclude professionals.* Chapter 3 discusses *dividend reinvestment plans* (DRIPs), which are programs that allow investors to buy stock directly from the company without a broker and often without paying any brokerage fees. In some DRIPs, you can even buy stock at a *discount* to the market price. This no-cost investment vehicle is available only to investors who register stock in their own name. Fund managers and other market professionals, who hold shares in "street" name, can't participate.

## GETTING STARTED HAS NEVER BEEN EASIER

Many investors remain on the sidelines because they don't know how to get started. They don't have a broker. They don't know how to go about getting a broker. They don't have enough money to open a brokerage account. (Some brokers require $1000 or more to open an account.) Fortunately, it's never been easier to get in the investment game. In many cases, a telephone is all you need to obtain the necessary information to purchase thousands of stocks and mutual funds. Chapter 3 discusses step-by-step strategies for buying stocks and mutual funds without using a broker and without laying out thousands to set up accounts.

### You Have Enough Money To Start Investing

One of the great misconceptions about investing is that it is a rich person's game. It is not. If you have $25 or $50, you can own stocks. If you have $100 or more, you can own mutual funds. If you can spare $5 or $10 from your paycheck each week, you can participate in your company's 401(k) plan.

Now some of you might be asking, "What can investing $25 or $50 a month do for my financial well-being?" In a year or two, not much. In 10 or 20 or 40 years, it can change your life. For example, a 22-year old who invests $50 per month and earns on average 10 percent a year will amass nearly $319,000 when he or she reaches the age of 62. In Chapter 3, I'll show you how to build stock portfolios with just $100, $500, and $1000. I'll also give you a list of top-rated fund families that allow you to get started with just $50 or $100.

### You Can't Afford NOT To Join
### The Individual Investor Revolution

You're probably going to live longer than you think. With life expectancy rates increasing and medical advances being announced almost on a daily basis, chances are that even if you are in your 60s today, you'll live at least another 20 years. And if you're in your 30s or 40s, you probably haven't even reached half-time yet. Given that we are living longer, our finances will have to last longer, too. This means that growing your financial resources is going to be very important whether you're 30 years old or twice that. You cannot grow your assets sitting on the sidelines. Furthermore, you cannot depend on the government to take care of you in retirement.

This latter statement is especially important in terms of the risks you run staying out of the revolution. As I've already stated, the government, by liberalizing retirement programs, is basically telling you that it's up to *you* to take care of your financial future. Apparently, many Americans don't think Uncle Sam is bluffing. According to a survey in *Smart Money* magazine, nearly twice as many young adults believe in the existence of extraterrestrial life than in the likelihood of ever cashing a Social Security check. That the long-term solvency of Social Security ranks below space aliens on young adults' believability scale may be hard to fathom for individuals currently cashing Social Security checks. Trust me—the fears of the eventual extinction of Social Security are quite real, and not just with young adults. Plenty of baby boomers in their 40s and 50s have similar feelings. I, for one, don't factor in any money coming from Social Security when I plan my retirement investment program.

Now some experts believe the fears of a bankrupt Social Security system are unfounded. Let's assume these experts are right. Does that mean that tomorrow's retirees can rest easy, relying exclusively on Social Security as a means to enjoy those golden years? It's important to understand that few people currently receiving Social Security checks live the life of Riley. The percentage of retirees who rely on Social Security for half or more of their income is 66 percent; the percentage of elderly who would fall below the poverty line without Social Security benefits is 54 percent. Regardless of whether Social Security will be around when you get the gold watch, it's clear that individuals will have an increasing responsibility for their financial well-being during retirement. What can you do to ensure a financially sound retirement? Obviously, the sooner you get started investing for retirement, the better. I'll give you ideas for retirement investing in Chapter 3.

## Avoiding Risk Can Be Hazardous To Your Wealth

Investors often avoid the markets because they're afraid of losing money. Avoiding risk, however, means relegating your portfolio to subpar returns. Risk and return are joined at the hip. You cannot have higher expected returns without assuming higher expected risks. (The only exception to this rule is generating higher returns by reducing transaction costs. This concept is discussed later in this book.) In order to grow your portfolio, you'll have to assume some risk.

How do you reduce your portfolio risk? Lengthening your investment time horizon is one way. Holding stocks for 10 years is a lot less risky than holding stocks for one or two years. From year to year, stocks may move up or down. The longer you hold stocks, however, the more likely you'll produce gains. Also understand that investment risk not only means being in stocks when they decline, but being out of stocks when they advance. I think this is perhaps the biggest risk of investing—the "lost" opportunity from being on the sidelines when stocks advance. How do you lessen this risk? Get in the market as soon as possible and stay in the market.

Another risk your portfolio faces is inflation risk, which is the risk that inflation will erode the value of your portfolio over time. How do you lessen inflation risk? Buy stocks and equity mutual funds. Stocks are the best investment for negating the effects of inflation.

The Pioneer Group, a financial-services firm, studied the returns of the 30 stocks in the Dow Jones Industrial Average from the end of 1974 to the end of 1994. What the firm found was that only one of the 30 Dow stocks, Bethlehem Steel (which is no longer a Dow 30 stock), failed to beat the cost of living. The cost of living increased roughly five percent a year over the 20-year time frame. Bethlehem Steel rose 1.6 percent annually for the period. The top five performers on the Dow during the 20-year period were Boeing (with an average annual rate of return of 25 percent for the period), Coca-Cola (21 percent), Disney (21 percent), Philip Morris (20 percent), and Exxon (nearly 18 percent). Bottom line: If you want to grow your portfolio, negate the effects of inflation, and maximize the power of time in an investment program, you must own stocks.

A rule of thumb says you should take your age minus 110, and that's the percentage of your portfolio you should have in stocks or stock mutual funds. Thus, a 70-year old could have as much as 40 percent of his or her portfolio in stocks. Of course, not all 70-year olds are alike. Financial situations, debt obligations, and health conditions dictate how far a 70-year old can stray from this 40 percent benchmark. Still, I see too many retirees get out of stocks entirely because of risk aversion. This is a mistake. You should always have some stock representation in a portfolio, whether you're 9 or 90 years old.

## You Know More Than You Think

Many individuals never join the individual investor revolution because they feel they don't know enough to succeed. Sure, maybe you aren't up on the latest investment lingo, or perhaps you may not be skillful in reading an income statement. However, you make choices every day in terms of what products or services you use based on price, quality, and service. Whether you realize it or not, the judgments you make about products and services relate directly to judgments about companies providing these goods and services. Some of the best investments I've ever made had nothing to do with analyzing a financial statement but everything to do with analyzing a company's product. Your role as a consumer is not the only source of investment information. You probably work in a particular industry. My guess is that you have a good sense whom the winners and losers are in that particular industry, if the industry is booming or hurting, and if the future is likely to be better than the past. This is all valuable information that can be put to use in an investment program.

On the following page is a list of companies that represent household names to most people. Chances are, all of you have used the companies' products at one time or another. These are hardly "undiscovered" stocks. You probably view them as solid companies. You also probably are saying to yourself that investing in any of these companies is not exactly rocket science; they're acknowledged industry leaders. That's precisely my point. Look how well these "obvious" investments have done over the last five years.

Some of these investments did better than the overall market for that time period; others trailed the market. *All*, however, did much better than your passbook savings account or bank certificates of deposit. Was the risk level higher for these investments? If you measure risk in terms of volatility, the answer is yes. However, holding stocks for a five-year time frame reduces the potential risk versus holding stocks for a single year. Also, if you measure risk in terms of opportunity costs ("lost" money due to poor returns over time), I'd argue that your bank passbook account is a "riskier" investment than stocks over a five-year period. The upshot is that you probably have the ability to do a decent job selecting individual stocks. And if you want to educate yourself, there have never been more inexpensive and accessible avenues to do so. For example, the Internet, discussed in Chapter 5, is truly an amazing tool for investment education and research.

| Company | Total Return (12/31/92–12/31/97) |
| --- | --- |
| American Express | 362 percent |
| Disney (Walt) | 138 percent |
| Eastman Kodak | 117 percent |
| Exxon | 145 percent |
| Ford Motor | 175 percent |
| General Electric | 291 percent |
| Gillette | 276 percent |
| Home Depot | 78 percent |
| IBM | 349 percent |
| McDonald's | 103 percent |
| Merck & Co. | 183 percent |
| Procter & Gamble | 234 percent |
| Sears, Roebuck | 217 percent |

Source: Microsoft Investor

## ▼ CONCLUSION . . .

The risk I run when I try to tell individual investors that there is a revolution at hand and that they can win on Wall Street is that I start to sound like that "self-help" blather on late-night infomercials. Don't get me wrong. Successful investing does not happen without effort on your part. (Buying this book is a good first step.) Still, if you take only one thing away from this chapter and, indeed, this book, I hope it's the following: *You can do it*. You can be a winner in the individual investor revolution. The rest of this book will show you how.

# CHAPTER TWO

# CARLSON'S 10 RULES OF ENGAGEMENT: DOING BATTLE IN THE INDIVIDUAL INVESTOR REVOLUTION

Go to the bookstore and find the personal finance/investment section. What you'll see on the shelves are lots of books with numbers in their titles—this "seven-point system" for success; that "nine-step program" for financial freedom; those "24 keys" to successful investing. Why all the numbers? Simple. Numbers imply a plan, a process, a blueprint for leading you from point A to point B. After all, isn't that what all of us want? Take my hand and lead me step-by-step down the path to prosperity.

Quite frankly, I'm a little burned out by all the numbers. However, in the interest of clarity and simplicity (and because my editor says numbers sell), I've put together my own set of numbers: Carlson's 10 Rules of Engagement.

Are *my* numbers better than *their* numbers? Of course. But if you adopted *any* system espoused by one of the plethora of personal finance books, you'd probably be better off than having no system or strategy at all. After all, you can't win a battle without a battle plan. And make no mistake—the individual investor revolution is a real battle, a war for your wallet. If you think I'm kidding, you've never met an investment banker, fund manager, or stockbroker.

## RULE #1: IF YOU'RE NOT IN THE GAME, GET IN THE GAME AS SOON AS POSSIBLE.

There is never a bad time to get started investing, and there is never a good excuse for not starting. I don't care if you think the market today (or tomorrow or next year) is too high. I don't care if you think you don't know enough about investing. I don't care if you think you don't have enough money. Get in the game as soon as possible, even if it's with just $10 or $25 or $50.

The reason that getting in the game is important is because the biggest success factor influencing your portfolio is how well you harness the power of time. The beauty of time is that it doesn't depend on how smart you are, how much money you have, or how well-connected you are. Time is the great equalizer for investors. Indeed, time is available to everyone. If time is the most influential factor on your portfolio's performance, it follows that the most important thing you can do is to get started on an investment program as soon as possible.

Now I know what some of you are thinking. The stock market has soared in the last three years. Stock valuations, according to the market experts, are at all-time highs. The market is due for a huge correction. Why should I be investing now? The problem with this thinking is that determining whether the market is "too high" is really a loser's game. For example, how many people refused to invest in 1994 because they thought the market was too high, only to see the market skyrocket in 1995. How many people refused to invest in 1996 because the market was strong in 1995? How many people refused to get started in 1997 because they felt that, after strong periods in 1995 and 1996, the market had to come down? In each case, those who waited lost out on huge gains.

The problem with trying to time your way into the market is that, in most cases, you'll fail to put your plan into action. Perhaps you tell yourself that you'll start once the market drops 10 percent from its current level. Now say the market does, in fact, decline as you hoped. What will you likely do? My guess is that you won't invest because you'll get scared that the market is going to drop even further. So you wait some more. Then what happens? The market starts to take off. What do you do? More than likely, you'll hold off buying because you don't want to chase stocks. And the cycle starts all over again—waiting for the market to drop, getting scared once it drops, watching the market rebound, and you're still on the sidelines. Remember: Every day you wait to invest, you diminish the power of the biggest success factor for your portfolio—time.

Neuberger & Berman, a mutual-fund family, calculated the results that would have been achieved by two hypothetical investors in the stock market following different strategies. One investor, "Early Bird," invested $2000 per year for 10 years beginning in 1967 (1967 through 1976). Early Bird's investing timing was terrible, as EB invested that $2000 each year at the exact market top. In other words, EB's market timing was the absolute worst it could be.

The other investor, "Late Bird," put up $40,000 in 20 annual increments of $2000 each from 1976 to 1995. Late Bird was a much better market timer. Indeed, LB's annual $2000 contribution was invested at the market's low point every year, a perfect 20-year timing record. So which bird had the bigger nest egg at the end of 1997 (using the Standard & Poor's 500 as a yardstick)? Surprisingly, Early Bird's portfolio had a value of approximately $500,000 versus around $425,000 for Late Bird. Even with investing twice as much and having perfect market timing each year for 20 years, Late Bird came out on the short end because of a later start. Bottom line: It's better to be early than smart in investing. Just ask Early Bird.

*If you're not in the market, there's never a bad time to start.*

A fairly dramatic example of the power of time in an investment program is provided by one of my subscribers to *DRIP Investor* newsletter. This subscriber invests approximately $4000 shortly after the birth of each grandchild. This $4000 is earmarked to fund the grandchild's retirement. Do you know how much that $4000 investment, without contributing another dime to it, will grow to when the grandchild retires at age 65? *Two million.* (That assumes a 10 percent annual return.) Now, some of you may be saying that $2 million won't be worth much 65 years from now. Let's say inflation cuts the real value in half or even by three-quarters. That means the grandchild will still have an after-inflation nest egg of $500,000 or more—not a bad legacy to leave to a grandchild.

*If you're not in the market, there's never a bad time to start.*

The last point I'll make concerning Rule #1 deals with this oft-asked question: As a market newcomer, am I better off investing all of my money at once or feeding my money into the market over time? Richard Williams and Peter Bacon of Wright State University, in a detailed study covering the years 1926 to 1991, suggest that nearly two-thirds of the time a lump-sum investment strategy significantly outperformed a strategy of feeding money into the market over time. One reason is that the stock market historically has risen more often that it has declined. Holding money on the sidelines generally costs investors in lost returns. Does that mean that a newcomer to the stock market should put all of his or her money into stocks immediately, regardless of market levels? Perhaps. Most people, however, find lump-sum investing nerve-racking. I don't see anything wrong with feeding money into the market over time if this strategy makes it easier for you to get started in the first place.

*Remember: If you're not in the market, there's never a bad time to start.*

## RULE #2: IF YOU'RE IN THE GAME, STAY IN THE GAME.

What is the biggest risk of investing?

You probably think it's being in the market when the market crashes.

You're wrong.

In my opinion, the biggest risk of investing is being out of the market when the market advances. Pulling money out of the market and sitting on the sidelines is often a recipe for disaster. Look at a chart of the Dow Jones Industrial Average in Figure 2.1. What is the overall trend of the market over the last 30 years? Up. To be sure, there have been periods of downward movement during the last 30 years. The fact is, however, that the market over time tends to move higher. According to the research company Ibbotson Associates, stocks have risen in more than two out of every three years since 1926. Anytime you pull money out of the market, you're bucking a strong long-term upward trend.

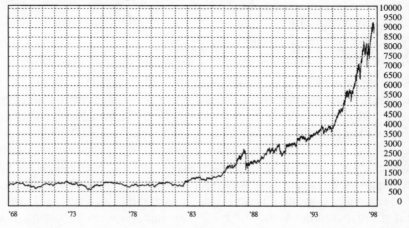

**Dow Jones Industrials Average**

**Figure 2.1**

Markets move in bursts and you have to be in the market to capture these bursts. Let's look at market action during 1997. Early in the year, the market underwent a fairly stiff correction that carried the Dow Jones Industrials to around the 6400 level. What happened next is what makes selling stocks so dangerous. From April to August, the Dow Industrials proceeded to rise more than 1800 points to an all-time high of more than 8259. Now I know there were plenty of investors who sold stock during the April 1997 decline but were left at the starting gate when the market exploded. To me, their biggest risk was not being invested during the decline to 6400, but being out of the market when it soared to 8259.

*If you're in the market, stay in the market.*

One of the best examples of how markets move in fits and starts was a 1991 study by two college professors, P.R. Chandy and William Reichenstein. They looked at monthly market returns from 1926 through 1987 and found that if the 50 best monthly market returns were eliminated, the S&P 500's 62-year return would be *zero*. In other words, if you had chosen the absolutely wrong 50 months to be out of the market but were invested in the market the remaining 93.3 percent of the time, your return would have been nil. This study clearly indicates that trying to time the market can expose you to more risk over time than merely riding through the market's up and downs with a buy-and-hold approach.

*If you're in the market, stay in the market.*

Ibbotson Associates looked at rolling five-year market periods since 1926 (1926–31, 1927–32, 1928–33, and so on). What Ibbotson found was that investors who held stocks for five years at a time would have lost money in only seven of the 60-plus rolling five-year periods since 1926, and four of the seven periods encompassed the 1929 crash.

*If you're in the market, stay in the market.*

I came across the following study in *Investor's Business Daily* that provides an interesting angle on the notion of timing the market versus a buy-and-hold strategy. The study looked at the difference in investment returns achieved by an individual who invested $1000 in the Dow Jones Industrials at the market high in each of the past 20 years versus an individual who invested $1000 in the Dow at the market low every year over the same period. What the study found was that if you invested at the market high every year, you would have earned roughly 80 percent of what you would have had with perfect timing (buying at the low every year). Thus, the reward for perfect market timing every year for 20 years was just 20 percent. When you consider the chances of achieving perfect market timing for 20 consecutive years (nonexistent) and the payoff if you beat these miraculous odds (surprisingly skimpy), you wonder why anyone tries to time the market. The study concluded, "The biggest mistake would have been not to invest at all." Unfortunately, being out of the market is usually what happens when investors sell stocks in hopes of buying them back at market lows.

*If you're in the market, stay in the market.*

Bottom line: Nobody knows for sure if stocks are "too high" or "too low." What we do know is that corporate earnings, which are ultimately the most important long-term driver of stock prices, will be higher five, 10, and 15 years from now. Higher corporate profits mean higher stock prices over time. Your odds of benefiting from this rise in stock prices will be a whole lot better if you refuse to play the "trading game."

---

### Invest Regularly

A critical aspect of staying in the game is investing regularly, in good markets and especially in bad ones. Indeed, it is the investor who has the courage to maintain a regular investment program during down market periods who wins big over time. Take a look again at Figure 2.1. If you are a long-term investor, you *have* to buy when the market falls. That's how you maximize the profit potential of a long-term investment strategy. Because the market's long-term trend is up, market declines must be viewed as opportunities rather than tragedies. Of course, you might have to wait two, five, or 10 years with your investments before the market's long-term upward trend kicks back in. Nevertheless, there's a strong probability that you'll eventually be rewarded for buying on declines.

Even if you always end up buying stocks at the worst possible time every year, you'll still get bailed out by the market's long-term upward trend. A study conducted by T. Rowe Price, the mutual-fund giant, examined stock purchases at the exact worst time each year from 1969 to 1989. In the study, $2000 was invested each year in the S&P 500 index at its annual peak, and dividends were reinvested. The study found that even if an individual invested at the market's high point each year, his or her account value at the end of the 20-year period would be more than four times the cumulative investment during that time. In other words, when buying and holding stocks, even when stocks are purchased at the top, investors usually do rather well over time. "For those with a long-term investment horizon and the discipline to stay the course, the commitment to invest may be more important than the timing of the investment," said the director of the T. Rowe Price study.

## Dollar-Cost Averaging

Successful investors invest as regularly as their finances allow. This means investing during down market periods as well as up market periods. In fact, the successful investor knows that investments made during market declines are usually the ones that provide the biggest bang over the life of the portfolio. One regular investment strategy that is especially effective for keeping you in the market and forcing you to buy during declines is *dollar-cost averaging* (DCA).

DCA is a mechanical strategy that takes all the guesswork and emotion out of investing. Instead of trying to time market purchases, investors who use dollar-cost averaging make regular investments, regardless of market levels. For example, an investor may allocate $100 per month to invest in a particular mutual fund or stock. DCA says that the individual makes the $100 investment each month regardless of the investment's price. If the stock is at high levels, the $100 purchases fewer shares; if the stock is at depressed prices, the $100 investment buys more shares. Using a DCA strategy, your average cost of a stock will always be less than the average of the prices at the time the purchases were made.

DCA is really a form of time diversification. Because your investments are done over a period of time, you are assured of not always buying at the top. Of course, DCA can be a dangerous strategy if the stock you are buying falls sharply and never rebounds. For that reason, I suggest sticking with high-quality, industry leaders when dollar-cost averaging.

Some investors may use a modified dollar-cost averaging program. For example, if a stock you own has been hit especially hard during a market correction, you can increase your regular investment a bit to take advantage of the big price decline. (I do this in my own investment portfolio.) Conversely, you might feel that one of your stocks is trading at especially high levels and you might reduce your regular investment a bit. Intuitively, modified dollar-cost averaging is appealing, as you leverage your investments on the downside while limiting investments on the upside.

The problem with such a program is that you are injecting timing into the equation on the basis of your perceptions of value, the very thing that you were trying to avoid with dollar-cost averaging. Perhaps your valuation model is flawed. You may be buying ever-decreasing dollar amounts of stock that will become a huge winner. The other potential problem with modified dollar-cost averaging based on valuation models is that you are buying greater dollar amounts as the stock drops than you would under basic dollar-cost averaging. Although this strategy will pay off when the stock turns around, it is especially disastrous if the stock continues to fall. For these reasons, if you tweak a dollar-cost averaging program to account for your perceptions of value, make sure the tweaks are small. Chapter 7 discusses effective "macro" tools for fine-tuning an investment program.

## Value Averaging

A form of dollar-cost averaging that is useful in keeping investors in the market is value averaging. Value averaging says that, instead of making the same investment each month in a stock or mutual fund, you vary the amount invested so that the value of the portfolio increases by a fixed sum or percentage each interval.

For example, let's say that, instead of investing $300 each month, you want the value of your investment to rise by $300 each month. In month 1, the value of your investment rises $200. Under value averaging, you would add $100 to the investment to achieve your plan of having the investment increase $300 each month. Now let's say that the investment rises $400 in a given month. Because you want the investment to rise $300, you would sell $100 worth of the investment. Conversely, let's say the value of the investment drops $200 in a given month. Because you want the value of the investment to rise $300 each month, you would contribute $500 for that month—$200 to offset the loss plus $300 to increase the value of the portfolio.

An easy way to compare value averaging with the basic dollar-cost averaging is to think in the following terms:

$   With dollar-cost averaging, you know how much you'll invest, but you don't know what the value will be at the end of your investment horizon.

$   With value averaging, you know how much your portfolio will be worth at the end of your investment horizon, but you don't know how much it will cost out of your pocket.

When examined in these terms, it's easy to see that value averaging is a more aggressive strategy than dollar-cost averaging. The total amount you invest is not constrained, as it is under dollar-cost averaging. Another negative of value averaging compared with dollar-cost averaging is that the strategy can create more transaction costs because you may have to sell shares to stay within your parameters. The selling also creates tax consequences. Finally, value averaging requires more monitoring than a basic dollar-cost averaging program.

Still, studies have shown that returns from value averaging compare favorably with dollar-cost averaging. Michael Edleson, who popularized value averaging with his book, *Value Averaging: The Safe and Easy Strategy for Higher Investment Returns* (International Publishing), ran 50 computer simulations over a variety of five-year market periods. More than 90 percent of the time, value averaging outperformed dollar-cost averaging.

Which method is appropriate for you? It depends to a large extent on how much time you want to spend monitoring your portfolio, how aggressive you want to be (remember that value averaging is more aggressive, because there is no cap on how much you invest to maintain the system), and how much you can afford to invest. If you invest $25 or $50 in a particular investment each month, it's easier to dollar-cost average. If you invest $1000 or more a month, however, value averaging may be more attractive to you.

Whichever strategy you choose, dollar-cost averaging, modified DCA, value averaging, or some other system, the key is that you stay in the game and invest regularly.

## RULE #3: KEEP YOUR BATTLE PLAN SIMPLE AND EFFICIENT.

Having a simple investment strategy has a variety of benefits. First, a simple investment approach is easier to implement and monitor over time. I see many investment programs get bogged down needlessly by investors making the investment process more complicated than need be. Here are some ways to keep your investment simple and efficient yet productive:

$ *Diversify—to a point.* Successful investors understand the importance of diversification when constructing an investment program. Proper diversification, however, does not mean owning 50 stocks, 12 mutual funds, and a partridge and a pear tree. An investor can achieve adequate diversification by owning 13 to 17 stocks, especially when these stocks are combined with mutual funds and other investments in a portfolio. Figure 2.2 shows the diminishing diversification benefits of adding stocks to a portfolio once you get more than 20 holdings. Having a diversified yet manageable number of holdings is the best way to maintain a reasonably simple investment plan, minimize risk, and leverage your best investment ideas.

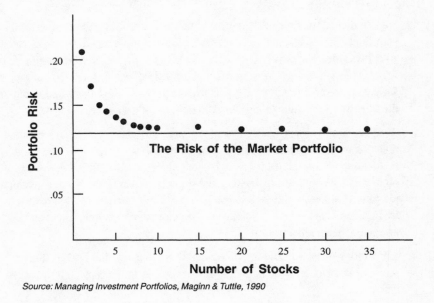

Source: Managing Investment Portfolios, Maginn & Tuttle, 1990

**Figure 2.2**

$ *Be a reluctant seller.* I talk about the pitfalls of frequent portfolio selling in detail in Chapter 8, but for our purposes here, being a reluctant seller of investments has many advantages in terms of portfolio simplicity and efficiency. Every time you sell, you incur transaction costs. You'll also incur a tax liability if you have a gain in the stock. Being transaction- and tax-efficient in your investment approach have a big impact on your portfolio over time. Selling investments frequently also complicates your strategy by having to reinvest the proceeds. Granted, some legitimate reasons to sell stocks exist. Rising debt levels and stupid acquisitions are two of my favorites. Still, selling stocks gingerly is an appropriate way to run a portfolio. The recent tax law change, which reduces the capital-gains tax to 20 percent for investments held for at least 12 months, puts an even greater premium on being a reluctant seller.

## RULE #4: PLAY TO YOUR STRENGTHS.

For more than 10 years, I've been a Chicago Bulls season ticketholder. That privilege has allowed me to see perhaps the greatest athlete of the 20th century, Michael Jordan, perform on a regular basis. The Bulls have won championship after championship because the team plays to its strengths, primarily Number 23. When you have the best player on the planet, you don't sit him on the bench. You maximize his talents. That may mean getting Michael 25 or 30 shots a game in order to win. It may mean using Michael as a decoy to free up another player for an open shot. Whatever the situation, your game plan is built around tapping the strengths you have as a team.

Investing is no different. It's foolish not to use whatever advantages you have when doing battle in the individual investor revolution. One advantage you can bring to the battle is special expertise in a particular industry. As discussed in Chapter 1, you probably know more than you think when it comes to a particular company or industry group. That's an advantage that should be reflected in your investment approach.

Another advantage you have is the ability to invest for the long term. Many institutional investors don't have the luxury of looking five or 10 years down the road. Their paychecks are predicated on performance today and tomorrow, not next year or next decade. Because you have the luxury of time, you should use this advantage in your investment program. How? One way is by buying stocks that may be out of favor in the near term but whose prospects are solid over the long term.

You also have the ability to invest in programs geared toward individual investors. *Dividend reinvestment plans* (DRIPs), discussed more fully in Chapter 3, allow investors to buy stock directly from companies, without a broker and without paying commissions in many cases. Certain DRIPs also allow participants to buy stock *at a discount* to the market price. (Chapter 6 provides a complete list of DRIPs offering discounts.) These programs are created specifically for individual investors; big, institutional investors cannot participate.

Another way you play to your strengths is by exploiting rule changes that favor you, such as the reduction in the capital gains tax rate. Under the new rules, individuals in the top tax bracket (39.6 percent) will see their capital-gains tax rate reduced from 28 percent to 20 percent on investments held more than 12 months. That rate will drop to 18 percent on investments bought after 2000 and held more than five years. The government, by reducing the capital gains rate, makes being a long-term investor a more profitable strategy. If you don't reflect this change in your investment strategy, you're wasting an advantage.

Another rule change that investors need to exploit is the new Roth IRA. I'll explain the Roth in greater detail in Chapter 3. For now, all I'll say is that by creating the Roth IRA the government has handed investors one of the best investing deals ever. The creation of 401(k) plans, in which contributions lower your taxable income and taxes on earnings are deferred, was yet another rule change that benefits individual investors. Successful investing means taking advantage of these "gimmies" when they come your way.

## RULE #5: TAKE WHAT YOUR OPPONENT GIVES YOU.

Continuing the sports analogy for a minute, successful teams maximize the charity of their opponents. How does this translate to the investment world? One way is by taking advantage of the huge price declines that hit stocks when they miss their earnings estimates. I'm sure some of you have owned good quality companies whose stock prices were blown out of the water when the company turned in quarterly earnings results that were just a shade below Wall Street's expectations. Does the fact that the company missed its earnings forecasts by a penny or two mean that its long-term prospects are in danger? Probably not. Sure, bad news may lead to further bad news in subsequent quarters. Still, I've seen instances where Wall Street's myopia shaved literally *billions* of dollars in value from a quality company in a single day. I'm not suggesting that investors should jump immediately into the fray every time a favored stock gets clobbered. What I am saying is that when Wall Street's nearsightedness hands you a potential long-term opportunity, it behooves you to at least consider it (Chapter 8 provides a step-by-step procedure for buying "crash" stocks).

## Corporate Spin-Offs

One area in which investors are often handed "gifts" are corporate spin-offs. A spin-off occurs when a company "spins off" ownership in a division or business to its existing shareholders and the division becomes an independent, publicly traded entity.

For example, in recent years AT&T has spun off Lucent Technologies and NCR to AT&T shareholders. The amount of shares you own in the spin-off depends on the number of shares you own in the main company. If you owned 100 shares of AT&T, you received roughly 32 shares of Lucent and six shares of NCR.

A firm may spin off a business because it no longer fits its long-term corporate strategy. A firm that believes it is undervalued can also spin off a business in the hope that the spin-off plus the old company will be worth more divided than as a single company.

The mechanics of a spin-off are reasonably straightforward. If you are the registered shareholder of a company spinning off a division, in most cases you will receive stock certificates representing whole shares in the spin-off company and cash for any fractional-share ownership. If your shares are held by the broker, the shares will be credited to your brokerage account. Spin-offs are usually classified as tax-free distributions and you do not incur a tax liability on spin-offs until you sell your shares. Following a spin-off, however, you have to readjust your cost basis on the shares of the former parent company. You'll also have to determine a cost basis for the new shares. Companies often disseminate a document showing the proper cost adjustments to make.

## Good News for Shareholders?

A number of spin-offs, especially Lucent Technologies, have done exceptionally well for investors in recent years. Several reasons exist that make spin-offs interesting investments. First, a company that is now out from under a large corporation has the chance to flex its entrepreneurial muscles, something it might not have been able to do as part of a bigger entity. Also, such a company may have a wider marketplace to sell its products than when it was part of a larger entity. In the case of Lucent Technologies, other telephone companies were probably a bit wary buying Lucent's telecommunications equipment while it was still part of AT&T. As an independent entity, Lucent has a wider marketplace to peddle its wares.

Another reason for the attractiveness of spin-offs is that managers understand it is now sink-or-swim time; the larger parent no longer subsidizes the firm. Having your back against the wall is often a great motivator for management.

Third, because they lack history, spin-offs are often difficult for Wall Street to evaluate. Thus, the opportunity exists for the spin-off to surprise analysts with better-than-expected earnings. Such positive earnings surprises often translate into a rise in the stock price.

Factors unique to spin-offs often cause investors to sell the shares regardless of their underlying value. For example, following a spin-off, it is not uncommon for the new company to offer an "odd-lot buyback program." Under an odd-lot program, the new company approaches investors holding "odd lots" (less than 100 shares) and offers to buy back the shares. Companies conduct odd-lot programs to help reduce the number of shareholders, thus reducing share-holder-servicing costs. Because many investors own less than 100 shares in a spin-off, the odd-lot program presents a way for these investors to bail out of the stock and pay little or no brokerage commissions.

Another factor that depresses the stock is that many spin-offs pay little or no divi-dends initially. An investor who likes to receive dividends may have limited interest in a stock that doesn't pay a dividend.

Finally, it's likely that the investor bought the former parent company because it liked its primary business. The investor may have little interest or knowledge about the spin-off's business.

The upshot is that investors who receive the spin-off shares probably have more reasons to sell the shares, such as pressure from the company to participate in the odd-lot buyback program, little or no dividend, little understanding of the spin-off's business, than to add to their holdings. When investors dump a stock for reasons unrelated to the company's earning power and appreciation poten-tial, buying opportunities are created.

To be sure, not all spin-offs are worth holding. Some spin-offs have a lot of debt and other long-term obligations dumped on them by the former parent company and can be unattractive. Still, investors should avoid dumping spin-off shares merely for convenience sake, as history has shown that you may be dumping investments with solid potential.

A spin-off in my personal portfolio about which I'm particularly excited is ChoicePoint. The company is a leading provider of risk-management and fraud-prevention information for the insurance industry. Equifax, a leading credit-verification company, spun off ChoicePoint in 1997. I like information-services companies as well as spin-offs, and ChoicePoint gives me the best of both worlds. I expect these shares to produce nice returns over the long term. The stock trades on the New York Stock Exchange under the symbol CPS. The company does not currently offer a dividend-reinvestment/direct-purchase plan, so purchases must be made via a broker.

## RULE #6: AVOID BATTLES YOU CAN'T WIN.

It's foolhardy to get into a battle you can't win. Unfortunately, the fact that Las Vegas exists indicates people ignore this advice. Las Vegas is not the only place where individuals are willing to assume long odds for a big payoff. Wall Street has its share of long-shot players as well, especially in the futures and options markets. Futures and options are forms of derivative securities. Derivatives are financial instruments whose prices are derived from other prices of underlying securities, assets, or indexes. Many market players use derivatives to hedge portfolio risk.

For example, let's say you own shares in IBM. You can hedge against a drop in IBM stock by buying a "put" option on IBM. Should IBM drop, the value of your "put" option rises, offsetting the loss on the common stock. (Chapter 6 provides various strategies for hedging portfolios using options.)

Using options and futures as portfolio insurance is not necessarily a bad game to play. However, *speculating* in futures and options is a game you can't win. When you speculate in the futures and options market, you are banking that you are smarter than the person taking the other side of the trade, and there's no margin for error. Wall Street professionals are the main players in the futures and options markets. Chances are, when you speculate in this market, you are doing so against investors who make their living scalping investors like you. The bottom line: The playing field in the futures and options market is far from level for the individual investor.

I've bought an occasional option on stocks as a speculation. Invariably, I lost money. One reason is that transaction costs for individual investors in the options and futures markets are higher than in the stock market. Second, because options and futures markets are short-term markets, whatever gains you make are taxed at your full tax rate; there's no capital gains break because you did not likely hold the derivative for the time required to earn the break. Finally, because most futures and options investments have time restrictions, you not only have to choose the right investment in the derivatives market, but your timing also has to be perfect. In other words, you have to pick the right investment *and* be right about the timing. You won't be able to do this consistently over time. I don't buy options any more. I found much greater success putting my ideas to work in the stock market where I had time on my side.

Now I know plenty of market "experts" preach the wisdom of using options and futures in an investment program. Not coincidentally, many of these guys have come out of the woodwork over the last three years, a time when doing virtually *any* wild-hair strategy probably would have made you money given the unprecedented strength in the financial markets. Don't get seduced by being lucky a time or two in the derivatives market. Investing is a marathon, not a sprint. You will not be able to win consistently in the options and futures markets over time. For that reason, unless you use options to hedge portfolio risk, stick with stocks and mutual funds.

## RULE #7: DON'T CLAIM YOUR VICTORIES PREMATURELY.

"You'll never go broke taking a profit" may be the worst investment advice ever given. Yes, you'll never go broke; you'll never get rich either. I hate to see investors claiming victories prematurely by selling stocks after they rise 25 percent or 50 percent. You'll never get rich taking such modest profits. When you take a 25 percent profit, keep in mind that your 25 percent profit shrinks rapidly when you take into account taxes and inflation. Good investment ideas are not a dime a dozen. If you feel you have two or three or 12, you should let time work its magic on those ideas. Constantly selling stocks after modest appreciation means you have to keep coming up with good ideas. Let's face it, perhaps the best investor of all time, Warren Buffett, owns less than two dozen stocks, many of which he's held for years. What makes you think you can crank out a dozen or two great investment ideas year-in, year-out?

When I look at my personal portfolio, what I see is probably not that different than what I would see if I looked at your portfolio—a few stocks that are not doing very well, several stocks that are treading water, and a few stocks that have done extremely well. It's those few stocks that go up, not 50 percent or 100 percent, but 1000 or 2000 percent, that will truly make a difference in your financial future. If you always sell stocks after they rise 50 percent, you'll never own the stock that goes up 500 percent or 5000 percent. *Those* are the stocks that will make you rich. One of my favorite expressions about selling winners early is the following: *Don't pull your flowers and water your weeds.* Don't sell your winners prematurely while keeping your losers. The best investment ideas usually have shelf lives longer than six or 12 months.

## RULE #8: HAVE THE COURAGE TO ACT ON YOUR CONVICTION . . . BUT . . . DON'T CONFUSE CONVICTION WITH STUBBORNNESS.

Wall Street is the only marketplace where the merchandise gets more popular as it gets more expensive. That's because the "herd" mentality on Wall Street says that, if a stock is rising, it must be worth buying. Invariably, however, those in the "herd" end up getting trampled when the stock's promise is not realized. Those who have the courage to act on convictions that may run counter to Wall Street's "group think" can find the rewards substantial.

One reason to stick with your own conviction is that it's unbiased. You can't say the same for Wall Street analysts' views of companies. The role of the stock analyst on Wall Street has changed dramatically in recent years. The main role of an analyst is no longer to assess the investment merit of companies; it's to bring in deals for the analyst's firm. If an analyst aggressively recommends a company's stock, the analyst's firm has a much better chance of doing underwriting and merger work for that firm. If you bad-mouth a stock, your firm could be shut out of lucrative advisory fees. As one market watcher puts it, on Wall Street, "independent research" is an oxymoron. Need proof? In May, 1998, *The Wall Street Journal* reported that 66 percent of the nearly 6000 stocks tracked by First Call Corp., a Boston earnings- and estimate-tracking service, had "strong buy" or "buy" recommendations from analysts. Only one percent had "sell" recommendations.

Of course, you can be as wrong as the next guy on Wall Street. Don't be too stubborn to admit you made a mistake if your scenario of the future does not pan out. On the other hand, if the reasons you made the investment still hold, be willing to stick with your story.

An example in my portfolio where I stuck with my story is H&R Block. I invested in H&R Block a few years ago primarily because of the company's tax business. I felt that any business that touched some 15 million people every year wasn't a bad business to own. This huge customer base gives Block the opportunity to sell other financial products and services. This huge customer base also makes Block an interesting takeover stock, and merger activity in the financial-services field has been heating up in recent years. Unfortunately, the stock fell from nearly $49 in 1995 to less than $24 in 1996, a 51 percent plunge. Problems with its CompuServe online unit caused Wall Street to give these shares the cold shoulder. It would have been extremely easy to bail on the stock. However, the reason I stayed with the stock was because my reasons for buying, 15 million customers and the prospects of a takeover, were still intact. So I bought more. I was rewarded for my patience when these shares rose more than 54 percent in 1997.

To be sure, not every stock that declines eventually rebounds and I don't want to understate the risks of buying stocks that tumble. Still, investors should not always jump to the often-easy conclusion that a stock that declines is a stock that should be sold. If the reasons that you bought the stock in the first place still hold, have the courage to act on your conviction and buy more. If, on the other hand, your reasons for buying the stock are no longer valid, don't be too stubborn to admit it's time to move on.

Because knowing why you buy a stock in the first place is so important to future investment decisions, jot down your thoughts on each investment in a journal. This journal will serve as a handy reference over time, especially when deciding to sell a particular investment.

## Rule # 9: Engage on All Fronts, Foreign and Domestic.

As an investor, you must be willing to go wherever value can be found. That may mean investing beyond the borders of the U.S. In recent years, many foreign stocks have underperformed the U.S. market, which has caused a number of market pundits to jump on the xenophobic bandwagon. This fear of foreign investment comes precisely at a time when the stock values overseas are perhaps the best they've been in a decade or more relative to the U.S. markets. If you want to be a successful investor over the long term, you can't ignore overseas investments. Fortunately, it's never been easier or cheaper to invest overseas. Chapter 4 provides a more detailed review of foreign investing and shows why every investor should have some international representation in a portfolio.

## Rule # 10: Develop Future Leaders of the Individual Investor Revolution.

Perhaps the most important job of a leader is to educate and train successors. I think part of the "wisdom package" parents and grandparents impart on children and young adults must include knowledge about investing. After all, kids have the most of the one ingredient so important to investment success—time. Judging from the letters I receive from kids, the interest in investing is there. Here are two letters I received over the last year (I've used the initials of the children in both cases):

*My name is E.R. I am nine years old. I am interested in buying stocks through a stock club, but to make my decision I need to get information on which companies have DRIPs. I thank you in advance for your help.*

\* \* \* \*

*Hello. My name is J.G. the third. I am 10 years old. I am writing to you because I want to know about buying stocks that avoid brokerage fees. You may think that I am too young for this stuff, but I am so crazy about stocks and other things that have to do with my careers. I also want to plan my careers now, instead of at the last minute. Oh, and one more thing. I am ultra-excellent in math. Everyone in my class says that I'm a human calculator. I know addition, subtraction, multiplication, division, fractions, ratios, percentages, binary, pre-algebra, squares, square roots, cubes, cube roots, and some trigonometry. The reason I really wrote to you is to ask you to please send the list of stocks that avoid brokerage fees.*

\* \* \* \*

The upshot is that if you instill good investing disciplines in a youngster today, you *will* change his or her life tomorrow.

Another reason to develop tomorrow's leaders of the revolution is that they can help you today. There's no denying young people are consumers. By one estimate, teenagers spent $122 billion in 1997. As a consumer, your kids probably have important insights into products and services, insights that can be useful when choosing investments.

What's the best way to get your kindergarten capitalists up and running? The next chapter provides a variety of investment vehicles geared nicely to young adults.

# ▼ Conclusion . . .

I freely admit that many of my "10 Rules of Engagement" may seem like Investing 101. You're right—this isn't brain surgery. You should be glad that successful investing doesn't require the mind of Einstein. This means *any* investor has the ability to be successful by following these simple, time-tested rules.

# CHAPTER THREE

# KEYS TO THE KINGDOM: STEP-BY-STEP STRATEGIES FOR ANY INVESTOR TO GET IN THE GAME

E G. Dickens, Jr., doesn't consider himself a Wall Street titan. The Lawrenceville, Georgia resident spends his days far away from the maddening Wall Street crowd as an accountant in the engineering department of Columbian Chemicals. Yet Mr. Dickens is a perfect example of the "new" individual investor, one who is participating in the financial markets directly, often for the first time, without an intermediary. Most importantly, he's participating on his own terms in dollar amounts that make sense to his pocketbook.

"Several years ago I was laughed at by a stockbroker when he found that I had only $1000 to invest," says Mr. Dickens. "He told me that he wasn't going to waste his time on such an insignificant amount. At that point, I wrote off the idea of ever owning stocks until a few years ago when I purchased seven stocks in order to use dividend reinvestment programs as a part of my savings strategy. Today I have 10 stocks and am really having fun watching them grow."

Mr. Dickens is not alone. Today literally millions of investors are finding that access to the financial markets, the "keys to the kingdom," is not the private domain of a privileged Wall Street few. Indeed, any investor—I repeat, *any* investor—now has the ability to buy quality stocks, mutual funds, and other investments directly, without a middleman.

## GETTING STARTED IN STOCKS

When most investors think of buying stocks, they think of using a stock broker. Most stock trades are still conducted using a stock broker.

The stock broker of today, however, often bears little resemblance to the broker of decades ago and, indeed, even a few years ago.

Deregulation of the brokerage industry had much to do with reshaping investors' relationships with brokers. Prior to 1975, commissions were fixed and, thus, there was little incentive for investors to educate themselves concerning investments. They were going to pay the same high brokerage rates regardless of whether they or the broker selected the investments.

The Securities and Exchange Commission changed everything when it eliminated fixed commissions on "May Day," May 1, 1975. May Day gave birth to a new player on the financial scene: the discount broker. Investors were now faced with the option of either using a full-service broker, and paying top dollar in commissions for his or her expertise and resources, or using a discount broker and saving a bundle on commissions. Practically overnight, the value of becoming a self-reliant investor jumped dramatically.

Consequently, over time, more and more investors began educating themselves on stocks and investing in general. In a way, the deregulation of the brokerage industry was an important step in cultivating the individual investor revolution because it helped spawn growing numbers of do-it-yourself investors. Gradually the discount brokerage business gave way to "super" discounters, or deep-discount brokerage firms, who drove commissions down further. Deep discounters provided even more incentive for individual investors to choose their own investments.

## ONLINE BROKERS

What sent the next tremor through the brokerage industry was technology, specifically the Internet. Online trading altered the relationship between investors and brokers and eliminated some of the worst aspects of using a broker—enduring broker cold calls, reaching your broker to make a trade, and having the broker pass judgment on your stock picks, while putting the power and control in the hands of individual investors. In short, online trading turned the broker into a nameless, faceless, and speechless entity that does only what self-reliant investors want a broker to do—provide easy and inexpensive access to the markets.

## ONLINE TRADING

Although a relatively recent phenomenon, the Internet's impact on the brokerage industry has been revolutionary. December 1997 will likely turn out to be a watershed month for the brokerage industry. Charles Schwab & Co. reported that 50 percent of retail commission trading for the month was done online. For all of 1997, Schwab reported that sales via electronic channels stood at 41 percent, up from 28 percent in 1996. By the end of 1997, Schwab had more than 1.2 million online accounts with more than $80 billion in assets.

Schwab is not the only brokerage firm benefiting from investors making trades in cyberspace. According to a report by broker Piper Jaffray, industry-wide online trading in 1997 accounted for an estimated 17 percent of all retail trading, more than double the 1996 level. Forrester Research estimates that the number of online accounts, about three million at the beginning of 1998, will jump to more than 14 million by 2002.

Investor interest in online trading has also caused a rapid growth in the number of brokerage firms going online. In early 1997, the number of online brokers was fewer than 15. That number grew to 33 by the end of the 1997 third quarter and stood at more than 60 at the beginning of 1998. Consequently, as usually happens when companies race to a new market, consumers benefit by lower prices. Online trading commissions have fallen from an average ticket price of $34.65 in the fourth quarter of 1996 to $15.95 by the fourth quarter of 1997. Today it is not uncommon to see online trades being done for $10 per trade or lower. Some online brokers actually make transactions for *free*.

## MY COMPUTER/MY BROKER

There's no denying that online trading has been a boon in providing low-cost and easy access to the financial markets. Interestingly, online trading provides a double-edged sword for the brokerage community. On one hand, cheap online trading has the potential to turn individual investors into trading machines, buying and selling stocks many times a day. That's good news for brokers. The bad news, for full-service brokerages in particular, is that online trading threatens their very franchises.

The following is a list of the more prominent online brokers:

| | |
|---|---|
| Accutrade | http://www.accutrade.com |
| | (800) 494-8939 |
| American Express | http://www.americanexpress.com |
| | (800) 658-4677 |
| AmeriTrade | http://www.ameritrade.com |
| | (800) 454-9272 |
| Brown & Co. | http://www.brownco.com |
| | (800) 822-2829 |
| Datek Online | http://www.datek.com |
| | (888) 463-2835 |
| Discover Brokerage | http://www.discoverbrokerage.com |
| | (800) 688-3462 |
| DLJ Direct | http://www.dljdirect.com |
| | (800) 825-5723 |
| E*Trade | http://www.etrade.com |
| | (800) 786-2575 |
| Fidelity | http://personal.fidelity.com |
| | (800) 544-8666 |
| National Discount Brokers | http://www.ndb.com |
| | (800) 888-3999 |
| Net Investor | http://www.netinvestor.com |
| | (800) 638-4250 |
| Quick & Reilly | http://www.quickwaynet.com |
| | (800) 672-7220 |
| Charles Schwab | http://www.schwab.com |
| | (800) 435-4000 |
| SureTrade | http://www.suretrade.com |
| | (212) 566-2031 |
| Wall Street Access | http://www.wsaccess.com |
| | (800) 925-5782 |

| Wall Street Electronica | http://www.wallstreete.com |
| | (888) 925-5783 |
| Waterhouse Securities | http://www.waterhouse.com |
| | (800) 934-4134 |
| A.B. Watley | http://www.abwatley.com |
| | (888) 229-2853 |
| Web Street Securities | http://www.webstreetsecurities.com |
| | (800) 932-0438 |

Source: *Barron's*

Notice you don't see Merrill Lynch on the list. Is that because Merrill Lynch has not figured out the online technology to allow a trade? Of course not. It's because they have a huge network of Merrill Lynch brokers who are getting top buck in the form of commissions and would revolt if Merrill Lynch started offering $8 trades. It's only a matter of time, however, before Merrill Lynch goes online. Schwab's on-line experience has been particularly telling. For example, Schwab still takes telephone orders, for which it charges a certain fee, but if you trade online, the fee is $29.95, up to 1000 shares. Interestingly, Schwab aggressively tells its customers that there is a cheaper way for them to trade and it courts online traffic.

Ultimately, all brokers will have to have an online presence. When that day comes, look for online commissions to go even lower. In fact, talk of rebates in the brokerage industry—in effect, *paying* customers for doing a trade—has already been heard from the lips of executives at online brokerage firms.

How can brokers charge $8 a trade, zero dollars a trade, or even pay for a trade? Brokerage firms make money by lending stock held in accounts and from the interest on margin loans. Brokers also earn interest on cash balances held in accounts. Another source of revenue, although it has been drying up a bit, is what's called "payment for order flow." This payment is, in effect, a kickback to brokers for steering trades to certain market makers. Also, keep in mind that many investors who use online systems pay rates considerably higher than $8 or $14 a trade. That's because many of these investors buy stock options, such as call and put options. Commissions on these investments tend to run much higher on average than commissions to buy and sell stock. The upshot is that, for large accounts, the time may come when investors are paid to make a trade. "I can see a time when, for a customer with a certain size margin account, we won't charge commissions," says J. Joe Ricketts, chairman of AmeriTrade Holding Corp., an online broker. "We might even pay a customer on a per trade basis to bring the account to us."

## THE ONLINE INVESTOR

What is it about online trading that has drawn so many individual investors so quickly? Obviously, the low commission is a major attraction, but price does not explain all of the allure. There's a high degree of independence and freedom that comes with the ability to turn on your computer and make a trade. No broker calls. No broker passing judgment on your decisions. The freedom to buy and sell any security you wish. In an age when more and more investors feel comfortable calling their own investment shots, online trading provides the power to trade instantaneously on their own terms, without a broker. Never mind that all of the trades are still going through a broker to be processed. All that concerns an investor is that he or she can punch a few keys on the computer to make a trade, without first having to talk to a broker. The ability to buy and sell stock for $8 a trade is such a powerful allure that even self-described "long-term investors" are trading on a daily basis. "Hey, at $8 a pop, you can't afford not to trade," one online enthusiast was quoted in *Smart Money* magazine.

Unfortunately, that type of mentality is what makes online trading both a blessing and a curse for certain investors. This broker-free access to instantaneous trading provides incredible power and freedom for investors. But power and freedom are double-edged swords if not used properly. One downside of on-line trading is that it is easy to fall into a trading mentality, buying and selling stocks at every blip in the market. This trading mentality can also affect mutual-fund investors, who are also increasingly able to trade their fund investments online either through brokerage fund "supermarkets" or via the fund families' own Web sites. Studies have shown that this is exactly the wrong way to build wealth in the stock market. Even purveyors of online trading concede that such easy and cheap access to the markets may not ultimately be in the best interest of certain investors. "Trading often and heavy is not something that makes you a lot of money," said J. Joe Ricketts, chairman of online broker AmeriTrade, in an interview with *Fortune* magazine. "Now that's contrary to my own interests, but it is the truth."

## Other Online Issues

A short-term trading mentality is not the only potential problem with online trading. Remember that online trading is only as good as the technology behind the trading system. Online investors have already tasted some of the downside to trading via computer and modem. Indeed, on October 27 and 28, 1997, when the Dow Jones Industrial Average fell 554 points and then rose 337 points in record trading of 1.2 billion shares, many investors experienced system crashes and were simply unable to execute a trade online. The problems may not always be related to system crashes at your broker. If your Internet service provider is having problems, you may not even be able to get onto the Internet, let alone connect to your broker. Of course, those two days were certainly not the norm, and investors using telephones to reach their brokers found plenty of delays as well. Still, if you believe that your online trades will always be conducted in nanoseconds, think again. For that reason, a prudent approach for the online investor is to open at least a couple of online accounts with brokers, preferably brokers who also take telephone orders. That way, you give yourself more options should system problems develop.

Also understand that any technology, including an online trading system, is vulnerable to security problems. Although Internet security has improved greatly in recent years, investors need to understand that security breaches are possible. For that reason, security provisions should be as important as commission schedules when considering online brokers, especially upstarts in the field.

Finally, computer-driven systems do make mistakes. In the case of online trading, mistakes can be whoppers. Make sure you review confirmations and other trading documents to avoid any surprises due to a stray keypunch on your computer.

## Empowering, If Used Properly

There will always be investors who confuse access with opportunity and believe that because you *can* trade many times a day online means that you *should*. For those people, online trading will likely be their investment ruin, especially when the markets turn ugly. For investors who couple the freedom of online trading with a prudent investment approach, however, the rewards should be ample.

When considering an online broker, look beyond commissions:

$ *What research services are available?* Many online brokers make a plethora of stock-picking tools and quote services available.

$ *What investments can I buy online?* Some online brokers don't allow you to buy certain investments online.

$ *How good is the company's customer support?* Send a few emails to the company and see how quickly the firm responds to your queries.

$ *Are there hidden fees?* Some online brokers charge you a start-up fee or an administrative charge per trade.

$ *How much does the broker require to establish an account?* Some online brokers require $2000 or more to establish an account.

Who's the best online broker? *Smart Money* magazine rated on-line brokers in its February 1998 issue on such criteria as commissions, availability of real-time quotes, research links, account information, technology support, fees, and product availability. The overall winner was Discover Brokerage Direct (http://www.discoverbrokerage.com). Several online brokers, however, had lower commissions and better technological support. I suggest you contact a number of online brokers and compare the features that mean the most to you.

## WHO NEEDS A BROKER?

"Stock brokerage is not a profession you want your children to go into." This quote reportedly came from the president of E*Trade Group, an online trading firm. Certainly, the advent of online trading and its low commissions are affecting the brokerage community, especially full-service brokers.

But online trading is not the only factor making the brokerage business a tougher place to make a buck these days. Many ways exist today for investors to access the market without *any* broker or financial intermediary. For example, no-load mutual funds (we'll discuss these later in the chapter), in which investors go directly to the fund family to buy funds, have been stealing brokerage customers for years. And if that wasn't enough, the growth in dividend reinvestment plans and what I call "no-load stocks," in which investors can invest directly with companies without a broker, represent yet another competitive threat to the traditional brokerage industry.

## DIVIDEND INVESTMENT PLANS (DRIPS)

Any of you who have read my other books know that I have a special fondness for dividend reinvestment plans (DRIPs). These are programs, offered by roughly 1100 publicly traded companies, which allow investors to buy stock directly from the company, without a broker and, in many cases, with little or no fees. Investors buy shares in two ways:

$ Companies take the shareholders' dividends and, instead of sending dividend checks, reinvest the dividends to purchase additional shares.

$ In nearly every plan, investors can make additional optional cash investments, which can be as small as $10 or $25 in certain cases. For investors with deeper pockets, these optional cash investments can be as large as $100,000 or $200,000 per year.

DRIPs are available in many of the bluest blue chips in America. For example, 29 out of the 30 Dow Jones Industrial stocks offer DRIPs (Travelers is the only Dow stock that does not offer a plan).

The benefits of DRIPs are many:

$ Investors buy full and fractional shares of stock through the plans, with the fractional share of stock entitled to a fractional share of the dividend. Thus, the plans are perfect for buying stock "on the installment plan" in amounts that make sense for your pocketbook.

$ In many cases, there are no fees to buy stock in the plans. If a firm charges a fee in its DRIP, the fee is usually lower than even the lowest online broker.

$ In a number of DRIPs, investors can actually buy stock cheaper than the market price. These discounts are usually two percent to five percent and can reach as high as 10 percent in a few instances. DRIPs with discounts are covered more extensively in Chapter 6.

The following list of high-quality DRIPs provides a nice sampling of the types of companies that charge no fees on the buy side and have investment minimums of $50 or less:

| | | | |
|---|---|---|---|
| Abbott Laboratories | Gannett Co. | Kellogg | Rite Aid |
| Anheuser-Busch | Harley-Davidson | Medtronic | Sara Lee |
| Coca-Cola | Heinz (H.J.) | Motorola | Schering-Plough |
| Emerson Electric | Intel | Pfizer | Schwab (Charles) |
| | Johnson & Johnson | Philip Morris Cos. | ServiceMaster |

## Getting Started in DRIPs

Joining a DRIP is easy. Here are step-by-step instructions on enrolling in a DRIP.

1. Pick a stock.

   When hunting for DRIP investments, be sure to focus only on those companies that offer the best long-term investment prospects. Just because a firm offers a DRIP does not make it a good investment. Investing in a DRIP of a bad company is a losing proposition, even if you are able to invest commission free. Concentrate your investment search on those companies with strong finances, favorable growth opportunities, and consistent earnings and dividend records. I've provided a number of DRIP recommendations in Chapter 8. Another good source for DRIP investment ideas is my newsletter (yes, I'm biased), *DRIP Investor*.

2. Once you've selected a stock investment, determine if the firm offers a DRIP.

   Helpful resources in determining whether a company offers a DRIP are my books, *Buying Stocks Without A Broker* (McGraw-Hill) and *No-Load Stocks* (McGraw-Hill), as well as my firm's *Directory of Dividend Reinvestment Plans* (Horizon Publishing). These books are available in bookstores or by calling 800-233-5922. You can also contact the company's shareholder services department to check if the firm offers a dividend reinvestment plan.

3. Know the plan specifics and eligibility requirements before investing.

   DRIPs differ dramatically from one company to another. Although most DRIPs require shareholders to own only one share in order to enroll, others require investors to own as many as 50 shares in order to be eligible. Also, although most programs charge no fees for participating in their DRIPs, some companies charge commissions and fees. The timing and frequency of optional cash purchases also differs between plans. How do you find out about the particulars? Call the company, talk to the shareholder services department, and get a copy of the plan prospectus, which provides all the details concerning the plan. Remember it is important to know the specifics of the plan, especially eligibility requirements, before investing in the stock. You don't want to buy one share of stock only to find out afterwards that you need 10 shares in order to enroll in the DRIP.

**4.** How to buy the first shares or shares.

In order to be eligible to enroll in most dividend reinvestment plans, you must be a shareholder. In other words, you have to own at least one share of stock in order to join, and the stock must be registered in your name, not the "street" or brokerage name. This is critical to understand in order to join a DRIP; the initial share or shares of stock you purchase in order to become eligible to join the DRIP must be registered in your own name, not the "street" name or the name of the broker. If you use a broker to purchase the first share (I use the discount broker **Kennedy, Cabot,** 800-252-0090, to make my initial purchases), make sure you tell the broker to register the share in your name, not the street name. Be aware that some brokers may charge you an additional fee to register the shares in your own name.

Another way to obtain the first share or shares needed to enroll in a DRIP is by using what I call the "buddy system." Let's say a friend or relative owns shares in a company that has a DRIP you want to join. You can have your friend transfer one share from his or her account into your name. This way, you become a shareholder of record and are now eligible to join the DRIP. I've transferred shares before and it is an easy process. In order to do so, you'll need a "stock power" form that can be obtained from a brokerage firm or the transfer agent administering the DRIP. Fill out the "stock power" form and include the name, address, and social security number of the individual to whom you are transferring the shares. You also must have a "medallion" signature guarantee stamp on the stock power form, which you can get from most banks. When you have completed the form and obtained the medallion stamp, return the form to the company or its transfer agent, along with a letter stating your intentions and specifying that you would like to enroll the individual directly into the DRIP. If the transfer agent does not enroll the individual directly into the plan, the individual will receive a stock certificate and a DRIP enrollment form. The individual will then need to fill out and return the DRIP enrollment form before he or she can be eligible to participate in the DRIP. The whole transfer process is fairly painless and is virtually free (you pay your bank a dollar or two for the medallion stamp).

**5.** Get your certificates in the mail.

Once you've made your purchase of initial shares through the broker, you'll have to wait for the trade to clear and for the company to receive your name as a registered shareholder before you can enroll in the DRIP. Once the firm and its transfer agent receive your trade information, a stock certificate is mailed to you. Unfortunately, it can take a few weeks or longer from the time you execute your trade with the broker until you receive the stock certificate and notification from the company. If the weeks start turning into months and you still haven't heard anything, contact the company's shareholder services department. Explain that you purchased stock and are checking to see if the firm has record of you as a registered shareholder. If the firm does not, contact your broker to determine if the shares were registered in your name. Oftentimes, prolonged delays are due to the fact that the broker registered the stock in "street" name. If this is the case, have the broker reregister the shares in your name.

**6.** Once you receive the certificates, notify the company of your desire to join the DRIP.

Request a DRIP enrollment form and a prospectus if you haven't received them already. In many cases, once a company has record of a new shareholder, the firm automatically sends the investor information about joining the DRIP. Once you have received the enrollment form, fill it out carefully. Be sure to specify on the enrollment form if you want all or just part of your dividends reinvested, as some companies permit partial dividend reinvestment. Then return the completed enrollment form to the company. Once the company receives your application, you can begin investing via the DRIP. Most DRIPs provide certificate safekeeping services, in which the company holds the certificate for you.

**7.** Know the plan's rules governing optional cash payments.

Once you've enrolled in a DRIP, you'll probably be anxious to begin investing via optional cash payments (OCPs). Make sure you know the various rules and restrictions governing OCPs. These rules are detailed in the company's DRIP prospectus. In most cases, companies invest optional cash payments once a month (often around the first or last business day of the month) or once a week. In order to be eligible to invest with an OCP in a particular month, the money must be received by the firm a specified number of days prior to the investment date. Don't send the money too far in advance of this date, as funds received by the company for OCP do not receive interest while awaiting investment. Also make sure that your investment falls within the minimum and maximum OCP limits permitted in the plan.

**8.** Keep good records.

Companies and their transfer agents do their best to help dividend reinvestment plan participants keep track of their investments. Investors receive statements, usually after each investment with dividends and optional cash payments. Make sure you keep track of this information, especially your cost basis for each purchase of stock. This information is essential when you sell shares and need to determine your cost basis for tax purposes. Also, at the end of the year, companies send 1099 forms showing the amount of dividend income that was reinvested during the year. This information is important because such dividends are taxable income each year, even though the dividends were reinvested in additional shares.

## NO-LOAD STOCKS™

If DRIPs have a downside, it's the way investors enter the plans. As you can see, in a traditional DRIP, there's a catch-22. You want to invest directly, but you can't until you're a shareholder. Although the eligibility requirement is usually just one share, getting that first share can be problematic. Fortunately, a growing number of companies are taking their DRIPs to the next level by allowing investors to make even their initial purchase of stock directly. I call these no-load stocks™.

No-load stocks work just like no-load mutual funds in that investors deal directly with the company without a broker. Enrolling in a no-load stock plan is quite simple:

$ Call the company's toll-free line to obtain a prospectus and enrollment form. A one-stop source for enrollment information for many no-load stock plans is the **Direct Stock Purchase Plan Clearinghouse**. The Clearinghouse, which is a joint venture between my firm and Shareholder Communications Corp., allows investors to order multiple enrollment forms via a single toll-free number, 800-774-4117. The 24-hour Clearinghouse hotline is a free call for investors. The costs of the Clearinghouse are shouldered by participating companies.

$ Once you receive the prospectus and enrollment information, it's important to read the information. The prospectus explains the details of the plan, including maximum and minimum investments, fees (if any), frequency of purchases and sales, and so on. Once you've read the prospectus, complete the enrollment form and cut a check. Make sure the check covers at least the minimum initial investment required in the plan. The minimum initial investment in more than half of the plans is $250 or less.

$ Return the completed enrollment form and check to the company. In most cases, you'll be dealing with a transfer agent that the company hires to administer the plan.

That's all there is to it. The shares are registered in book-entry form, meaning no stock certificate is created unless you request stock certificates, and you will be sent regular statements to assist you in your recordkeeping.

I call these programs no-load stocks because they've adopted a number of features found in no-load mutual funds. In addition to direct investing, many of these plans also feature:

$ *Automatic monthly debit services*: With most mutual funds, you can set up an automatic investment program whereby the fund electronically debits your bank account each month to buy stock. Automatic electronic debit is also available in many no-load stock plans.

$ *Frequent purchases and sales*: You can buy and sell shares in a mutual fund daily. So, too, can you buy and sell shares in many no-load stock plans daily. On the sell side, many plans now allow investors to sell their shares over the telephone.

$ *IRAs*: Mutual funds are popular investments for individual retirement accounts. A growing number of no-load stocks also have IRA options built into their plans. Via the IRA option, an individual can invest directly with a company and have the investment earmarked for an IRA. Several no-load stocks, such as Fannie Mae, Chrysler, and Philadelphia Suburban, even have Roth IRA options.

As you can see, the types of services offered in these plans are comparable to mutual funds. In fact, in some no-load stock plans, you can borrow against the value of the shares held in the plan. Ameritech, for example, allows an investor who holds $3000 or more of Ameritech stock to take out a line of credit of up to 75 percent of the shares' value. In the not-too-distant future, I would expect to see other services offered as part of no-load stock plans, including money-market accounts and limit orders for buying and selling stock.

## How to Invest $100, $500, or $1000

One of the major attractions of direct-purchase plans is the small minimums required to get started. Through these plans, *any* investor, regardless of the size of his or her pocketbook, has the ability to buy stocks in the world's best companies. This section discusses ways investors with modest sums can initiate and maintain an investment program in no-load stocks. Additional model portfolios are provided in Chapter 8.

## $100 Portfolio

One danger that's common for many newcomers to the financial markets is that they delay getting started because of their tiny "starter" funds. Unfortunately, delaying an investment program often results in no investment program at all. It's better to start an investment program as early as possible, even if it means starting with a modest amount of money, than to defer investing until your bankroll increases.

Obviously, $100 isn't enough money to construct a fully diversified portfolio, but it may be all a newcomer to the markets can squeeze out of his or her finances. It's important to understand that the initial $100 investment is not an end, but a beginning to a long-term investment program. Fortunately, with just $100, investors have a variety of quality no-load stocks from which to choose.

The investor with $100 has a couple of ways to go when starting. He or she could choose one or two stocks with the funds. Plans that charge fees in their direct-purchase programs may be too punitive for an investor who has only $100 or so to invest. Quality, "fee-friendly" direct-purchase plans with initial minimums of $100 or less include **Johnson Controls** *(NYSE: JCI; $50 minimum initial investment),* **Wisconsin Energy** *(NYSE: WEC; $50 minimum initial investment),* and **WPS Resources** *(NYSE: WPS; $100 minimum initial investment).*

An alternative approach would be to focus on companies that have modest requirements if an investor agrees to automatic monthly debit from a bank account. For example, **Becton, Dickinson** *(NYSE: BDX)*, a leading health-care company, has a $250 minimum initial investment. The firm will waive the minimum, however, if an investor agrees to automatic monthly debit of at least $50. The firm charges purchase fees of just three cents per share and no enrollment fee. Another "fee-friendly" firm that will waive its initial minimum if an investor agrees to an automatic monthly investment of just $25 is **Interstate Energy** *(NYSE: LNT)*, a Wisconsin-based electric utility.

What would I do with $100? I'd spread it over two stocks—Becton, Dickinson and Johnson Controls. Because neither charges fees, all my money is working for me and I'd have a monthly commitment going forward of just $50. Of course, I could invest more money if I wanted each month, but at least I wouldn't be obligated to invest more than the $50 automatic debit in the Becton, Dickinson plan.

## $500 Portfolio

With $500, I might include positions in some quality firms that charge modest fees. Of course, fees matter, but the fees make up a smaller percentage of a $500 investment. If you're willing to incur modest fees, several quality companies will waive their initial minimums if you agree to automatic monthly debit. These companies include **Fannie Mae** *(NYSE: FNM; $25 minimum with automatic debit)* and **Tribune** *(NYSE: TRB; $50 automatic debit minimum)*. **Walgreen** *(NYSE: WAG)* charges fees but has a $50 minimum initial investment. A $500 investment bankroll also allows you to consider a few stocks with higher investment minimums. One alternative would be to choose a couple of stocks with initial minimums between $100 and $250. Two "fee-friendly" stocks in this category are **Eastman Kodak** *(NYSE: EK; $150 minimum initial investment)* and **Exxon** *(NYSE: XON; $250 minimum initial investment)*.

What would I do with $500? I'd buy Johnson Controls and Becton, Dickinson and add Exxon, Tribune, and Walgreen. The total outlay to get started in this portfolio would be $450 plus $20 in one-time enrollment fees for Tribune and Walgreen. My ongoing monthly commitment due to automatic debit obligations would be $100 ($50 each for Becton, Dickinson and Tribune).

## $1000 Portfolio

With $1000, you could make a case that you have enough to establish a brokerage account to purchase the first share needed to enroll in traditional DRIPs. However, I'll be consistent and stay with direct-purchase plans to fill out this portfolio.

If you were concerned about committing yourself to monthly obligations via automatic debit services, $1000 would allow you to buy a nice portfolio without having monthly obligations. For example, you could purchase Johnson Controls ($50 minimum), WPS Resources ($100 minimum), Exxon ($250 minimum), and **Regions Financial** *(NASDAQ: RGBK; $500 minimum initial investment)*, a leading regional bank. Total cost for this portfolio is $900. None of these companies charges fees, so all of your money works for you. This portfolio also alleviates the need for you to commit to monthly investments via automatic debit.

What would I do with the $1000? I'd take the $500 portfolio and add **Finova** *(NYSE: FNV; $500 minimum initial investment)*, a financial-services concern, or Regions Financial.

As you can see, putting a little money to work for you in direct-purchase plans can be done in a variety of ways. Of course, when investing small amounts, be extra sensitive to fees. It's also not enough to just start an investment program; you need to continue making regular investments. For that reason, some individuals may find the "forced" savings afforded by automatic monthly debit an attractive way to go. Before investing in any direct-purchase plans, obtain copies of the plan prospectuses. The toll-free numbers for enrollment information for the stocks mentioned in this section are listed in the table on the next page.

## COMPANY BENEFITS

Companies derive a number of benefits from offering dividend-reinvestment/no-load stock plans.:

$ *Raising Equity Capital.* One of the biggest benefits a no-load stock program provides is a source of cheap equity capital. Companies have the option of either issuing new shares in their programs or going into the open market to purchase shares for participants. When a firm buys shares on the open market, no

## No-Load Stocks

### $100 Portfolio

| Company | Minimum Initial Investment | Initial Fees |
|---|---|---|
| Becton, Dickinson | $50* | 0 |
| Johnson Control | 50 | 0 |

### $500 Portfolio

| Company | Minimum Initial Investment | Initial Fees |
|---|---|---|
| Becton, Dickinson | $50* | 0 |
| Exxon | 250 | 0 |
| Johnson Control | 50 | 0 |
| Tribune | 50* | 10 |
| Walgreen | 50 | 10 |

### $1000 Portfolio

| Company | Minimum Initial Investment | Initial Fees |
|---|---|---|
| Becton, Dickinson | $50* | 0 |
| Exxon | 250 | 0 |
| Finova | 500 | 0 |
| Johnson Control | 50 | 0 |
| Tribune | 50* | 10 |
| Walgreen | 50 | 10 |

* Automatic monthly debit minimums

| | |
|---|---|
| Becton, Dickinson | 800-955-4743 |
| Eastman Kodak | 800-253-6057 |
| Exxon | 800-252-1800 |
| Fannie Mae | 888-289-3266 |
| Finova | 800-774-4117 |
| Interstate Energy | 800-356-5342 |
| Johnson Controls | 800-524-6220 |
| Regions Financial | 800-922-3468 |
| Tribune | 800-924-1490 |
| Walgreen | 800-774-4117 |
| Wisconsin Energy | 800-558-9663 |
| WPS Resources | 800-236-1551 |

new equity capital is created; the firm merely acts as a broker in buying shares for investors. The money that is sent to the company to purchase stock is not kept by the company but instead is used to purchase shares on the open market. When a firm chooses to issue new shares via a no-load stock program, the money sent to the company goes directly into its coffers. This capital can be used to buy equipment, reduce debt, make acquisitions, or fund research. Selling stock in this fashion is attractive to a company because equity can be raised much more cheaply via a no-load stock plan than it can via an investment banker.

$ *Cementing Relationships.* Another benefit corporations obtain by offering no-load stock programs is to cement relationships with shareholders. These relationships can be especially helpful in industries, such as utilities, telecommunications, and banking, in which competitive pressures are rising due to deregulation. The synergy between a shareholder as a consumer of the company's goods and services is a reason many no-load stock programs are offered by consumer-products companies. For example, McDonald's offers a program that allows individuals to buy even their initial shares of stock directly from the company. McDonald's knows that if it can turn you into a shareholder, you're more likely to buy Big Macs instead of Whoppers next time you go fast-food hunting. This competition for the consumer is one reason the growth of these plans has been dramatic in recent years. The retail sector is a good example. Once Wal-Mart and Home Depot offered direct-purchase plans, other retailers, such as Sears, Dayton Hudson, and J.C. Penney, followed suit. In the oil sector, Texaco's plan was quickly followed by direct-purchase plans from Exxon, Mobil, Amoco, Chevron, Royal Dutch Petroleum, and British Petroleum.

$ *Diversify Shareholder Base.* A common complaint from corporate America is the myopic investment vision of institutional investors. If a company fails to meet or exceed earnings estimates each and every quarter, look out. Individual investors, on the other hand, are more stable and long-term-oriented. Some corporations like small investors because they help to stabilize the stock price. For companies that want a greater representation of small investors, offering a no-load stock program is an excellent way to draw small investors to its shareholder ranks.

A related benefit is that small investors tend to be more loyal to company management, or at least silent on corporate governance issues. Institutional investors have been rather vociferous in recent years concerning certain corporate matters. Companies that are under siege from institutional shareholders might find more friendly faces by boosting the ranks of small investors via a no-load stock program. Another reason that certain corporations might want to broaden representation among small investors is to help ward off an unwanted takeover attempt. A large number of small investors can help level the playing field during proxy battles.

## PLAN FEES

When I first started covering no-load stocks, these plans were truly "no load," in other words, no fees on the buy side. In the last two years, however, fees have been creeping into these plans. These fees usually come in the form of one-time enrollment fees (usually $5 to $15) and per-transaction fees (usually $1 to $10 plus five cents to 10 cents per share). Companies are charging these fees in order to help defray the costs of operating the plans.

For example, it's estimated that a company spends $12 to $16 per year on registered shareholder services. These costs include printing and mailing quarterly and annual reports and proxy statements. Obviously, fees matter, so it is important to evaluate fees when choosing no-load stocks, but don't ignore a company's plan merely because it charges fees. Fees impact investors differently depending on investment styles and amounts.

## CYBER-INVESTING IN DIRECT PURCHASE PLANS

One of the most exciting developments in the direct-purchase world is the migration of traditional DRIPs and no-load stock plans to cyberspace. This development is not surprising given the huge success online brokers have had in garnering customers. A pioneer in cyber-investing directly with companies is Equitable Companies, the insurance and financial-services firm. This company was the first firm to allow investors to purchase shares in its DRIP via the Internet. Participants in the company's DRIP can log on to the company's Web site at http://www.eqshare.com to make optional cash purchases and check on their accounts.

Another firm that helped pioneer DRIP cyber-investing is Fannie Mae, the mortgage lender. Interested investors can make their initial purchase directly over the Internet by logging on to http://www.netstockdirect.com and looking up the Fannie Mae section of the site. Another Web site promising DRIP-like investing for online investors is http://www.buyandhold.com. The site is expected to be up and running by the end of 1998. My guess is that, within the next two years, virtually all DRIPs and no-load stocks will allow purchases over the Internet, either at company Web sites or "Clearinghouse"-type Web sites, such as www.buyandhold.com and netstockdirect.com.

## DIRECTORY OF NO-LOAD STOCKS

Investors should note that companies frequently change details of their plans, so it's always a good idea to read the plan prospectus before enrolling to make sure there are no surprises. Also note that companies are implementing no-load stock plans at a furious pace. The number has grown from just over 50 plans at the end of 1994 to more than 400 at the time of this writing. That number includes many foreign companies that now allow investors to buy initial shares directly. (Directories of foreign no-load stocks are provided in Appendix C.) To obtain a free, updated list of all no-load stocks, send your request for the list and a self-addressed envelope to DRIP Investor, 7412 Calumet Avenue, Hammond, Indiana 46324-2692. I've also provided a complete directory of U.S. no-load stocks in the Appendix at the back of the book.

For a complete review of DRIPs and no-load stocks, see my two other books *Buying Stocks Without A Broker* (1996) and *No-Load Stocks* (1997), both published by McGraw-Hill. For continuous coverage of DRIPs/no-load stocks, my newsletter, *DRIP Investor*, is an excellent source. Subscription information is available in the back of the book.

## INVESTMENT CLUBS—ARMIES OF THE REVOLUTION

Another way to get started in stocks is by joining an investment club. Think of investment clubs as the "armies" of the individual investor revolution. The number of investment clubs has exploded in the last three years. The National Association of Investors Corporation, based in Madison Heights, Michigan (248-583-6242), is the umbrella organization for many investment clubs in this country. According to the

NAIC, there are now more than 37,000 NAIC investment clubs, up from 12,429 in 1994. The NAIC estimates that its members control some $175 billion in assets.

Through the course of the year I speak to thousands of investment club members attending various NAIC functions. What I have found is that many of these individuals knew nothing about investing prior to joining the investment club but quickly learned a great deal thanks to the efforts of the club members. I've also found that investment clubs offer a rich environment for building lasting friendships. Another benefit of investment clubs is that they provide a way for individuals to invest with little money. Many clubs have monthly dues of just $25 to $50.

Please see Appendix B for information on a local NAIC group near you.

## GETTING STARTED IN MUTUAL FUNDS

Mutual funds are investment companies that take in funds from many individuals, commingle the money, and buy a portfolio of stocks (or bonds or other investments) that they manage. Popular fund families include Vanguard, Janus, Fidelity, Strong, and T. Rowe Price. Mutual funds provide a way for investors with limited dollars—many mutual funds have minimum investments of $2500 or less—to have portfolio diversification as well as professional money management.

Investors can purchase mutual funds through a broker or directly with the fund family. "No-load" funds are sold to investors without a broker and without an up-front sales fee. To join most no-load funds, you call the fund family directly via a toll-free number, and the fund group sends you the necessary enrollment information and fund prospectus. The prospectus explains the details of the fund—fees, management styles, and so on. "Load" funds carry a sales fee, which can range from as little as one percent of your investment to five percent or more of your investment, and are usually sold by brokers. All mutual funds have annual management fees, which are paid to the investment company for managing the portfolio. These fees can vary dramatically from as low as 0.25 percent of a fund's assets to two percent or more a year.

Investors buy and sell shares in the fund at the "net asset value." This is the total of the fund's assets minus any liabilities. Many mutual funds list their net asset values daily in *The Wall Street Journal*.

An excellent source for ongoing coverage of mutual funds is *Morningstar Mutual Funds*. The guide is found in most libraries or by calling 800-735-0700. (Chapter 5 provides other ways to research mutual funds using the Internet.)

Most investment advisers believe that mutual funds represent the only way individual investors should venture into the markets. The professional management and "instant" portfolio diversification afforded by funds are two huge benefits that are tough for individual investors to replicate on their own.

I have a different slant on funds. Funds represent an excellent avenue for investors who don't have the time or inclination to call their own investment shots to get in the investing game. However, the hype that proclaims funds as the "perfect investment" is misleading. In many respects, individual stocks have advantages over equity funds in terms of expenses and taxes. Nevertheless, I don't view funds versus stocks as an "either/or" issue; an investor can hold both stocks and funds in a single portfolio. Certainly for new investors who feel uncomfortable, funds can be excellent "starter" investments. For investors who are confident in their stock-picking abilities, funds represent a useful tool in complementing your stock investments in a well-rounded investment program.

How should you choose a mutual fund? One point I'll make here is that, all things being equal, funds with the lowest expenses make the best investments. Thus, investors should focus on no-load funds with low annual expenses. Chapter 8 goes into great detail on what I think are key factors when selecting mutual-fund investments.

Many mutual funds allow investors to get started with minimal amounts of money if the investor agrees to automatic monthly investments via electronic debit of a bank account. Below is a listing of prominent fund families that waive the minimum initial investment requirement if an investor agrees to automatic monthly investments:

| Fund Family | Minimum Automatic Monthly Deposit | Phone Number |
|---|---|---|
| Dreyfus | $100 | 800-645-6561 |
| Founders | $50 | 800-525-2440 |
| Invesco | $50 | 800-525-8085 |
| Strong | $50 | 800-368-1030 |
| T. Rowe Price | $50 | 800-638-5660 |
| USAA | $50 | 800-382-8722 |

You should also note that many fund families lower the minimum initial investment if you are opening an IRA.

## FUND "SUPERMARKETS"

Fund investing has become extremely convenient due to the growth of fund "supermarkets." These one-stop shops for funds are offered by a variety of brokerage and fund concerns. Perhaps the best-known fund supermarket is Charles Schwab's OneSource program. Through OneSource, Schwab customers have literally thousands of mutual funds offered by many fund families in which they can invest. The advantage of using a supermarket such as OneSource is that you can hold all your fund investments with a single entity.

As an example, let's say you want to invest in six funds offered by Charles Schwab's OneSource plan. If the funds are no-load funds, you could make those investments directly with the fund families without Schwab. However, you'll have to make six phone calls, fill out six enrollment forms, and deal with six monthly or quarterly statements from the various fund families. If you use Schwab's OneSource plan, you can make all six investments directly through Schwab and your six fund investments appear on your consolidated statement you receive from Schwab. Furthermore, you'll pay no additional fees by buying the funds through Schwab. (Schwab charges the fund families a fee for carrying their funds in the OneSource program.)

Of course, just because it's easy to buy and sell funds through fund supermarkets doesn't always make it appropriate. Don't use the convenience of fund supermarkets to trade your fund investments. Granted, trading no-load funds doesn't generate transaction costs because no-load funds are sold without sales charges, but you'll still likely generate tax liabilities if you trade funds frequently. For this reason, be careful that you don't abuse the convenience of buying and selling funds via fund supermarkets or even within the same no-load mutual-fund family.

## RETIREMENT INVESTING

Look at any poll surveying the reasons people invest. At the top is usually "retirement." For many of us, retirement represents the ultimate "cliff dive," the big jump into the great unknown. Will I have enough money? What if my health fails? Will Social Security be around to help?

Some advisers say you'll need about 80 percent of your pre-retirement income to live comfortably. If your annual salary before retirement was $50,000, you'll need $40,000 annually to maintain your lifestyle. I've always wondered why you need less money in retirement than you do while you are still working. Presumably, it's because the house is paid off, the kids are out of college, and your household "overhead" is reduced. This may be true for some people, but not all. Individuals are having children later, which means those financial responsibilities associated with kids may not stop at age 62. Perhaps you're one of those "sandwich" couples, taking care of children as well as aging parents. Will you need less money at retirement? What if inflation, which has been benign in recent years, skyrockets over the next 20 years, reducing the real value of your retirement stash? What if Social Security truly turns out to be a giant Ponzi scheme?

The upshot is that things change and what you assume is a satisfactory nest egg today could be woefully lacking 10 years from now. Bottom line: You just don't know how much is going to be enough. The best way to invest for retirement is maximizing your retirement opportunities as soon as possible, even if it means starting with just $10 or $20 a month. Fortunately, many excellent retirement vehicles are available even to individuals with modest incomes. This section explores these vehicles.

### 401(k) Plans

Section 401(k) of the Internal Revenue Code allows employers to offer a way for their employees to delay payment of taxes while saving for retirement. Not all companies offer a 401(k) program, but the number of firms that do has been rising rapidly in recent years.

The 401(k) is the best investment deal you'll ever get for saving for retirement. Under a 401(k) plan, part of your pay is deposited into an account in your name. These contributions are made with *pre-tax* dollars. In other words, neither federal nor state income taxes are withheld from this money, and because the amount you contribute to your 401(k) is not included on your W-2 form as taxable wages or income, your 401(k) contributions reduce your yearly tax bite. Therefore, funds in your 401(k) plan will grow tax-deferred; you'll pay no taxes until the funds are withdrawn.

Let's say you invest $300 per month in your company's 401(k) plan. (If you work for a nonprofit organization, the counterpart to the 401(k) plan is the 403(b) plan.) Assuming you are in the 28 percent tax bracket, you would have to pay a little more than $1000 in taxes on these earnings if you did not contribute the money to the 401(k) plan. In other words, your $3600 investment in the 401(k) is really costing you only about $2600 when you account for the tax savings. Let's look at it another way: Say you want to make a $3600 investment outside of a 401(k) plan. You would have to earn $5000 in order to net a $3600 investment after taxes (assuming a 28 percent tax bracket).

But there's more to the 401(k) story than tax benefits. In many cases, your employer matches a portion of your contribution. That's free money, and, because the contributions are made via payroll deduction, you don't even have to worry about making the investments.

To summarize, a 401(k) plan offers the best of all possible worlds:

$ *Convenience.* Payroll deductions mean the program runs sort of on autopilot; you don't have to do much besides choose the investments and how much you want deducted from your pay.

$ *Low minimums/greater maximums than IRAs.* You can get started in a 401(k) plan by saving as little as one percent of your salary. Even if you earn as little as $100 per week, you can still set aside $1 a week in your 401(k) plan. And for those with deeper pockets, the maximum contribution to a 401(k) plan in 1998 is $10,000, well above the $2000 maximum for an IRA.

$ *Tax advantages.* Money contributed to a 401(k) plan will not incur federal or state income taxes and lowers your taxable income. Your money also grows tax-deferred.

$ *Free money.* If your employer matches part of your investment, $1 contributed to a 401(k) plan instantly becomes $1.50 or $2 once you consider employer matching and tax savings (depending on your tax bracket). And that's before you consider the positive effects of that money growing tax-deferred over time.

$ *Flexibility.* You can raise or lower your 401(k) contribution over time to take into account increases or decreases in your salary. You can also stop and restart contributions if need be. This flexibility also extends to your investment options. In most plans, you'll have a variety of investments from which to choose (usually mutual funds or stock in your company). You'll also have the ability to change your investment mix over time. Most plans allow participants to change investments at least every three months, while others, such as my company's 401(k) plan, allow investment switches daily.

## Managing Your 401(k) Plan

It doesn't matter that the 401(k) plan is the best deal around for investors if you don't manage your plan properly. The following list contains issues you should consider when managing your 401(k) plan:

$ *This is a retirement account, not a savings account.* Your access to 401(k) monies is limited. Penalties are usually associated with withdrawals of 401(k) money before age 59, so consult a tax adviser before dipping into these funds.

$ *Don't eliminate risk from your 401(k) portfolio.* Purging a portfolio of risk means relegating your portfolio to returns that are inadequate for building and sustaining a retirement nest egg. If you're someone in his or her 20s or 30s, focus on equity mutual funds. If you're in your 50s or 60s, you should still have some portion of your 401(k) money in stock funds.

$ *If you change jobs, be sure to "roll over" your 401(k) funds into another retirement plan.* What you don't want to do is take possession of this money when you change jobs. Investors have 60 days in which to perform their 401(k) rollover if they take possession of funds. However, individuals who take possession of 401(k) funds rather than having them transferred directly to a qualified plan may be in for a surprise. If funds are distributed to you, 20 percent of the amount will be withheld for income taxes. In order to roll the whole amount into an IRA (a qualified plan in which you can roll over 401(k) funds), you have to make up the 20 percent. If you do this, you'll get the 20 percent back when you file your tax return. In most cases, if you do not invest the entire amount, including the 20 percent that is withheld, you will be taxed on that 20 percent as ordinary income, plus be liable for a penalty if you are under the age of $59^1/_2$. The best approach is to have your old employer roll over the 401(k) money directly into a new qualified account or the 401(k) of your new employer.

$ *Don't trade your 401(k) money.* The flexibility of many 401(k) plans, including the ability to switch investments daily in some plans, makes it extremely easy to trade your 401(k) money. Unfortunately, just about the time you move money out of stocks and into bonds or a money-market account, it's probably the time you should be buying equity mutual funds, not selling. The best strategy for managing your 401(k) plan is to pick an asset allocation that makes sense for your age, income level, and investment time horizon. Once you've determined your asset allocation, buy the appropriate investments on the basis of this allocation. Don't get caught up moving money in and out of funds. Be patient and do as little trading as possible. Figure 3.1 shows some possible asset allocation mixes. (I borrowed this information from a brochure handed out by my company's 401(k) plan administrator.) I think this information does a pretty good job of breaking down possible mixes based on age and risk aver-

**Some Typical Allocation Mixes**

| CONSERVATIVE | | BALANCED | | AGGRESSIVE | |
|---|---|---|---|---|---|
| **Age 20-40** | | **Age 20-40** | | **Age 20-40** | |
| Stocks | 40-60% | Stocks | 60-75% | Stocks | 90-100% |
| Fixed-income | 20-40% | Fixed-income | 15-25% | Fixed-income | 0-10% |
| Short-term | 15-30% | Short-term | 10-20% | Short-term | 0% |
| **Age 40-50** | | **Age 40-50** | | **Age 40-50** | |
| Stocks | 30-50% | Stocks | 40-60% | Stocks | 75-100% |
| Fixed-income | 25-45% | Fixed-income | 25-40% | Fixed-income | 15-25% |
| Short-term | 25-40% | Short-term | 20-30% | Short-term | 0% |
| **Age 55-65** | | **Age 55-65** | | **Age 55-65** | |
| Stocks | 0-30% | Stocks | 30-50% | Stocks | 50-75% |
| Fixed-income | 40-75% | Fixed-income | 40-75% | Fixed-income | 20-50% |
| Short-term | 30-40% | Short-term | 25-35% | Short-term | 0-20% |

**Figure 3.1**

sion. Of course, when applying any asset allocation model to your situation, be sure to consider your other assets, income, and investments.

$ *Manage your 401(k) money with your other investments in mind.* When I think of how to allocate my investments, I don't ignore investments that I hold outside of a 401(k) plan, especially if these investments are earmarked for retirement, too. For example, I own more than 20 stocks outside of my 401(k), but I don't own any foreign mutual funds. Thus, I usually have at least 20 percent of my 401(k) money invested in international funds. Likewise, I don't want to own all small-cap, aggressive stocks outside of a 401(k) plan only to duplicate these investments within a 401(k) plan by investing in only small-cap growth mutual funds.

$ *Don't get caught holding your company's stock exclusively in your 401(k) plan.* Not all company "matching" plans are the same. In my company's plan, my employer usually matches around 25 percent of my contribution up to the first six percent of my income. I get this match regardless of where I invest my money in the plan. Some companies offer company stock as a matching contribution. Owning company stock is not necessarily a bad thing. In fact, having your interest aligned with company shareholders by being a stockholder is good—to a point. The problem arises when you have too much of a good thing. Indeed, employer matching plans with company stock can be quite seductive. After all, who wouldn't want to buy stock 50 cents or 75 cents on the dollar? Such discounts on company stock are common in 401(k) plans. But don't be seduced. Follow prudent portfolio diversification strategies when building your 401(k) plan. Try to limit your company's stock in your plan to 25 percent or less. Remember: You already have a lot at stake with your company by virtue of having a job with the firm. Don't get killed twice, losing your job and retirement funds, in the event the firm goes belly up.

For further information about your company's 401(k) plan, including eligibility requirements and investment options, consult your firm's benefits department. If your company does not offer a 401(k) plan, bring up the idea to your supervisor. You'll probably have plenty of allies if you decide to bring the issue to management.

## Roth IRA

The 1997 Taxpayer Relief Act contained a lot of good news for investors. First, the Act reduced the capital-gains tax rate for investments held more than 12 months to 20 percent from 28 percent. Second, the Act created two new savings tools: the Roth IRA and the Education IRA.

The Roth IRA, named after Senator William Roth, Jr., is the best investment deal to come along since the 401(k). Despite the Roth IRA's many benefits, millions of investors are still not taking advantage of this new IRA. My guess is that investors feel the Roth is too complicated. Sometimes I think the best way to make a subject or concept easy to understand is by approaching it in a "question and answer" format. The following is a "Q&A" on the new Roth IRA:

**Q.** How does the Roth IRA differ from the traditional IRA?

**A.** In a traditional IRA, earnings on contributions grow tax-deferred, which means they are subject to taxes when withdrawn. In contrast, although the annual contribution to a Roth IRA is not tax deductible, the account's value is not taxed upon distribution, including earnings. In other words, your money grows tax-*free*.

**Q.** Can anyone open a Roth IRA?

**A.** It depends on your income. Single individuals with an adjusted gross income of up to $95,000 ($150,000 for couples filing jointly) can make a full $2000 annual contribution. Partial contributions are allowed for individuals whose adjusted gross income is between $95,000 and $110,000 ($150,000 and $160,000 for joint filers).

**Q.** What are the benefits of the Roth IRA over a traditional IRA?

**A.** As mentioned, your money grows tax free in a Roth IRA, not tax-deferred as in a traditional IRA. In order to withdraw your money tax-free, your account has to have been open at least five years and your withdrawal occurs either after you reach $59^{1}/_{2}$ or due to disability, death, or if the money is used for expenses under the "first-time homebuyer" rule. Another advantage of the Roth IRA is that you aren't required to withdraw money ever, even after the age of $70^{1}/_{2}$. With a Roth IRA, if you die, your beneficiary won't have to pay income taxes on money withdrawn from the account. This makes a Roth IRA an interesting estate-planning tool.

**Q.** Can I make contributions to a Roth IRA even after I turn $70^{1}/_{2}$?

**A.** Yes, as long as you have earned income.

**Q.** What are the downsides to Roth IRAs?

**A.** If you withdraw your money before your Roth account has been open five years, your earnings may be subject to federal income taxes plus a 10 percent penalty. You also don't get a federal income tax deduction for money you contribute to a Roth IRA.

**Q.** If I'm opening a new IRA, would you preference a Roth IRA?

**A.** If you are not eligible to make tax-deductible contributions to a traditional IRA because of income levels, the Roth may be preferable. If you qualify for tax-deductible IRA contributions, the choice is not so simple. If you have many years until retirement or want an estate-planning tool, a Roth IRA may still be preferable.

**Q.** Can I contribute to both a Roth IRA and a traditional IRA?

**A.** Yes, but your total annual contribution to all IRAs (traditional and/or Roth) cannot exceed $2000.

**Q.** Should I quit contributing to my employer's 401(k) plan in order to put money into a Roth IRA?

**A.** I would advise against that. One reason is that in many 401(k) plans, the employer matches a certain percentage of your contribution. This matching, in effect, is money that you would lose if you failed to contribute. I would still opt for maximizing the contribution to your 401(k) plan before opening an IRA, including a Roth IRA.

**Q.** Can I convert an existing traditional IRA into a Roth IRA?

**A.** Yes, as long as your adjusted gross income isn't more than $100,000 for the year in which you convert. Obviously, being able to shift from tax-deferred growth to tax-free growth is a big incentive to convert from a traditional IRA to a Roth IRA. However, when you convert a traditional IRA, you incur a tax liability. The size of the tax liability differs depending on whether you are converting deductible or nondeductible IRA funds. If you are converting IRA funds that were tax-deductible upon contribution, the entire amount is considered ordinary income for tax purposes. In other words, if you are converting a deductible IRA of $28,000 to a Roth IRA, you'll have to pay taxes on the full $28,000. If you are converting a nondeductible IRA, only the earnings are subject to tax, not the contributions, which were made with after-tax dollars. Investors who make conversions in 1998 qualify for a special tax treatment that allows them to spread their tax burden over four years. Returning to our previous example, an individual who converts a deductible IRA with $28,000 spreads the tax hit over four years by recording as income $7,000 in the years 1998 through 2001.

**Q.** When does it make the most sense to convert?

**A.** Conversion makes sense if the following items are true:

$ You have a lot of time until retirement to make up for the tax hit you'll absorb when converting.

$ You expect to be in a higher tax bracket at retirement.

$ You have a relatively small IRA with the bulk of the money being nondeductible contributions.

$ You have the money to pay the tax without using retirement funds.

**Q.** What types of investments can I hold in a Roth IRA?

**A.** Investors have a variety of investment choices with the Roth IRA. The most popular choice for IRAs is mutual funds. You should follow the same rules in terms of investing in your Roth IRA as you would any retirement program. What's Rule #1? The longer you have until retirement, the more concentrated your funds should be in growth investments, such as equity mutual funds. An index fund that mimics the performance of the Standard & Poor's 500, such as the **Vanguard Index 500** fund (800-662-7447), would provide a solid core holding for a Roth IRA.

**Q.** I like what I've read here. How do I get started investing in a Roth IRA?

**A.** Once you've determined that a Roth IRA makes sense for you, the next step is to choose your investment. If you go with mutual funds (such as those funds recommended here or in Chapter 8), contact the fund and request enrollment information for the fund, as well as an application for a Roth IRA. When you get the fund enrollment and Roth IRA materials, fill them out and return them to the fund. Make sure you include your check for the initial investment. Many mutual funds have lower investment minimums for investors opening IRAs, so individuals with limited finances still may find it possible to get started investing in a Roth IRA.

## Education IRA

Another investment vehicle created by the 1997 Taxpayer Relief Act was the Education IRA. Actually calling this investment an "IRA" is a misnomer; the Education IRA has nothing to do with saving for retirement. The vehicle was created to assist parents in setting aside funds for a child's post-secondary education.

The Education IRA allows individuals to set aside up to $500 per child per year. The money grows tax-deferred and can be withdrawn without paying any taxes if the funds are used for post-secondary education expenses. Contributions can be made to an Education IRA by anyone such as parents, grandparents, friends, and relatives. Full contribution is allowed only if the contributor's adjusted gross income is less than $95,000 (single) or $150,000 (married filing jointly).

Don't be dismayed if your income exceeds these levels; you still may be able to provide the funding for an Education IRA. Let's say you are a wealthy uncle who wants to set aside $500 per year for five nieces and nephews. Even though your income requirements may not allow you to open the account, you still may be able to provide the funding by giving the parents of the children a gift in the dollar amount required to fund the accounts. Remember: You can give anyone a tax-free gift of up to $10,000 per year. As long as the parents' incomes don't exceed the limits, the parents can take your gift and use the money to fund the Education IRAs. What if the parents' income exceeds the upper limits to contribute to an Education IRA? The parents could give "gift" money to a friend or relative whose income is within allowable limits to make an Education IRA contribution. The friend or relative could then be the contributor. Regardless of who contributes the money, the account is controlled by the parents until the funds are distributed or the child reaches the age of 30, which is also when the funds must be distributed. Earnings are taxed and penalized if not used for education expenses by age 30 (but not the contributions, because they are made with after-tax dollars).

One of the positive aspects of the Education IRA is that you can shift the funds from one child to a sibling if need be. For example, let's say you open Education IRAs for your two children. After saving for many years, one of the children decides against enrolling in college. Rules governing Education IRAs allow you to take that money and combine it with the funds from the Education IRA for your other child.

The downside of an Education IRA is that the money contributed is not tax-deductible. Also, because of the newness of the Education IRA, it's uncertain how colleges will view Education IRAs within the context of financial-aid decisions. Finally, because the annual limits are only $500 per child, the plans don't provide an opportunity to set aside big dollars, especially for a youngster in his or her teens. Still, I think anything that helps make it easier for investors to save money, whether for college education or retirement, is a worthwhile investment. How should these monies be invested? Mutual funds are likely to be the investment of choice for an Education IRA. How aggressive you should be with these funds depends primarily on the amount of time until the funds are likely to be withdrawn. For example, if you are setting aside money for a two-year old, you should focus exclusively on growth. Quality long-term growth funds to consider include the **Vanguard Index 500** fund (800-662-7447) or the **T. Rowe Price Mid-Cap Growth** fund (800-638-5660). As you get closer to the date on which funds will be withdrawn, you should focus less on growth and more on safety. The **Vanguard Wellington** fund (800-662-7447), which invests about two-thirds of its funds in stocks and one-third in bonds, represents a solid choice for more conservative investors.

## Traditional IRA

With the creation of the Roth IRA, the traditional IRA has sort of taken a backseat. Actually, many individuals turned away from the traditional IRA several years ago when contributions to the traditional IRA became nondeductible for millions of Americans. For individuals who cannot deduct IRA contributions but are eligible to contribute to a Roth IRA, the traditional IRA *is* inferior to the new Roth IRA, not to mention a 401(k). For that reason, investors should first "max" out investments to a 401(k) before contributing to a traditional IRA. However, many investors who have the financial wherewithal to make the maximum contribution to their 401(k) and still have money left for an IRA may not be eligible for the Roth IRA. In this case, should these investors consider a traditional IRA?

Some financial advisers will tell you that a traditional IRA is a bad idea for those who can't make deductible contributions. I disagree. Any investment vehicle that helps investors set aside money for retirement is worth considering. The traditional IRA, while not having the bells and whistles of the Roth IRA, still allows you to set aside money that grows tax-deferred, and that isn't all bad. That's one reason why I still fund a traditional IRA with nondeductible contributions.

Here are some rules and eligibility requirements governing traditional IRAs:

$ If you are not covered by a qualified retirement plan at your place of employment, your contributions to a traditional IRA are deductible, regardless of your income. Thus, if you make $200,000 per year at your job, yet you are not covered by a qualified retirement plan, you can make a deductible contribution to a traditional IRA of up to $2000 per year.

$ If you are covered by a qualified plan, you may still be able to deduct contributions to a traditional IRA. For 1998, a full deduction is available to individuals with adjusted gross incomes of $30,000 or less (single filer) or $50,000 (married, filing jointly). For incomes between $30,000 to $40,000 (single filer) and $50,000 to $60,000 (married, filing jointly), partial deduction of contributions is permitted. For incomes above $40,000 (single filer) and $60,000 (married, filing jointly), no deductible contributions are permitted. (These income levels are indexed for inflation.) However, you still can make nondeductible contributions to an IRA of up to $2000. For married couples, the maximum contribution is $2000 per spouse.

Where do I invest my traditional IRA contributions? I have my entire IRA in the Strong Dow 30 Value no-load fund (800-368-1030). I manage this fund with Richard Moroney. (I guess you can say I eat my own cooking.) Other ideas for IRA investments include an S&P index fund or an international equity fund, such as the T. Rowe Price International Stock fund (800-638-5660).

## GETTING JUNIOR STARTED

This chapter has discussed a number of low-cost and easy ways for you to get into the investment game, including stocks, mutual funds, 401(k) plans, and IRAs. The individual investor revolution, however, is not strictly an "adult thing." Maybe you have a budding Warren Buffett in your household who has an interest in the market. Or, more likely, you'd like your child to avoid the investment mistakes you made. Indeed, I wish I had a dollar for every time I receive a phone call or a letter from a subscriber regretting that he or she didn't invest sooner.

It doesn't have to be that way for your child or grandchild.

The power of time in an investment program is an often-discussed topic in these pages—for good reason. Enough studies have shown that investment success is directly related to how effectively an investor harnesses the power of time. An individual who starts investing in his or her teens or 20s has a huge advantage over someone in his or her 50s or 60s who is just beginning to set aside money. Of course, starting an investment program at any age is better than having no investment program at all. Still, it's hard to overstate the importance of time in an investment program.

For example, if a 10-year old sets aside just $16 per month (perhaps with a little help from mom and dad and the grandparents) in an individual stock or equity mutual fund and maintains this investment discipline for 50 years, he or she will have more than $277,000 at age 60 (assuming an average annual return of 10 percent). You may not fully realize the power of time in this example until you understand the following: That 10-year old invested only $9600 over the course of those 50 years to amass more than $277,000.

Now, if one of the many jobs of being a parent or grandparent is making sure your mistakes are not repeated by your children and grandchildren, I think it follows that you owe it to your children and their children to get them started investing as soon as possible.

### Easy To Get Started

There are two important factors to consider when initiating an investment programs for kids. First, the learning process is enhanced if the child is able to invest in a company to which he or she can relate. In other words, don't expect your child to show much interest in some obscure biotechnology company. Instead, invest in a company in which your youngster uses or is familiar with the product. I'm not advocating that you invest in a lousy toy company, for example, just because junior plays with the toys, but there are plenty of consumer products and services that are quality investments and are probably familiar to your child or grandchild.

Although you could use any of the investment vehicles mentioned here for creating your kindergarten capitalist, I'm especially partial to DRIPs and no-load stocks for getting youngsters started. Dividend reinvestment plans make solid "starter" investments for kids for several reasons. First, many DRIPs have minimum investment requirements of just $10 to $25. Such small amounts make it easier for a youngster to make periodic contributions to the plan. Second, the growth of direct-purchase plans has made it easier for youngsters to get started without ever having to open a brokerage account.

The following quality companies offer DRIPs and provide products and services that would be recognizable to most children and young adults:

| | | |
|---|---|---|
| * Cadbury Schweppes (*7-Up*) | Harley-Davidson | PepsiCo |
| Coca-Cola | Hershey Foods | * Procter & Gamble |
| Colgate-Palmolive | * Home Depot | * Quaker Oats (*Gatorade*) |
| * Compaq Computer | Intel | * Sony |
| * Diageo (*Burger King, Pillsbury*) | * International Business | * Tribune (Chicago Cubs) |
| * Disney (Walt) | Machines | * Wal-Mart Stores |
| * Exxon | * Mattel | * Walgreen |
| * Ford Motor | * McDonald's | Wendy's International |
| | | Wrigley (William) |

* Initial purchases may be made directly.

## Fannie Mae's "Kid-Friendly" Direct-Purchase Plan

One company that is making it especially easy to create a kindergarten capitalist is **Fannie Mae,** the largest mortgage lender in the country. Fannie Mae's direct-purchase plan includes a "Young Shareowner Investment Option." This option is available for children and young adults eligible for the Uniform Gifts or Transfers to Minors Account (UGMA) registrations (UGMAs are explained below). Participants in the Young Shareowners Option can open an account with just $100. The company will waive the $100 minimum if an investor agrees to automatic monthly debit of at least $12. Subsequent investments can be made for as little as $10, and for investments of $10 to $100 made with a check, there is no purchase fee. For invest-ments of $100 to $2500, the purchase fee is $5 ($2 if made with automatic debit). For purchases over $2500, the fee is $5 plus com-missions ($2 plus commissions if made with automatic debit). There are no fees to reinvest dividends. Another interesting feature of the plan is the availability of an Education IRA. For further informa-tion and an enrollment form, call 888-289-3266.

Obviously, just because a DRIP is an easy way to invest in a com-pany doesn't make it a good investment. Fortunately, Fannie Mae has an excellent track record of growth. Although these shares will likely be volatile due to interest-rate movements, the stock has excellent long-term potential.

## Registering Investments

Whether you set up DRIPs appropriate for a youngster, non-DRIP stocks, or mutual funds, how the investment is registered is an important consideration when starting an investment program for a child. A parent or grandparent could merely open a DRIP or mutual-fund account in the name of the parent or grandparent and simply earmark the account for the youngster. In this way, the par-ent or grandparent controls the account. However, a disadvantage to this approach is that the account holder will be taxed on the income earned in the plan at his or her tax rate.

An alternative is to set up the investment in the child's name under a Uniform Gifts to Minors Account (UGMA). Funds in the account are in the minor's name and social security number and are consid-ered to be owned by the minor. Dividends paid on the account are taxable, most likely at a preferred tax rate. The adult custodian is responsible for the account until the minor reaches the age of majority. Any withdrawals from the account are payable to the cus-todian on the minor's behalf until that time. However, once the youth has reached the age of majority, 18 in many states, control of the account reverts to the child to do with as he or she sees fit. This is the downside of setting up a UGMA. Parental control is lost at the age of majority. Another consideration is that college financial aid decisions could be impacted if a child has sizable assets in a UGMA account. It is important to understand the pluses and minuses of UGMAs before registering the investments in that form.

## Buying Other Investments Directly

Investors have a plethora of other financial investments that can be bought directly, in most cases via the computer, and usually without any intermediary:

$ Dollar Bank of Pittsburgh offers U.S. savings bonds for sale over the Internet. Customers of its "Netbanking" service complete an order form telling the bank which account to charge. A Series EE bond is then mailed in about a week. Customers will soon be able to buy savings bonds directly from the Bureau of the Public Debt's Web site using a credit card (http://www. savingsbonds.gov).

$ Investors can buy treasury securities directly without a broker and without a service charge via the Treasury Department's Treasury Direct program. The program recently added three new features. The "Pay Direct" option allows investors to buy Treasury securities without sending a check via automatic debit of a bank account. "Reinvest Direct" allows investors to reinvest maturing securities over the phone. "Sell Direct" allows direct investors to sell their securities before maturity without enlisting the aid of a broker for the first time. Investors are charged $34 per sell transaction. Future plan refinements include allowing individuals to buy and sell treasury securities via the Internet. For further information about the program, visit the Bureau of Public Debt's Web site at http://www. publicdebt.treas.gov or obtain a copy of "Buying Treasury Securities at Federal Reserve Banks," a booklet available for $4.50 from the Federal Reserve Bank of Richmond, Public Services Department, P.O. Box 27622, Richmond, VA 23261.

$ Initial public offerings (IPOs) for smaller companies are migrating to the Internet. IPOs occur when a private company "goes public," or sells shares to investors. IPOs are usually done in the following way: A company hires an investment bank, such as Goldman Sachs or Merrill Lynch, to sell the new shares to the public. The investment bank heads a syndicate of other brokers and bankers who are responsible for selling the shares directly. For its efforts, the investment banker takes a fee, which can be as high as seven percent of the amount of the funds raised. This fee is essentially for bringing a buyer and seller of stock together. As we've seen with direct-purchase plans, however, technology and communications now make it unnecessary to use an intermediary. A growing number of small companies are using the Internet to go public, making available their IPOs directly to individual investors. To be sure, many of the firms using the Internet for IPOs are extremely speculative. For that reason, investors who are interested in these Internet IPOs should proceed with caution. My guess is that over time, as the market for Internet IPOs matures and the number of Internet investors grows, you'll see larger companies going public directly without using an investment bank. The following are Web sites focused on Internet IPOs (Source: *Barron's*):

Direct IPO http://www.directipo.com

Direct Stock Market http://www.direct-stock-market.com

Niphix http://www.niphix.com

InterBourse http://www.interbourse.com

Wit Capital http://www.witcapital.com

IPOnet http://www.e-iponet.com

Virtual Wall Street http://www.virtualwallstreet.com

Internet Capital http://www.inetcapital.com

IPO Data Systems http://www.ipodata.com

$ For investors who want to make venture capital investments, the Internet provides a starting point. Private Capital Clearinghouse, Inc.'s PriCap Web site (http://www.pricap.com) provides a place for budding venture capitalists to explore various venture capital opportunities. Technology Funding, a venture capital firm, sells shares of a new fund exclusively over the Web. Individual investors can buy shares in the fund, which focuses on information technology, medical technologies, and industrial-automation investments, with a minimum $1000. For further information, visit the Web site at http://www. techfunding.com. Of course, it's important to remember that venture capital investments carry a high degree of risk, including the loss of your entire investment.

# ▼ Conclusion . . .

Low-commission online trading, direct investing through DRIPs, no-load stocks, no-load mutual funds, and investor-friendly retirement programs including 401(k)s and Roth IRAs are opening doors for millions of small investors who are either only limited players in the financial markets or have been shut out of the game altogether. It is important, however, that investors understand that with increased access comes increased responsibility for your investment actions. Don't assume, for example, that just because a company makes its IPO available on the Internet that it's a worthy investment. In fact, you can bet that the increased ability for individual investors to buy investments directly will fuel an increase in investor scams. For this reason, it's imperative that investors use time-tested investment tools and strategies when taking advantage of this increased investor accessibility. Several of these tools will be described in the following chapters of this book.

# CHAPTER FOUR

# THE BORDERLESS REVOLUTION: INDIVIDUAL INVESTORS GO GLOBAL

Ｔrue revolutions know no borders. Such is the case with the individual investor revolution. Today *any* investor has at his or her fingertips easy, inexpensive vehicles for investing in every part of the globe. I know that may seem hard to believe for someone who is new to the markets and barely understands how to invest in U.S. stocks, but the fact is that in many cases buying foreign investments is no different than buying U.S. stocks or funds. You don't need a broker located in Singapore or Hong Kong or London. In fact, you don't need a broker *at all* to invest overseas.

Of course, it's one thing to invest in U.S. household names such as General Electric, Wal-Mart, Home Depot, or McDonald's. It's quite another story to invest in companies where the CEOs speak a different language and George Washington doesn't appear on the petty cash. Yet most investors would be surprised to discover that many products and services they use every day are produced and sold by overseas companies. The table below lists brand names familiar to many U.S. investors and in every case the products are produced by a foreign company (the country where the firm is headquartered is in parentheses). Furthermore, each of these foreign companies allows *any* U.S. investor to buy shares directly, the *first* share and every share:

| Products/Services | Company |
|---|---|
| Pillsbury food products, Burger King restaurants | Diageo (United Kingdom) |
| Nokia cellular phones | Nokia (Finland) |
| Wisk detergent, Dove soap | Unilever NV (Netherlands) |

| Products/Services | Company |
| --- | --- |
| Canon copiers | Canon (Japan) |
| Panasonic televisions | Matsushita Electric Industrial (Japan) |
| Hard Rock Café | Rank Group (United Kingdom) |
| PlayStation home video game system | Sony (Japan) |
| Stop & Shop stores, Giant supermarkets | Ahold (Netherlands) |
| Seven-Up soft drink | Cadbury Schweppes (United Kingdom) |
| Fila footwear | Fila (Italy) |
| Luxottica eyewear, LensCrafters outlets | Luxottica (Italy) |
| Tagamet antiulcer medication | SmithKline Beecham (United Kingdom) |
| Novolin insulin | Novo-Nordisk (Denmark) |
| TDK cassette tapes | TDK (Japan) |
| Eureka and Frigidaire home appliances | Electrolux (Sweden) |

Investing overseas doesn't have to be investing in the dark. Information on foreign companies is more plentiful than ever. Furthermore, by virtue of using certain products, you probably know more about some foreign companies than you think. The upshot is that you have the access, knowledge, and research tools to invest overseas.

Of course, just because an investor can buy companies based in China or Russia or Argentina doesn't necessarily mean that he or she should. Plenty of market experts will tell you that the benefits of going global are illusory and that buying foreign companies is an investment minefield. Given the performance of many international investments in the last few years, it would be difficult to argue the contrary. However, Wall Street is famous for its short-term memory. In the late 1980s and early '90s, for example, international investing was all the rage, with investors reaping huge returns on investments in emerging countries. It was only after a few years of licking its wounds that Wall Street developed its current investing xenophobia. Bottom line: Real benefits exist for the investor who includes overseas investments in a well-rounded investment portfolio. This chapter discusses investing globally and evaluates a number of ways individual investors can add a foreign flavor to their portfolios.

## DIVERSIFICATION BENEFITS

The essence of portfolio diversification is a correlation of returns among the portfolio's holdings. A portfolio in which all investments move in the same direction and magnitude is not a diversified portfolio. A diversified portfolio has assets that are not closely correlated. In that way, when one group of investments is doing poorly, other investments in the same portfolio are picking up the slack. Diversification speaks to limiting risk. Risk is usually thought of by most investors as volatibity. Diversified portfolios usually are less volatile, precisely because the assets are less correlated.

A long-time argument for investing overseas is that international investments enhance a portfolio's diversification because the returns on these investments are not closely correlated with returns of U.S. stocks. Now some analysts argue that due to advanced communications, global markets, and technology, the world is becoming a much smaller place. This interdependence of world economies is causing a convergence among market returns across countries. In short, the movements of the U.S. markets are becoming much more correlated with movements in international markets.

I would agree that over *short* periods of time, convergence is possible and, indeed, probable, especially during times of worldwide crises. However, over longer periods of time, the diversification benefits increase.

Figure 4.1 shows what analysts call an investor's "efficient frontier." The frontier shows the percent return and the percent risk level (as measured by standard deviation) for a given basket of stocks and bonds. The concept of an efficient frontier is to show a balance in a portfolio between return and risk. Ideally, the best place to be on the frontier is in the northwest portion. At this point, investors maximize return while minimizing risk. For the period 1970 through 1996, a portfolio of all U.S. stocks would have returned, on average, less than 12.5 percent per year with a standard deviation exceeding 15 percent. A portfolio of all bonds, on the other hand, had an average annual return of less than 11 percent annually with a standard deviation of around 11 percent. Now by adding international investments along the curve, the benefits of diversification can be readily seen. For example, a portfolio of one-third non-U.S. stocks and two-thirds

U.S. stocks had a higher average annual return (more than 12.5 percent) and a lower standard deviation (less than 15 percent) than a portfolio of 100 percent U.S. stocks. And as the curve shows, adding international stocks improved return and reduced risk at every point along with curve. Thus, for this lengthy period, international exposure boosted portfolio returns while lowering risk.

**Efficient Frontiers**

Non-US Stocks, US Stocks and US Bonds
1970-1996

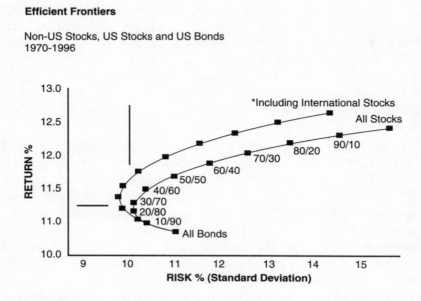

Source: Stocks: S&P 500 Index, Bonds: Lehman Bros. US Long-Term Government Bond Index. International stocks = MSCI EAFE Index.

*International stocks represent one-third of the total stock portfolio.

**Figure 4.1**

## COSTS OF DIVERSIFICATION

Of course, if you look at shorter time frames, you'll find periods when international exposure hindered returns. That's precisely the case in the last few years when U.S. markets have outpaced international markets dramatically. In hindsight, you would have been better off in most cases investing solely in U.S. stocks rather than mixing U.S. investments with foreign investments. Remember, however, that diversification means investing in assets that are not closely correlated. In some ways, foreign investments in recent years gave investors exactly what they promised—a low correlation to returns of U.S.

investments. It's just that during strong U.S. markets investors don't want diversification; they want to maximize returns.

Interestingly, it's precisely during times when international markets underperform the U.S. markets that investors should expand their international exposure in order to capitalize on the inevitable comeback. The following is an example taken from a *Wall Street Journal* column written by Jonathan Clements: "In the eight years prior to year-end 1978, U.S. markets (as measured by the *Standard & Poor's* 500) posted average annual returns of just 4.6 percent. On the other hand, foreign stocks (as measured by Morgan Stanley Capital International's Europe, Australasia, and Far East (EAFE) index) rose more than 13 percent. Was it a time to be selling U.S. securities? Of course not. It was a time to buy. Now jump ahead to today. Since year-end 1988, foreign stocks have returned, on average, just 4.3 percent per year versus more than 18 percent for the S&P 500. I ask you—is it time to sell foreign securities? Or time to buy?"

## WE ARE NOT ALONE

Although many U.S. investors believe that the investing world doesn't extend beyond our borders, the truth is just the opposite. For example;

$ According to International Finance Corp., over three-quarters of the world's companies are listed on foreign stock exchanges.

$ Non-U.S. companies already account for over 60 percent of the world's stock market size, and their share is expected to exceed 70 percent in less than 10 years.

The fact is that a plethora of investment opportunities exist outside the U.S. and many of these investments have turned in stellar results over the years. Why? One reason is fast-growing economies in many foreign countries. For example, by one estimate, the Gross Domestic Products (GDPs) of at least 16 countries have grown faster than the U.S. GDP. Economic activity in developing countries is on average growing at rates well above those of developed countries. To ignore such economic growth is to ignore the investment opportunities that often accompany such growth. Investors, regardless of where they live, cannot afford to do that. Even if you don't buy the diversification benefits of investing abroad, it still makes sense to include selected foreign investments in a portfolio due to the fact that, in many cases, their growth opportunities exceed those of many U.S.-based corporations.

## Other Factors Fueling Foreign Equities

In addition to fast-growing foreign economies, several other factors point to higher stock prices abroad in the coming years:

$ *Values relative to U.S. stocks.* International stocks as a group have lagged badly behind U.S. equities in the last few years. This underperformance has created excellent values in many international markets relative to U.S. equities. To be sure, value doesn't always equate with immediate price rises, and patience and a long-term focus are necessary when investing overseas. Still, the value should eventually be realized.

$ *Fall of Communism.* The fall of Communism has led to a worldwide shift toward free markets. Countries are seeing the wisdom of shifting the control of corporations from the government to the private sector. Of course, adjustments to new economic systems don't occur overnight, and many countries will see their fortunes worsen before they improve under free markets. Still, over the long term, the shift toward more capitalistic societies can only be positive for investors in foreign equities.

$ *Global competition.* The increasing cost-consciousness of U.S. companies and the continued paring of corporate fat have not gone unnoticed overseas. U.S. companies have become even more formidable competitors in the global marketplace. Foreign companies now understand that in order to be successful in the global markets of the future, they too will have to cut costs, shed losing operations, and improve productivity. These measures should help profitability and, in turn, stock prices.

$ *Increased flow of U.S. pension dollars into foreign stocks.* According to *The Wall Street Journal*, U.S. pension funds have increased their international holdings over the past five years at a 30 percent average annual rate. U.S. pension funds could have 14 percent of their total assets in non-U.S. investments within the next five years, up from 11 percent currently.

$ *Changing attitudes toward equity investment in foreign countries.* Many countries are seeing slow but steady progress in changing their citizens' attitudes toward stocks. For example, changing regulations should fuel greater equity participation in countries such as Japan. Pension funds are also becoming more common outside the U.S. Foreign investors putting money into foreign stock markets will provide further buying support for foreign equities.

$ *Global merger activity.* U.S. investors have reaped the benefits of the massive merger activity that has occurred in U.S. markets in recent years. As global markets develop, this merger activity will expand beyond our own borders. International merger activity is already taking place in such areas as utilities, steel, health care, and financial services and will likely be commonplace in nearly every industry sector by the turn of the century. Cross-border mergers could accelerate even more if relative valuations between U.S. and international companies persist and U.S. concerns find it cheaper to buy than build abroad.

## PITFALLS OF FOREIGN INVESTING

Although overseas investing offers plenty of pluses for investors, I would be remiss if I didn't point out some of the pitfalls of investing overseas. One of the biggest potential problems is currency risk. Currency fluctuations impact the performance of your international investments. When local currencies weaken versus the U.S. dollar, your returns suffer. Conversely, if you own shares in a country whose stock market is rising and whose currency is strengthening against the dollar, you're getting a double-powered boost to your portfolio.

A common argument against investing overseas is that individual investors do not have the necessary insights and data to make informed investment choices when investing in foreign companies. Other considerations include accounting standards that are rarely uniform and can hinder fundamental analysis of a particular foreign company, the tax consequences of buying foreign securities, and the ability to obtain financial information in a timely fashion.

Although these are important concerns, they should not automatically prevent an investor from considering investing overseas. As far as obtaining financial information on most foreign companies, annual and quarterly reports are readily available by contacting the company's U.S. agent. Furthermore, Value Line, Standard & Poor's, and other purveyors of independent research materials provide ample coverage of international firms. Online services and the Internet are rich sources for information on foreign companies. Three Web sites in particular with useful information are www.bankofny.com/adr, www.jpmorgan.com/adr, and www.global-investor.com. More on researching international companies is discussed in Chapter 5.

The tax complications of owning foreign investments primarily concern dividends. Most nations require companies to withhold tax from dividend payments going abroad, and investors are entitled to a credit or a deduction on their tax return to offset all or a portion of these foreign taxes. You can obtain year-end tax help and the necessary paperwork from the U.S. depository handling the foreign company's securities or the international mutual-fund family.

A final potential pitfall is the political/economic instability of many foreign countries. Volatile political and economic systems can create major shocks, such as rampant inflation, oppressive regulations, and currency devaluations—all of which are not positive for stock prices. For that reason, investors should diversify investments across a number of regions, especially when investing in emerging countries.

## WHICH FOREIGN MARKETS?

Of course, to say one should invest overseas without providing further direction is like sending a person on a trip around the world without a map and a Fodor's guide. Investments in Russia and the United Kingdom both constitute "foreign investing," yet investments in these countries have dramatically different risk and return profiles. And specific stocks within each of these countries have different risk and reward profiles. For example, British Petroleum and British Airways both constitute international stocks, but shares of this oil and airline issue, respectively, will probably behave quite differently. Looking at the table below shows just how differently annual returns can be in specific foreign markets (the returns are in percentages of gain or loss in U.S. dollars from the Dow Jones World Stock indexes):

| Country | 1997 Return |
|---|---|
| Mexico | 54.21 percent |
| Portugal | 51.04 percent |
| Denmark | 34.05 percent |
| United States | 31.69 percent |
| Netherlands | 24.19 percent |
| Austria | -1.72 percent |
| South Africa | -11.52 percent |
| Japan | -26.39 percent |
| Singapore | -37.83 percent |
| Philippines | -62.36 percent |
| Thailand | -75.83 percent |

Source: Wall Street Journal

So how does an investor go about choosing the right geographic sectors for investment? One way is to focus on those countries that limit government intervention in their economies. Limited government restrictions on such things as wages, prices, and capital flows should foster economic growth over time. Each year, the Heritage Foundation of Washington, D.C. and *The Wall Street Journal* publish an Index of Economic Freedom, which ranks countries according to the level of government intervention in the economy. The latest index is provided in the table beginning on the next page.

The rankings focus on the following 10 areas:

- $ Trade
- $ Taxation
- $ Government intervention
- $ Monetary policy
- $ Foreign investment
- $ Banking
- $ Wage/prices
- $ Property rights
- $ Regulation
- $ Black market activity

Each of these areas is given a ranking of one to five. The higher the score, the greater the level of government interference. A cumulative score is the basis for the overall ranking. Of course, a country's pro-economic freedom does not always make that country a strong investment candidate year-in, year-out. Indeed, companies new to the freedom process may have to go through gut-wrenching changes that hinder economic output initially but stimulate it later. This list is not meant to be an end of your search, but rather a beginning.

## AROUND THE GLOBE

When I look around the world, the areas that stand out as solid investments over the next year or two are Europe and Latin America. Europe is still the safest bet for overseas investors and is benefiting from many of the same factors that have fueled corporate profits in the U.S., namely restructuring and cost cutting. Also, the environment for investing should improve via the development of the European

Heritage Foundation/The Wall Street Journal Index of Economic Freedom Rankings

| Rank | Country | 1998 Score | 1997 Score | 1996 Score | 1995 Score | Trade | Taxation | Gov't Intervention | Monetary | Foreign Policy | Banking Investment | Wage/Prices | Property | Regulation Rights | Black Market |
|---|---|---|---|---|---|---|---|---|---|---|---|---|---|---|---|
| 1 | Hong Kong | 1.25 | 1.25 | 1.25 | 1.25 | 1 | 1.5 | 1 | 2 | 1 | 1 | 2 | 1 | 1 | 1 |
| 2 | Singapore | 1.30 | 1.30 | 1.30 | 1.25 | 1 | 3.0 | 1 | 1 | 1 | 2 | 1 | 1 | 1 | 1 |
| 3 | Bahrain | 1.70- | 1.60 | 1.70 | 1.60 | 2 | 1.0 | 3 | 1 | 2 | 2 | 2 | 1 | 2 | 1 |
| 4 | New Zealand | 1.75 | 1.75 | 1.75 | - | 2 | 3.5 | 2 | 1 | 2 | 1 | 2 | 1 | 2 | 1 |
| 5 | Switzerland | 1.90 | 1.90 | 1.80 | - | 2 | 3.0 | 3 | 1 | 2 | 1 | 2 | 1 | 3 | 1 |
| 5 | United States | 1.90 | 1.90 | 1.90 | 1.90 | 2 | 4.0 | 2 | 1 | 2 | 2 | 2 | 1 | 2 | 1 |
| 7 | Luxembourg | 1.95+ | 2.05 | 1.95 | - | 2 | 3.5+ | 3 | 1 | 2 | 2 | 2 | 1 | 2 | 1 |
| 7 | Taiwan | 1.95 | 1.95 | 1.95 | 1.95 | 2 | 2.5 | 2 | 1 | 3 | 3 | 2 | 1 | 2 | 1 |
| 7 | United Kingdom | 1.95 | 1.95 | 1.95 | 1.95 | 2 | 4.5 | 2 | 1 | 2 | 2 | 2 | 1 | 2 | 1 |
| 10 | Bahamas | 2.00 | 2.00 | 2.00 | 2.10 | 5 | 1.0 | 2 | 1 | 3 | 2 | 2 | 1 | 1 | 2 |
| 10 | Ireland | 2.00+ | 2.20 | 2.20 | 2.20 | 2 | 5.0 | 2 | 1 | 2 | 2 | 2 | 1 | 2 | 1+ |
| 12 | Australia | 2.05+ | 2.15 | 2.10 | 2.20 | 2 | 4.5 | 3 | 1 | 2 | 1 | 2 | 1 | 3 | 1+ |
| 12 | Japan | 2.05 | 2.05 | 2.05 | 1.95 | 2 | 4.5 | 1 | 1 | 3 | 3 | 2 | 1 | 2 | 1 |
| 14 | Belgium | 2.10 | 2.10 | 2.10 | - | 2 | 5.0 | 2 | 1 | 2 | 2 | 2 | 1 | 3 | 1 |
| 14 | Canada | 2.10 | 2.10 | 2.00 | 2.00 | 2 | 5.0 | 2 | 1 | 3 | 2 | 2 | 1 | 2 | 1 |
| 14 | United Arab Emirates | 2.10 | 2.10 | 2.10 | - | 2 | 1.0 | 3 | 1 | 4 | 3 | 3 | 1 | 2 | 1 |
| 17 | Austria | 2.15 | 2.15 | 2.05 | 2.05 | 2+ | 4.5 | 3 | 1 | 2 | 2- | 2 | 1 | 3 | 1 |
| 17 | Chile | 2.15+ | 2.25 | 2.45 | 2.50 | 2 | 3.5 | 1 | 3 | 2 | 3 | 2 | 1 | 2 | 2+ |
| 17 | Estonia | 2.15+ | 2.35 | 2.35 | 2.25 | 1+ | 3.5 | 2 | 4 | 1 | 2 | 2 | 2 | 2 | 2+ |

| | | | | | | | | | | | | | | | |
|---|---|---|---|---|---|---|---|---|---|---|---|---|---|---|---|
| 20 | Czech Republic | 2.20- | 2.05 | 2.00 | 2.10 | 2- | 4.0- | 2 | 2 | 2 | 1 | 2 | 2 | 2 | 3+ |
| 20 | Netherlands | 2.20- | 2.00 | 1.85 | - | 2 | 5.0 | 3 | 1 | 2 | 1 | 3- | 1 | 3- | 1 |
| 22 | Denmark | 2.25- | 2.05 | 1.95 | - | 2 | 4.5 | 4 | 1 | 2 | 2 | 1 | 1 | 2 | 3- |
| 22 | Finland | 2.25+ | 2.30 | 2.30 | - | 2 | 4.5- | 3 | 1 | 2 | 3 | 2+ | 1 | 3 | 1 |
| 24 | Germany | 2.30- | 2.20 | 2.10 | 2.00 | 2 | 5.0 | 2+ | 1 | 2 | 3- | 2 | 1 | 4- | 1 |
| 24 | Iceland | 2.30+ | 2.50 | - | - | 2 | 4.0 | 3 | 2+ | 2 | 3 | 2+ | 1 | 3 | 1 |
| 24 | South Korea | 2.30+ | 2.45 | 2.30 | 2.15 | 3 | 4.0+ | 2 | 2 | 2+ | 2 | 2 | 1 | 3 | 2 |
| 27 | Norway | 2.35+ | 2.45 | 2.45 | - | 2+ | 4.5 | 3 | 1 | 2 | 3 | 3 | 1 | 3 | 1 |
| 28 | Kuwait | 2.40 | 2.40 | 2.40 | - | 2 | 1.0 | 4 | 2 | 4 | 3 | 3 | 1 | 2 | 2 |
| 28 | Malaysia | 2.40+ | 2.60 | 2.40 | 2.15 | 3+ | 3.0 | 2 | 1 | 3 | 3 | 3 | 2 | 2 | 2 |
| 28 | Panama | 2.40+ | 2.50 | 2.40 | 2.70 | 3+ | 3.0 | 3 | 1 | 2 | 1 | 2 | 3 | 3 | 3 |
| 28 | Thailand | 2.40- | 2.30 | 2.30 | 2.30 | 3 | 3.0 | 2- | 1 | 2+ | 3 | 3 | 2- | 3 | 2 |
| 32 | El Salvador | 2.45+ | 2.55 | 2.45 | 2.65 | 3 | 2.5 | 1+ | 3 | 2 | 2 | 2 | 3 | 3 | 3 |
| 32 | Sri Lanka | 2.45 | 2.45 | 2.65 | 2.80 | 3 | 3.5 | 2 | 2 | 3 | 2 | 1 | 3 | 2 | 3 |
| 32 | Sweden | 2.45 | 2.45 | 2.55 | 2.65 | 2 | 4.5 | 5 | 1 | 2 | 2 | 2 | 2 | 3 | 1 |
| 35 | France | 2.50 | 2.50 | 2.30 | 2.30 | 2 | 5.0 | 3 | 1 | 3 | 2 | 3 | 2 | 2 | 1 |
| 35 | Italy | 2.50+ | 2.60 | 2.70 | 2.50 | 2+ | 5.0 | 3 | 2 | 2 | 2 | 2 | 2 | 3 | 2 |
| 35 | Spain | 2.50+ | 2.60 | 2.70 | 2.60 | 2 | 5.0 | 2 | 2 | 2 | 2+ | 3 | 2 | 3 | 2 |
| 38 | Trinidad & Tobago | 2.55 | 2.55 | 2.50 | - | 5 | 4.5 | 2 | 2 | 1 | 2 | 2 | 1 | 3 | 3 |
| 39 | Argentina | 2.60+ | 2.65 | 2.65 | 2.85 | 4 | 3.0+ | 2 | 5 | 2 | 2 | 2 | 2 | 2 | 2 |
| 39 | Barbados | 2.60+ | 2.80 | 3.00 | - | 3+ | 5.0 | 3 | 1 | 2 | 2 | 2+ | 2+ | 3 | 3 |
| 39 | Cyprus | 2.60 | 2.60 | 2.60 | - | 3 | 4.0 | 3 | 1 | 2 | 2 | 3 | 3 | 2 | 3 |

| Rank | Country | 1998 Score | 1997 Score | 1996 Score | 1995 Score | Trade | Taxation | Gov't Intervention | Monetary Policy | Foreign Policy | Banking Investment | Wage/Prices | Property Rights | Regulation | Black Market |
|---|---|---|---|---|---|---|---|---|---|---|---|---|---|---|---|
| 39 | Jamaica | 2.60 | 2.60 | 2.70 | 2.80 | 2 | 3.0 | 2 | 4 | 2 | 2 | 3 | 2 | 3 | 3 |
| 39 | Portugal | 2.60 | 2.60 | 2.60 | 2.80 | 2 | 5.0 | 3 | 2 | 2 | 3 | 2 | 2 | 3 | 2 |
| 44 | Bolivia | 2.65+ | 2.85 | 2.75 | 3.20 | 2 | 2.5 | 3+ | 3 | 2 | 2 | 1 | 3 | 4 | 4 |
| 44 | Oman | 2.65+ | 2.75 | 2.85 | 2.65 | 2+ | 3.5 | 4 | 1 | 3 | 4 | 3 | 2 | 2 | 2 |
| 44 | Philippines | 2.65+ | 2.80 | 2.90 | 3.30 | 3+ | 3.5 | 1 | 2 | 3 | 3 | 2 | 2 | 3 | 4 |
| 47 | Swaziland | 2.70+ | 2.80 | 2.90 | 2.90 | 3+ | 3.0 | 2 | 2 | 2 | 3 | 3 | 2 | 3 | 4 |
| 47 | Uruguay | 2.70 | 2.70 | 2.80 | 2.90 | 2 | 3.0 | 3 | 5 | 2 | 2 | 2 | 2 | 3 | 3 |
| 49 | Botswana | 2.75+ | 2.85 | 2.80 | 3.05 | 3+ | 2.5 | 4 | 2 | 3 | 2 | 2 | 2 | 3 | 4- |
| 49 | Jordan | 2.75- | 2.70 | 2.80 | 2.90 | 4 | 2.5+ | 3- | 2 | 2 | 2 | 3 | 2 | 3 | 4 |
| 49 | Namibia | 2.75+ | 2.95 | - | - | 4 | 3.5 | 4 | 2 | 2 | 2 | 2+ | 2 | 3+ | 3 |
| 49 | Tunisia | 2.75 | 2.75 | 2.65 | 2.85 | 5 | 3.5 | 3 | 2 | 2 | 3 | 2 | 3 | 2 | 3 |
| 53 | Belize | 2.80- | 2.70 | 2.70 | 2.70 | 5 | 4.0 | 2 | 1 | 2 | 3 | 2 | 3 | 3 | 3 |
| 53 | Costa Rica | 2.80 | 2.80 | 2.80 | 2.90 | 4 | 3.0 | 2 | 3 | 2 | 3 | 2 | 3 | 3 | 3 |
| 53 | Guatemala | 2.80 | 2.80 | 2.85 | 3.05 | 3 | 3.0 | 1 | 3 | 3 | 2 | 3 | 3 | 4 | 3 |
| 53 | Israel | 2.80 | 2.80 | 2.90 | 3.10 | 2 | 5.0 | 4 | 3 | 1 | 3 | 2 | 2 | 2 | 4 |
| 53 | Peru | 2.80+ | 2.90 | 3.00 | 3.40 | 2+ | 3.0 | 1 | 5 | 2 | 2 | 2 | 3 | 4 | 4 |
| 53 | Saudi Arabia | 2.80 | 2.80 | 2.90 | - | 4 | 4.0 | 4 | 1 | 4 | 3 | 3 | 1 | 2 | 2 |
| 53 | Turkey | 2.80 | 2.80 | 3.00 | 3.00 | 2- | 4.0+ | 2 | 5 | 2 | 2 | 3 | 2 | 3 | 3 |
| 53 | Uganda | 2.80+ | 2.90 | 2.83 | 2.94 | 5- | 4.0 | 2+ | 5 | 2 | 3 | 1 | 2 | 2+ | 2 |
| 53 | Western Samoa | 2.80 | 2.80 | 2.80 | - | 3 | 4.0 | 2 | 2 | 3 | 3 | 3 | 3 | 3 | 2 |

| Rank | Country | | | | | | | | | | | | | | |
|---|---|---|---|---|---|---|---|---|---|---|---|---|---|---|---|
| 62 | Indonesia | 2.85 | 2.85 | 2.85 | 3.35 | 2 | 3.5 | 1 | 2 | 2 | 3 | 3 | 3 | 3 | 5 |
| 62 | Latvia | 2.85+ | 2.95 | 3.05 | - | 2+ | 2.5 | 3 | 5 | 2 | 2 | 2 | 3- | 3 | 4 |
| 62 | Malta | 2.85 | 2.95 | 3.05 | 3.25 | 4 | 3.5 | 2 | 1 | 2 | 3 | 4 | 2+ | 3 | 4 |
| 62 | Paraguay | 2.85- | 2.75 | 2.65 | 2.75 | 2 | 2.5 | 2 | 4 | 1 | 2 | 3 | 4 | 3 | 5 |
| 66 | Greece | 2.90- | 2.85 | 2.80 | 2.80 | 2 | 4.0- | 3 | 3 | 2 | 4 | 3 | 2 | 3 | 3 |
| 66 | Hungary | 2.90 | 2.90 | 2.90 | 2.80 | 4 | 4.0 | 3 | 4 | 2 | 2 | 2 | 2 | 3 | 3 |
| 66 | South Africa | 2.90+ | 3.00 | 3.00 | 3.00 | 4+ | 4.0 | 3 | 3 | 2 | 3 | 2 | 3 | 2 | 3 |
| 69 | Benin | 2.95 | 2.95 | 2.95 | - | 4 | 3.5 | 3 | 1 | 3 | 3 | 3 | 3 | 3 | 3 |
| 69 | Ecuador | 2.95+ | 3.05 | 3.15 | 3.25 | 3 | 2.5 | 1 | 5 | 2 | 3 | 2+ | 3 | 4 | 4 |
| 69 | Gabon | 2.95 | 2.95 | 3.05 | 3.06 | 5 | 4.5 | 3 | 1 | 2 | 2 | 3 | 3 | 3 | 3 |
| 69 | Morocco | 2.95- | 2.75 | 2.70 | 2.90 | 5- | 3.5 | 3 | 1 | 2 | 3 | 3 | 3 | 3- | 3 |
| 69 | Poland | 2.95+ | 3.15 | 3.05 | 3.25 | 2+ | 3.5 | 3 | 5 | 2 | 3 | 3 | 3- | 3 | 3 |
| 74 | Colombia | 3.00+ | 3.10 | 3.00 | 2.90 | 3+ | 4.0 | 2 | 4 | 2 | 2 | 2 | 2 | 3 | 5 |
| 74 | Ghana | 3.00+ | 3.20 | 3.20 | 3.30 | 3+ | 3.0 | 3 | 4 | 3 | 3 | 2 | 3 | 4 | 2 |
| 74 | Lithuania | 3.00+ | 3.10 | 3.50 | - | 1+ | 3.0 | 3 | 5 | 2 | 3 | 3 | 3 | 3 | 4 |
| 77 | Kenya | 3.05 | 3.05 | 3.05 | 3.05 | 4 | 3.5 | 3 | 2 | 3 | 2 | 3 | 3 | 4 | 3 |
| 77 | Slovak Republic | 3.05 | 3.05 | 3.05 | 2.75 | 3- | 4.5 | 3 | 2+ | 3 | 3 | 3 | 3 | 3 | 3 |
| 77 | Zambia | 3.05- | 2.85 | 2.95 | 3.05 | 3- | 3.5 | 3- | 5 | 2 | 3 | 3 | 3 | 4 | 3 |
| 80 | Mali | 3.10 | 3.10 | 3.10 | 3.50 | 3 | 5.0 | 3 | 1 | 2 | 3 | 3 | 3 | 3 | 5 |
| 80 | Mongolia | 3.10+ | 3.30 | 3.50 | 3.33 | 1+ | 4.0 | 3 | 5 | 3 | 3 | 3 | 3 | 3 | 3 |
| 80 | Slovenia | 3.10 | 3.10 | 3.35 | - | 4 | 4.0 | 3 | 5- | 2+ | 2 | 3 | 2+ | 3 | 3 |
| 83 | Honduras | 3.15 | 3.15 | 3.15 | 3.15 | 4 | 3.5 | 1+ | 3- | 3 | 3 | 3 | 3 | 4 | 4 |

| Rank | Country | 1998 Score | 1997 Score | 1996 Score | 1995 Score | Trade | Taxation | Gov't Intervention | Monetary Policy | Foreign Investment | Banking Investment | Wage/Prices | Property Rights | Regulation Rights | Black Market |
|---|---|---|---|---|---|---|---|---|---|---|---|---|---|---|---|
| 83 | Papua New Guinea | 3.15- | 3.10 | 3.10 | - | 5 | 2.5+ | 3 | 1 | 3 | 4 | 3 | 3 | 4- | 3 |
| 85 | Djibouti | 3.20 | 3.00 | - | - | 4 | 2.0 | 5- | 1 | 3 | 3 | 3 | 3 | 4 | 4 |
| 85 | Fiji | 3.20 | 3.20 | 3.10 | 3.30 | 5 | 3.0 | 3 | 1 | 3 | 3 | 3 | 3 | 4 | 4 |
| 85 | Pakistan | 3.20- | 3.10 | 3.05 | 3.15 | 5 | 4.0 | 3 | 2 | 2 | 3 | 3 | 3- | 4 | 3 |
| 88 | Algeria | 3.25 | 3.25 | 3.25 | 3.15 | 5 | 3.5 | 3 | 3 | 3 | 3 | 3 | 3 | 3 | 3 |
| 88 | Guinea | 3.25+ | 3.45 | 3.35 | 3.35 | 3+ | 4.5 | 3 | 3 | 3 | 2 | 2 | 4 | 4 | 4+ |
| 88 | Lebanon | 3.25- | 2.95 | 2.95 | - | 5- | 2.5 | 2 | 5 | 3 | 2 | 2 | 3 | 3 | 5 |
| 88 | Mexico | 3.25+ | 3.35 | 3.35 | 3.05 | 3 | 3.5 | 2+ | 5 | 2 | 4 | 3 | 3 | 4 | 3 |
| 88 | Senegal | 3.25 | 3.25 | 3.40 | - | 4+ | 4.5 | 3 | 1 | 3 | 3 | 4 | 3- | 4 | 3 |
| 88 | Tanzania | 3.25 | 3.25 | 3.45 | 3.50 | 3 | 3.5 | 3 | 4 | 3 | 3 | 2 | 3 | 4 | 4 |
| 94 | Nigeria | 3.30- | 3.20 | 3.25 | 3.15 | 5 | 3.0 | 2 | 5- | 2 | 4 | 2 | 3 | 4 | 3 |
| 94 | Romania | 3.30+ | 3.40 | 3.70 | 3.55 | 2 | 5.0 | 3 | 5 | 2 | 3 | 2 | 4 | 4 | 3+ |
| 96 | Brazil | 3.35 | 3.35 | 3.45 | 3.30 | 4 | 2.5 | 3 | 5 | 3 | 3 | 3 | 3 | 3 | 4 |
| 96 | Cambodia | 3.35+ | 3.55 | - | - | 3+ | 2.5 | 3+ | 5- | 3 | 3 | 3 | 4 | 4 | 3 |
| 96 | Egypt | 3.35+ | 3.45 | 3.45 | 3.50 | 5 | 4.5 | 3 | 3 | 3 | 2+ | 3 | 3 | 4 | 3 |
| 96 | Ivory Coast | 3.35 | 3.35 | 3.25 | 3.25 | 5 | 3.5 | 3 | 1 | 3 | 3 | 3 | 4 | 4 | 4 |
| 96 | Madagascar | 3.35- | 3.25 | 3.35 | 3.50 | 5- | 3.5 | 2 | 3 | 4 | 4 | 2 | 3 | 3 | 4 |
| 96 | Moldova | 3.35 | 3.35 | 3.45 | 4.10 | 3 | 3.5 | 3 | 5 | 3 | 3 | 3 | 3 | 3 | 4 |
| 102 | Nepal | 3.40+ | 3.60 | 3.50 | - | 3+ | 3.0 | 2+ | 2 | 4 | 4 | 4 | 3 | 4 | 5 |
| 103 | Cape Verde | 3.44 | 3.44 | 3.44 | - | 5 | N/A | 3 | 2 | 2 | 5 | 4 | 2 | 4 | 4 |

| | | | | | | | | | | | | | | | |
|---|---|---|---|---|---|---|---|---|---|---|---|---|---|---|---|
| 104 | Armenia | 3.45 | 3.45 | 3.75 | - | 2 | 3.5 | 3 | 5 | 4 | 3 | 3 | 3 | 4 | 4 |
| 104 | Dominican Republic | 3.45 | 3.45 | 3.45 | 3.40 | 5 | 2.5 | 2 | 5 | 3 | 3 | 2 | 3 | 4 | 4 |
| 104 | Russia | 3.45+ | 3.65 | 3.50 | 3.50 | 4+ | 3.5 | 3+ | 5 | 3 | 2 | 3 | 3 | 4 | 4 |
| 107 | Burkina Faso | 3.50 | 3.50 | 3.70 | - | 5 | 4.0 | 3 | 1 | 2 | 4 | 4 | 4 | 4 | 5 |
| 107 | Cameroon | 3.50- | 3.60 | 3.60 | 3.60 | 5 | 4.0 | 3 | 1 | 3 | 4 | 3 | 3 | 4 | 5 |
| 107 | Lesotho | 3.50+ | 3.65 | 3.65 | - | 3+ | 4.0+ | 3 | 3 | 3 | 4 | 4 | 4 | 4 | 4 |
| 107 | Nicaragua | 3.50+ | 3.60 | 3.60 | 3.90 | 4+ | 3.0 | 2 | 5 | 2 | 3 | 3 | 3 | 4 | 5 |
| 107 | Venezuela | 3.50+ | 3.60 | 3.50 | 3.00 | 3+ | 4.0 | 3 | 5 | 3 | 3 | 3 | 3 | 3 | 5 |
| 112 | Gambia | 3.60 | 3.60 | - | - | 4 | 4.0 | 3 | 2 | 4 | 4 | 4 | 2 | 4 | 5 |
| 112 | Guyana | 3.60- | 3.50 | 3.35 | - | 5- | 4.0 | 3 | 5 | 3 | 3 | 2 | 3 | 4 | 4 |
| 114 | Bulgaria | 3.65- | 3.60 | 3.50 | 3.50 | 4- | 4.5+ | 3 | 5 | 3 | 3 | 3 | 3 | 4 | 4 |
| 114 | Georgia | 3.65+ | 3.85 | 3.85 | - | 3 | 2.5 | 2+ | 5 | 3 | 4 | 4 | 4 | 4 | 5 |
| 114 | Malawi | 3.65- | 3.55 | 3.40 | 3.40 | 5 | 4.5 | 3 | 4+ | 3 | 3 | 3 | 3 | 4 | 4 |
| 117 | Ethiopia | 3.70- | 3.60 | 3.70 | 3.80 | 5- | 4.0 | 3 | 2 | 4 | 4 | 4 | 4 | 4 | 4 |
| 117 | India | 3.70 | 3.70 | 3.75 | 3.70 | 5 | 4.0 | 3 | 2 | 3 | 4 | 3 | 3 | 4 | 5 |
| 117 | Niger | 3.70 | 3.70 | 3.70 | - | 5 | 4.0 | 3 | 1 | 4 | 4 | 4 | 3 | 4 | 5 |
| 120 | Albania | 3.75- | 3.65 | 3.45 | 3.55 | 3 | 3.5 | 5 | 5 | 2 | 4 | 3 | 4 | 3 | 5 |
| 120 | Bangladesh | 3.75- | 3.70 | 3.65 | 3.90 | 5 | 3.5+ | 3- | 2 | 3 | 3 | 4 | 4 | 5 | 5 |
| 120 | China | 3.75+ | 3.80 | 3.80 | 3.80 | 5 | 3.5+ | 5 | 3 | 3 | 3 | 3 | 4 | 4 | 5 |
| 120 | Congo | 3.75 | 3.75 | 3.80 | 3.90 | 5 | 4.5 | 3 | 1 | 4 | 4 | 4 | 4 | 4 | 4 |
| 120 | Croatia | 3.75- | 3.70 | 3.70 | - | 3 | 3.5- | 5 | 5 | 3 | 3 | 4 | 4 | 4 | 5 |
| 125 | Chad | 3.80 | 3.80 | - | - | 5 | 4.0 | 3 | 1 | 4 | 4 | 4 | 4 | 4 | 5 |

| Rank | Country | 1998 Score | 1997 Score | 1996 Score | 1995 Score | Trade | Taxation | Gov't Intervention | Monetary | Foreign Policy | Banking Investment | Wage/Prices | Property | Regulation Rights | Black Market |
|---|---|---|---|---|---|---|---|---|---|---|---|---|---|---|---|
| 125 | Mauritania | 3.80 | 3.80 | 3.80 | - | 5 | 4.0 | 3 | 2 | 3 | 5 | 4 | 4 | 4 | 4 |
| 125 | Ukraine | 3.80- | 3.75 | 4.00 | 3.90 | 4 | 4.0+ | 3 | 5 | 3 | 4 | 3 | 4- | 4 | 4 |
| 128 | Sierra Leone | 3.85 | 3.85 | 3.75 | 3.75 | 4 | 4.5 | 3 | 5 | 3 | 4 | 3 | 4 | 3 | 5 |
| 129 | Burundi | 3.90- | 3.80 | - | - | 5 | 4.0 | 3 | 2- | 4 | 4 | 4 | 4 | 4 | 5 |
| 129 | Suriname | 3.90+ | 4.00 | 3.90 | - | 5 | 4.0+ | 3 | 5 | 3 | 4 | 3 | 3 | 4 | 5 |
| 129 | Zimbabwe | 3.90- | 3.70 | 3.70 | 3.50 | 5 | 4.0 | 4- | 4 | 4 | 3 | 3 | 4- | 4 | 4 |
| 132 | Haiti | 4.00 | 4.00 | 4.20 | 4.20 | 4 | 3.0 | 3 | 3 | 4 | 4 | 4 | 5 | 5 | 5 |
| 132 | Kyrgyzstan | 4.00 | - | - | - | 4 | 4.0 | 3 | 5 | 3 | 4 | 4 | 4 | 4 | 5 |
| 132 | Syria | 4.00+ | 4.20 | 4.20 | - | 5 | 5.0 | 3 | 3+ | 4 | 5 | 4 | 4 | 2 | 5 |
| 135 | Belarus | 4.05- | 3.85 | 3.55 | 3.65 | 4+ | 4.5 | 3 | 5 | 4 | 3 | 4- | 4- | 4- | 5 |
| 136 | Kazakstan | 4.10 | - | - | - | 4 | 4.0 | 3 | 5 | 4 | 4 | 4 | 4 | 4 | 5 |
| 136 | Mozambique | 4.10- | 4.00 | 4.05 | 4.40 | 5- | 4.0 | 3 | 5 | 4 | 3+ | 3 | 4 | 5 | 5 |
| 136 | Yemen | 4.10- | 3.90 | 3.75 | 3.75 | 5 | 3.0 | 4 | 5 | 4+ | 4 | 3 | 4 | 4 | 5 |
| 139 | Sudan | 4.20 | 4.20 | 4.10 | 4.22 | 5 | 5.0 | 3 | 5 | 4 | 4 | 4 | 4 | 4 | 4 |
| 140 | Myanmar (Burma) | 4.30 | 4.30 | 4.30 | - | 5 | 3.0 | 5 | 4 | 4 | 4 | 4 | 4 | 5 | 5 |
| 140 | Rwanda | 4.30- | 4.20 | - | - | 5 | 5.0 | 4 | 2- | 4 | 5 | 3 | 5 | 5 | 5 |
| 142 | Angola | 4.35 | 4.35 | 4.35 | 4.35 | 5 | 3.5 | 4 | 5 | 4 | 4 | 4 | 4 | 5 | 5 |
| 143 | Azerbaijan | 4.40+ | 4.60 | 4.70 | - | 5 | 4.0 | 5 | 5 | 4+ | 4 | 5 | 4 | 4 | 4+ |
| 143 | Tajikistan | 4.40 | - | - | - | 5 | 5.0 | 4 | 5 | 4 | 4 | 4 | 4 | 4 | 5 |
| 145 | Turkmenistan | 4.50 | - | - | - | 5 | 5.0 | 4 | 5 | 4 | 5 | 4 | 4 | 4 | 5 |

| | | | | | | | | | | | | | | | |
|---|---|---|---|---|---|---|---|---|---|---|---|---|---|---|---|
| 146 | Uzbekistan | 4.55 | - | - | 5 | 4.5 | 4 | 5 | 4 | 5 | 5 | 4 | 4 | 5 | 5 |
| 147 | Congo (former Zaire) | 4.70- | 4.20 | 4.20 | 5- | 5.0 | 4- | 5 | 4 | 5- | 4 | 4 | 5- | 4 | 5 |
| 147 | Iran | 4.70 | 4.70 | 4.70 | 5 | 5.0 | 5 | 4 | 5 | 5 | 5 | 5- | 4 | 4 | 5 |
| 147 | Libya | 4.70 | 4.70 | 4.70 | 5 | 5.0 | 5 | 2 | 5 | 5 | 5 | 5 | 5 | 5 | 5 |
| 147 | Somalia | 4.70 | 4.70 | 4.70 | 5 | 5.0 | 5 | 5 | 4 | 5 | 3 | 5 | 5 | 5 | 5 |
| 147 | Vietnam | 4.70 | 4.70 | 4.70 | 5 | 5.0 | 5 | 5 | 4 | 4 | 4 | 5 | 5 | 5 | 5 |
| 152 | Bosnia | 4.80 | - | - | 5 | 5.0 | 5 | 5 | 4 | 5 | 4 | 5 | 5 | 5 | 5 |
| 153 | Iraq | 4.90 | 4.90 | 4.90 | 5 | 5.0 | 5 | 5 | 5 | 5 | 4 | 5 | 5 | 5 | 5 |
| 154 | Cuba | 5.00 | 5.00 | 5.00 | 5 | 5.0 | 5 | 5 | 5 | 5 | 5 | 5 | 5 | 5 | 5 |
| 154 | Laos | 5.00 | 5.00 | - | 5 | 5.0 | 5 | 5 | 5 | 5 | 5 | 5 | 5 | 5 | 5 |
| 154 | North Korea | 5.00 | 5.00 | 5.00 | 5 | 5.0 | 5 | 5 | 5 | 5 | 5 | 5 | 5 | 5 | 5 |

**Note:** Scores followed by a plus sign (+) have improved from last year. Those followed by a minus sign (-) have worsened.
Source: Heritage Foundation/The Wall Street Journal

Common Market. I expect increased merger activity to fuel these markets as well.

Latin America has always been huge on promise, but ill-advised economic policies seem to short-circuit companies in this region. Still, certain countries in this region offer good potential. I remain a fan of Mexico, where rising standards of living and an emerging middle class should help retailers, media companies, and other consumer-oriented firms. Chile is another interesting area.

For aggressive investors, it may be time to do nibbling in Asia/Pacific Rim. Much of the recent news coming from this region has been bad. Japan's financial markets have been stuck in low gear and other Pacific Rim countries have been experiencing difficult economic times. Interestingly, the Pacific Rim was the toast of Wall Street in the 1980s. Long term, I still think the Pacific Rim poses perhaps the biggest challenge to the U.S. in many world markets. For more aggressive investors, China presents perhaps the biggest opportunities, but you'll have to be patient.

Of all the regions, Eastern Europe may be the most difficult to analyze. Some countries, such as Poland, seem well ahead of the curve relative to certain regions of the former Soviet Union. Also, the dislocations caused by the fall of Communism will continue to hamper near-term prospects. This may be the riskiest area in the short term.

## How to Invest Abroad

Never before have individual investors had such convenient and low-cost ways to invest overseas. The following sections examine a number of avenues for investing overseas.

### Mutual Funds

Most investment advisers believe that mutual funds represent the only way individual investors should venture into foreign markets. International funds have professional managers who have special expertise in navigating the "treacherous" international investment landscape. Funds provide the necessary diversification when investing in such potentially volatile markets. Funds also take care of the tax problems that can arise when investing overseas. The downside is that investment companies managing the funds don't work for free. Morningstar estimates that the average annual expense ratio of an international equity fund is roughly 1.9 percent. In other words, for every $50,000 in the typical international equity fund, an investor pays

$950 per year in "carrying fees." And fees are only part of the costs. Another downside of international mutual funds is the unwanted tax liabilities created every time the fund manager distributes capital gains to fund holders.

Regarding international funds, a well-diversified mutual fund offers an excellent way to invest overseas, providing expenses are not too high and you don't have the time or inclination to pick individual stocks. Be aware, however, that not all international funds are alike. Some focus exclusively on a specific country, while others target a particular region. Some international funds focus on bond investments; others may hold bonds and stocks. "Global" mutual funds may also invest in both U.S. and foreign stocks. For that reason, make sure you know what you are buying when you consider an international fund. If you already have ample U.S. stock exposure, a global fund may not be the best choice. Also, a fund that claims it's diversified across the world, but in reality has 40 percent of its assets in the Pacific Rim, may not be the best choice. Finally, an international mutual fund may focus on small-capitalization foreign companies, which can increase not only the fund's expected return but also its risk. Make sure you understand the investment objectives and holdings of an international fund before investing.

Most major no-load fund families offer international funds. Two that I particularly like are the T. Rowe Price International Stock Fund (800-638-5660), a diversified international fund, and Acorn International Fund (800-922-6769), an international small-cap fund.

## Closed-End Funds

Closed-end funds are similar to open-end funds in that each permits investment in a basket of stocks selected and managed by an investment company. However, there are a few major differences. Open-end funds continually sell new shares to the public and redeem shares at the fund's net asset value, which is the market value of the firm's portfolio of stocks, minus short-term liabilities. Closed-end funds, however, sell only a certain number of shares at the initial public offering, just like a stock. Once the shares are sold, the fund is "closed" and new money is not accepted.

Another major difference is that closed-end funds trade on the stock exchanges, while open-end funds do not. Because closed-end funds are publicly traded, their prices are set by supply and demand among various investors, just like common stocks. Thus, unlike open-end funds that always redeem shares at the net asset value, it is not unusual to see a closed-end mutual fund trade above or below its net asset value, and sometimes these premiums or discounts are quite large. How do you know if a closed-end fund is trading at a discount or premium? Such information is given regularly in *The Wall Street Journal* and *Barron's*.

A number of closed-end funds focus on international investments. These funds include both international bond and stock funds. When considering international closed-end funds, evaluate the following:

$ Merely because an international closed-end fund trades at a discount does not make it a good investment. It is important to evaluate if the fund meets your investment objective, abides by an investment strategy that makes sense to you, and fits with the rest of your portfolio. This latter factor is crucial. If your only investment is a closed-end fund, for example, it probably isn't a good idea to buy a single-country, closed-end fund.

$ Closed-end funds charge expenses and these expenses can be rather high. One rule of thumb is to avoid investing in closed-end funds where the discount is not at least 10 times the fund's annual expenses. A closed-end fund with annual expenses of 1.5 percent should trade at a discount of at least 15 percent before being considered.

$ Keep in mind that the disparity between an international closed-end fund's price and the net asset value may be the result of potential pricing problems for fund investments that do not trade frequently and that current prices to establish net asset value are estimates of the true value of the investment. This may be the case with international closed-end funds that focus on illiquid bond investments.

$ Never buy any closed-end fund at the initial public offering. Most closed-end funds perform poorly immediately following the initial public offering. You'll probably dodge a bullet or two by waiting and taking a fresh look at the fund six months or so after it is issued.

Although most closed-end funds require a broker to make the purchase, a small but growing number of funds are allowing investors to make their initial and subsequent fund purchases directly without a broker. Boston EquiServe, a transfer agent for closed-end funds, has been a leader in bringing out direct-purchase closed-end funds.

The terms are the same for each closed-end fund offering direct purchase:

$ The minimum initial investment is $250, with a $10 fee for initial purchases.

$ Subsequent investments can range from $100 to $100,000 annually.

$ Optional cash payments are invested weekly.

$ Purchasing fees are $5 plus eight cents per share.

$ Selling fees are $10 plus 15 cents per share.

$ There are no fees for reinvestment of dividends.

$ Automatic investment services via electronic debit of a bank account are available.

In addition to these fees, investors in the funds will incur expense charges related to the fund's management fees. These fees differ between funds, so make sure you review the plan prospectus before investing.

The following five closed-end funds offer direct-purchase plans through Boston EquiServe. For enrollment information, call the appropriate toll-free numbers:

$ **Brazilian Equity Fund** *(NYSE: BZL*, 800-969-3306) invests primarily in Brazilian equities.

$ **Emerging Markets Infrastructure Fund** *(NYSE: EMG*, 800-969-3365) invests in infrastructure plays, such as electric generators, telecommunications providers, and building-materials firms, in emerging countries. The fund believes that these are the types of sectors that should benefit most from economic growth in developing economies.

$ **Emerging Markets Telecommunications Fund** *(NYSE: ETF*, 800-969-3364) invests exclusively in telecommunications companies that service emerging countries.

$ **First Israel Fund** *(NYSE: ISL*, 800-969-3321) invests at least 65 percent of assets in Israeli securities. The fund has a heavy weighting in technology and financial stocks.

$ **Indonesia Fund** *(NYSE: IF*, 800-969-3294) invests at least 65 percent of assets in Indonesia equity and debt securities. This area of the world has been extremely volatile in recent years.

Of these funds, my preference is the Emerging Markets Infrastructure Fund. To be sure, this fund will be extremely volatile, which is typical in emerging market investments. Still, I like the focus of the fund and expect it to perform well over the long term.

## World Equity Benchmark Shares (WEBS)

*World Equity Benchmark Shares* (WEBS) are a relatively new way to invest overseas. They are portfolios indexed against various *Morgan Stanley Capital International* (MSCI) country benchmarks. WEBS trade on the American Stock Exchange, so investors have a liquid market to buy and sell these investments. The difference between international closed-end funds and WEBS is that WEBS generally trade in line with their net asset values. You can buy and sell WEBS to gain exposure to the following countries' stock indexes:

| | | | |
|---|---|---|---|
| Australia | Germany | Mexico | Switzerland |
| Austria | Hong Kong | Netherlands | United Kingdom |
| Belgium | Italy | Singapore | |
| Canada | Japan | Spain | |
| France | Malaysia | Sweden | |

WEBS offer a way to target specific countries for international investing, but investors seeking diversified international exposure have to buy multiple WEBS. Investors should also note that WEBS must be purchased via a broker; no WEBS offer direct purchase. I'm a fan of companies based in the Netherlands, and their WEBS offer a way to pinpoint investments across the country.

## American Depository Receipts (ADRs)

The easiest way to invest in specific overseas companies is via *American Depositary Receipts* (ADRs), which are securities that trade on U.S. exchanges and represent ownership in shares of foreign companies. ADRs are issued by U.S. banks against the actual shares of foreign companies held in trust by a correspondent institution overseas. Often, ADRs are not issued on a share-for-share basis. Instead, one ADR can be the equivalent of five or 10 of the company's ordinary shares.

ADRs have become increasingly popular in recent years. According to the Bank of New York, trading volume in ADRs in 1997 reached 15 billion shares, a 23 percent increase over 1996, with an associated dollar value of $555 billion, a 53 percent increase over 1996. There are now some 1600 ADRs, up from 109 in 1988.

One reason for the growing popularity of ADRs is convenience. Investors can buy and sell ADRs just like they buy and sell any security of a U.S. company in liquid and ready trading markets. ADRs are also quoted in U.S. dollars and pay dividends in U.S. dollars. In fact, most investors who buy well-known foreign companies, such as Sony or Royal Dutch Petroleum, probably don't even know they are actually buying the ADR, not common stock. That's because the difference between the stock and ADR is transparent to the investor.

The table beginning on the next page is a list of the 50 most actively traded listed ADRs in 1997. As you can see from the list, ADRs are available in companies around the globe, from Italy (Fila Holdings) and Argentina (Banco de Galicia) to Japan (Sony) and Israel (Teva).

An index that tracks the performance of ADRs is now available from the Bank of New York. The Bank of New York ADR Index consists of 431 companies from 36 countries and contains a composite index and four regional indices: The Europe ADR Index, the Asia ADR Index, the Latin America ADR Index, and the Emerging Market ADR Index. Information regarding the Bank of New York ADR Index is available on the firm's Web site at http://www.bankofny.com/adr.

### Buy ADRs Without a Broker

The traditional way to buy ADRs is via a stock broker, but individual investors now have the option of bypassing the broker and investing directly in a growing number of ADRs. Indeed, more than 150 ADRs offer direct-purchase programs whereby individual investors can purchase ADRs directly, including their first share and every subsequent share, from the companies' U.S. agents. Shares are purchased in the same way as shares are purchased in U.S. companies offering direct purchase. Investors call a toll-free phone number to receive a plan prospectus and enrollment information that is filled out and returned with the check. The minimum initial investment in all ADR direct-purchase plans is $250 or less. Once the initial investment has been made, you can make subsequent purchases directly. The plans make it easy even for investors with limited funds to buy quality ADRs and build a diversified international stock portfolio over time.

You might be wondering why foreign companies would offer direct-purchase plans. Given the increasingly global marketplace, international companies are seeing the importance of courting U.S.

The 50 Most Actively Traded Listed ADRs of 1997 (by 1997 Dollar Volume)

| Company/Symbol | Country | Share Volume | Dollar Volume | Exchange |
| --- | --- | --- | --- | --- |
| Telebras (Pref. Shares)/TBR | Brazil | 747,844,500 | 86,620,035,586 | NYSE |
| Royal Dutch Petroleum Co./RD | Netherlands | 392,152,600 | 30,346,441,616 | NYSE |
| Telefonos de Mexico (Series L)/TMX | Mexico | 573,043,900 | 25,576,691,550 | NYSE |
| Ericsson Telephone Co. (B Shares)/ERICY | Sweden | 583,697,300 | 22,409,044,013 | NASDAQ |
| Nokia Corporation/NOKA | Finland | 257,922,100 | 18,853,470,097 | NYSE |
| British Petroleum/BP | UK | 177,974,900 | 17,899,764,903 | NYSE |
| ASM Lithography Holding/ASMLF | Netherlands | 182,597,900 | 17,899,764,903 | NYSE |
| SmithKline Beecham/SBH | UK | 190,031,700 | 11,872,555,056 | NYSE |
| Unilever/UN | Netherlands | 88,688,000 | 11,276,978,984 | NYSE |
| Bann Co. NV/BAANF | Netherlands | 167,811,600 | 9,339,915,969 | NASDAQ |
| Philips Electronics NV/PHG | Netherlands | 143,786,000 | 9,102,086,619 | NYSE |
| Teva Pharmaceutical Ind./TEVIY | Israel | 160,352,100 | 8,767,121,397 | NASDAQ |
| Gucci Group NV/GUC | Netherlands | 139,052,900 | 8,010,970,575 | NYSE |
| YPF Sociedad Anonima (D Shares)/YPF | Argentina | 241,272,400 | 7,401,238,775 | NYSE |
| Glaxo Wellcome/GLX | UK | 175,875,700 | 6,808,605,566 | NYSE |
| Danka Business Systems/DANKY | UK | 194,581,200 | 6,528,825,531 | NASDAQ |
| Reuters Holdings/RTRSY | UK | 101,454,200 | 6,528,825,531 | NASDAQ |
| Telefonica de Argentina/TAR | Argentina | 147,445,300 | 4,819,241,309 | NYSE |

| Company | Country | | | Exchange |
|---|---|---|---|---|
| Telefonica de Espana/TEF | Spain | 59,456,100 | 4,637,089,644 | NYSE |
| British Telecommunications/BTY | UK | 64,546,800 | 4,629,970,534 | NYSE |
| SGS-Thomson Micro-electronics/STM | Netherlands | 56,276,100 | 4,280,550,603 | NYSE |
| News Corporation (Pref.)/WS+ | Australia | 238,854,900 | 4,041,523,513 | NYSE |
| Grupo Televisa/TV | Mexico | 135,689,100 | 3,972,170,478 | NYSE |
| Elf Aquitaine/ELF | France | 63,277,900 | 3,411,965,525 | NYSE |
| Elan Corp./ELN | Ireland | 76,352,500 | 3,288,374,709 | NYSE |
| CANTV-Nacional Telephonos de Chile/VNT | Chile | 87,567,000 | 3,188,897,856 | NYSE |
| Compania de Telecom de Chile/CTC | Chile | 101,157,400 | 3,008,725,388 | NYSE |
| CBT Group/CBTSY | Ireland | 47,675,200 | 2,930,570,538 | NASDAQ |
| Imperial Chemical Industries/ICI | UK | 51,313,900 | 2,907,377,342 | NYSE |
| Banco de Galicia y Buenos Aires/BGALY | Argentina | 111,388,800 | 2,907,001,870 | NASDAQ |
| Fila Holdings/FLH | Italy | 63,284,400 | 2,871,241,622 | NYSE |
| Saville Systems/SAVLY | Ireland | 62,284,400 | 2,871,241,622 | NYSE |
| Repsol S.A./REP | Spain | 66,289,100 | 2,736,156,400 | NYSE |
| Vodaphone Group/VOD | UK | 54,603,600 | 2,724,928,981 | NYSE |
| Astra (Series A)/A | Sweden | 92,525,700 | 2,596,081,428 | NYSE |
| News Corporation/NWS | Australia | 129,154,600 | 2,534,654,556 | NYSE |
| Petroleum Geo-Services/PGO | Norway | 51,434,900 | 2,463,917,488 | NYSE |
| TOTAL/TOT | France | 52,630,300 | 2,452,640,125 | NYSE |

| Company/Symbol | Country | Share Volume | Dollar Volume | Exchange |
|---|---|---|---|---|
| British Steel/BST | UK | 92,186,300 | 2,389,910,531 | NYSE |
| Tubos de Acero de Mexico/TAM | Mexico | 108,792,100 | 2,219,201,709 | NYSE |
| Aegon/AEG | Netherlands | 29,170,800 | 2,171,214,381 | NYSE |
| Unibanco-Uniao de Bancos Brasileiros/UBB | Brazil | 63,679,100 | 2,143,194,091 | NYSE |
| Telefonica de Peru/TDP | Peru | 88,821,800 | 2,043,909,506 | NYSE |
| Gallaher Group/GLH | UK | 109,759,500 | 2,030,046,806 | NYSE |
| Telecom Argentina STET-France Telecom/TEO | Argentina | 53,772,700 | 2,018,648,916 | NYSE |
| Shell Transport & Trading Co./SC | UK | 29,123,000 | 1,933,679,375 | NYSE |
| Rhone Poulenc (Series A)/RP | France | 49,873,500 | 1,917,563,338 | NYSE |
| Sony Corp./SNE | Japan | 22,265,300 | 1,865,359,916 | NYSE |
| Alcatel Alsthom/ALA | France | 73,218,800 | 1,723,313,247 | NYSE |
| De Beers Consolidated Mines/DBRSY | | 57,862,900 | 1,721,354,175 | NASDAQ |

Source: Bank of New York

customers. A company such as Sony, for example, understands that every U.S. investor who owns Sony represents a lifetime Sony customer. Direct-purchase plans provide a way for foreign-based companies to build brand-name recognition and consumer goodwill in the U.S. Direct-purchase plans also provide a way for foreign companies to diversify their shareholder base geographically.

## J.P. MORGAN'S SHAREHOLDER SERVICES PLAN

Prior to 1996, no ADR offered a direct-purchase plan. That changed in mid-1996 when J.P. Morgan, a major administrator of ADRs, started its Shareholder Services Program. The program allows investors to make initial investments in many foreign companies whose ADRs are administered by Morgan. The following are the terms of the J.P. Morgan plan:

$ Initial purchases are available to investors in all 50 states.

$ Minimum initial purchase is $250.

$ Subsequent purchases can range from $50 to $100,000 per year.

$ Purchases are made at least weekly, and daily if practical.

$ There is a one-time enrollment fee of $15.

$ Per-transaction fees are $5 plus 12 cents per share.

$ Investors are charged a proportion of approximately 12 cents per share to reinvest dividends.

$ Automatic monthly investments via electronic debit of a bank account are available.

$ Shares can be sold via the telephone.

## BANK OF NEW YORK'S GLOBAL BUYDIRECT PLAN

Following Morgan's lead, Bank of New York offered its Global BuyDIRECT program for ADR clients beginning in 1997. The following are the terms of Bank of New York's ADR direct-purchase plan:

$ Initial purchases are available to investors in all 50 states.

$ Minimum initial purchase is $200.

$ Subsequent purchases can range from $50 to $250,000 per transaction.

$ Shares are purchased at least weekly, and daily if practical.

$ There is a one-time enrollment fee of $10.

$ Per-transaction fees are $5 plus 10 cents per share.

$ Reinvestment fee is 10 cents plus five percent of the amount of reinvested dividends ($5 maximum).

$ Automatic monthly investment services are available.

$ Shares can be sold via the telephone.

Please see Appendix C for an extensive list of the ADRs under the J.P.Morgan Shareholder Services Plan and a list of those that participate in the Global BuyDIRECT program under the Bank of New York.

## CITICORP'S INTERNATIONAL DIRECT INVESTMENT PROGRAM

Not to be outdone, Citicorp launched its International Direct Investment Program for ADR clients in 1998. The following are terms of Citicorp's plan:

$ Initial purchases can be made by investors in all 50 states.

$ Minimum initial investment is $250.

$ Subsequent investments can range from $50 to $100,000 per year.

$ There is a $10 enrollment fee.

$ Purchasing fees are $5 plus 10 cents per share.

$ Selling fees are $10 plus 10 cents per share.

$ Sell instructions must be submitted in writing. All sell instructions are processed no later than five business days after the order is received.

$ There is no charge to reinvest dividends other than a brokerage charge of 10 cents per share.

$ Automatic monthly investment services are available.

The only client of Citicorp's new plan at the time of this writing is **AEGON NV** (NYSE: AEG). AEGON, headquartered in the Netherlands, is an international insurance company providing primarily life insurance and financial and investment products. AEGON USA is the largest non-USA owned life insurance holding company. The company's earnings have grown at a steady rate in recent years.

Further growth is expected. AEGON is one of my favorite international direct-purchase investments and I rate it five stars (*****). For enrollment information for AEGON and future International Direct Investment Program members, call 800-808-8010.

Another client of Citicorp that is not a member of the International Direct Investment Program but does offer a direct-purchase plan is **Nokia** (NYSE: NOKA). Based in Helsinki, Finland, Nokia is a leading provider of wireless telecommunication systems and equipment with customers in 120 countries. Per-share profits have jumped sharply in recent years. I like these shares for long-term growth and give them four stars. Nokia's direct-purchase plan permits initial purchases with a minimum $250. Subsequent purchases can range from $50 to $100,000 per year. Fees for initial and subsequent purchases are $2.50, plus brokerage fees of a maximum eight cents per share. For enrollment information, call 800-483-9010.

## Low-Cost International Investing

As you can see, all ADR direct-purchase plans have a variety of fees in their plans. Depending on investment styles and investment amounts, the fees will impact investors differently. Even with fees, these programs are still very cost-competitive versus buying ADRs through brokers. Also, ADR direct-purchase plans are very cost-effective when compared to the typical international mutual fund, especially if you are investing for the long term. Compare $50,000 invested in an international mutual fund earning an average 11 percent per year (before annual carrying charges of 1.9 percent) and a portfolio of ADRs worth $50,000 earning an average of 11 percent per year. At the end of 20 years, the $50,000 in the mutual fund (deducting for the annual expenses) will grow to less than $300,000. On the other hand, the $50,000 ADR portfolio, which has no carrying charges, grows to approximately $403,000—a difference of more than $100,000.

Of course, a mutual-fund manager would argue that an international mutual fund provides immediate diversification for investors, diversification that can be more difficult to achieve by buying individual ADRs. Keep in mind, however, that international investments are usually part of an individual's portfolio, not a portfolio unto itself. You don't necessarily have to own 50 ADRs to be "properly diversified." An investor can have adequate portfolio diversification with

13 to 20 U.S. and foreign stocks. Just by adding a few ADRs to a stock portfolio, an investor should enjoy the benefits of investing overseas.

## IRA/401(k) Investments

In many cases, the biggest pool of money an individual controls is in his or her IRA/401(k) plans. Because of the size of these assets, it is imperative that investors properly diversify them in order to control risk. I think an individual who has no overseas representation in his or her retirement plan is making a big mistake. In my 401(k) plan, I try to keep 20 percent to 25 percent of the assets invested in international stock funds. Yes, this exposure has limited my returns in recent years due to the sluggishness of foreign markets, but over the long haul I think this exposure will serve me extremely well.

How can you include international investments in a retirement program? Check with your 401(k) plan administrator to see if a foreign stock fund is one of your investment options. If so, check out the record of the fund in Morningstar. (Your plan administrator should have performance reports on the fund as well.) Make sure you compare the performance of the fund relative to other foreign funds pursuing a similar investment approach. Also be sure to look at performance over at least the last one, three, five, and, if possible, 10-year periods. Don't compare the fund's performance strictly to U.S. equity funds. Most foreign funds have underperformed general U.S. equity funds in recent years. If the performance is acceptable, you might want to put some of your 401(k) money into the fund.

You should feel very comfortable having at least 10 percent of your retirement assets in international stock funds. If you have a choice among international funds, I would choose the one with the broadest geographic exposure.

In your individual retirement accounts, you can hold both mutual funds and stocks. If you prefer funds, focus on quality international funds with moderate expenses. Again, I prefer the Acorn International and T. Rowe Price International Stock Funds. (I have a portion of my 401(k) money in these two funds.) If you prefer individual stocks in your IRA, focus selections on those ADRs I've rated with four or five stars. Personal favorites among ADR direct-purchase investments (these would be appropriate for IRAs as well as investments outside a retirement account) include AEGON (insurance/financial services), Ahold (supermarkets), Baan (software), British Airways (airline), Dassault Systemes (computer-aided design systems), Elan (pharmaceuticals), New Holland (farm equipment), Nokia (cellular telephones), Novo-Nordisk (drugs/chemicals), Royal Dutch Petroleum (oil), Reuters Group (financial-information services), Unilever NV or PLC (consumer products), Saville Systems (billing systems), and Vimpel Communications (cellular telephone services).

# ▼ CONCLUSION . . .

I n order to maximize portfolio profits in the future, investors cannot ignore investment opportunities outside the United States. Fortunately, the individual investor revolution has created an environment in which it is as easy to invest overseas as it is in the U.S. No-load international mutual funds, closed-end international funds, WEBS, and ADR direct-purchase programs all provide investors with access to foreign markets that far surpass what was available even five or 10 years ago. Of course, access is no assurance of investment success; investors must still choose wisely when venturing overseas.

This chapter also touched briefly on some useful Web sites for obtaining information on international investments. Chapter 5 provides an expansive look at the wealth of investment information and decision-making tools available on the Internet..

# CHAPTER FIVE

# FINDING THE NEXT MICROSOFT IN CYBERSPACE: DOING INVESTMENT RESEARCH ON THE INTERNET

When I first started in the investment business more than 16 years ago, I didn't own a computer. I didn't use a computer at work. I wrote my newsletter articles on an electric typewriter. My stock-picking tools included pen, paper, calculator, and file cabinets filled with various companies' quarterly and annual reports.

No Pentiums. No spreadsheets. No modems. No hard drives.

And certainly no Internet.

Although my research tools seem a bit underwhelming by today's standards, I was light-years ahead of most individual investors. In addition to quarterly and annual reports, I had access to *Standard & Poor's* and *Moody's* research material, *Value Line Investment Survey*, charting books, financial magazines, and newsletters. Of course, these research materials weren't free; my firm spent thousands of dollars each year buying these services.

For the typical small investor, however, stock research meant something quite different. Unless you were willing to part with big sums of money, doing stock research usually meant going to the local library and praying that *Value Line* and *The Wall Street Journal* weren't checked out or stolen.

Now fast-forward to today. I'm writing this book on a desktop computer that has more power than the behemoth machines that filled entire rooms decades ago. And with a few keystrokes, I can retrieve stock quotes, balance sheets, income statements, brokerage reports, stock charts, news updates, trading data, and much more on virtually any stock in the world. In seconds, I can screen thousands of mutual funds to find the few that fit my strict investment criteria. In short, I can do the sort of high-level research about which I couldn't even dream 16 years ago. And I can do it without ever leaving my chair.

Funny thing is—so can you.

## THE INTERNET LEVELS THE PLAYING FIELD

I already discussed how the Internet and online trading have provided millions of individual investors with low-cost access to the financial markets. The Internet has also leveled the playing field in terms of information. Individual investors today have an unbelievable amount of research power at their fingertips. Best of all, this power comes with an extremely low price tag. Indeed, $15 to $20 a month buys you more market information and intelligence today than most market pros received when they paid tens of thousands of dollars a few years ago. This chapter explores the Internet and provides simple, straightforward strategies for making this information resource work for you.

### What's the Internet?

Although Internet fever is a relatively new phenomenon, the Internet has actually been around for about a quarter century. The Internet was spawned by a government effort to connect together a U.S. Defense Department computer network, called the ARPAnet, with various other radio and satellite networks. The aim of the network was to allow any computer on the network to talk with any other computer. The communication was done through Internet Protocol (IP) packets. Over time, many organizations started building their own computer networks in hopes of hooking up with ARPAnet. One important network was commissioned by the National Science Foundation (NSF), an agency of the U.S. government. These systems formed what is now the backbone of the Internet system. Today, the Internet has grown into a collection of interconnected computer networks encompassing educational, research, and commercial entities.

### What The Internet Is NOT

Admittedly, it is difficult to overstate the power of the Internet in terms of empowering individual investors. Never before has *any* investor had such powerful tools both for accessing the markets and research investments. The danger of the Internet, however, is that investors use this power irresponsibly.

In Chapter 3, we talked about the misuse of the power of the Internet in terms of online trading. Cheap online brokerage commissions have caused many investors to discard prudent investment disciplines in the name of "trading" your way to riches. Unfortunately, online commissions can't be cheap enough to compensate for the long-term damage done to a portfolio due to short-term trading.

This misuse of the Internet can also extend to using the Internet for picking investments. Remember the Internet's strength is information, not advice. Yes, the Internet is an excellent research source, but you'll still have to do the reading and the analysis. The key to your investing success won't depend on being able to obtain company financial records online or screen for stocks using various criteria. Your success depends on what you do with this information.

Another factor to consider when using the Internet is the following: don't assume that everything you read online is fact. I think most Web sites do their best to verify their information, but some sites do a much better job than others in terms of providing accurate information. Don't be bashful in checking the veracity of information obtained online, especially if it's information you plan to use to make decisions. Crosscheck information on one site against information found on another.

Finally, don't assume everyone voicing opinions online is unbiased. One of the strengths of the Internet, anonymity, is also one of its weaknesses. You never know who is touting this particular stock or that particular financial product. People have their own agendas and this goes doubly in the online world. Your success in using the Internet depends on your ability to cut through the clutter and separate fact from fiction.

## Getting Started

Obviously, before you can use the Internet as your private research department, you have to get online. Now I'm no computer geek. Most of the time I use my computer as a glorified typewriter, so I'm not going to make any specific recommendations concerning computers, servers, modems, printers, Internet providers, and all of that other mumbo jumbo. Rather, I'll tell you what I think is important to know when you are assembling the products necessary to surf the Net:

$ *Computer/Monitor*: Who makes the best computers? Quite frankly, I am probably the last person to make that judgment. I do know at some point, your computer will not work properly.

This means placing a service call or receiving some kind of assistance over the phone. If you buy a cheap computer from "Stinky's Computer and Bagel Emporium" that Stinky slapped together in his basement, you might find that going cheap at the front end is going to be much more expensive, in the long run, than sticking with the tried and true and paying a bit more up front. Another thing to consider when buying a computer is that, what seems blazing fast today (we're talking computer speed here) will be turtle-like tomorrow. Also, if you use a computer for any length of time, you become a "speed freak," someone who just can't wait that extra nanosecond for the computer to pull up a file. Speed is especially important in the Internet world. There's nothing more frustrating than hitting a key to visit your favorite Internet spot and having to wait for the information to appear on your screen. So don't skimp on your computer when it comes to speed and processing guts. At a minimum, you'll want a computer with a 150-megahertz chip and 16MB in memory. Don't skimp on a monitor either, especially given the graphics-heavy Web sites that are being developed.

$ *Modem*: A modem is the device that connects your computer to the Internet, currently done over telephone lines. Just as with a computer, you shouldn't take the cheapest route when buying a modem. Modems have certain speed rates that describe how fast they transmit data. Common speed rates, or "bauds" as they are called, are 28.8 or 33.6 kilobits per second. When buying a modem, make sure you buy one that provides speeds of at least 28.8K and preferably 33.6K or the new 56K modems. The reason is that even if you have the fastest, meanest PC on the planet, it won't make a difference if your modem transmits data slowly. In many cases, a modem is built into the computer.

$ *Printer*: You don't need a printer to surf the Net, but you'll need one if you want to print out any information. It is still much easier to read paper than a computer screen. In terms of printers, you have many choices.

$ *Internet Service Provider (ISP)*: You'll also need some place to plug into if you want to do some net-surfing and an Internet Service Provider will be your gateway to the Internet. For the most part, fees are similar across ISPs, usually $15 to $25 per month for unlimited usage. You'll connect to your ISP via an 800-number or local phone number, so long-distance charges are not an issue. What makes a good ISP? Reliability and avail-ability. A problem for many ISPs has been keeping their equip-ment from breaking down under the strain of the rapid growth of the Internet. Related to this increasing use of the Internet is the occasional inability to gain access to the Internet via the ISP. There's nothing worse than dialing up your ISP only to get a busy signal because the system is overloaded. You also want to make sure that your ISP is compatible with the fastest modem speeds. Some ISPs only support 28.8K modem speeds. Try to find an ISP with at least 33.6K modem compatibility. When searching for an ISP, check out the offerings of AT&T and MCI. Chances are your local phone company has also gotten into the ISP business. Finally, America Online offers Internet access as part of its membership package.

$ *Web browser*: The last piece of equipment you'll need is soft-ware to allow you to navigate the Internet. This software is called a Web browser. Microsoft (Microsoft Internet Explorer) and Netscape (Netscape Navigator) make the most popular Web browsers. I've used both and found them relatively user-friendly. Chances are, when you purchase your computer, a Web browser will already be loaded on the PC.

$ *Telephone line*: Your home telephone line is adequate for access-ing the Internet. Keep in mind that if you have only one phone line, no one will be able to call you when you are online. For that reason, many people are adding a second line for Internet access. The cost of installing such "dedicated" lines varies but can run about $200, plus a monthly fee. Depending on your usage, as well as the number of online users in your household, you might find a second line a necessity.

## America Online

Once you have all the necessary equipment, the next step is going online. For millions of people, going online means logging onto America Online. Actually, AOL isn't really the Internet but a sepa-rate online system that is controlled by AOL. The benefit of AOL is that it provides a ready-made, well-organized place for investors to obtain information. AOL's content is divided into various channels ranging from personal finance and news to entertainment and sports. These channels are organized in such a way that even novice com-puter users should be able to navigate them easily.

The value of AOL is that it is a structured environment. For many investors, such structure takes the confusion out of the online process. On the other hand, AOL is not the Internet; it does not offer anywhere near the breadth of information available on the Internet. Fortunately, AOL users are not stranded in this closed system. AOL provides a gateway onto the Internet. One of the reasons AOL has become so popular is that an AOL user has access to AOL's content as well as all the information of the Internet. For roughly the monthly fee you'd pay a typical ISP, AOL provides Internet access and a whole lot more.

AOL's popularity also makes it difficult at certain times of the day to hook up. AOL has come a long way in the last year or so in solving some of its capacity issues. Still, don't be surprised to get a busy signal or two when attempting to log on to AOL. Also, AOL has had some well-publicized outages in recent years. To be fair, all ISPs have experienced such problems, although AOL's outages, due to its high profile, seem to be the most publicized. Again, the online world is not perfect, regardless of your equipment or ISP. For that reason, many people have multiple ISPs, perhaps AOL and a national ISP firm. In this way, you have backups in case your main ISP has service problems.

## Navigating the World Wide Web

The most popular side of the Internet is the World Wide Web. The Web is a graphical system that allows you to view information contained on many different Web sites and easily navigate between them. Web sites are found by entering the site's address in your Web browser software. The Web address is also known as the *uniform resource locator* (URL). Most URLs start with the following letters: http://www. (name of web site).com. For example, my newsletter on dividend reinvestment plans, *DRIP Investor*, has its own Web site. The URL is http://www.dripinvestor.com. In order to visit my site, you merely need to type in this address on the Web browser, punch the "enter" key, and you're on your way.

### Web Links

One of the nice things about the Web is that you can easily move between pages within the same site or from one site to another via links that are distinguished by colored text or buttons. Clicking such a link sends you directly to that other site or page. Most Web sites provide several links, so finding one site of interest will likely lead to other sites offering more information.

**Search Engines**

One key to finding what you want on the Web depends to a certain extent on your ability to use Internet search engines. Search engines are Internet services that assist you to find the Web sites you need. Most search engines work in the following way:

$ Go to the Web site of a popular search engine such as Alta Vista (http://www.altavista.digital.com), Yahoo! (http://www.yahoo.com), Lycos (http://www.lycos.com), or Excite (http://www.excite.com).

$ Enter your request in the space provided, being as specific as possible. Let's say you have an interest in vintage wines and want to see what information is available on the Web. If you just type the word "wine" into the search engine, you'll likely have thousands of sites that match your request, so narrow your search as much as possible using specific words and phrases.

$ In case you have questions or problems, read the site's help instructions to know the best way to conduct a search.

Using search engines can be extremely frustrating for beginners. A lot of your searches will pull up sites that have nothing to do with the topic of interest. Over time, however, as you play with different search techniques and engines, you'll likely gain a reasonable amount of proficiency in finding what you want. For further tips on using search engines, visit the Search Engine Watch site (http://searchenginewatch.com).

One nice feature of Web browsers is that, while it may take you a long time to find a gem of a site, you can "bookmark" it and make sure you'll never lose the address. The "Bookmark" or "Favorites" feature on the menu bar allows you to store and organize Web sites you visit often for quick and easy retrieval.

## Finding the Next Microsoft in Cyberspace

Now that we've gone over the basics, let's get to specific Web sites that will make you a better investor. One thing I won't do is inundate you with thousands of Web sites on investing. I cannot begin to provide a comprehensive listing of all that's out there for the individual investor. Many "Internet Yellow Pages" exist that provide listings of specific Web sites. Of course, with content on the Internet growing exponentially every week, any "all-inclusive" directory on the Internet is quickly outdated. What I'll do is narrow the universe to a few selected sites that I think are especially useful for investors.

Before I give specific Web addresses, you should realize that in order to use many of these sites, you'll probably have to register as a user. In many cases, the registration process is free of charge. Still, you'll have to provide the site with certain information, such as your name and email address. I have registered for many sites and have found this to be fairly painless. Yes, you might receive email from these Web sites at some point alerting you to new features of their site or new products that they would like to sell you, but I've found the registration process a small inconvenience relative to the wealth of information you'll receive. Make sure you register without incurring a financial obligation. Some Web sites charge various fees to enter parts of their sites. I'll discuss "free versus fee" sites later in this chapter.

## CASE STUDY 1—FINDING A VALUE STOCK IN A VALUE-SCARCE MARKET.

The best way to show the power of the Internet is to walk you through a step-by-step stock research project, using different Internet sites along the way.

### Step 1—Stock Screening

The first step in the research project is to develop your own ideas on what constitutes a value stock. For example, you might decide that a good value stock for your purposes has the following attributes:

$ A P/E ratio of 15 or under.

$ A yield of at least 1.5 percent.

$ Earnings growth of at least eight percent per year for the last five years.

$ A strong balance sheet with long-term debt to equity of no more than 25 percent.

$ A market capitalization (the stock price times the number of shares outstanding) of no more than $5 billion.

$ A stock price that is no more than twice the company's book value.

$ Return on equity of at least 10 percent.

$ A stock price no greater than $30.

Please note that I'm using these criteria merely for example purposes. You may feel that only stocks with P/E ratios below 10 constitute true value stocks. What I plan to show you is that the Internet provides a lot of flexibility to find stocks that meet your specific criteria.

The value of the Internet is that it allows you to screen thousands of companies based on your specific screening criteria to give you stocks for further research. Simply go to one of the many stock screening sites on the Web. The following Web sites provide a variety of screening tools:

$ http://www.marketplayer.com    This extremely robust screening tool may be a bit intimidating for beginners. You'll need to register to use this site. After entering your user name and password, click the "screening" section on the left-hand side of the page, which takes you to a screening page showing a variety of screening tools. Click "Sample Reports" at the top of page. This section provides a variety of "canned" screening formats, including a "Warren Buffett Stable Growth Screen" that is already set up to follow the investment criteria used by Warren Buffett, arguably the most successful investor of all time. If you want to customize your own screen, you can do so using hundreds of screening criteria.

$ http://www.irnet.com    This site has a variety of screening tools to help you find a stock of interest. This site also contains the capability to screen stocks based on written commands. Click the Search button on your toolbar and you'll see a number of screening tools appear. One tool is the English Query Search tool, which allows you to request information in plain English. This site's Java Stock Screener is another useful screening tool.

$ http://www.rapidresearch.com    This site offers a variety of screening tools, including basic and more advanced screening techniques. On the site's home page, you'll see a variety of screening criteria. If you want more screening options, click the "advanced screener" button on the left-hand side of the home page.

$ http://www.wsrn.com    This is a fairly user-friendly screening tool, although it does not allow you to screen for as many criteria as, say, marketplayer. Click "stock screening" on the left-hand side of the home page and you're off and running.

$ http://www.stockscreener.com    This is a solid, user-friendly screening tool offering plenty of criteria by which to screen stocks. You'll want to bookmark this one.

$ http://www.marketguide.com   This screening tool is part of the Market Guide cadre of online tools. It is easy to use and fairly robust. To get to the screening tools, click the "screening" button at the top of the home page.

Besides the fact that these are extremely useful sites, they are also free. For our research project, let's use Stock Point (www.irnet.com). Click on the Search button at the top of the home page. The Java Stock Screener allows me to enter my specific search criteria. After entering the criteria, I start the search by hitting the Search key. After a few seconds, the screen provides a list of stocks that meet my criteria with direct links to further information on each company. This list of stocks provides my starting point for further research.

### Step 2—Research the Screen Candidates

It's now time to narrow the stocks even more using fundamental research. First, you'll probably want to go the companies' Web sites for information. I think you'll be surprised by both the number of companies that have their own Web sites and the breadth of information available on these Web sites. Often, all you need to do to find a company's Web site is use the company name in the URL. One place to find links to companiess Web sites is the New York Stock Exchange Web site (http://www.nyse.com). At the site's home page, click "Listed Companies" on the left-hand side of page. On the next page, click "Listed Company Links." This page provides links to Web sites of many companies whose shares trade on the New York Stock Exchange. I've also provided Web addresses for many U.S. and foreign companies offering direct-purchase plans in the directories in Appendices A and C.

Once you've obtained information from the companies' Web sites, the next place to search is the various research outlets available on the Internet. The easiest way to find these services is by going to an "aggregator" site. These Web sites pull together in a single area literally hundreds of links to research services. Most of these aggregator sites use the company's stock symbol to start the search. Once you've entered the stock symbol, plenty of financial data is at your fingertips. Some useful aggregators include:

$ http://www.yahoo.com   Part of the Yahoo site is a useful consolidation of many sites devoted to fundamental stock research. Simply go to this Web address, click Stock Quotes, which is near the top of the page, put in the company's stock symbol, and you are introduced to a number of links providing a variety of different information about the company. For example, key in the symbol for Olsten (OLS), which is one of the stocks that met our screening criteria. What pops up is the latest quote on the stock, as well as a variety of news stories on the company. You'll also see links to other data pertaining to Olsten, such as charts, securities and exchange filings, research material, and other pieces of information. Click each of these items and you'll find a wealth of information on the company. The Yahoo site is laid out nicely and provides a place to do one-stop shopping for research information on a particular company.

$ http://www.quicken.com   This site, from the people who brought you Quicken personal finance software, is one of the better sites for links to a bounty of useful sites for doing research.

$ http://www.dailystocks.com   This is another excellent aggregator of Web research links. Like Yahoo, Daily Stocks uses the stock symbol to key its information search. I use this site quite often to obtain large amounts of information quickly.

$ http://www.stockfever.com   This site is yet another provider of important links to research information on a particular company.

$ http://www.nasdaq.com   This site provides information on stocks that trade on the Nasdaq market. One particularly useful feature is a research report on most Nasdaq-traded stocks. On the home page, type in the stock symbol of a company in the upper right-hand box, then click "Get Info Quotes." You are taken to a page that offers a variety of information options on that particular company. Click "Stock Reports," and then click Open Stock Report on the next page that appears. This opens a page with a variety of data on the company.

$ http://www.investor.msn.com   This is one of the best starting points on the Web for finding information on companies. Just type the company's stock symbol on the upper left-hand corner of the home page and hit Enter.

$ http://www.stockmaster.com   This site also has a lot of good research links for finding information on companies.

For our purposes, let's use http://www.dailystocks.com as a starting point for research on Olsten. On the home page of Daily Stocks, you'll have at your fingertips a plethora of general market news and summaries. When you enter the stock symbol, you'll go to a separate page showing all the various links to information on Olsten. Information that's available includes:

$ Company SEC filings

$ Company earnings estimates

$ Balance sheet

$ Income statement

$ Five-year revenues and earnings history

$ List of competitors

$ Comparison of company to others in industry group

$ Charts—daily, weekly, or monthly prices

$ Newspaper and magazine articles in which the company is mentioned

$ Historical pricing data

$ Discussion forums in which investors have been talking about the company

As you can see, the site provides a wealth of data on the company to assist you in making judgments. Best of all, most of the information is free.

## Step 3—See What Others Are Saying About the Stock

Once you've done your research, you might want to check what others may be thinking about the companies. Be warned, however, that the strong suit of the Internet is information, not advice. Keep in mind that entities providing opinions on the Web probably have an agenda. For example, those positive comments about the company in some discussion forums or Usenet groups may come from an individual with a huge position in the stock. Likewise, those negative comments could be coming from somebody who is selling the stock short and is trying to rally sentiment against the company. Even brokerage reports on companies need to be looked at with a skeptical eye. Brokers are never quick to pan companies because a sell recommendation could hurt the brokerage's chances of getting underwriting work from the firm. Still, you might learn something you didn't know or gain an insight you didn't have that may help you decide whether to invest in the stock. Here are some ideas for getting outside viewpoints on stocks:

$ A number of brokerage firms make their research available on the Web for free. Two decent brokerage research sites are Lehman Brothers (http://www.lehman.com) and Hambrecht & Quist (http://www.hamquist.com). Lehman organizes its online information by industry group. Scroll down the home page and click "Research." If you're interested in stocks, click "Equity Research." Hambrecht & Quist provides a lot of research reports on high-technology companies. Click the "Research" button on the home page.

$ Daily Stocks, as most aggregators, has links to various discussion groups and chat rooms. These groups provide a fertile ground for back-and-forth discussion about a stock. One of the more popular technology discussion forums is Silicon Investor Forum, to which you can get from the Daily Stocks site.

$ Usenet groups are Internet discussion groups offered on literally thousands of topics. Many of these topics are investment-related. If the company is large enough, you'll probably find a Usenet group dedicated exclusively to the company. How do you find these Usenet groups? A good portal to Usenet groups is http://www.dejanews.com. At this Web site, you can search Usenet groups by describing your area of interest. Another way to find investment-related information is by clicking the business/money section on the Dejanews home page.

$ The Motley Fool (http://www.fool.com) has a number of bulletin boards where investors can place questions about stocks or investments in general. Motley Fool has an especially big presence on America Online and is one of the more popular sites for beginners.

### Step 4—See What the Insiders Are Doing

I think it's always useful to know whether corporate insiders are buying or selling the stock. I generally put more weight on insider buying than I do insider selling. Insiders may sell stock for many reasons unrelated to the company's prospects—estate planning, portfolio diversification, tuition bills, home purchase, and so on. An insider who is buying his or her company's stock, however, is usually making a statement that he or she feels the stock is undervalued. The following Web sites offer insider-trading information:

$ http://www.insidertrader.com   This site provides an easy way to monitor insider-trading activity.

$ http://www.dailystocks.com   This site's home page features insider-information links.

$ http://www.dailyrocket.com   This site offers a lot of interesting information, including insider-trading data. Click "Notes from the Inside," which is located on the left-hand side of the site's home page.

For our research project, let's use www.insidertrader.com to check out if any insiders have been buying or selling. When you arrive at the home page, you'll see that this site offers free information as well as premium services that require a fee. Click "Free Stuff" and enter a stock symbol to see if there has been any insider trading in the stock. Our search shows that Olsten has had no insider buying since March 1997 and a couple instances of insider selling in the last year.

## Step 5—Check Out a Stock Chart

After you've done fundamental research on the company, it's a good idea to check out a stock chart to see how the stock has been trading. The Internet has a number of excellent sources for stock charts:

$ http://www.bigcharts.com   This site allows you to create a variety of charts on stocks. You can use daily, weekly, or monthly price data. You can also lay over the chart a variety of technical indicators to give you further insight into the stock's trading pattern. On the site's home page, enter the stock symbol and get charting.

$ http://www.quicken.com   This site has a useful feature that combines charts with news stories. Enter the stock symbol for Olsten (OLS) on the home page and click "Go." The page that pops up shows the latest quote and other information. At the top of the left-hand side of the page is "Charts." Click this to go to a chart of Olsten. On the chart, you'll notice red dots. Just click the red dot on the chart to get the news behind the stock's move for that day.

## Step 6—Check for Breaking News

Perhaps the last step in the investment selection process is to check for breaking news on the company. Many sites provide excellent news sources for stocks:

$ `http://www.newsalert.com` This site links to a variety of news sources.

$ `http://www.bloomberg.com` This site contains a wealth of news on the markets.

$ `http://www.cnnfn.com` This is the Web site for CNN's financial news network.

$ `http://dailystocks.com` This site has a lot of news links.

$ `http://www.yahoo.com` Click "Stock Quotes" on the home page, and you can obtain the latest news on a stock of interest.

$ `http://www.moneynet.com` This is the site for Reuters news information.

## Step 7—Picking the Stock

One thing you won't find on the Internet is a Web site that tells you for certain what stocks will go up. Make no mistake—the Internet is not the Holy Grail of stock picking. It is merely a tool. Ultimately, you'll have to synthesize all the research information you've collected and choose what stock makes sense given your analysis.

## Step 8—Monitor Your Investments

Your work is not done once you've made your stock choice. You need to monitor the stock and the rest of your investments. The Web provides a number of excellent sites that make it easy to monitor your investments:

$ `http://www.investor.msn.com` This site has one of the best portfolio trackers on the Web. Click "Portfolio Manager" on the left-hand side of the site's home page and download the needed portfolio software.

$ `http://www.yahoo.com` Another helpful site for portfolio tracking. Click "stock quotes" on the site's home page. On the next page, click "Register," which is near the top of the page. Once you've registered, you'll be able to create a portfolio.

$ `http://www.dailystocks.com` I track the Dow 30 stocks on this site. To track your portfolio, click "Portfolios" at the top right-hand side of the site's home page and follow the directions.

$ `http://www.quicken.com` This is another portfolio tracking option. Click "Portfolios" on the left-hand side of the home page. Once you've registered, you'll be able to create a portfolio.

$ http://www.newsalert.com   This interesting Web site has a variety of monitoring tools. One of these tools will automatically send you news updates on stocks of interest. Click "My Portfolio" on the left-hand side of the site's home page to get started.

$ http://www.riskview.com   This is an interesting site that allows investors to assess the risk level of their portfolio. The site is a joint venture between Dow Jones & Co., Infinity Financial Technology, and IBM. The site allows an investor to measure his or her portfolio's return and risk profile for a given time frame. This site is not the most user-friendly site I've come across, but more sophisticated investors and experienced Web users may find this site an especially powerful tool for constructing a portfolio.

$ http://www.sec.gov   Known as "Edgar," this site for the Securities and Exchange Commission is an extremely useful tool for keeping track of corporate filings on companies of interest.

## CASE STUDY 2—FINDING A QUALITY MUTUAL FUND

As shown, the Internet is an extremely effective tool for doing stock research. The Web is also extremely useful for researching mutual-fund investments. The following is a step-by-step approach to finding the next great mutual fund.

### Step 1—Screening Funds

A number of Web sites provide excellent tools to screen funds based on a variety of criteria:

$ http://www.morningstar.net   This is the Web site for Morningstar, arguably the leading purveyor of mutual-fund information. This is a "must-bookmark" site for investors interested in mutual funds. Click "Fund Selector" on the left-hand side of the site's home page.

$ http://www.stockpoint.com   This investment Web site offers a fund screening tool. Click "analysis" at the top of the home page and you are taken to a page featuring a variety of analysis tools. Scroll down the page until you come to the Mutual Fund Quick Search tool.

$ http://www.quicken.com   This site provides useful screening information on funds. Click "Mutual Funds" on the left-hand side of the home page. On the next page, click on "Fund Finder" on the left-hand side of the page.

$ http://www.smartmoney.com   This is the site for *Smart Money* magazine and has a variety of investment information, including a mutual fund screen. Click "Mutual Fund Finder" on the left-hand side of the home page. You'll find an easy-to-use tool for finding various fund criteria, from asset size to expenses.

## Step 2—Visit the Fund Family's Web Site

The second step is to visit the Web site of a mutual fund of interest. Most fund families have useful Web sites that provide information about their funds—who manages the fund, what are the fund's top holdings, year-to-date performance results, and other relevant data. The easiest way to find the fund family's Web site is to key in the fund family's name in the URL.

## Step 3—Do Additional Research on the Fund

At this point, you'll probably want to check out other sites for further research on funds. Many of the sites use the fund's symbol to key the search. Two worthwhile Web sites for general information on funds are http://www.morningstar.net and http://www.quicken.com. A third, http://www.stocksmart.com, has useful fund information as well. Click "Mutual Funds" at the top of the site's home page. Other sites with fund information include http://www.investor.msn.com (click "Funds" at the top of the home page) and http://www.fundsinteractive.com.

## Step 4—Tracking your Fund

Most of the portfolio-tracking Web sites highlighted in the first case study can also be used to track funds. Another useful mutual-fund tracking service is offered by http://www.fundalarm.com. This site focuses on when to sell mutual funds. One feature of the site keeps track of fund manager changes.

## Answers to Other Investment Questions

These two case studies show how investors can use the Web to pick stocks and mutual funds. Of course, you might have other personal finance needs to address. Many of these questions can be answered using the Web. For example:

$ *How do I research foreign stocks?* In most cases, the sites for researching U.S. securities work well when researching foreign stocks whose American Depository Receipts (ADRs) trade in this country. All you'll need is the ADR's trading symbol. Other Web sites catering to foreign investments include http://www.global-investor.com, http://www.ifc.org, http://www.bankofny.com/adr, http://www.jpmorgan.com/adr, http://www.ft.com, http://www.newsalert.com (click "Global Stocks" on left-hand side of home page), and http://www.tradershaven.com. Also, http://www.nasdaq.com provides information on American Depository Receipts that trade on the Nasdaq market.

$ *How do I know if I should convert my traditional IRA to a Roth IRA?* The Web has many sites that are useful in answering such personal finance questions. One site that is an excellent source for making a variety of financial calculations, including Roth conversion, is http://www.financenter.com.

$ *Where can a beginner get good information on investing?* The Web has several sites catering to beginners. My favorites include http://www.aaii.org (American Association of Individual Investors), http://www.better-investing.org (National Association of Investors Corporation), and http://www.investorama.com (links to many educational sites). Click "The Directory" at the top of this site's home page.

$ *Where can I find some high-level investment research studies?* Ibbotson Associates, an investment research firm based in Chicago, has a very useful site at http://www.ibbotson.com. When you go to this site, click the "Research" section at the top of the site's home page. This takes you to many links, including a link to "Investment Research via the Internet." This link connects to several interesting research and information sites on the Internet.

## Free versus Fee Web Sites

The amount of free information on the Internet is truly staggering. Indeed, virtually all the sites mentioned thus far are, for the most part, free. If you're willing to pay a fee, even more Web information is available. Fees for "premium" Internet services are usually moderate, perhaps $5 to $15 per month. One site that has an excellent "premium" service is `http://www.investor.msn.com`. For $9.95 per month, you can obtain a variety of additional information sources. One premium service on the site is the capability to obtain an extremely comprehensive research report on a company of your choice with a single click. Another premium service worth checking out is `http://www.wsj.com`. This is the site for *The Wall Street Journal*. For $49 per year ($29 for subscribers to the *Journal*), you can have free reign on this site. One of the benefits is access to *The Wall Street Journal Interactive Edition*, *Barron's Online*, and *Smart Money Interactive Edition*. You also have access to a wealth of corporate information and news. If you are considering a "premium" service on the Internet, see if there's a free 30-day trial offered.

# ▼ Conclusion . . .

This chapter is not meant to be a complete source of Internet investment information. New investment sites are being developed almost daily, and existing sites continue to add content. I'm sure what will be available two or three years from now will make today's offerings look rather paltry. When using the Internet, always remember to consider the source of the information and advice. What is the agenda of the person or Web site providing the information/advice? What are the credentials of the site provider? How does the site's information compare with other Internet information sources? If you approach the Internet with a healthy degree of skepticism and awareness of its shortcomings, you'll be in a much better position to exploit its many opportunities.

# CHAPTER SIX

# CAPTURE THE CRUMBS

D avid Komansky, who heads Merrill Lynch, earned more than $9 million in stock and cash in 1997. Donald Marron, who runs PaineWebber Group, took home about $11 million in cash and stock. Philip Purcell, the head of Morgan Stanley Dean Witter, received about $14 million in cash and stock. The firms where these and other Wall Streeters work didn't do too shabbily either. Merrill Lynch, the brokerage giant, had 1997 *profits* of $1.9 billion. Charles Schwab, the leading discount broker, had a 1997 net profit of $270 million. Fidelity, the mutual-fund giant, is a private company and thus is not required to publicly disclose revenues and income. But by some estimates, the Fidelity Magellan fund, which is just one fund within the vast Fidelity stable, generates several hundred million dollars each year in management fees.

The point of all of these mind-numbing numbers is something you already know—a lot of money is made on Wall Street each year. That's obvious. *How* that money is made, however, may not be. Interestingly, Wall Street's billions, in many cases, are made by what I call "capturing the crumbs." Brokerage commissions, mutual-fund fees, stock and bond trading profits, interest earned on margin accounts, interest float on dividend income that has yet to be sent to investors—all of these are ways Wall Street captures crumbs.

One example of how Wall Street gets rich one crumb at a time is a mutual fund. A typical mutual fund might have a management fee of one percent of the fund's assets. Now one percent of $100 (that's $1 for the mathematically challenged among us) is not getting anybody rich. But take one percent of $1 billion in fund assets (that's $10 million), and you can see just how quickly capturing the "crumb" of one percent can add up to big money.

Stock brokers, fund managers, and stock and bond traders all talk in terms of "basis points." Basis points are often how Wall Streeters are paid. One basis point is one-hundredth of one percent. Thus, 50 "basis points" translates to one-half percent (0.5 percent). When a Wall Streeter talks about "100 basis points," that's a fancy way of saying one percent. On Wall Street, the battle between competing brokers, investment banks, mutual funds, and the like isn't a battle for a big piece of any particular business; it's really a battle for crumbs, for basis points.

What's also important to understand is that Wall Street battles for these crumbs during good times and bad. In fact, Wall Street often exploits good market times to extract even more "crumbs" from investors. Let's return to our example of mutual funds. In the last 10 years, assets in mutual funds have skyrocketed to more than $5 *trillion* paced by soaring stock markets. Yet despite record inflows to mutual funds, some fund families have raised fees. In other words, fund groups are actually capturing even greater numbers of crumbs.

Fund families and other Wall Street institutions capture more crumbs during strong market periods because individual investors let them. Why? Individual investors don't seem to pay as much attention to one-half percent here or one-quarter percent there, because they haven't had to pay attention in recent years. For the three-year period that ended in 1997, the Standard & Poor's 500 had an average annual return of more than 31 percent. Such returns, which are well in excess of the stock market's long-run average annual return of roughly 11 percent, have made many individuals fat and happy, but also a bit sloppy. Who cares if you're losing 1.5 percent or two percent in transaction costs or mutual-fund fees when you're earning 30 percent a year on your money?

Of course, these good times won't last forever. More normal market returns, not to mention some years when the market declines for the year, will put a premium on being able to wring out more return from your portfolio each year. This chapter provides a number of "crumb-capturing" strategies for individual investors.

## CRUMBS MATTER

I've discussed how crumbs in the forms of commissions, fund fees, interest float, and margin interest matter to Wall Street institutions. Crumbs matter to individual investors as well, especially over time.

Figure 6.1 shows the effects of small percentage changes in portfolio returns over five, 15, and 30-year periods. As the tables show, the importance of crumbs increases as your investment sums grow and investment time horizon lengthens. For example, the difference between earning an average 10 percent and 12 percent per year over a 30-year period (assuming a $10,000 initial investment) is a whopping $125,105.

Of course, it's one thing to understand that capturing crumbs is important to portfolio success; it's another to capture these small increments without unduly boosting the risk characteristics of your portfolio. Fortunately, ways exist to generate greater investment returns without increasing your risk.

## TRIM TRANSACTION AND MANAGEMENT FEES

Perhaps the easiest way to improve expected portfolio returns without boosting risk is by reducing transaction and management fees. Every basis point you save as a result of paying lower brokerage or mutual-fund fees boosts your portfolio returns.

Here are some ways to save on transaction and management fees:

$ *Buy no-load mutual funds.* Research has shown that buying funds that have sales charges (also called "loads") does not guarantee superior fund performance. That's not surprising. A fund that charges a four percent or five percent sales charge digs itself a deep hole relative to a fund that charges no sales fees. Granted, a number of load funds have provided solid returns for investors, but when 70 percent or more of all equity funds, load and no-load funds alike, fail to perform as well as the S&P 500, buying a load fund stacks the odds against you even more.

$ *Focus on funds with low expenses.* One of the great success stories in the fund industry in recent years is the index fund. An index fund mimics the performance of a particular equity index. The most popular index funds mirror the Standard & Poor's 500 index. Index funds have beaten the pants off actively managed funds in recent years. Although many reasons are given for this superior relative performance of index funds, a big reason is that annual expenses for index funds are much lower than expenses for actively managed funds. It is not unusual for an equity fund to have an annual expense ratio of 1.5 percent or more. At 1.5 percent, an investor with $50,000 in the fund pays $750 per year in fees. Conversely, a typical index fund will have annual

### How $10,000 Grows Over 5 Years . . .

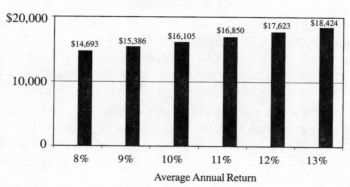

Average Annual Return

### How $10,000 Grows Over 15 Years . . .

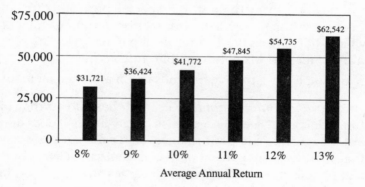

Average Annual Return

### How $10,000 Grows Over 30 Years . . .

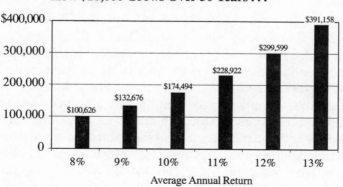

Average Annual Return

**Figure 6.1**

expenses of 25 basis (0.25 percent) to 60 basis points (0.6 percent) of assets. It is no wonder that actively managed funds with expense ratios five or six times that of an index fund fail to beat the index fund. I know most fund groups will tell you that what matters is performance, not fees. However, it's indisputable that the higher the fund's annual expenses are, the higher the hurdle for that fund to provide market-beating returns. If you are ambivalent between two fund investments, always choose the one with lower annual expenses.

$ *Shop for brokerage commissions.* A huge disparity exists between the commissions charged by brokerage firms. This gap has widened as a result of the increase in inexpensive online brokers. If you make your own investment decisions and still use a full-service broker, evaluate whether you are getting your money's worth. You might be able to find a better, less-expensive option.

$ *Beware of hidden brokerage fees.* Some brokers charge an annual administrative fee on your account, while others charge an inactive account fee if you don't meet a minimum number of trades each year. Many brokers charge extra to register shares in your own name rather than a "street" name.

$ *Compare broker money-market rates.* When shopping for brokers, make sure you compare rates each broker pays on funds being held for investment. By shopping smart, you might be able to pick up 10 or 20 basis points on funds parked at your brokerage firm.

$ *Compare broker margin loan rates.* Brokers are allowed to loan investors up to 50 percent of the purchase price of stock. The 50 percent that is put up by the broker is called "margin." Investors use margin to leverage their investments in stocks. Let's say you buy 100 shares of a $50 stock. The investment would normally cost you $5000, but you have a margin account with your broker that allows you to borrow up to half the amount of your $5000 investment. The broker doesn't loan you this money out of the goodness of his or her heart; as is the case with any loan, you'll pay interest. An investor using margin believes that gains in the investment will more than offset the interest on the loan. If you think you will use margin in your investment program, be sure to shop for the best margin rates.

$ *Don't ignore dividend reinvestment plans/direct-purchase plans.* Chapter 3 discussed DRIPs and direct-purchase plans, which are programs in which investors can buy stock directly from companies. Shares are purchased in two ways: with dividends that the company reinvests on behalf of the individual and with optional cash payments that participants send directly to companies. DRIPs and direct-purchase plans are excellent investment vehicles in terms of improving access to financial markets for investors, especially those with limited pocketbooks. DRIPs are also extremely cost-effective ways for investors to buy stock. Most DRIPs/direct-purchase plans charge little or no fee for purchasing stock. For investors who are willing to forgo exact precision over the buy and sell price for cheaper commissions, these programs offer an excellent alternative.

## Buying Stocks at a Discount

One way to boost investment returns without increasing risk is to buy stock cheaper than the market price. This can be done by investing in certain DRIPs. A number of dividend reinvestment plans provide discounts for plan participants that usually range from two to five percent of the prevailing market price. Most companies apply the discounts only to shares purchased with reinvested dividends, but several companies apply the discounts to stock purchased with both reinvested dividends and optional cash payments.

The notion of companies allowing DRIP participants to purchase stock at a discount goes counter to the belief that companies want to maximize their stocks' purchase price. However, companies that offer discounts derive an important benefit: the ability to raise money more cheaply than via traditional capital-raising avenues. A company that issues stock through its DRIP becomes, in effect, its own underwriter, thus eliminating the middleman's fees. If a company can induce more investors to purchase stock through its DRIP via a two or five percent discount, the company can sell more stock and do it in a more cost-effective manner than using an investment banker.

From an investor standpoint, the biggest benefit of buying stock at a discount through a DRIP is the ability to accumulate shares more cheaply than buying the stock outside the DRIP. The discount, in effect, provides an "instant" profit as well as a cushion against price declines. Discounts also provide a boost to the stock's yield. For example, buying shares with reinvested dividends at a five percent discount is the equivalent of adding 10 to 20 basis points to your yield. The table below lists nine DRIPs with five percent discounts on reinvested dividends. The current yield is one that participants outside the DRIP earn. The "discount-adjusted" yield reflects the five percent discount on reinvested shares:

| Company | Price | Dividend | Yield | "Discount-Adjusted" Yield |
|---|---|---|---|---|
| Ball | $39 | $0.60 | 1.5% | 1.6% |
| Blount | 29 | 0.29 | 1.0 | 1.1 |
| Cousins Prop. | 29 | 1.44 | 5.0 | 5.2 |
| Fleming | 18 | 0.08 | 0.4 | 0.5 |
| Green Mt. Pw. | 14 | 1.10 | 7.9 | 8.3 |
| Hibernia | 20 | 0.36 | 1.8 | 1.9 |
| New Plan Realty | 25 | 1.49 | 6.0 | 6.3 |
| Philadelphia Sub. | 20 | 0.65 | 3.3 | 3.4 |
| United Mobile | 11 | 0.75 | 6.8 | 7.2 |

Yield is a component of a stock's total return (which is equal to the issue's price appreciation plus the dividend yield), so enhancing a stock's yield by 10 to 20 basis points automatically boosts the stock's total return by a similar amount. Remember a person buying the stock at the discount is not assuming any greater level of risk than an investor who buys the same stock outside the DRIP.

## Poor Man's Arbitrage

One way Wall Street makes its billions is by taking advantage of "arbitrage" opportunities. Arbitrage in the investment world, in its simplest form, is the practice of capturing investment crumbs by taking advantage of price discrepancies in different markets for the same security. For example, let's say that Sony is trading in Japan's Nikkei market at a price that is higher in dollar terms than the price of Sony's American Depository Receipts (ADRs) trading in the U.S. market. A Wall Street arbitrageur would buy the Sony ADRs in the U.S. market and sell the Sony stock in the foreign market and pocket the difference. This difference might only be a few pennies per share, but such crumbs add up when the transaction entails thousands of shares. To be sure, most arbitrage opportunities are not available to individual investors because arbitrage opportunities often last for only seconds before they are "arbitraged away" by Wall Street firms.

A "poor man's" arbitrage exists, however, with DRIPs that apply their discounts to shares purchased with optional cash payments.

DRIPs with discounts on optional cash payments are tailor-made for arbitraging because the shares purchased through a DRIP are cheaper than shares purchased on the open market. Consequently, it is not uncommon for investors to perform the following "poor man's" arbitrage:

1. Enroll in a DRIP that offers a discount.
2. Purchase the maximum amount of stock permitted via optional cash payments.
3. Immediately sell the stock.

Such activity presents a quandary for companies. On the one hand, companies like discounts because they enhance the DRIPs' capability to raise money. On the other hand, such arbitrage activity can heighten the stocks' volatility. Furthermore, some companies resent the fact that arbitrage activity is conducted by professional investors when their plans are intended primarily for small investors. For that reason, most companies reserve the right to terminate a DRIP account if the firm believes the account is being used to arbitrage the discount.

If you attempt this type of arbitrage, keep in mind the following:

$ *The arbitrage is best done using DRIPs that offer discounts on optional cash investments.* The profit potential from arbitraging the discount on reinvested dividends is limited unless you hold many shares.

$ *Consider the amount of optional cash payments (OCPs) permitted and how often the OCPs are invested.* The larger the maximum amount of OCPs permitted in the plan is, the larger the potential profit. It is also better to be able to take advantage of the arbitrage monthly instead of quarterly, because you triple your profit opportunities.

$ *Size of discount.* Obviously, profit potential is greater with a five percent discount than with a three percent discount.

$ *Pricing periods.* This is a crucial point to consider. Many companies with discounts have implemented multiday pricing periods, five to 10 days and even longer in some cases, which are used to determine the purchase price in the DRIP (pricing periods, along with all the other details of the DRIP, are explained in the plan prospectus). These pricing periods make it more difficult to determine at what price you'll be purchasing shares. For example, if I know the company buys stock on the last day of the month with optional cash payments and the purchase price will be the average price on that day, then I know at what price I must short the stock in the market (or sell shares from my own inventory) to lock up the profit. However, when a company uses a pricing period to compute the price—such as if the purchase price is the average of the high and low price per day over a 10-day period—it is more difficult to determine my purchase price.

Such pricing periods can distort the size of the discount. For example, let's say a stock's average price during a 10-day pricing period is $10. Then on the close of the tenth day, the stock is trading for $9. The discount (let's say five percent) would be applied to the average price over the 10-day period ($10), giving DRIP participants a purchase price of $9.50 ($10 multiplied by 0.95). In this scenario, you'd be better off buying the stock at the market price because it's cheaper than the "discounted" price. Understanding how the pricing period works is critical to a successful arbitrage.

$ *Trading volume of the stock.* If you plan to short the stock in the market in order to lock up your profit, make sure the daily trading volume of the stock is sufficient to support short selling. In some cases, it can be difficult to execute the short sale if the stock is thinly traded.

$ *Commissions matter.* Keep in mind that commissions you pay to sell the stock on the open market reduce your profit spread. Make sure you are not paying too much in commissions.

As you can see, the "poor man's" arbitrage may not be as simple as it first appears. For this reason, I usually recommend that individual investors view the discount as a nice bonus and leave the arbitrage activity to more sophisticated investors.

## Taxes on DRIP Discounts

Historically, DRIP discounts have been taxed the same as ordinary income. If you bought a $50 stock through your DRIP and received a five percent discount, your purchase price would be $47.50 per share ($50 multiplied by 0.95). The difference between your purchase price and the actual market price, $2.50, was considered income and was consequently taxed at your ordinary rate. In 1994, a private IRS ruling was passed that changed how these discounts are taxed. The ruling states that if you buy stock at a discount, the amount of the discount does not constitute income to you. In effect, the new ruling allows you to convert what was once considered dividend income into long-term capital gains. Of course, if you are arbitraging the discount, your profits are taxed as ordinary income because you are not holding the shares for the mandatory holding period for long-term capital gains. I suggest you consult with your tax adviser concerning this ruling and other tax questions you may have concerning DRIPs with discounts.

Below is a list of companies offering discounts. The list indicates the size of the discount and whether the discount is offered on reinvested dividends (RD) and/or OCPs. Stock symbols and contact numbers are provided and companies that permit initial purchases directly are highlighted. Among the issues on the list, I especially like Atmos Energy, Duke Realty Investments, Old National Bancorp, Philadelphia Suburban, Piedmont Natural Gas, Popular, Time Warner, and United Mobile Homes. Investors should note that companies change their discount policies frequently, so always double-check with a company of interest to make sure it still offers a discount before investing.

## DRIPs with Discounts

| Company | Discount | |
|---|---|---|
| | RD* | OCP* |
| **American Realty Trust** *(NYSE: ARB)* (800) 278-4353 | 10% | —— |
| **American Water Works** *(NYSE: AWK)* (800) 736-3001 | 2 | 2% |
| +**Atmos Energy** *(NYSE: ATO)* (800) 774-4117 | 3 | —— |
| **Ball** *(NYSE: BLL)* (765) 747-6100 | 5 | —— |
| +**Bedford Property** *(NYSE: BED)* (800) 842-7629 | 0–3 | 0–3 |
| **Berkshire Gas** *(NASDAQ: BGAS)* (413) 442-1511 | 3 | 3 |
| **Blount** *(NYSE: BLTA)* (334) 244-4000 | 5 | —— |
| +**Capstead Mortgage** *(NYSE: CMO)* (800) 468-9716 | 2 | 2 |

| Company | Discount | |
|---|---|---|
| | RD* | OCP* |
| **Carolina First** *(NASDAQ: CAFC)* (864) 255-4919 | 5 | —— |
| **CBL Associates** *(NYSE: CBL)* (423) 855-0001 | 5 | —— |
| **CNB Bancshares** *(NYSE: BNK)* (812) 464-3416 | 3 | —— |
| **Commerce Bancorp** *(NYSE: CBH)* (609) 751-9000 | 3 | 3 |
| **Commercial Net Lease** *(NYSE: NNN)* (407) 422-1574 | 3 | —— |
| **Continental Mortgage & Equity Trust** *(NASDAQ: CMETS)* (800) 278-4353 | 5 | —— |
| **Countrywide Credit** *(NYSE: CCR)* (818) 225-3550 | 0–5 | —— |
| **Cousins Properties** *(NYSE: CUZ)* (770) 955-2200 | 5 | —— |
| **Crestar Financial** *(NYSE: CF)* (804) 782-5619 | 5 | —— |
| **+CRIMMIE MAE** *(NYSE: CMM)* (888) 266-6785 | 0–5 | 0–5 |
| **+Duke Realty** *(NYSE: DRE)* (800) 774-4117 | 4 | —— |
| **+Equity Resident. Prop.** *(NYSE: EQR)* (800) 733-5001 | —— | 0–5 |
| **+Entergy** (NYSE: ETR) (800) 225-1721 | —— | 0–3 |
| **Essex County Gas** *(NASDAQ: ECGC)* (978) 388-4000 | 5 | —— |
| **FCNB** *(NASDAQ: FCNB)* (301) 662-2191 | 3 | —— |
| **First American** *(NASDAQ: FATN)* (615) 748-1500 | 5 | —— |
| **First Commonwealth Fin.** *(NYSE: FCF)* (724) 349-7220 | 5 | 5 |
| **Fleming Co.** *(NYSE: FLM)* (405) 840-7200 | 5 | —— |
| **Fuller (H.B.)** *(NASDAQ: FULL)* (612) 645-3401 | 3 | —— |
| **Green Mt. Power** *(NYSE: GMP)* (802) 864-5731 | 5 | —— |
| **Health Care REIT** *(NYSE: HCN)* (419) 247-2800 | 4 | 4 |

| Company | Discount | |
|---|---|---|
| | RD* | OCP* |
| **Hibernia** *(NYSE: HIB)*<br>(504) 533-3333 | 5 | —— |
| **+Home Properties NY** *(NYSE: HME)*<br>(800) 774-4117 | 3 | 3 |
| **Income Opportunity Realty** *(ASE: IOT)*<br>(800) 278-4353 | 5 | —— |
| **INMC Mortgage** *(NYSE: NDE)*<br>(818) 225-3550 | 1 | 3 |
| **Lafarge** *(NYSE: LAF)*<br>(703) 264-3600 | 5 | —— |
| **+Liberty Property** *(NYSE: LRY)*<br>(800) 944-2214 | 3 | —— |
| **Media General** *(ASE: MEGA)*<br>(804) 649-6000 | 5 | —— |
| **Merry Land & Investment** *(NYSE: MRY)*<br>(706) 722-6756 | 5 | 5 |
| **+Michaels Stores** (NASDAQ: MIKE)<br>(800) 577-4676 | — | 0-5 |
| **Monmouth REIT** *(NASDAQ: MNRTA)*<br>(732) 542-4927 | 5 | 5 |
| **National City** *(NYSE: NCC)*<br>(800) 622-6757 | 3 | 3 |
| **National Health Investors** *(NYSE: NHI)*<br>(615) 890-9100 | 5 | —— |
| **New Plan Realty** *(NYSE: NPR)*<br>(212) 869-3000 | 5 | —— |
| **North Carolina Natural Gas**<br>*(NYSE: NCG)* (910) 483-0315 | 5 | —— |
| **+Old National Bancorp**<br>*(NASDAQ: OLDB)* (800) 774-4117 | 3 | —— |
| **+Philadelphia Suburban** *(NYSE: PSC)*<br>(800) 774-4117 | 5 | —— |
| **+Piedmont Natural Gas** *(NYSE: PNY)*<br>(800) 774-4117 | 5 | —— |
| **Popular** *(NASDAQ: BPOP)*<br>(787) 756-3908 | 5 | —— |
| **+Pub. Service Co. of NC** *(NYSE: PGS)*<br>(800) 774-4117 | 5 | —— |
| **+ Redwood Trust** *(NYSE: RWT)*<br>(800) 774-4117 | 2 | 0–2 |
| **Saul Centers** *(NYSE: BFS)*<br>(301) 986-6000 | 3 | —— |
| **+Security Capital Pacific** *(NYSE: PTR)*<br>(800) 842-7629 | 0–5 | 0–5 |

| Company | Discount | |
|---|---|---|
| | RD* | OCP* |
| +Sunstone Hotel *(NYSE: SSI)*<br>(800) 774-4117 | 0–5 | 0–5 |
| +Thornburg Mtge. *(NYSE: TMA)*<br>(800) 509-5586 | 0–5 | 0–5 |
| Time Warner *(NYSE: TWX)*<br>(800) 279-1238 | 5 | —— |
| Transcontinental Realty *(NYSE: TCI)*<br>(800) 278-4353 | 5 | —— |
| Union Planters *(NYSE: UPC)*<br>(901) 580-6000 | 5 | —— |
| United Mobile Homes *(ASE: UMH)*<br>(732) 542-4927 | 5 | —— |
| +UtiliCorp United *(NYSE: UCU)*<br>(800) 647-2789 | 5 | —— |
| York Financial *(NASDAQ: YFED)*<br>(717) 846-8777 | 10 | —— |

+ Permits initial purchases directly.

## Avoid Uncle Sam

Taxes have an insidious effect on your portfolio returns, especially over time. Every dime you pay Uncle Sam in taxes, such as capital gains taxes or taxes on dividend income, is a dime that will never earn you any future returns. It's gone forever. Here are some ways to avoid Uncle Sam in your investment program:

$ *Avoid frequent trading* : One reason I like a buy-and-hold investment philosophy is that it is extremely tax-friendly. In many cases, selling stock means incurring a tax liability if you have a gain in the stock. And depending on how long you've owned the stock and your tax bracket, your tax liability could be as much as 39.6 percent of your profit.

One alternative to selling stocks is using options to protect yourself on the downside. I talked about the dangers of speculating in options in Chapter 2, but options can provide an effective way to hedge your portfolio's risk if used properly, while giving you an alternative to selling stocks. Let's say you've owned Coca-Cola stock for many years and are sitting with huge capital gains. You're also concerned about these stocks and the market, but you don't want to get hit with a huge tax bill by selling them.

You can protect yourself by buying put options on Coca-Cola. Investors buy put options on stocks that they believe will drop in value. One put option gives you the right to sell 100 shares of a stock in the future at a "strike" price specified today. If the stock drops, the profits on the put option help defray the losses on the underlying stock. If the stock doesn't drop, the put expires worthless. As with any insurance, investors pay a price for protection—the price of the puts. However, investors can opt for the insurance rather than sell the shares and incur a big tax bite. As a rule, the use of puts makes more sense as your capital gains and exposure to the stock become greater and greater. Remember each put represents 100 shares. If you own, say, 500 shares of Coca-Cola, you'll need to buy five puts in order to provide adequate protection.

Another option strategy is to "buy a put" and "sell a call." A call option gives the holder the option of buying a stock at a set price. The option seller receives a premium when selling a call, which reduces the downside risk in the underlying stock by the premium amount that the seller receives. In this insurance strategy, the investor sells a call against his position and uses the proceeds from the sale of the call to buy put options. This strategy provides the protection of a put without the expense. Your gain or loss is limited to the trading range between the two options. Keep in mind that when an investor sells calls, he or she runs the risk of having the shares "called away." In other words, the holder of the call option can exercise the option and buy the stock from the seller of the call, in which case the investor is forced to sell the issue (and incur tax liabilities) unless he or she buys back the call option at the higher price. As you can see, selling calls has its own set of risks. However, if you are concerned that your stock holdings will decline yet don't want to sell the shares due to tax reasons, selling calls provides a way to build an income stream (and fund purchases of put options for additional insurance) that can help offset some of the price drop in your stocks.

$ *Stocks are usually better investments than mutual funds when it comes to avoiding Uncle Sam.* With individual stocks, you control your tax destiny; you incur a tax liability only when you decide to sell the shares. With stocks, you can defer taxes indefinitely. You can even wipe out any tax liability on investments if you pass along the investments to your heirs when you die.

That's because your heirs receive a "stepped-up" cost basis on stocks that they inherit. Unfortunately, with mutual funds, you have no say over the tax issue. The fund manager decides whether you'll receive a taxable distribution. If you're ambivalent between owning mutual funds and individual stocks, keep in mind the tax advantages of stocks.

$ *If you invest in mutual funds, make sure they are "tax-friendly."* One way to assess the tax-friendliness of a mutual fund is to examine its turnover ratio. This ratio measures the level of selling in the fund. A turnover ratio of 100 percent means that the fund manager turned over the entire portfolio once during that year. The lower the turnover ratio, the lower the amount of selling that is done in the portfolio, and the lower your potential tax hit. A number of mutual fund families are developing what they call "tax-efficient" funds. Characteristics of these funds include:

- Infrequent selling of fund positions.

- Minimizing the taxable gain on sales by assigning the highest cost basis possible to the sold shares.

- Offsetting gains by selling fund holdings with losses.

- Favoring stocks with modest dividends because dividends are taxed as ordinary income.

- When considering a tax-friendly fund, don't ignore index funds, which tend to be very tax-friendly.

$ *Consider the tax status of the particular investment account when deciding on investments.* Retirement accounts, because they are tax preferenced, are probably better vehicles for holding less tax-friendly investments, such as mutual funds. Retirement accounts are also good vehicles for holding income-generating investments, such as bonds and dividend-paying stocks. Does this mean that you should never hold stocks in an IRA or 401(k) plan? Certainly not. It does mean, however, that it's not a bad idea to weight your retirement portfolio a bit toward higher-yielding investments like total-return stocks or balanced mutual funds in order to maximize the tax benefits. Also, by including mutual funds in a tax-preferenced account, you mitigate the effects of unwanted capital-gains distributions. Conversely, higher-growth investments, such as stocks, should be held outside of retirement accounts. In this way, you limit the tax bite by owning stocks (being able to defer indefinitely capital gains taxes) and have the ability to exploit losses.

**$** *Avoid "avoidable" tax transactions.* Before buying a mutual fund toward the end of the year, for example, make sure the fund has already made its capital gains distribution for that year. There's nothing more galling than buying a mutual fund, perhaps showing a loss on paper in the fund, yet having to pay taxes on a capital gains distribution that you receive shortly after buying the fund. Most fund families will tell you the approximate date when a capital gains distribution is planned. Other common taxable transactions to avoid include writing checks on your bond mutual fund (every time you do this, you incur a potential tax liability) and frequent switches between funds within the same mutual fund family (which constitute taxable transactions). Another tax mistake is putting tax-preferenced investments (such as municipal bonds) in tax-preferenced accounts, such as IRAs.

## ▼ CONCLUSION...

I f you can earn just one percent a month on your portfolio, your annual portfolio return is more than 12 percent. That's above the market's long-run annual return of around 11 percent and it means your money doubles every six years or so. Although that may not sound all that exciting given market returns of recent years, I think most experienced investors would give their first-born to average 12 percent a year over the next 10 years. In an environment of more traditional returns, it is important to maximize your return opportunities.

This chapter presented a number of ways in which investors should be able to eke out an additional one or two percent each year. Best of all, these strategies entail virtually no additional risk. Remember: Don't be sloppy when it comes to capturing crumbs. Every little bit adds up over time. If you are to be successful in the individual investor revolution, it's important to pay attention to the details. Therein lie the crumbs that can mean the difference between a winning and losing portfolio.

# CHAPTER SEVEN

# SIMPLE YET POWERFUL "MACRO" INVESTMENT TOOLS FOR WINNING THE REVOLUTION

W e all like to take simple things and make them complicated. Our belief that what's simple is often inadequate applies to our perception of investment tools. Many investors fall into the trap of believing that the best investment tools are the most complex. The age of the computer and the ability to slice and dice billions of pieces of data in seconds fuel the myth that you cannot do good investment analysis without a hard drive and a Pentium processor. Yet my experience has been that often the best investment tools are the simplest. Why? As most statisticians will tell you, the cleanest, simplest models usually provide the most consistent and robust conclusions. Simple models are not cluttered by extraneous variables that make it difficult to discern cause and effect.

Now don't confuse "consistent" with "infallible." Wall Street is strewn with the bodies of economists and analysts who clung to a single indicator to predict the market only to see that indicator betray them. It's a fool's game to base your entire investment approach on a single weapon. The best you hope when employing any investment tool is to swing the odds in your favor, improve the probability of a desired outcome, and not bet the farm.

What do I mean by simple? First, simple tools can be used and understood by any investor, including beginners. Simple tools don't discriminate across investors; they're available whether you have a little money or a lot, whether you have access to the Internet or still use a pen or pencil as your computer of choice. Simple tools are also relevant and adaptive during changing market conditions. This is especially important when markets have moved to unprecedented levels.

Indeed, what you want is not necessarily a tool that compares the present to the past but one that compares the present to some relative measure that is adaptable over time.

## THE IMPORTANCE OF SIMPLICITY IN A CONFUSING INVESTMENT WORLD

Simplifying your investment tools is becoming more important precisely because the market is becoming a more confusing place to do business. For example, during 1997, the Dow Jones Industrial Average registered one-day moves of 100 points or more over 50 times. In fact, the Dow Jones Industrials fell 554 points on October 27, 1997—the largest one-day decline in the Average's history—only to rebound 337 points the next day—the Average's largest one-day rise in history. On nearly one-third of the trading sessions in 1997, the Dow Industrials rose or fell more than one percent, only the fourth time it has been so volatile in 20 years.

Seeing the market gyrate 100 points or more from day to day or even during the same trading day is unsettling for many investors, regardless if the 100-point move represents only a small percentage of the Dow Industrials or Standard & Poor's 500. And when investors become unsettled, they often behave irrationally. Having a few simple yet powerful "macro" investment tools to keep you on the right path during such erratic market periods is invaluable.

### The Dangers of Using "Macro" Tools

Talk to some of the best money managers and many of them will tell you it is a waste to spend time, energy, and money on "macro" tools that look at the big picture—economy, interest rates, and overall market risk—and purport to make you a better market timer or interest-rate predictor. To a certain extent, I agree. The biggest success factor for any portfolio is not how skillfully you employ such tools to time the market; it's how effectively you harness the power of time. Time is the greatest ally your portfolio has. Using macro tools aggressively can also cause you to do things that run counter to maximizing time in your investment program. For example, let's say you have a tool that tells you when to be in or out of the market, and it flashes a sell signal. You obey the signal and dump all your stocks. Smart? No. Anytime you pull out of the market, you're bucking the market's historical tendency to the upside.

The biggest benefit of using macro investment tools is to help your investment portfolio at the margin. If a tool is telling you that market prices are dropping, for example, you might want to readjust your portfolio a bit to focus on quality, as opposed to selling all of your stocks outright. If a macro tool is telling you that the market's risk level over the next 12 months is extremely high, you might want to consider this indicator when deciding on how aggressively to put new money into the market. Again, we're not talking about making wholesale portfolio changes based on these tools, but perhaps changes at the margin. At the very least, even if you don't react at all to the information provided by these tools, it can help you feel more secure during dramatic market moves and less like a leaf blowing in the wind.

## What You Need to Know

When you strip the investment process down to its barest essentials, what does an investor really need to know about the "macro" world?

$ *The market's "primary" trend.* When people refer to the market as being "bullish" or "bearish," they are referring to the direction of the market's "primary" trend. It's important to know if the market's primary trend is trending higher or lower. Notice I didn't say the market's daily or weekly trend, but the "primary" trend. The primary trend generally lasts 18 months or more. If you know whether the market's primary trend is bullish or bearish, you'll feel much more comfortable ignoring the unsettling trading that occurs on a daily or weekly basis and be less likely to do something you'll regret later. The tool I use to discern the primary trend dates all the way back to the turn of the century yet is perhaps even more powerful today.

$ *The market's intermediate risk level.* There's value in knowing how risky the market is at any given point in time. If nothing else, it gives you a snapshot of the risk you are taking relative to your position in the market. I'll show you how to determine the market's 12-month risk level using one simple statistic.

$ *The direction of interest rates.* Interest rates are important to the stock market because rates, in effect, price the attractiveness of alternative investments to stocks. If rates are low or falling, investors are less apt to sell stocks to buy fixed-income investments. If rates are rising, the attractiveness of other investments increases, which can cause investors to dump stocks. The best tool for predicting interest rates, as you'll soon discover, is found every day in *The Wall Street Journal*.

Armed with just these three tools, any investor should become more confident in his or her decisions, especially during those difficult market times when it is easy to lose your way.

## THE DOW THEORY

My favorite tool for determining market trends is the Dow Theory. The theory gets its name from Charles Dow, the founder and first editor of *The Wall Street Journal*.

To say that the Dow Theory has stood the test of time would be an understatement; the theory's roots date to the late 1890s. The genesis of the Dow Theory was Charles Dow's work explaining price fluctuations in the stock market. Dow's examination of the market pointed to an overall market trend: individual stocks may show divergent price movements, but nevertheless the great body of stocks moves more or less in unison. This "trend" behavior led to the development of a trend theory and ultimately the Dow Theory. A protégé of Charles Dow, William Peter Hamilton, is often credited with refining the Dow Theory.

### Tools of the Theory—Dow Industrials and Transports

To measure the movement of the overall market trend, in 1896 Dow devised a market index—the Dow Jones Industrial Average. This index consisted of 12 industrial stocks (only General Electric still remains today from the original 12 Dow Industrial stocks). Prior to 1896, Dow had been devising an index consisting primarily of railroad stocks that would later become the Dow Jones Transportation Average. Dow felt that the rails did not provide a full barometer of economic activity. When combined with the Industrial index, however, the combined indices could act as co-confirmers of broader market trends. Dow felt these two indices could present a fairly representative picture of broad market trends.

### About the Averages

Before we continue our history lesson on the Dow Theory, it's important to understand how the Theory's primary tools, the Dow Industrials and Transports, are computed. To compute the respective averages, all the closing prices of the stocks are added together and divided by a divisor. The divisor is adjusted to reflect stock splits, spinoffs, and other capitalization changes.

The following are the components of the Dow Industrial and Transportation Averages:

## Dow Industrials

| | | |
|---|---|---|
| AT&T | Exxon | Minnesota Mining |
| Allied-Signal | General Electric | and Manufacturing |
| Aluminum Company | General Motors | Morgan (J.P.) |
| of America | Goodyear Tire & Rubber | Philip Morris |
| American Express | Hewlett-Packard | Companies |
| Boeing | International Business | Procter & Gamble |
| Caterpillar | Machines | Sears, Roebuck & Co. |
| Chevron | International Paper | Travelers |
| Coca-Cola | Johnson & Johnson | Union Carbide |
| Disney (Walt) | McDonald's | United Technologies |
| Du Pont (E.I.) | Merck | Wal-Mart Stores |
| Eastman Kodak | | |

## Dow Transports

| | | |
|---|---|---|
| AMR | Delta Air Lines | UAL |
| Airborne Freight | FDX | Union Pacific |
| Alaska Air | GATX | US Airways |
| Alexander & Baldwin | Norfolk Southern | USFreightways |
| Burlington Northern | Roadway Express | XTRA |
| CNF Transportation | Ryder System | Yellow |
| CSX | Southwest Airlines | |

It's important to understand that the Dow Averages are price-weighted. Higher-priced stocks carry greater weight in the index than lower-priced stocks. For example, at the time of this writing, Merck is trading for $115 per share; Philip Morris, $38. If Philip Morris rises 10 percent, the stock's impact on the Dow Industrials is approximately 15 points (3.8, which is 10 percent of 38, divided by the divisor, currently 0.25089). If Merck rises 10 percent, the favorable impact on the Dow Industrials is 45 points (11.5, which is 10 percent of 115, divided by 0.25089).

The fact that the Dow Averages are price-weighted is a bone of contention with many market watchers who prefer indexes that are weighted by market capitalizations (stock price times number of shares outstanding). Market capitalization-weighted is how the Standard & Poor's 500, for example, is computed. Keep in mind, however, that when Charles Dow developed the Averages more than 100 years ago, the fastest computer was a brain and pencil. Thus, the easiest way to construct and track the index was to just add up the prices of the stocks each day.

Surprisingly, despite being price-weighted, the Dow Industrials generally track quite closely with indexes consisting of many more stocks and computed based on market capitalization. The table below shows the tight correlation between the performance of the Dow Jones Industrial Average and the S&P 500 over many years (perfect correlation is 1.0):

### Correlation of Dow Jones Industrial Average to S&P 500

| | | | |
|---|---|---|---|
| 1920s | 0.976972 | 1960s | 0.976804 |
| 1930s | 0.983407 | 1970s | 0.930982 |
| 1940s | 0.996008 | 1980s | 0.997842 |
| 1950s | 0.993357 | 1990s | 0.991673 |

Source: *The Dow Jones Averages 1885–1995*, edited by Phyllis S. Pierce (Irwin)

One reason for the close correlation between the indices is that the stocks in the Dow Industrials make up a hefty portion of the S&P 500 stocks. Thus, when market watchers decry the Dow as being too narrow and not as representative of the overall market as, say, the S&P 500, the numbers simply do not bear this out.

A couple of quirks about the Dow Averages are worth noting. First, because higher-priced stocks carry greater weight in the index, it seems that Dow components are a bit slower to split their shares than other issues. One reason may be that stock splits reduce the clout a company has on the index. If the market is doing well and the high-priced stocks are leading the charge, an incentive may exist for Dow stocks to remain at higher prices rather than split their shares.

Another quirk is that the divisor, because it is less than 1.0, is in effect a multiplier. In other words, with every adjustment in the divisor, the price movements of the Dow become more exaggerated. For example, if each Dow Industrial stock rises one point in a day, the total gain in the index is 119 points (30 divided by 0.25089). If the divisor, perhaps because of a split, shrinks to 0.2005, a one-point advance in each Dow stock translates to an increase in the Average of nearly 150 points (30 divided by 0.2005). Given the drop in the divisor over the last five years, it's not surprising that the Dow Industrials have seen a significant increase in the number of 100-point days to the upside and downside.

## The Three Movements

Continuing with our history lesson, Dow and Hamilton discovered that market trends, as measured by the Dow Industrials and Transports, consisted of three movements:

1. A primary trend
2. Secondary reactions
3. Daily fluctuations

The early Dow theorists compared these three movements to the action of the ocean. The primary trend is the tide that moves during a comparatively long space of time with no regard for waves or ripples. Secondary reactions are the waves that sometimes seep far up the beach in apparent contradiction of an ebbing tide or fall back in a trough in defiance of a rising tide. These reactions develop swiftly and frequently and are difficult to distinguish from a turn in the tide. The daily fluctuations are the ripples and splashes on the surface.

The Dow Theory is concerned primarily with the movement of the tide, or the market's primary trends. These are the movements of lasting importance. The Dow Theory believes that daily fluctuations, although having value when taken as a whole over a lengthy time period, have no forecasting value when looked at individually.

## Tenets of the Dow Theory

The following is an examination of the key tenets of the Dow Theory:

$ *The Averages tell the story.* A fundamental principle of the Dow Theory is that the Dow Industrials and Transports "see all and know all of financial importance." The Dow Averages represent all that is known and all that can be foreseen by financial and layminds concerning financial matters. One could think of the Averages as being "efficiently priced" in the sense that the Averages reflect all relevant information analyzed by the brightest (and not-so-brightest) minds on and off Wall Street.

$ *The Dow Theory is based on closing prices in the Dow Industrials and Transports.* Wall Street loves to look to intraday pricing for indications of market direction, but the Dow Theory measures the market strictly on closing prices in the indexes. Only closes in the Dow Industrials and Transports above or below old highs or old lows have value under the Dow Theory, not intraday price movements above or below critical points.

$ *The movement of the Dow Industrials and Transports must confirm one another in order for any signal under the Dow Theory to be authentic.* Movement of one Average that is confirmed by the other provides the strongest signals under the Dow Theory. The notion of confirmation is an often misunderstood piece of the Dow Theory. Investors should think of confirmation between the two Dow Averages in terms of direction as opposed to magnitude of the move. For example, it's highly unlikely that the Dow Industrials and Transports will both rise or fall the exact same amount in percentage terms. In 1997, for example, the Dow Industrials rose 22 percent; the Dow Transports, 44 percent. However, despite the disparity in percentage gain, the Averages certainly confirmed one another in terms of direction, and that's the key point. Another key point to understand about confirmation is that the Averages need not necessarily confirm direction every day. For example, a move by one Average to new highs that is not confirmed by the other on the same day is not necessarily nonconfirmation.

$ *Prolonged divergence between the Averages is often a red flag.* Movement by one Average that is not confirmed by movement in the other Average after a reasonable period of time can often lead to a secondary reaction and, in some cases, a change in the primary trend.

## BULL MARKETS

The Dow Theory defines a "bull market" as a long, broad, upward movement of prices that is interrupted at uncertain intervals by important reactions. In the 100 years during which the Averages have been recorded, there have been 26 clearly defined bull markets, according to the Dow Theory. The average length of the 25 completed bull markets was approximately 31 months.

### First Phase

Bull markets generally have three phases. The beginning of a new bull market is often characterized by a period of weeks, and perhaps even several months, during which the Dow Averages make a succession of small movements. These viewed all together form a "saw-toothed" pattern, with rallies making successively higher tops, while successive declines fail to penetrate previous lows. This pattern is normally accompanied by small volume.

This trading action is often accompanied by market observers and the financial media spouting gloom and doom about the markets. Pessimism is in the air, yet the Averages refuse to retreat further. This resiliency in the face of bearish sentiment is often an indication of a market that has bottomed.

What usually occurs next is that the old lows in both Dow Averages hold with the Industrials and Transports rallying above their previous high points. The move to new highs by both Averages signals a new bull market.

Figure 7.1 shows the movements of the Dow Industrials and Transports in 1990 and 1991. The charts provide an excellent case study showing the beginning of a bull market. Notice that both the Dow Industrials and Transports, after plunging to new lows toward the end of 1990, failed to go to new lows in early 1991. The resiliency of the Averages developed into a breakout above previous resistance levels in January 1991. The move to new intermediate highs by both Averages completed the evidence of a turn in the tide to a new bull market.

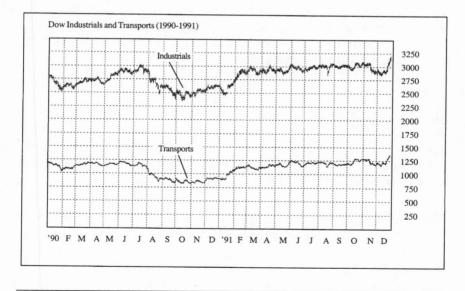

**Figure 7.1**

## Second Phase

The second phase of a bull market is often the longest. Stock prices adjust and readjust themselves to improving business and increased earnings. This is often the "gravy train" phase of bull markets, when Dow Theorists buy stocks knowing that the bullish primary trend should reward them for their courage.

### Final Phase

The third and final phase of a bull market has some distinguishing characteristics. It is usually punctuated by frequent and sharp reversals. Optimism is generally running to extremes on the part of the investing public. Interestingly, however, the Averages are usually telling a different story. Market reversals are followed by failed attempts to move above old highs. These rebounds are often accompanied by diminishing market volume. Finally, after failing to move to new highs, both Averages close below their lowest points of the preceding shakeout. At this point, the market's primary trend, according to the Dow Theory, has turned bearish.

## BEAR MARKET

Dow theorists define a primary bear market as the long, broad, downward movement of prices that is interrupted at irregular intervals by important reversals (rallies in this case). Like bull markets, bear markets generally have three phases.

### First Phase

The first phase of a bear market occurs after the Averages fail to rise to new highs and break below important low points established during a reversal. One characteristic of the first phase of a bear market is the surrender of "get-rich-quick" hopes by late participants in the bull market, who sell aggressively.

### Second Phase

The second phase of a bear market is likely to be a long, drawn-out affair. The economy usually is in a recession, and corporate earnings are slipping. Interestingly, this phase usually still has investors clinging to hopes that the market is poised for a rebound, with bargains abounding in the market. These investors are usually proved wrong, however, as stocks continue to slip, even in the face of periodic good news.

### Third Phase

The third phase of bear markets is when things turn truly ugly. Stock prices collapse with high-quality and speculative stocks getting creamed. However, at some point, while investor sentiment is usually at its most bearish, the Averages refrain from retreating. Small volume, the refusal of the Averages to retreat in the face of bad news, and an all-pervading pessimism make the Dow theorist alert for the signal—a breakout to new highs in both Averages, as discussed earlier—which will mark the coming of a new bull market.

## TIME ELEMENTS IN PRIMARY TRENDS

The duration of bull and bear markets has varied significantly over the years. The tables below show the lengths of bull and bear markets since 1897, the year the Averages were instituted.

TWENTY-SIX PRIMARY BULL MARKETS

| Bull market which began in | lasted approximately (months). |
|---|---|
| 1896 | 33 |
| 1900 | 28 |
| 1903 | 27 |
| 1907 | 25 |
| 1910 | 28 |
| 1914 | 24 |
| 1917 | 24 |
| 1921 | 15 |
| 1923 | 62 |
| 1932 | 57 |
| 1938 | 11 |
| 1939 | 6 |
| 1942 | 49 |
| 1947 | 15 |
| 1949 | 42 |
| 1953 | 31 |
| 1957 | 21 |
| 1960 | 15 |
| 1962 | 45 |
| 1966 | 29 |
| 1970 | 31 |
| 1974 | 31 |

| Bull market which began in | lasted approximately (months). |
|---|---|
| 1978 | 22 |
| 1982 | 60 |
| 1987 | 32 |
| 1990 | *N.C. |

Bull markets' average length is approximately 31 months.
*N.C. Not completed at time of printing.

TWENTY-FIVE PRIMARY BEAR MARKETS

| Bear market which began in | lasted approximately (months). |
|---|---|
| 1899 | 15 |
| 1902 | 5 |
| 1906 | 11 |
| 1909 | 9 |
| 1912 | 27 |
| 1916 | 14 |
| 1919 | 22 |
| 1922 | 11 |
| 1929 | 35 |
| 1937 | 13 |
| 1939 | 4 |
| 1939 | 34 |
| 1946 | 12 |
| 1948 | 12 |
| 1953 | 9 |
| 1956 | 20 |
| 1959 | 15 |
| 1961 | 7 |
| 1966 | 9 |
| 1969 | 18 |
| 1973 | 24 |
| 1976 | 17 |
| 1981 | 15 |
| 1987 | 4 |
| 1990 | 4 |

Source: Dow Theory Forecasts
Bear markets' average length is approximately 15 months.

Two things should jump out at the reader immediately. First, bull markets, on average, tend to last twice as long as bear markets. This statistic reinforces the notion that the stock market generally trends higher over time. Second, bull markets have gotten longer in recent years, while bear markets have been much more compact. Some market watchers attribute the brevity of recent bear markets to the huge selling activity that can sweep through the stock market in a short period of time due to the "unwinding" of futures, options, and other financial derivatives. Another plausible explanation is that the recent abnormal durations of bull and bear markets are just that—abnormal—and investors can expect future bull and bear markets to assume more traditional durations.

## SECONDARY REVERSALS

Perhaps the greatest function of the Dow Theory is helping investors discern the difference between changes in the primary trend and mere, short-term pullbacks within the bullish primary trend. *Secondary reversals* or *corrections* are important declines in a primary bull market or important rallies in a bear market. Although such movements are often unsettling for investors, secondary corrections serve an important purpose, especially during bull markets. Secondary corrections help release some of the steam that often occurs when the bullish primary trend is starting to overheat. In effect, the reversal helps restore sanity and values to the market, which helps sustain the vitality of the bull market. Such reversals also represent the best time to add to stock positions.

A reversal is caused by conditions within the market itself. Any important piece of current news can touch off a reversal, such as the release of disturbing economic data or economic or political problems abroad. Dow theorists know, however, that fundamental conditions leading to a big primary movement do not change overnight. Still, distinguishing a reversal from an actual turn in the tide presents a delicate problem. Fortunately, secondary corrections have several tell-tale signs:

$ The movement of the Averages is more rapid and violent in a secondary correction than in the primary trend.

$ The length of time consumed is shorter than the preceding primary movement. Most secondary corrections last three weeks to three months.

$ Secondary corrections generally retrace one-third to two-thirds of the primary movement since the conclusion of the last secondary correction.

As is usually the case when discussing the Dow Theory, it's easier to show the Theory at work than to describe it in words. Let's look at the movement in the Averages during 1997 (see Figure 7.2) to see how a typical secondary correction unfolds.

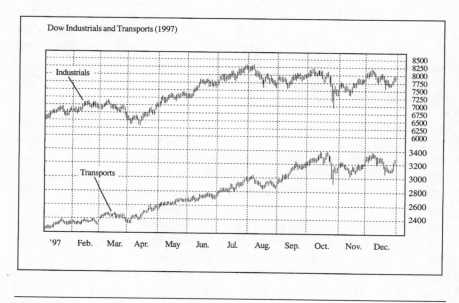

**Figure 7.2**

The market breakdown in 1997, kicked off with a 554-point drop on October 27, was extremely disconcerting to investors and brought the bears out in droves. A sane look at the decline through the lens of the Dow Theory, however, shed important meaning on what was a classic secondary correction. Notice that the Dow Industrials bottomed around 6400 in April. The decline represented the lows made during the previous secondary correction. From April to August, the Dow Industrials rose more than 1800 points to a new high at 8259. The Dow Theory says a secondary correction generally is extremely violent and rapid, and few investors would argue that the market break in October was not violent and rapid.

Second, the Dow Theory states that secondary corrections generally retrace one-third to two-thirds of the advance since the last correction low. Since the market rose some 1800 points, a correction could carry the market down some 1200 points, to roughly the 7100 level on the Dow, and still be a correction in a bull market. Interestingly, the Dow fell to 7161, a two-thirds correction.

Third, the secondary correction lasted about three months, which is within the time parameters of a secondary correction. Investors familiar with the Dow Theory would have realized that the sharp drop in the market was not atypical of secondary corrections and would have been more confident in taking advantage of the sharp drop in stock prices to buy. Indeed, the Dow Industrials and Transports would eventually move to all-time highs in early 1998, thus reconfirming the bullish primary trend.

## DOW THEORY'S TRACK RECORD

That the Dow Theory has stood the test of time speaks volumes of its capability to keep investors on the right side of the market's primary trend. But don't take my word for it. William N. Goetzmann of Yale School of Management, along with Stephen Brown of New York University and Alok Kumar, also of Yale, decided to put the Theory under the microscope. In their 1997 paper, "The Dow Theory: William Peter Hamilton's Track Record Re-Considered," the professors found that there was merit to the theory. The professors used artificial intelligence software to identify technical trading patterns associated with the buy-and-sell signals issued by Hamilton. The software then applied these patterns to subsequent markets. What the professors found was that a portfolio that followed the signals would have outperformed a buy-and-hold strategy by about two percentage points per year while incurring about one-third less volatility.

Of course, past performance is not indicative of future results, and tools that work over long periods of time can turn south during shorter time frames. Nevertheless, the usefulness of the Dow Theory cannot be ignored. I would argue further that the Theory's effectiveness has become even greater in recent years due in part to its capability to keep investors focused on the market's primary trend during markets that have exhibited huge short-term swings.

## WHAT THE DOW THEORY WON'T DO

When using the Dow Theory, it's important to know the theory's limitations. For example, the theory does not tell you how high or low a primary market move will carry. The theory merely tells you the direction of the primary trend. Don't expect the Dow Theory to get you in at the exact bottom of bear markets or get you out at the exact top of bull markets. The theory aims to capture the bulk, but not all, of any market move. One final note—my experience with the Dow Theory has been that the theory is more effective in discerning the change in the primary trend from bearish to bullish. Discerning changes from bullish to bearish are a bit more tricky using the theory.

## SUMMARY OF THE DOW THEORY

We've covered a lot of ground here, so it might be worth restating the tenets of the Dow Theory one more time for clarity's sake:

$ The Dow Theory looks solely at the movements of the Dow Industrial and Transportation Averages.

$ The Dow Theory's signals are based on market closes, not intra-day movements in the Averages.

$ These Averages express the sum of all pertinent information. In other words, the Averages "tell the story."

$ The market as a whole has a primary trend.

$ The trend is interrupted by reversals.

$ The best time to buy during primary bull markets is during secondary corrections within the primary trend. Conversely, the best time to sell stocks is during rallies within primary bear markets.

$ A signal is made only by confirmation between the two Averages, either to new highs (bullish) or to new lows (bearish).

$ Signals made in third phases have diminishing authority.

$ Manipulation and short-selling have no lasting influence on the primary trend.

$ Conditions that bring about bull markets and bear markets change slowly.

For further reading on the Dow Theory, pick up a copy of William Peter Hamilton's classic, *The Stock Market Barometer*.

## INTERMEDIATE POTENTIAL RISK INDICATOR

One of the best tools I've ever seen for determining the market's risk level over a 12-month period is the Intermediate Potential Risk indicator. The Intermediate Potential Risk indicator takes the percentage of New York Stock Exchange stocks trading above their 200-day moving averages and quantifies this percentage in terms of market risk. A reading of 70 percent or more of the NYSE stocks trading above their 200-day moving averages constitutes "higher risk;" readings below 40 percent constitute "lower risk."

The percentage of NYSE stocks trading above their 200-day moving average can be found in every issue of *Investor's Business Daily* newspaper. The information appears on what is called the "Market Charts" page, which is highlighted every day in the table of contents. Once you locate the "Markets Charts" page, you'll see three large charts on the page: Nasdaq Composite, S&P 500, and Dow Jones Industrials. On the Dow Industrials chart, you'll see a box showing price changes of the Dow 30 components for that particular day. Just under that box you'll find the piece of information showing the percentage of NYSE stocks trading above their 200-day moving average.

The indicator also provides a true picture of the popularity of stocks. It's useful for providing a snapshot of how stocks may have moved to extremes, relative to their average price level of the last 200 days. What underlies the indicator's effectiveness is the concept of "reversion to the mean." Basically, this concept means that, over time, stock prices tend to return to their long-term averages. A stock that is trading well above its 200-day moving average is likely trading at an unsustainable level and will eventually migrate back to its long-run average. Likewise, a stock trading well below its 200-day moving average should, over time, move back toward its long-run average.

Keep in mind that the long-run average can change over time to reflect higher stock prices (which is why most 200-day moving averages trend upward), and this is another reason why I like to use this indicator. Indeed, it doesn't depend on P/E ratios, dividend yields, or other data with ranges that can change over time. The indicator provides a *relative* tool at that particular market period.

Figure 7.3 shows the Intermediate Potential Risk indicator and the Dow Jones Industrial Average over the last five years (you can create and maintain this chart yourself by recording the daily percentages in a computer spreadsheet). In looking at the charts, you can see that during the April 1997 market pullback, the risk level fell sharply into neutral territory and was well below the "higher risk" levels seen in 1995. This occurred despite the Dow Industrials in 1997 being sharply higher than 1995 levels, which is noteworthy. The indicator doesn't use absolute levels in the Dow Industrials to formulate its risk levels. It looks at the popularity of stocks relative to current market levels.

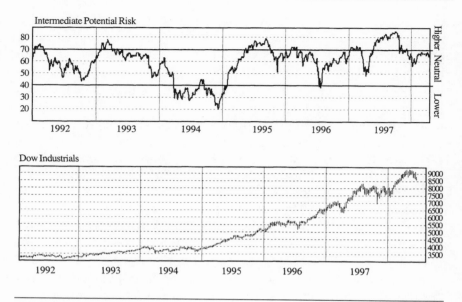

**Figure 7.3**

As you can see by Figure 7.3, the Intermediate Potential Risk indicator has had a good record of spotting intermediate-term excesses in the stock market. During the last five years, a move into "higher risk" territory (above 70 percent) was usually followed by a correction in the Dow Industrials. Conversely, a reading in "lower risk" territory, which is below 40 percent—1994 and 1996 were good examples of this—coincided with attractive buying opportunities.

## Strong Correlation Between Intermediate Potential Risk And Market Returns

With the help of my fund partner Richard Moroney, I put the Intermediate Potential Risk indicator to the test by running a series of regressions comparing Intermediate Potential Risk levels to 12-month changes in the Dow Jones Industrial Average. Regression analysis allows you to see how correlated one set of data is with another set, and whether the correlation is statistically significant. In other words, you learn how much of the correlation is due to chance and how much of the correlation is a result of cause and effect.

One set of regressions showed a strong correlation between diminishing market returns and rising Intermediate Potential Risk levels. Another set of regressions compared year-ahead returns in the Dow

Jones Industrial Average to the Intermediate Potential Risk indicator in the period since 1990. This set of regressions yielded the following:

$ If Intermediate Potential Risk was in "low risk" territory (less than 40 percent), the average year-ahead return was 18.7 percent, 2.6 percentage points above the average return for periods in which the Intermediate Potential Risk was not in the low-risk territory. The average year-ahead return rose to 19.6 percent, a 3.5 percentage point premium, when the risk level fell below 35 percent and 20.6 percent, a 4.3 percentage point premium, when the risk level fell below 30 percent.

$ When the risk level moved into "high risk" territory (more than 70 percent), the average year-ahead returns were 15.3 percent versus 17 percent for periods when Intermediate Potential Risk was not in high-risk territory. When the risk level rose above 75 percent, average year-ahead returns fell to 14.3 percent, down from 16.8 percent in all other periods.

When looking at this data, keep in mind that the period being analyzed has been part of one of the greatest bull markets in history. Thus, investors made money regardless of when they invested. Still, returns were nicely correlated with risk levels—the higher the Intermediate Potential Risk, the lower the year-ahead return.

Should investors trade aggressively based on this indicator? No. The indicator's greatest value is for determining how aggressively to put new money into the market. For example, if you make regular monthly investments to stocks or mutual funds, you might adjust the size of these investments depending on intermediate risk levels. Say the Intermediate Potential Risk is 75 percent. You might want to trim your regular investments by perhaps 10 percent to 20 percent until the risk returns to at least neutral (below 70 percent). Notice I didn't say eliminate your investments. We're talking about fine-tuning a portfolio.

Also, I don't think investors should alter investment programs based on minor moves in the risk level. Rather, the indicator is most useful when it runs to extremes, either on the upside (above 70 percent and especially above 75 percent) or the downside (below 40 percent). For example, I would not alter investment programs based on movements within neutral territory (40 percent to 70 percent).

You can also use this indicator to guide you when buying stocks on margin. Obviously, you can feel more comfortable using margin if the

Intermediate Risk Level is below 40 percent. Conversely, maintaining high margin debt when the risk level is north of 70 percent may be too risky.

## INTEREST RATES

One of the major drivers of this market in recent years has been interest rates. Stable or falling interest rates are important for stock prices for several reasons. First, because interest rates price the cost of capital, low rates make it easier for companies to borrow to fund corporate expansion. Second, interest rates influence the attractiveness of alternative investments to stocks. If rates are low, CDs and other fixed-income investments are not very attractive, which means investors' money stays in stocks. As rates rise, the incentive increases for investors to dump stocks and switch into less-risky investments. The fact that interest rates have been favorable for the last three years has limited investorss willingness to sell stocks.

Keeping in mind that many an economist has lost his or her job trying to predict interest rates, I think investors can better their odds of determining future interest-rate trends by looking at the action of the Dow Jones Utility Average. The Dow Utility Average, found daily in *The Wall Street Journal*, is comprised of 15 electric and natural-gas utilities. The following stocks comprise the Dow Jones Utility Average:

| | | |
|---|---|---|
| American Electric Power | Edison International | Public Service |
| Columbia Energy | Enron | Enterprise Group |
| Consolidated Edison | Houston Industries | Southern Company |
| Consolidated Natural Gas | PECO Energy | Texas Utilities |
| Duke Energy | PG&E | Unicom |
| | | Williams Companies |

What does the Dow Utility Average have to do with interest rates? Utilities are sensitive to interest-rate movements for a number of reasons. They require a constant stream of capital to fund their operations. Therefore, utilities are sensitive to the cost of that capital, and thus, interest rates. Second, utilities are often perceived as "surrogate" income investments. If interest rates are falling, income investors often turn to utilities as a source of return due to their high yields and moderate capital-gains potential. When rates rise, utilities become less attractive relative to other income investments, causing investors to pull money out of utilities.

Figure 7.4 compares the Dow Jones Utility Average to the interest rate on the 30-year treasury bond. As you can see, the movements of the Dow Utilities and the rate on the 30-year treasury bond are inversely correlated. When the Utility Average rises, the interest rate on the 30-year treasury bond declines, and vice versa.

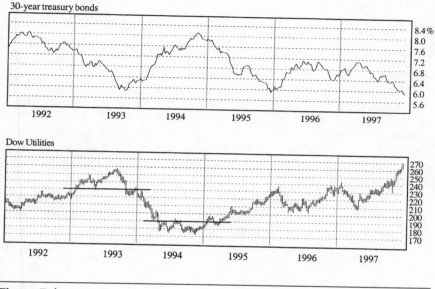

**Figure 7.4**

When using the Utility Average as a barometer for future interest-rate direction, it's important to focus on significant moves in the Average. A big move in the Average on a daily or even weekly basis does not necessarily signal a change in the interest-rate outlook. Look for significant moves above former highs or lows in the Average to signal a changing rate climate. Let's return to the chart on the Dow Utilities. In late 1993, the Dow Utilities were starting to deteriorate. When the average went below 220 in early 1994, that represented a significant breakdown below previous lows. The weakness in the Utilities was the precursor of a dramatic rise in interest rates in 1994. Indeed, the rate on the 30-year treasury bond rose from under 6.4 percent at the beginning of 1994 to over eight percent toward the end of the year. The weakness in the Utilities at the beginning of the year presaged the rise in rates that occurred during the year. Interestingly, in early 1995, the Dow Utilities started to improve and registered a nice breakout above the 190 level. The strength in the Dow Utilities signaled a change in the interest-rate environment. Indeed, as the charts show, the Dow Utilities continued to move higher for the rest of the year. At the same time, the interest rate on the 30-year treasury bond fell from just under eight percent in early 1995 to around six percent by year-end. Had you been watching the action of the Dow Utilities in the early part of 1995, the decline in interest rates during the year should not have been a surprise.

## Use Tools as Confirming Indicators

When used in conjunction, the three tools discussed in this chapter can be an effective means of confirming indicators. Although any one indicator can give a false signal, it is less likely that two or three indicators, when confirming one another, will be wrong. For example, let's say that the Intermediate Potential Risk indicator has moved into high-risk territory above 70 percent. At the same time, the Dow Jones Utility Average has broken down dramatically and is making new lows. A market in which values have run to extremes against a backdrop of rising interest rates is likely to be a market on borrowed time. Conversely, when the market's primary trend has moved from bearish to bullish and the Intermediate Risk Indicator is in the 35 percent range, you have a market that is ripe for aggressive buying.

## ▼ Conclusion...

It could be said that investing, like football, is a game of inches. Small victories, such as earning an extra percent per year on your investments using the strategies and tools discussed in Chapters 6 and 7, can have a huge impact on your investment success over the long term. If you remember to use the tools discussed in this chapter like scalpels and not sledgehammers, you should find them effective weapons for winning the individual investor revolution.

# Putting It All Together: The Ultimate Individual Investor Portfolio for the 21st Century

**M**uch of this book has been devoted to providing tools to succeed in the individual investor revolution. Chapters 1 and 2 examined the seeds of the individual investor revolution and Chapter 2 provided 10 simple rules for doing battle in the revolution. Chapters 3 and 4 focused on exploiting the low-cost access individual investors have to the markets. Chapter 5 showed how individual investors now have a wealth of information and analytical tools at their disposal via the Internet. Chapter 6 provided strategies on maximizing portfolio returns while minimizing risk levels and Chapter 7 provided simple yet powerful "macro" tools to fine-tune your portfolio strategies.

Now comes the hard part.

Indeed, having the tools to fight the individual investor revolution does not ensure an investor of *winning* the individual investor revolution. Even armed with all the tools and strategies provided in Chapters 1 through 7, investors can still lose the war if their stock and fund selections perform poorly. Of course, no surefire stock or fund selection system exists; even the smartest investors usually have portfolios where a third or more of their selections are losers. Big portfolio returns often owe much of their performance to just a few investments that pay off handsomely while the rest of the portfolio merely breaks even. The goal of this chapter is to incorporate the lessons learned in the first seven chapters to help increase your odds of owning those stocks and funds that can change your financial future while minimizing exposure to the investments that can cripple it.

## SUCCESSFUL INVESTING

Probably hundreds of ways exist to invest successfully. Successful value investors focus on buying low P/E ratio stocks, successful momentum investors focus on buying stocks that are rising in price, income investors focus on current yield to pick stocks, and growth investors require a company's earnings to grow at rates in excess of the overall economy. All ways have their pluses and minuses, and all ways run in and out of Wall Street's favor over time. My strategy for choosing stocks may be dramatically different from yours. That's OK, especially if you have been successful. I certainly haven't cornered the market on stock-picking prowess. I do believe, however, that all successful investors share common characteristics.

### Harness the Power of Time

I know I've said this *ad nauseam* already, but it bears repeating. The most significant success factor in an investment program is time. If time is the most influential factor on your portfolio's performance, it follows that the most important thing you can do is to get started in an investment program as soon as possible. Every day you wait to invest, you diminish the value of the one factor that can help your investments the most—time. There's never a bad time to start investing.

### Focus on the Long Term

Another common characteristic among successful investors is a focus on the long term. Investors who trade stocks on a daily or weekly basis are ultimately wasting their time and money. The seduction of such short-term trading is akin to a first-timer in Las Vegas. You might get lucky and win the first time, but if you keep going back to the casino, you'll likely end up on the short end. Successful investing is a marathon, not a sprint, and the odds are highly unlikely that you'll be able to time successfully what amounts to fairly random daily market movements.

### A Reluctance to Sell

I have never sold any of my DRIP shares. I know some investors may find that hard to believe (and, perhaps, incredibly stupid), but it's true. It's been easy to be a buy-and-hold investor given the market's performance over the last several years. Of course, the future may not mirror the past, and I have no doubt that my "no-sell" policy will likely be tested over the next few years. I'm also confident that I won't detour far from my past investment practices. One reason is that, for the most part, patience has its rewards on Wall Street.

A nice example from my own portfolio is Bristol-Myers Squibb. I've owned the stock for several years and have been extremely pleased with the performance, especially in the last two years. The stock has risen from a 1996 low of $39 (split adjusted) to a 52-week high (at the time of this writing) of more than $117. But the times have not always been so kind to Bristol-Myers. The stock fell from $45 in 1992 to a 1993 low of around $25, a drop of more than 43 percent. The stock failed to rebound much in 1994. Concerns over major health-care reform crimped these shares. As the clouds lifted concerning health-care reform and Wall Street began to focus on the company's fundamentals, however, the stock exploded. Instead of selling shares when times were tough, I took advantage of the price dips in 1992 through 1994 to buy more stock. My patience was rewarded when the stock skyrocketed.

Remember that when you sell, you're assured of at least two (and more likely three) bad things happening. Every time you sell, you incur transaction costs. You'll also incur a tax liability if you have a gain in the stock. Transaction costs and taxes can have a big impact on your portfolio over time.

A third reason to sell reluctantly is that you may be selling certain stocks at precisely the time you should be buying them. A study that appeared in *The Wall Street Journal* showed that most individual investors are better off buying what they sell and selling what they buy. The study, conducted by economist Terrance Odean, found the stocks that small investors buy tend to trail the overall market, but stocks they sell beat the market after the sale. The study showed that investors hurt themselves by trading stocks even before including the adverse effects of transaction costs. Odean attributed this masochistic behavior to several factors. First, investors suffer from the "disposition effect." That is, people don't like to admit defeat, which is why investors are more likely to sell winners than losers. This impulse to sell winners and keep losers—in effect, to refuse to admit you made a mistake—is so strong that it runs counter to the strong tax incentives that exist for selling losers and keeping winners. Odean also attributes frequent trading of stocks to investors' unawareness of the hazards of trading, such as taxes, transaction costs, and opportunity costs. Of course, all studies have their outliers, those individuals who do show the ability to time properly buys and sells. However, the average investor who thinks he or she is one of the favored few when it comes to timing buys and sells often finds out the opposite is true—much to the detriment to portfolios. Granted, taxes should only be one piece of the investment puzzle. Still, when studies show that most investors sell at the exact wrong time and that such selling creates tax liabilities, it makes sense to be a reluctant seller.

## Stupid Acquisitions

Of course, legitimate reasons exist to sell stock. One reason is because the company's debt load has become too great. I generally shy away from companies whose debt levels are north of 50 percent of total capital (total capital is long-term debt plus shareholders' equity). Because I like to invest for the long term, I want companies that are going to be around for the long term. A heavy debt load can lead to an early exit.

Another reason to sell stock is what I call the "stupid acquisition." I'm not a huge fan of corporate takeovers, for several reasons:

$ In many cases, companies overpay for acquisitions. Why? Unfortunately, CEOs' egos and empire building often supplant shareholders' interests. The result is that the acquirer pays more than the acquiree is worth. This is especially true when two or more companies compete for the same target.

$ Combining companies, especially in this age of multiple technological platforms, people's different skill levels, and distinctive corporate cultures, is an extremely difficult job. It takes a lot of managerial talent to combine companies in a way that the new whole is greater than the sum of its parts.

$ Although takeovers can provide a short-term pop for one of your stock holdings, I often wonder if the short-term gains outweigh the "lost" long-term appreciation potential. Just think how much Microsoft shareholders would have given up in capital gains if the firm had been acquired four or five years ago.

I bring up the "stupid" acquisition topic primarily because of the recent wave of merger activity. Megabillion-dollar mergers seem to be announced daily with Wall Street feverishly speculating on who will next tie the corporate knot. Wall Street pundits are quick to point out that the current merger activity, especially in banking and financial services, makes sense. Size and scale mean distribution and marketing clout. Although that may be well and good, investors should note a variety of ironies in the latest merger cavalcade:

$ Much of the merger activity in recent years has been focused in the financial-services areas. Yet these are the same Wall Street institutions that have been advising corporate America to restructure, spin off, lay off. Why is "bigger is better" OK for these companies, but "focused is better" for the rest of corporate America? Why aren't financial-services firms taking their own advice?

$ The thrust behind many of these takeovers is the creation of financial "supermarkets" where investors can "one-stop shop" for all their financial needs. The success of such supermarkets is predicated on the capability of financial-services organizations to cross-sell products to investors. One-stop financial shops have been tried in the past, however, with limited success. Furthermore, although some Wall Street shops have had success cross-selling products, others have been much less successful in cross-selling products to their customers, especially commercial banks. After all, how many of you buy stocks, bonds, mutual funds, insurance products, annuities, and the like from your neighborhood bank? I know I don't.

Here are some words of advice: First, be especially wary of "late-in-the-game" deals. Such deals spring more from desperation than common sense. Second, if your stocks have been left out of the latest merger activity, don't be dismayed. In the end, you might be a lot better off.

## An Emphasis on Quality as Well as Price

When you buy a car, you don't rush out to buy the cheapest one available. If that were the case, Yugos would be in every garage. You instead try to find the best value for your money. Investing should be no different. Yet many individuals look only at the price tag when buying investments. If investors focused on quality first and price second, they would make better investment decisions. I can't think of anytime in my investing experience when paying up for a proven quality stock turned out to be a bad decision. Notice I said "proven." A newfangled Internet stock that may or may not have a quality product a year from now is not my idea of a "proven" quality company and, thus, does not merit being bought at a P/E ratio of 200. A proven, quality company is one that has performed well over time and has a strong, defensible, leadership position in its particular market. Where I've gotten into trouble is trying to buy stocks on the cheap, only to find out that the cheap price was justified.

## PICKING STOCKS

There is no Holy Grail for picking stocks. Talk to 100 successful stock investors and you'll likely get 100 different answers to the following question, "What makes a good stock pick?" What I can tell you is what has worked well for me over the years:

$ *Have an owner's mentality*: Investors would make dramatically different investment decisions if they bought a stock on the basis of whether they actually wanted to own the company, not the stock. Having an owner's mentality makes you think more closely about such important issues as:

- Do I like the industry's long-term prospects?

- How much is the government going to be poking its head in my business?

- How dependent is my business on a couple of big customers?

- Who are my main competitors and can I compete successfully against them?

- Is current management worth owning?

- How quickly will I recoup my investment?

Notice I didn't say anything about the stock's P/E ratio, its recent earnings growth, and other factors that often dominate the investment decision-making process. These things are important. Nevertheless, if you approach buying a stock as you would buying the entire company, you'll likely make more prudent and thoughtful investment choices.

$ *Focus on consistency*: Past performance is no assurance of future results. Still, how a company has performed in the past is probably a good guide of how it will perform in the future, particularly if it's a company that has been around awhile and has survived and thrived over several business cycles. Wall Street usually rewards companies for their consistency.

$ *Stay with quality*: My portfolio includes a lot of household names. Industry leaders rarely falter over a multiyear period. I've missed a lot of opportunities over the years in this fast-growing Internet stock or that blazing small-cap technology issue. I've also avoided a lot of disasters. If you plan to be a long-term investor, you need to invest in companies that will be around for the long term. Staying with quality stocks with strong and defensible industry positions increases your odds of staying in the game.

$ *Emphasize growth industries*: If I'm investing for the long term, I want to own companies in industries where the growth potential is well above that of the overall economy. For that reason, my portfolio is sprinkled with companies in steady, growing industries—health care, information services, outsourcing firms, financial services, telecommunications, technology, and consumer nondurables. I don't do much in the cyclical areas. Cyclical stocks are more trading-oriented vehicles due to their dependence on the economy and the up-and-down nature of their earnings. Successful investing in cyclicals requires three good decisions: what to buy, when to buy, and when to sell. I've found that if I stick with growth stocks, I'm more likely to find stocks that have steady upward price trends, which means I don't have to worry so much about the sell side in order to achieve gains. Do I miss opportunities in cyclical stocks because of my inability to time these stocks properly? You bet. But the biggest fortunes in the stock market are not made off the backs of autos, metals, or heavy-industry stocks. Real wealth in the market comes from buying and holding good growth stocks. Remember: Over time, stock prices follow earnings. The relationship between earnings and stock price can get out of whack over short-term periods. In the long term, however, rising earnings streams will lead to rising stock prices.

## Dividends Matter

If you asked a sampling of investors how to compute a stock's total return, you'd probably be surprised by their answers. To most casual investors, a stock's return is measured by the performance of the stock price in a given year. A stock that goes from $5 to $10 has a total return of 100 percent, right? Not quite. A stock's total return has two components: price appreciation and dividends. Of course, the total return is the same as the price appreciation for a stock that doesn't pay a dividend. But for a stock that does, the total return is the sum of the dividends plus the price appreciation.

Dividends are the forgotten heroes of many portfolios. Dividends not only enhance a portfolio's return; they serve as a portfolio hedge during rocky market periods. Picking stocks based, in part, on dividends is a bit like the "bird-in-the-hand" adage. Say you buy a stock at the beginning of the year with a yield of three percent. You know that unless the company cuts or eliminates the dividend, you are already up three percent in one of the two components that will determine the stock's total return for the year. On the other hand, a person who buys a stock with no dividend is relying exclusively on price appreciation for return. The three percent cushion provided by the yield can prove invaluable during declining market periods and can help to bail out a portfolio's performance.

One of the mistakes dividend investors make is focusing on a stock's current yield rather than dividend-growth prospects. This is especially true when investing in utility stocks. Unfortunately, the highest-yielding utilities are often the most dangerous. A stock's yield, in some respects, is a proxy for risk. Stocks yielding two or three percentage points above their industry average are probably issues in which the future stream of dividends is in jeopardy. Avoid chasing yield when investing for dividends. Instead, focus on dividend growth. This is especially important if you buy and hold stocks. When considering stocks, don't overlook issues just because their current yield may be on the skimpy side; consider their dividend-growth prospects.

Another factor to consider when evaluating a company's dividend outlook is examining its payout ratio. The payout ratio is found by dividing a company's annual per-share dividend by 12-month earnings per share. For example, a company that pays $1 per share in dividends and earns $2 per share in profits has a payout ratio of 50 percent (1 divided by 2). Because companies ultimately fund dividends from earnings, a high payout ratio means a company has less room to expand its dividend (a ratio of one indicates that all a company's earnings are going to the dividend). Many companies like to maintain a consistent payout ratio, so it follows that firms with strong earnings-growth prospects usually are those with solid dividend-growth prospects.

One argument against focusing on dividends is the preferential tax treatment of capital gains versus dividends, which are taxed as ordinary income. If you are in the top tax bracket, your dividend income is taxed at a 39.6 percent rate. Conversely, the top tax on capital gains is 20 percent if securities are held for 12 months or more. For investors in the highest brackets, capital gains are preferable to dividends. Certainly taxes matter in a portfolio, but a rising dividend stream is generally indicative of a quality investment, one that should not be avoided merely because of tax implications. Indeed, during declining markets, you'll be happy to pay taxes on dividend income, especially if your nondividend paying stocks—the ones that are tax-preferenced—are underwater for the year.

## Crash Stocks

One problem with investing in turnarounds is that investors are usually too early. My experience has been that it's better to be late than early in crash stocks. A true rebound stock will show huge gains over time. Thus, investors are usually better off buying a crash stock after it has moved higher than buying it on the way down. Of course, buying a "crash" stock that has bottomed is easier said than done. How do you know that the stock has bottomed? You can swing the odds in your favor by following these rules for buying "crash" stocks:

$ *Patience is a virtue.* I use this analogy all the time for new investors who want to find the next Chrysler. It's better to wait for an axe to hit the ground than to try to catch it on the way down. One positive sign that a stock may be bottoming is that the stock trades within a narrow price range—say five percent from the top of the range to the bottom—for at least two months.

$ *Look for a catalyst for change.* Crash stocks usually need some event to jump-start Wall Street's interest in the company. This event may be new management, a major restructuring, or a stock buyback announcement.

$ *Bet with the insiders.* Corporate insiders—executives, directors, and majority stockholders—presumably know more about a company than outside investors. If you see corporate insiders buying a stock that is dramatically depressed, chances are they are expecting a turnaround in the company's business. How do you know what insiders are doing? *The Wall Street Journal* reports on insider trading every Wednesday, and *Barron's* reports on it in every weekly issue. If you have access to the Internet, a number of Web sites provide insider-trading information (see Chapter 5 for insider-trading sites on the Internet).

$ *Look for improving earnings momentum.* It is difficult for companies to sustain a rally without earnings momentum. That goes doubly for crash stock. Earnings momentum doesn't mean that you have to wait until the company is showing positive quarterly earnings gains. Earnings momentum can mean that a company's losses are declining. Earnings need to improve before most crash stocks pay off handsomely.

$ *Bet on strong balance sheets.* Avoid crash stocks whose debt is at huge levels. These companies have a difficult time coming back.

$ *Avoid industries with steep and shifting technology learning curves.* I generally don't recommend hunting for crash stocks among small technology companies. Technology markets move so quickly and are filled with such strong and dominant players that small, underfinanced technology groups quickly find themselves shut out of the markets. The fact that products have such short lives and that product prices generally drop over time makes it doubly difficult for a crippled technology company to regain its footing.

The best turnaround investment I ever made was CBS, formerly Westinghouse. One reason I was successful was that I followed my own advice. I bought CBS only after insiders were buying the stock, management was overhauled, and the company underwent a major restructuring by focusing on radio and television broadcasting and selling other businesses. Interestingly, I didn't catch CBS at the absolute bottom. However, as is the case with real turnaround stocks, I didn't have to in order to make a lot of money.

## PICKING MUTUAL FUNDS

I'll admit I'm a stock guy. I buy stocks primarily through DRIPs and no-load stocks. Nevertheless, I also own a few mutual funds in my IRA and 401(k) plans, including the Strong Dow 30 Value Fund, a fund I manage along with Richard Moroney. Although I prefer investing in stocks, I also understand that funds provide a worthwhile tool for achieving proper portfolio diversification. Funds offer an excellent way to target certain asset classes. Funds also offer an avenue for leveraging investments in certain focused industries or foreign countries.

Interestingly, a lot of parallels exist between picking stocks and picking funds. The following is a brief primer on what are the best approaches to picking winning mutual funds.

### Fees Matter

A first step in selecting a mutual fund is to focus on a fund's annual fees. This information is available in the fund prospectus.

What's a fair fee structure? Obviously, the lower the better. You should never pay annual management fees of two percent or more.

Expect to pay higher annual management fees in funds that specialize in international or small-cap investments.

## Keep Turnover Low

I already discussed the importance of limiting short-term trading with your investments. I believe the same philosophy applies to mutual-fund investing. A fund that is constantly turning over its portfolio is one in which fundholders will likely feel the brunt of transaction costs and tax liabilities (yes, brokerage commissions come out of the fund's assets). In general, you'll likely be better off in a fund with a low turnover rate. A turnover ratio of 50 percent means the fund manager turns over half of the fund's investments in a year. Avoid funds in which the turnover ratio is 100 percent or more. This information is found in Morningstar or by calling the fund.

## Maintain a Focused Approach

One of the selling points of mutual funds is that with a little money investors can diversify their investments across many stocks. Fortunately, although portfolio diversification is important as a risk-reduction strategy, investors don't need a portfolio of several hundred stocks to be properly diversified. Having a concentrated portfolio instills discipline into an investment program and forces you to know what's happening with your investments.

The same principle applies nicely to mutual-fund investing. A fund manager who concentrates his or her holdings in a fairly small number of stocks will likely be more in tune with those investments than a fund manager who invests in hundreds of companies.

Also, keep in mind that as the number of individual stocks in a portfolio grows, so does the fund's likelihood for producing mediocre returns. After all, the more stocks in a fund, the more that fund begins to mirror the overall market. Remember: If you want to match market returns, buy an index fund. Index funds mirror the performance of certain market indices. The most popular index fund mirrors the performance of the Standard & Poor's 500. If you are investing in mutual funds to outperform the overall market, you need to give yourself the chance to do so. One way is buying a fund that's dependent upon a small number of stocks. In this way, the fund avoids watering down its performance by holding a lot of stocks. Granted, the volatility of the fund may be greater due to a small number of holdings, but your chances for market-beating performance are improved.

In terms of total holdings, I would focus on funds that have fewer than 50 stocks in their portfolios.

## Asset Size Matters

A common sequence of events in the fund industry is short-term success breeds long-term mediocrity. It's not uncommon for a small fund that shows impressive performance to begin producing lackluster results as the fund's assets swell. Judging from comments by fund managers, it is much harder to manage a large fund than a small fund. The fact that funds often close their doors to new investors when they reach a certain asset size validates the idea that size matters.

Several reasons explain the difficulty of managing large and rapidly growing funds. First, a fund that may have made its mark with a certain investment style may not be able to continue investing money in the same manner when money is flooding in. For example, a fund that invests in companies that meet certain value criteria may not be able to find enough of those stocks for its new money. What usually happens is that the fund manager alters his or her style a bit to accommodate money flows. Also, large funds are forced to hold a larger number of individual stocks. As the number of individual stocks grows in a portfolio, the road to mediocrity often shortens. Finally, a large fund does not have the same flexibility as a small fund. A mutual fund with assets of $200 million has many more stocks from which to choose (big-cap stocks, small-cap stocks, fast-growing stocks, and so on) than a $10 billion fund that cannot buy certain stocks because the fund's buying would alter the stock price too greatly.

Another factor that probably gives smaller funds a leg up in beating the market is that a fund family's risk/reward parameters shift as a fund grows. For example, a fund with billions of dollars in assets generates millions of dollars a year in management fees even if the fund doesn't earn a dime for investors. Thus, the mind-set for a large fund is likely to lean toward minimizing risk (and avoiding a big decline in the fund's net asset value), rather than maximizing fundholder returns. Conversely, a fund with a small asset base has much more incentive to shoot for big returns. Big returns mean greater press coverage, which means bigger inflows.

## All in the Family

Perhaps the simplest way to pick a mutual fund is to find a fund family with depth of research and a track record of strong returns across various equity funds. As starting points, I'd check out Fidelity (800-544-8888), T. Rowe Price (800-638-5660), Neuberger & Berman (800-877-9700), Vanguard (800-662-7447), and Strong (800-368-1030). Look at the fund choices among these and other fund families, focusing on general equity funds with moderate asset sizes.

Why do I like this strategy? The small size gives the fund manager a lot of flexibility in terms of what stocks to purchase. The fund manager has every incentive to do well because strong performance draws money. A small fund within a big and successful fund family can leverage off that fund family's research department.

## BUILDING BLOCKS

It's always dangerous to create a "one-size-fits-all" investment portfolio because a person's time horizon, investment objectives, risk aversion, and financial situations differ dramatically. For that reason, I'm taking a slightly different tack for constructing the "ultimate" individual investor portfolio for the 21st century.

To build our portfolio, we'll use securities from each of the following three categories (see following table):

$ High octane, low sleep stocks/funds

$ Less octane, more sleep stocks/funds

$ Yield boosters

### Outline of the "Ultimate" Individual Investor Portfolio

**High Octane/Low Sleep**

Stocks

Baan

Compaq Computer

Diebold

Elan

Equifax

Guidant

Intel

Investors Financial Services

Lucent Technologies

Microsoft

Nokia

Oracle

Paychex

Reuters Group

Schwab (Charles)

Southwest Airlines

Strayer Education

Vimpel Communications

WEBS–Netherlands

**Mutual Funds**

Acorn International

White Oak Growth

## Less Octane/More Sleep

**Stocks**

AEGON

AFLAC

AT&T

Becton, Dickinson

BellSouth

Block (H&R)

Bristol-Myers Squibb

CBS

Coca-Cola

Disney (Walt)

Emerson Electric

Exxon

Fannie Mae

Finova

Gannett

General Electric

Hewlett-Packard

Home Depot

International Business Machines

Johnson & Johnson

Johnson Controls

Merck & Co.

Motorola

New Holland

PepsiCo

Popular

Procter & Gamble

Regions Financial

Royal Dutch Petroleum

SBC Communications

ServiceMaster

Tribune

Walgreen

Wal-Mart Stores

**Mutual Funds**

L. Roy Papp Stock

Mairs & Power Growth

Strong Dow 30 Value

Strong Schafer Value

T. Rowe Price International Stock

T. Rowe Price Mid-Cap Growth

Vanguard Growth and Income

Vanguard Index 500

## Yield Boosters/Risk Reducers

**Stocks**

Duke Realty Investments

Energen

IPALCO Enterprises

Old National Bancorp

Philadelphia Suburban

Southern Company

WICOR

**Mutual Funds**

>Strong Advantage
>Vanguard Bond Index Total Bond Market Fund
>Vanguard Wellington

You could think of these three groups as portfolios unto themselves. I prefer to use them as categories from which to mix and match stocks and funds to build portfolios based on different risk levels and investment objectives.

## High Octane/Low Sleep

As the name implies, these investments offer high growth potential, but also high potential volatility. The stocks were chosen for several reasons. All are involved in industries that should show rapid growth over the next decade and beyond, and many of these companies are leaders in their growth niches. These stocks have also produced solid track records of earnings growth. Another factor that went into my choices was the ease of owning the stocks. For example, many of these stocks offer direct-purchase plans that allow investors to buy even initial shares directly. Others offer traditional dividend reinvestment plans in which investors who are already shareholders can buy additional shares directly from the company.

The following are reviews of the companies in this group. You'll also find many of the companies in the directories of U.S. and foreign direct-purchase plans. The best way to use these recommendations is to focus on companies that pique your interest and do further analysis by obtaining annual and quarterly reports from the company and using research techniques discussed in Chapter 5. Note that the stock symbols are in parentheses.

$ **Baan NV** (NASDAQ: BAANF): Baan is one of the world's largest providers of enterprise resource planning software. This software is used by corporations to increase efficiencies across various functions. This Netherlands-based company has grown dramatically since 1995 with net income increasing more than fourfold in that time. The stock has been a big performer as well, rising from a split-adjusted price of around $5 in 1995. The stock has all the attributes of a high-flier, including a high P/E ratio. However, this firm provides an interesting way to play the software market. The ADR can be bought via a broker or the company's direct-purchase plan (see the directory in Appendix C for further details and performance ratings on Baan and other

ADR direct-purchase plans). Enrollment information for the plan is available by calling 800-428-4237 or 800-774-4117.

$ **Compaq Computer** (NYSE: CPQ): Compaq has carved out a strong position in the personal computer market and the acquisition of Digital Equipment expands its computer offerings to larger systems. Wall Street seems to be taking a wait-and-see attitude concerning the Digital deal. Compaq has had inventory problems in the past, which has caused the selling of these shares. Price dips represent good opportunities to buy these shares. Compaq will prove to be a survivor in these competitive markets, offering interesting long-term potential. The stock can be purchased via a broker or through the company's direct-purchase plan. (See the directory in Appendix A for details and performance ratings for Compaq Computer and other U.S. direct-purchase plans.) Enrollment information is available by calling 888-218-4373.

$ **Diebold** (NYSE: DBD): Diebold is a leader in the ATM market. The company also offers various security services for the ATM industry. Other businesses include developing transaction systems using electronic "smart cards." ATM growth has been strong in the U.S. and abroad due to bank mergers and the use of ATMs as surrogate bank branches. With ATM technology now allowing a variety of products and services to be disseminated via the machines, ATM use should increase. The stock took a big hit in 1998 when earnings disappointed Wall Street, and it may take some time for these shares to rebound. Still, I like the company's long-term prospects. The shares can be purchased via a broker. Diebold also offers a dividend reinvestment plan for individuals who own at least one share. A brochure on the plan is available by calling 800-643-4296.

$ **Elan** (NYSE: ELN): This Ireland-based company has activities in a variety of pharmaceutical markets. The firm is a leader in developing controlled-release drug delivery systems. Elan has also been developing its own stable of pharmaceuticals. Profits have been rising at a rapid rate in recent years, and further growth is likely. The "graying of America" assures strong demand for pharmaceutical products, which should help the bottom line of Elan. The stock provides an excellent way to provide international flavor to a portfolio. Shares can be bought via a broker or through the company's direct-purchase plan. Enrollment information for the plan is available by calling 800-943-9715 or 800-774-4117.

**$ Equifax** (NYSE: EFX): I like information-services companies and Equifax is one of the best. Although you may not be familiar with this company, chances are the firm is very familiar with you. Equifax is a major provider of credit-verification services. This business has generated huge profits in recent years and should continue to be a money-maker. Geographic expansion and new products should fuel further growth. I own Equifax and am glad I do, as the stock has increased approximately four-fold since 1994. The stock can be bought through a broker or via the company's direct-purchase plan. Enrollment information for the plan is available by calling 888-887-2971.

**$ Guidant** (NYSE: GDT): Guidant, spun off from Eli Lilly in 1994, manufactures products used in cardiac rhythm management and coronary disease treatment. The company is a leader in coronary angioplasty products. Per-share profits more than doubled from 1994 to 1997. Medical technology companies, such as Guidant, should also benefit from an aging population. The stock offers an interesting way to play healthcare markets. The stock can be bought via a broker or through the company's direct-purchase program. Enrollment information for the plan is available by calling 800-537-1677.

**$ Intel** (NASDAQ: INTC): The world's largest chip maker, Intel is situated nicely to prosper from the ongoing technology revolution in this country. No chip maker is better financed, better managed, and better situated to keep ahead of the steep learning curve in this business. Chip makers run hot and cold on Wall Street, and Intel will show periods of price weakness. Yet, these shares represent a core technology holding. I own the stock and expect it to perform well over the next several years. The stock can be bought via a broker. Intel also offers a dividend reinvestment plan for investors owning at least one share. As is the case with all DRIPs, the share must be registered in your own name, not in the "street" name, or name of broker. A brochure for the plan is available by calling 800-298-0146.

**$ Investors Financial Services** (NASDAQ: IFIN): This company provides asset administration services for the financial-services industry. Services include accounting, transfer work, performance measurement, and mutual-fund administration. Rapid earnings growth has helped boost these shares in the last two years. The growth in the mutual-fund industry should work to the advantage of this company. The stock has been trading publicly only since November 1995 and is tied to the financial markets via its services. Thus, rising interest rates or a prolonged bear market would be bad news for these shares. Still, this undiscovered gem offers good appreciation potential. Shares can be purchased via a broker or the company's direct-purchase plan. Enrollment information for the plan is available by calling 888-333-5336.

$ **Lucent Technologies** (NYSE: LU): I am a big fan of telecommunications equipment providers such as Lucent. One reason is the huge growth opportunities for equipment providers as telecommunications providers expand and upgrade systems both in this country and abroad. Lucent Technologies, formerly a part of AT&T, has been winning its share of contracts. One ace the company holds is one of the premier research departments in the world, Bell Laboratories. The stock is a bit pricey and is vulnerable to weakness during market corrections. Even so, the stock has been a big winner for me and should continue to be a market leader. The stock can be purchased via a broker or through the company's direct-purchase plan. An enrollment form is available by calling 888-582-3686 or 800-774-4117.

$ **Microsoft** (NASDAQ: MSFT): Microsoft is truly the dominant player in the technology markets. This domination is one reason the company is usually in the sights of federal regulators, who seem especially keen on eroding Microsoft's market dominance. Government regulatory intervention represents a potential risk to these shares, but it is hard to imagine a technology revolution over the next decade and beyond in which Microsoft is not the key player. The stock is never cheap but should outperform most equities over the next three to five years. The stock does not offer a direct-purchase plan or a DRIP and, thus, must be purchased via a broker.

$ **Nokia** (NYSE: NOKA): Another interesting play in the telecommunications field is Helsinki-based Nokia. The firm is a leader in cellular-telecommunications products. Profits have been uneven over the years, but earnings in the last two years have shown strong growth. Nokia has some worthy competitors in its markets, including Motorola and Sweden-based Ericsson. Nevertheless, this high-octane performer is positioned nicely to garner its fair share of the burgeoning worldwide cellular market. The ADRs can be purchased via a broker or the company's direct-purchase plan. An enrollment form for the plan is available by calling 800-483-9010.

$ **Oracle** (NASDAQ: ORCL): Oracle is a leading provider of database software. Given the new world of data-hungry corporations and consumers, Oracle should find continued strong demand for its products that help users make sense of all that data. Oracle, as is the case with most technology companies, is not immune to periodic selling by Wall Street. However, with data likely to be the real currency of the information age, a portfolio would do well to hold these shares. I own the stock and recommend purchases. The stock does not have a DRIP or direct-purchase plan and must be purchased via a broker.

$ **Paychex** (NASDAQ: PAYX): This company may not be a household name to many investors, but its growth record has surely been noticed on Wall Street. The stock has registered huge gains over the last five years. Although Paychex may have trouble maintaining such heady growth, I'm optimistic that happy days are still ahead. The company provides payroll processing and other business services for small and medium-sized companies. I own Paychex for the simple reason that, if you believe in the entrepreneurial spirit of America and continued business creation, Paychex should remain on the fast track. The stock can be purchased via a broker. The company also offers a dividend reinvestment plan for investors owning at least one share of stock. A brochure on the plan is available by calling 800-937-5449.

$ **Reuters Group** (NASDAQ: RTRSY): Companies that provide data and information should remain solid market performers in the 21st century. One stock I own in this sector is Reuters. The United Kingdom-based concern is a world leader in financial-information services. The stock hit a rough patch in 1998 following allegations that the company misappropriated a competitor's data. Some analysts on Wall Street are fearful that the company's best days are behind it. I remain bullish on these shares, however, and expect this company to remain shareowner focused. The company's ADRs can be purchased via a broker or the company's direct-purchase plan. An enrollment form is available by calling (800) 428-4237 or (800) 774-4117.

$ **Schwab (Charles)** (NYSE: SCH): Financial-services firms should remain in vogue over the next decade as aging baby boomers continue to prepare for their golden years. Schwab has clearly been one of the most innovative players in this sector. The firm provides play on brokerage as well as the mutual-fund industry via its OneSource fund "supermarket" business. Management is clearly several cuts above the typical management found in the financial-services field. The stock will ride the highs and lows of the stock market yet should produce above-average returns for investors. Schwab can be purchased through a broker. In one of the great ironies of the financial markets, Schwab also offers a DRIP for individuals owning at least one share and doesn't charge any fees to purchase shares through its DRIP. A brochure on the plan is available by calling 800-670-4763.

$ **Southwest Airlines** (NYSE: LUV): The airline industry is probably the least growth-oriented sector represented in this group, yet Southwest Airlines meets the parameters of a classic growth stock. Per-share profits have risen annually since 1992, increasing more than threefold in that time. Cost controls, profitable route expansion, and industry-leading customer service should keep the airline flying above its competitors. The stock offers perhaps the best way to gain exposure to the transportation sector. Southwest Airlines does not offer a DRIP or direct-purchase plan and must be purchased via a broker.

$ **Strayer Education** (NASDAQ: STRA): Job training, especially to meet the needs of the fast-growing technology sector, will be a huge market in the next century. One firm that is poised to exploit this demand is Strayer Education. The company offers undergraduate and graduate degree programs at campuses in Washington, D.C., northern Virginia, and Maryland. Per-share profits have risen annually since 1991. The shares have been publicly traded only since 1996. The lack of a long-term track record lends some uncertainty to these shares, but there's no doubt that education markets offer above-average growth potential over the next decade, which should help these Nasdaq-traded shares. The company offers a DRIP plan for shareholders of at least one share and there are no fees on the buy side. The stock can be purchased via a broker and a brochure on the plan is available by calling 800-937-5449.

$ **Vimpel Communications** (NYSE: VIP): Here's a real flier. The company provides cellular-telephone services in Russia. Lest you think that cellular communication in Russia means soup cans and string, you might be surprised to know that Vimpel Communications has posted higher per-share profits every year since 1994. I'll admit I thought long and hard about throwing these shares into the mix, but for investors who want a high-octane, high-risk overseas situation, these shares certainly fit the bill. The fact that the company is involved in a business with excellent long-term prospects made my decision a bit easier. Even though the company is based in Russia, its American Depository Receipts trade on the New York Stock Exchange. You can buy the ADRs via a broker or through the company's direct-purchase plan. An enrollment form is available by calling 800-943-9715 or 800-774-4117.

$ **Mutual Funds: Acorn International** focuses on international investments, but with a twist. The fund invests in small-capitalization foreign firms. This small-cap focus energizes potential returns but also boosts risk. On the plus side, the fund's track record has been stellar, especially in light of the beating that many international funds have taken in recent years. In addition, the fund is tax-friendly. A fund's tax efficiency ratio is determined by taking a fund's after-tax return divided by pre-tax return. Acorn International's three-year tax efficiency ratio is 94 percent. The fund is also expense-friendly relative to other international funds. Fund assets are roughly $1.7 billion, a bit higher than I normally would like but still small enough to allow flexibility for the fund manager. Acorn is a no-load fund and can be bought directly from the Acorn fund family. For an application, call 800-922-6769. Another high-octane growth fund that focuses on U.S. companies is the **White Oak Growth Stock Fund** (888-462-5386). The firm has turned in impressive performance in recent years due partly to astute picking in the technology sector. The fund has added assets at rapid clip over the last 12 months, which will make a more challenging environment for the fund manager. Still, the fund is a good choice for the aggressive growth portion of a portfolio.

$ **WEBS–Netherlands:** If you remember from Chapter 4, *World Equity Benchmark Shares* (WEBS) are securities traded on the American Stock Exchange that allow an investor to target a specific geographic region. WEBS trade just like stocks and can be bought and sold intraday, unlike open-end mutual funds that are priced at the end of each trading day. One of my favorite overseas sectors is the Netherlands. I'm amazed by the quality of companies based in this rather small country. Indeed, AEGON, Baan, ING Groep, New Holland, Philips, Royal Dutch Petroleum, and Unilever are just some of the investment-worthy companies headquartered in the Netherlands. Of course, targeting a single country leaves you exposed to adverse changes in that country's economic and political conditions. With that said, I think WEBS provide an interesting way to spice up the international portion of a portfolio, and the WEBS focused on the Netherlands are my preferred way to go. You'll have to purchase WEBS through a broker.

## Less Octane/More Sleep

The second group of stocks offers less growth potential but a higher degree of stability. That's not to say that these stocks won't fall during down markets. Still, the companies are a bit more seasoned in many cases and are less apt to follow the feast-or-famine trading patterns that are more common with the first grouping of stocks. I own several of these stocks and believe that all the stocks would fit nicely into the growth portion of a portfolio. Adding further appeal is the ability to buy many of these stocks directly from the company, thus making their acquisition easy and relatively inexpensive. Again, use this group as a source of growth ideas, following up on companies you find especially interesting by doing further research. You'll notice that the number of stocks is greater in this group. I did this purposely, as I feel that most readers probably would feel a bit more comfortable owning more of these stocks in a portfolio than the stocks in the "high-octane" group.

$ **AEGON NV** (NYSE: AEG): I like financial-services firms and AEGON offers investors an international play on this sector. The company, based in the Netherlands, is a world leader in insurance and financial products. The company's AEGON USA unit is the biggest non-U.S. insurance company in the country. Rising profits have fueled big gains in the last year, and the stock is a suitable holding in any portfolio. An enrollment form for the plan is available by calling 800-808-8010 or 800-774-4117. An alternative insurance selection is **AFLAC** (NYSE: AFL), which is a leading provider of supplemental insurance. Insurance companies are linked to interest rates, so rising rates could cause selling in these shares. However, the stock offers a quality choice in the insurance sector. Adding further appeal is the company's fee-friendly direct-purchase plan. An enrollment form is available by calling 800-227-4756.

$ **Disney (Walt)** (NYSE: DIS): One market destined for long-term growth is the entertainment sector. The one company that's perhaps the best situated to capitalize on this sector is Disney. The firm's theme park business has excellent expansion opportunities in this country and abroad. The film business continues to crank out winner after winner. The one slow spot has been its ABC network broadcasting business. But Disney rarely accepts mediocrity for long, so look for improvement in this area soon. The company knows the value of a brand, and no brand is more identifiable around the globe. Given its child-friendly businesses, this issue makes an excellent "starter" stock for a youngster. The stock can be bought via a broker or Disney's direct-purchase plan. An enrollment form is available by calling 800-948-2222. An alternative entertainment choice is **CBS** (NYSE: CBS). The company, formerly Westinghouse, has reengineered itself in recent years to become a force in radio and television broadcasting. Although the stock has moved sharply higher over the last two years, I think the stock has plenty of upside as Wall Street continues to realize its full potential. I own CBS and recommend these shares. The stock can be purchased via a broker. The company also has a DRIP that is available to shareholders of at least one share of stock. A brochure is available by calling 800-507-7799.

**$ Exxon** (NYSE: XON): Exxon has been a long-time holding in my portfolio, and the issue has rarely disappointed. The company's global energy business helps fend off weakness in any one geographic region. The firm is my first choice for representation in the oil sector. Exxon can be purchased via a broker or the company's extremely investor-friendly direct-purchase plan. The plan offers an IRA option and automatic monthly debit services. Exxon picks up all fees on the buy side. An enrollment form is available by calling 800-252-1800. An alternative energy issue is **Royal Dutch Petroleum** (NYSE: RD). The firm is also a global leader and should produce solid results over time. Royal Dutch offers a direct-purchase plan as well. An enrollment form is available by calling 800-428-4237 or 800-774-4117.

**$ Finova Group** (NYSE: FNV): Finova is one of the better companies that is not well known among individual investors. The firm is a leading lender to medium-sized businesses. Profits have risen at a rapid rate in recent years and further growth is expected. But the stock is dependent on favorable interest rates. Still, I like niche financial-services firms, and Finova is one of the best. The stock can be bought via a broker or the company's direct-purchase plan. Finova picks up all fees on the buy side in its program. An enrollment form is available by calling 800-774-4117. An alternative lending company is **Fannie Mae** (NYSE: FNM), the leading mortgage company in the country. The stock has performed extremely well over the last two years and I expect further gains to occur as long as interest rates remain accommodating. The stock can be purchased via a broker or the company's direct-purchase plan. An enrollment form is available by calling 888-289-3266.

$ **General Electric** (NYSE: GE): GE has operations in a variety of industries, from appliances and financial services to television broadcasting and jet engines. The one common thread is that the company is a leader in every market it pursues. Strong management and consistent earnings growth have made these shares a favorite of investors. GE should continue to be a solid market performer. The stock can be bought via a broker or its direct-purchase plan. An enrollment form is available by calling 800-786-2543. An alternative play is **Emerson Electric** (NYSE: EMR). Emerson is what I consider to be a "growth cyclical" stock. Despite fairly mundane electrical-equipment markets, the company has posted higher annual profits for more than a decade. Strong cost controls are a key. The company offers a DRIP for shareholders of at least one share. A brochure on the plan is available by calling 314-553-2197.

$ **Hewlett-Packard** (NYSE: HWP): One of the best diversified technology plays is Hewlett-Packard. The firm's strengths have been in the printer and instruments business. The company has developed a strong PC and server business in recent years. The firm's management is perennially considered one of the best in corporate America, and betting on strong management is rarely a losing proposition. Hewlett-Packard can be purchased via a broker or the company's DRIP. The DRIP requires ownership of at least 10 shares before enrolling. A brochure on the plan is available by calling 800-286-5977. An alternative technology issue is **International Business Machines** (NYSE: IBM): IBM appears to be steering a more profitable course following rough sledding a few years ago. The company's size and financial strength make it a formidable competitor. The stock can be purchased via a broker or its direct-purchase plan. An enrollment form is available by calling 888-421-8860.

$ **Home Depot** (NYSE: HD): One of the finest retailers around is Home Depot. The company's track record of growth is impressive, and its wining formula shows no signs of waning. The stock is rarely cheap. Nevertheless investors who want representation in the retailing sector should consider this issue for its healthy three to five year potential. The stock can be purchased via a broker or its direct-purchase plan. An enrollment form is available by calling 800-774-4117. An alternative retailing choice is **Wal-Mart Stores** (NYSE: WMT). This leading discounter has ample growth potential, both in the U.S. and abroad. The company also offers a direct-purchase plan for first-time buyers. An enrollment form is available by calling 800-438-6278.

$ **Johnson & Johnson** (NYSE: JNJ): These stocks have performed well in recent years, but demand in this country and abroad should fuel earnings gains well in excess of the average stock. Johnson & Johnson is one of the strongest diversified companies in the healthcare sector. The stock represents a core holding for any portfolio and can be purchased via a broker. The company also offers a DRIP for shareholders of at least one share. A brochure on the plan is available by calling 800-328-9033. An alternative company in healthcare products is **Becton, Dickinson** (NYSE: BDX). The firm produces a variety of hospital supplies and diagnostic products. Per-share profits have risen every year since 1983. The stock's three- to five-year appreciation prospects are well-above average. Becton, Dickinson also offers an extremely fee-friendly direct-purchase plan. An enrollment form is available by calling 800-955-4743.

$ **Johnson Controls** (NYSE: JCI): Johnson Controls manufactures automotive seating components and building-control systems. Despite its cyclical bent, the company has posted solid earnings growth in recent years. The stock has performed well, and further gains are expected. Especially appealing about the company is its investor-friendly direct-purchase plan. Minimum initial investment is just $50, and the firm picks up all fees on the buy side. The stock makes an excellent "starter" issue for a portfolio. An enrollment form is available by calling 800-524-6220. An alternative among cyclicals is **New Holland NV** (NYSE: NH). The company, based in the Netherlands, is a leading provider of farm equipment, especially in Europe and the Pacific Rim. The firm is not widely followed on Wall Street, but that should change as earnings expand. The stock is a solid pick in the agricultural sector. The stock can be bought via a broker or the company's direct-purchase plan. An enrollment form is available by calling 800-428-4237 or 800-774-4117.

$ **Merck** (NYSE: MRK): Like Johnson & Johnson, Merck is a member of the Dow Jones Industrial Average and a leader in healthcare products. Merck's stable of pharmaceuticals is impressive and includes several billion-dollar sellers. The company spends billions on research and development, which assures a well-stuffed product pipeline. Shares can be purchased via a broker or the company's direct-purchase plan. An enrollment form is available by calling 800-774-4117. An alternative drug company is **Bristol-Myers Squibb** (NYSE: BMY). I own these shares and have enjoyed their solid price gains in recent years. Bristol-Myers offers a DRIP for shareholders owning at least 50 shares. A brochure on the plan is available by calling 800-356-2026.

$ **Motorola** (NYSE: MOT): I like telecommunications-equipment companies, which is partly why I own Motorola. I also believe that the company, because of its problems in recent years, is one of the few companies in this group that is still reasonably priced. Wall Street will likely play "show me" with this company, which means Motorola may not generate huge gains over the next 12 months until investors see clearer signs of an earnings turnaround. Nevertheless, the company has the finances, technological savvy, and management to engineer a turnaround. The stock can be bought via a broker. Motorola has a DRIP for shareholders of at least one share. A brochure on the plan is available by calling 800-704-4098. An alternative is **AT&T** (NYSE: T). Many on Wall Street left these shares for dead in 1997, but new management has rejuvenated investors' interest in this company. AT&T has formidable competition in its markets, yet I'm betting this company will make the changes necessary to prosper in the telecommunications markets of the future. The stock's DRIP requires ownership of 10 shares in order to participate. A brochure on the plan is available by calling 800-348-8288.

$ **PepsiCo** (NYSE: PEP): PepsiCo is thought of as a soft-drink producer, and rightly so because it is the world's second-largest player in this market. What I especially like about the company is its food operations under the Frito-Lay banner, which is the world leader in salted snack foods. This business represents an important springboard into foreign markets. I own the stock and recommend it for growth investors. The company's DRIP requires ownership of at least five shares in order to enroll. A brochure on the plan is available by calling 800-226-0083. An obvious alternative to PepsiCo is **Coca-Cola** (NYSE: KO). The company continues to surprise Wall Street with its ability to post healthy volume increases. Although I think PepsiCo is probably a better value, it has been dangerous to bet against Coca-Cola in the past. The company offers a DRIP for shareholders of at least one share. A brochure on the plan is available by calling 888-265-3747.

**$ Regions Financial** (NASDAQ: RGBK): I like regional banks, and Regions Financial is one of the best of the bunch. The company, based in Alabama, has an excellent record of earnings growth. The company has been actively expanding via acquisitions, and Regions itself is an interesting takeover issue. I own the stock and recommend purchases. The stock can be purchased via a broker or the company's fee-friendly direct-purchase plan. An enrollment form is available by calling 800-922-3468. An alternative choice is **Popular** (NASDAQ: BPOP), the holding company for Banco Popular. This banking concern specializes in banks located in Hispanic communities across the country and Puerto Rico. The Hispanic population is a fast-growing ethnic group, and Popular is positioned nicely to benefit from this growth. The stock offers an interesting demographic play. The stock can be bought via a broker. ADRIP is offered to shareholders of at least one share. One attraction of the DRIP is a five percent discount paid on shares purchased with reinvested dividends. A brochure on the plan is available by calling 787-756-3908.

**$ SBC Communications** (NYSE: SBC): SBC is a leading regional Bell. The firm's service region in Texas and parts of the South and Southwest has good growth potential. The acquisition of Pacific Telesis expanded operations to the West Coast. SBC has a booming cellular-telephone business, which enhances long-term growth prospects. The stock should be a big winner in the telecommunications markets of the future. The stock can be bought via a broker or the company's direct-purchase plan. An enrollment form is available by calling 888-836-5062. An alternative choice among the baby Bells is **BellSouth** (NYSE: BLS). The company's service region in the Southeast should show growth well in excess of the national average. Strong finances should fuel further dividend hikes. The stock is suitable for any portfolio. BellSouth can be purchased via a broker or its direct-purchase plan. An enrollment form is available by calling 888-266-6778.

$ **ServiceMaster** (NYSE: SVM): In many respects, ServiceMaster is the quintessential service company. The firm provides both consumer and business services ranging from housekeeping, lawn care, and food service to home health care and pest control. This amalgam of operations has produced fairly consistent earnings growth over the last decade. This growth has fueled a tripling in the stock price from its 1995 low. This well-run company should prosper from continued outsourcing of duties by both consumers and corporations. The stock can be bought via a broker. The firm offers a DRIP for shareholders of at least one share. A brochure on the plan is available by calling 800-858-0840. An alternative service company is **H&R Block** (NYSE: HRB). The continued tinkering with tax laws is good news for Block. What I like best about Block is its large customer base of some 15 million tax-payers. Such a customer base gives Block ample opportunities to cross-sell other financial products. This base also makes Block an attractive target for other financial-services firms. The stock can be bought via a broker. The company has a DRIP for share-holders owning at least one share of stock. A brochure on the plan is available by calling 888-213-0968.

$ **Tribune** (NYSE: TRB): Tribune is a leading publisher and broad-casting company. Flagship newspapers include the *Chicago Tribune* and the *Orlando Sentinel*. The company also owns super-station Channel 9 as well as the Chicago Cubs baseball team. Strong fiscal controls, an eye for value, and profitable strategic investments (the firm was an early investor in America Online) have helped the company. The stock's consistency should con-tinue to find admirers on Wall Street. Tribune can be purchased via a broker or the company's direct-purchase plan. An enroll-ment form is available by calling 800-924-1490. An alternative choice in the publishing sector is **Gannett** (NYSE: GCI), the publisher of *USA Today* and a host of smaller newspapers. Gannett can be purchased via a broker. The company also offers a DRIP for shareholders of at least one share. A brochure on the plan is available by calling 800-778-3299.

$ **Walgreen** (NYSE: WAG): One of my favorite holdings is Walgreen, the drugstore chain. I view Walgreen as a way to play the growing need for pharmaceuticals in this country. Walgreen fills nearly nine percent of the nation's prescriptions. That amounts to more than 200 million prescriptions per year. The business will continue to provide the growth punch to the bottom line. The stock has performed well in the last three years. The stock can be purchased via a broker or its direct-purchase plan. Minimum initial purchase in the plan is just $50. An enrollment form is available by calling 800-774-4117. An alternative in the consumer-products area is **Procter & Gamble** (NYSE: PG), which is a world leader in a variety of consumer products. The firm's strong global representation should help it as overseas markets mature. I also own Procter & Gamble and look for decent gains. The stock offers a direct-purchase plan for first-time buyers. An enrollment form is available by calling 800-764-7483.

$ **Mutual Funds:** The following funds are "no loads" (no sales fees) and offer reasonable growth at average or moderate risk. **T. Rowe Price International Stock Fund** (800-638-5660) is a broad-based diversified international fund. The fund's performance record over the last five years has been extremely consistent. Another T. Rowe Price fund with a strong track record is its **Mid-Cap Growth Fund** (800-638-5660). The company has achieved good growth at acceptable risk and is a solid way to gain exposure in this stock sector. Among index and "enhanced" index funds, the **Vanguard Index 500** (800-662-7447) and **Vanguard Growth and Income** (800-662-7447) funds offer appeal. The Index 500 mimics the performance of the Standard & Poor's 500. The Growth and Income fund is an "enhanced" index fund in that the fund invests in many of the stocks that comprise the S&P 500, but in different weightings from the index. By preferencing certain S&P 500 stocks, the fund hopes to outperform the index. We do a similar strategy in the mutual fund I co-manage with Richard Moroney, the **Strong Dow 30 Value Fund** (800-368-6010). This new fund invests exclusively in the 30 stocks that comprise the Dow Jones Industrial Average. The fund invests 50 percent of the assets in the price-weighted positions of the Dow 30 stocks. In effect, 50 percent of the fund attempts to mirror the Dow. The remaining 50 percent of the funds are invested in the 30 Dow stocks, overweighting what we perceive as cheap stocks in the Dow and underweighting expensive Dow stocks. We use a nine-factor valuation model as a guide to help choose stocks to overweight and underweight (please obtain a copy of the prospectus before investing). A Strong fund with an excellent track record is **Strong Schafer Value Fund** (800-368-6010). Schafer Value invests in stocks that have higher growth prospects than the S&P 500 but trade at earnings multiples that are less than the S&P 500. Two smaller no-load growth funds worth considering include the **Mairs & Power Growth Fund** (800-304-7404), which is not available to investors in all 50 states, and the **L. Roy Papp Stock Fund** (800-421-4004). Both have good track records and low expenses.

## Yield Boosters/Risk Reducers

This third category of stocks and mutual funds provides a way to boost a portfolio's income stream while dampening volatility. All these stocks offer direct-purchase plans for new investors. Also note that several apply discounts to shares purchased through their DRIPs/direct-purchase plans. To research further these and other stocks highlighted in this chapter, use the techniques discussed in Chapter 5.

$ **Duke Realty Investments** (NYSE: DRE): Duke is a real estate investment trust. The company has a diversified portfolio of properties including industrial, office, and retail space. The company has expanded at a rapid clip in recent years. I'm not a huge fan of REITs, but this issue has been a consistently above-average performer. The stock can be bought via a broker or the company's fee-friendly direct-purchase plan. Participants in the plan receive a four percent discount on shares purchased with reinvestment dividends. An enrollment form is available by calling 800-774-4117.

$ **Energen** (NYSE: EGN): Energen is a top utility holding. Dividends have grown at a healthy clip, and the payout should continue to rise at a rate in excess of the typical natural-gas utility. I like these shares and would feel comfortable owning them. Energen can be purchased via a broker or the company's fee-friendly direct-purchase plan. An enrollment form is available by calling 800-774-4117.

$ **IPALCO Enterprises** (NYSE: IPL): IPALCO Enterprises provides electricity to parts of Indiana. Although Indiana is not known as a high-growth state, its economic performance has been fairly consistent over the years, which has helped these shares. Given the location of its service region, the utility is a prime takeover candidate. The stock can be purchased via a broker or the company's fee-friendly direct-purchase plan. An enrollment form is available by calling 800-774-4117.

**$ Old National Bancorp** (NASDAQ: OLDB): Old National Bancorp is a growing regional bank located in Indiana. The firm's solid performance in recent years may eventually draw a suitor looking to expand in the Midwest. Even without a takeover, these shares have ample growth potential. The stock can be bought via a broker or the company's direct-purchase plan. The plan provides a three percent discount on shares purchased with reinvested dividends. An enrollment form is available by calling 800-774-4117.

**$ Philadelphia Suburban** (NYSE: PSC): Philadelphia Suburban is a leading water utility in Pennsylvania. The company has been expanding aggressively via acquisitions. Profit growth has been decent, especially for a utility. The stock offers a top pick in the water sector. Philadelphia Suburban's direct-purchase plan is extremely user-friendly and includes a no-fee IRA option (regular and Roth IRAs are available) as well as a five percent discount on shares purchased with reinvested dividends. The company charges no fees on the buy side. An enrollment form is available by calling 800-774-4117.

**$ Southern Company** (NYSE: SO): Southern is one of the top electric utilities in the country. The firm's service region in the Southeast should experience above-average growth. Strong finances and low generating costs put the company in good position to prosper as electric utility markets become more competitive. The stock can be purchased via a broker or the company's direct-purchase plan. An enrollment form is available by calling 800-774-4117.

**$ WICOR** (NYSE: WIC): WICOR is a Wisconsin-based natural-gas utility. What puts the shine on these shares are strong finances and growing nonutility businesses in fluid-handling and water-processing equipment. I like Wisconsin-based utilities due, in part, to the state's regulatory environment. These shares should do at least as well as the average natural-gas utility. The stock can be purchased via a broker or the company's fee-friendly direct-purchase plan. An enrollment form for the plan is available by calling 800-236-3453.

**$ Mutual Funds**: The three no-load mutual funds in this group have differing approaches to income. The **Vanguard Wellington**

**Fund** (800-662-7447) invests two-thirds of its assets in stocks and roughly one-third of its assets in bonds. This approach has served the fund well over the years, as risk-adjusted performance has been impressive. For more bond exposure, the **Vanguard Bond Index Total Bond Market Fund** (800-662-7447) provides an attractive way to gain greater bond exposure in a portfolio. The **Strong Advantage Fund** (800-368-6010) is a short-term bond fund. Short-term bond funds, because of the nature of their bond holdings, generally are less volatile when interest rates change. The Advantage Fund has been a leader in the short-term bond sector and provides a way to increase the yield component of a portfolio without taking on undue interest-rate risk.

## The Ultimate Individual Investor Portfolio

Now that I've covered the stocks in the three categories, it's time to mix and match them in a single portfolio. When you go through this process, keep in mind the following items:

$ As you move from one category to the next, your expected return and expected risk levels decline. By risk, I'm referring to the volatility of expected returns. For example, Microsoft may have an annual expected return of 20 percent over the next decade, but the volatility of the returns on an annual basis may be extremely high. On the other hand, a company in the "less octane" group may have expected annual returns of 15 percent over the next decade, but the annual volatility is likely to be much lower. The longer your investment time horizon, the greater your ability to handle volatility. Thus, a 30-year old may preference high-octane stocks at a much higher rate than a person who is 50 or 60 years old.

$ When you're done picking assets from each of the three groups, examine the degree of diversification across various industry groups. For example, you don't want a 10-stock portfolio that has five utility stocks. Avoid having too large an exposure to any one industry sector.

The portfolio discussed in this section (and outlined in the following table) should not necessarily be considered the best portfolio that can be constructed using the three groups of stocks. Rather, it's a portfolio that is consistent with my own risk parameters. I constructed the portfolio exclusively with companies that offer direct-purchase plans. Of course, the other issues discussed in these groups that don't permit initial purchases directly may be considered as well. The portfolio covers most investment sectors. The Strong Dow 30 Value Fund provides exposure to big blue-chip stocks, such as Merck, Disney, Wal-Mart, GE and the like. T. Rowe Price Mid-Cap Growth gives me exposure to another segment of stocks. The Acorn International gives me a way to play growth in small- and mid-capitalization stocks overseas. The individual stock selections (save Southern Company and Philadelphia Suburban, which provide a bit of ballast to the portfolio) focus on issues in attractive industry groups with big upside potential and, in most cases, good dividend growth prospects over the next decade and beyond.

Not surprisingly, my personal portfolio contains several of the stocks and funds listed here. To be honest, I wouldn't quibble with using any of the stocks and funds listed in these three groups in a single portfolio, as long as you follow prudent diversification practices and stay within your own risk parameters. In addition to the growth potential of the portfolio, I also like the fact that all of the components may be purchased directly without a middleman, without laying out money as a deposit to set up a brokerage account, and with very little initial money in many cases. In fact, an investor who wants to own this portfolio in its entirety would need to shell out $11,550 to get started (minimum initial investment amounts are in parentheses next to each investment). While $11,550 is not an insignificant amount of money, my guess is that it's a lot less than most people think is required to own a portfolio of 15 stocks and three mutual funds. Furthermore, if you are willing to commit to automatic monthly debits each month, your start-up requirements are much less. For example, the Strong Dow 30 Value Fund has a minimum initial investment of $2500, but the fund will waive the minimum if an investor agrees to automatic monthly debit of just $50. Lucent will waive the $1000 minimum if an investor agrees to automatic monthly debit of at least $100.

## The Ultimate Individual Investor Stock Portfolio

**Stocks**

AEGON ($250)

Compaq Computer ($250)

Elan ($200)

Equifax ($500)

Finova Group ($500)

Guidant ($250)

Home Depot ($250)

Johnson Controls ($50)

Lucent Technologies ($1000)

Philadelphia Suburban ($500)

Regions Financial ($500)

SBC Communications ($500)

Southern Company ($250)

Tribune ($500)

Walgreen ($50)

**Mutual Funds**

Acorn International ($1000)

T. Rowe Price Mid-Cap Growth ($2500)

Strong Dow 30 Value ($2500)

What are the total fees to implement this portfolio? Because the mutual funds are no load, there are no sales fees to buy these investments. For the individual stocks, the total fees to make initial investments in all 15 stocks are about $110. And if you invest more than the minimums required in each of these stocks, your fees won't be much higher than $110. In addition to fairly low initial investment requirements and start-up fees, this portfolio should be gentle on investors relative to investment fees and annual expenses going forward.

How would I divvy up my dollars in this portfolio? I would probably put 15 to 20 percent in the Acorn International Fund. Another 15 to 20 percent could be put into the T. Rowe Price Mid-Cap Growth Fund; then approximately 30 percent could be put into the Strong Dow 30 Value Fund (more conservative investors might want to boost this a bit). The remaining 30 to 40 percent could be distributed evenly across the 15 stocks.

Keep in mind that you'll want to construct this portfolio with your retirement investments in mind. For example, if you already have, say, 30 percent of your 401(k) plan in international equity funds, you may not want to have a big position in the international sector in this portfolio.

## Portfolio Fine-Tuning

One could argue that the best approach to running an investment portfolio is to leave it alone. More harm than good comes from tinkering and toying with the investments. Once you choose your risk level and portfolio components, set your percentages and go away. I think there's a lot of value to that approach, which is why I don't do a lot of tinkering to my stocks and funds. Still, I think it's important for investors to understand that things do change over time and making minor modifications to a portfolio is not necessarily a bad thing.

You should always be aware of how your investments are diversified in your portfolio. You might make a great investment in a particular stock or fund that, over time, swells in importance in your portfolio. At some point, the value of this single investment may swamp other investments. Although you're obviously glad the investment did well, you may also have more exposure to a single investment than you would like. Investors should always be watchful for the need to rebalance a portfolio to bring certain investments and asset groups back in line with risk parameters.

Rebalancing is also important as investment objectives and time horizons change. For example, this portfolio focuses primarily on high growth stocks that carry reasonably high risk. Although this may be suitable for me today, the same portfolio may be inappropriate for me 20 years from now. At that time, I may have different financial responsibilities (such as tuition or medical costs) and income levels. Rebalancing a portfolio over time to reflect these changing objectives is imperative.

Another way to tweak a portfolio is by using some of the macro tools and strategies described in Chapter 7. Remember that the operative word here is "tweak," not "overhaul."

# ▼ Conclusion . . .

W e've covered a lot of ground in this chapter, from discussing specific building blocks for a portfolio, to constructing it, to fine-tuning a portfolio over time. I'm sure many of you might quibble with some stock or fund selections I've included. More likely, with a universe of some 10,000 publicly traded stocks and more than 8,000 mutual funds, I've left out stocks and funds that you might think would make good holdings. I don't claim to have a monopoly on the best stock and fund picks, but I do believe that harnessing the power of time, focusing on quality as opposed to price, and maintaining a disciplined investing program, are some of the best ways for investors to succeed in the financial markets of the future. Furthermore, when you combine these investment strategies with the low-cost/no-cost market access and the information now available to all investors, the power to win the individual investor revolution is within the reach of *every* investor.

# DIRECTORY OF U.S. DIRECT PURCHASE PLANS

T he following directory of U.S. direct purchase plans provides pertinent information concerning plan details and fees. Here are some things to consider when using the directory:

$ Each listing includes the stock symbol and stock exchange on which the stock trades (NYSE: New York Stock Exchange; ASE: American Stock Exchange; NASDAQ: Nasdaq market).

$ You can assume that companies in the directory allow investors in nearly or all 50 states to make their initial purchases directly.

$ OCP is the abbreviation used for optional cash payments, the voluntary payments that shareholders may make directly into the plan in order to purchase additional shares.

$ Some plans permit partial dividend reinvestment. This option allows participants to receive dividends on part of the shares held in the plan while reinvesting dividends on the remainder. This option is addressed in the Plan Specifics.

$ Each listing indicates if a discount is available and, if so, the amount of the discount and whether it applies to just reinvested dividends or both reinvested dividends and OCPs.

$ Each listing provides the monthly dividend payment dates for the stock. Individuals who like to receive at least some of their dividends may find this listing useful, especially for constructing a portfolio of stocks in which dividends are paid every month.

$ Each listing provides, when available, the company's Web site address. The Web site is a good source for additional information on the company.

$ Often, the best source of information about a particular plan is the plan administrator. For that reason, many listings contain more than one contact number. If you call the company for information, ask for the shareholder services department.

I also provide performance ratings to assess the investment merit of each company. The performance ratings range from the highest (*****) to the lowest (*). In the case of some firms, I lacked sufficient information on which to rate them and such firms are listed as not rated (NR). These ratings take into account the companies's earnings and dividend growth records, financial positions, industry growth prospects, and the overall suitability for investment. I've also provided, when possible, a performance history of the stock. The performance data shows what a $1000 investment at the end of 1992 would have become five years later. (I'd like to thank the Microsoft Investor Web site, http://www.investor.msn.com, for the performance information. This data is available on thousands of companies, U.S. and foreign, at this Web site.) For enrollment information, use the contact numbers provided for each company. Because companies change plan details frequently, you should always obtain and read the plan prospectus before investing.

---

**ABT Building Products Corp. (NASDAQ:ABTC)**
**One Neenah Center, Suite 600**
**Neenah, WI 54956-3070**
**(800) 774-4117, (800) 286-9178**
www.abtco.com

*Business Profile:* Manufacturer of specialty building products for the home repair, remodeling, and construction markets.

*Performance History:* $1000 invested on 12/31/92 was worth $1200 on 12/31/97, a 20 percent increase in five years.

*Plan Specifics:*

- Initial shares can be purchased directly from the company ($250 minimum).
- No discount.
- OCP: $50 to $100,000 per year.
- Stock is purchased weekly with OCPs.
- Purchasing costs are $5 plus eight cents per share.
- Termination fee is $10.

- Selling costs are $10 plus eight cents per share.
- Automatic investment services are available ($1.50 plus eight cents per share).
- The company does not pay a dividend.

*Performance Rating:* \*\*\*


**Aetna, Inc. (NYSE:AET)**
**PO Box 2598**
**Jersey City, NJ 07303**
**(800) 955-4741, (800) 446-2617, (860) 273-0123**
www.aetna.com

*Business Profile:* Provider of insurance and financial services.

*Performance History:* $1000 invested on 12/31/92 was worth $1811 on 12/31/97, an 81 percent increase in five years.

*Plan Specifics:*

- Initial shares can be purchased directly from the company ($500 minimum or automatic monthly investment of at least $50 for 10 consecutive months). There is a one-time enrollment fee of $10.
- Partial dividend reinvestment is available.
- No discount.
- OCP: $50 to $250,000 per year.
- Stock is purchased weekly with OCPs.
- Purchasing costs are $5 plus 12 cents per share.
- Selling costs are $15 plus 10 cents per share.
- Automatic investment services are available ($1 plus 10 cents per share).
- Dividend reinvestment fee: five percent of amount invested ($3 maximum) plus three cents per share.
- Shares can be sold via the telephone.
- Safekeeping services are available.
- Gift share transfers are available.
- Direct deposit of dividends is available.
- Dividends are paid February, May, August, and November.

*Performance Rating:* \*\*\*


**AFLAC, Inc. (NYSE:AFL)**
**Worldwide Headquarters**
**1932 Wynnton Rd.**
**Columbus, GA 31999**
**(800) 227-4756, (800) 774-4117, (706) 323-3431**
www.aflac.com

*Business Profile:* Holding company with insurance and broadcasting interests.

*Performance History:* $1000 invested on 12/31/92 was worth $3190 on 12/31/97, a 219 percent increase in five years.

*Plan Specifics:*

- Initial shares can be purchased directly from the company ($750 minimum).
- Partial dividend reinvestment is available.

- No discount.
- OCP: $50 to $120,000 per year.
- Stock is purchased bimonthly with OCPs.
- No purchasing costs.
- Selling costs are five cents per share.
- Automatic investment services are available.
- Safekeeping services are available.
- Direct deposit of dividends is available.
- Dividends are paid March, June, September, and December.

*Performance Rating:* \*\*\*\*


**AGL Resources, Inc. (NYSE:ATG)**
**303 Peachtree St., NE**
**PO Box 4569**
**Atlanta, GA 30302**
**(800) 774-4117, (800) 633-4236, (404) 584-9470**
www.aglr.com

*Business Profile:* Largest natural-gas utility in the southeastern portion of the United States.

*Performance History:* $1000 invested on 12/31/92 was worth $1420 on 12/31/97, a 42 percent increase in five years.

*Plan Specifics:*

- Initial shares can be purchased directly from the company ($250 minimum).
- Partial dividend reinvestment is available.
- No discount.
- OCP: $25 to $5000 per month.
- Stock is purchased monthly with OCPs, generally on the first business day of the month.
- Selling costs include brokerage fees and transfer taxes.
- Automatic investment services are available.
- Safekeeping services are available.
- Gift share transfers are available.
- Dividends are paid March, June, September, and December.

*Performance Rating:* \*\*\*\*


**Air Products & Chemicals, Inc. (NYSE:APD)**
**7201 Hamilton Blvd.**
**Allentown, PA 18195-1501**
**(800) 519-3111, (888) 694-9458, (800) 774-4117, (610) 481-4911**
www.airproducts.com

*Business Profile:* Manufacturer of industrial chemicals, equipment, and gases.

*Performance History:* $1000 invested on 12/31/92 was worth $2190 on 12/31/97, a 119 percent increase in five years.

*Plan Specifics:*

- Initial shares can be purchased directly from the company ($500 minimum or automatic monthly investment of at least $100 for 10 consecutive months). There is a one-time enrollment fee of $10 plus 10 cents per share.
- Partial dividend reinvestment is available.
- No discount.
- OCP: $100 to $200,000 per year.
- Stock is purchased weekly with OCPs.
- Purchasing costs are $5 plus 10 cents per share.
- Selling costs are $10 plus 12 cents per share, and applicable transfer taxes.
- Dividend reinvestment fee: five percent of amount invested up to $3.
- Shares can be sold via the telephone.
- Safekeeping services are available.
- Automatic investment services available ($2 fee).
- Gift share transfers are available.
- Direct deposit of dividends is available.
- Dividends are paid February, May, August, and November.

*Performance Rating:* *****

**AirTouch Communications, Inc. (NYSE:ATI)**
**One California St., 21st Floor**
**San Francisco, CA 94111**
**(800) 727-7033, (800) 233-5601, (415) 658-2000**
www.airtouch.com

*Business Profile:* Leading provider of cellular communications services.

*Performance History:* $1000 invested on 12/31/92 was worth $1629 on 12/31/97, a 63 percent increase in five years.

*Plan Specifics:*

- Initial shares can be purchased directly from the company ($500 minimum).
- No discount.
- OCP: $100 to $10,000 per transaction.
- Stock is purchased weekly with OCPs.
- Purchasing and selling costs are $7.50 plus brokerage fees.
- The company does not pay a dividend.

*Performance Rating:* ****

**American Electric Power Co., Inc. (NYSE:AEP)**
**1 Riverside Plaza**
**Columbus, OH 43215**
**(800) 955-4740, (614) 223-1000**
www.aep.com

*Business Profile:* Major electric utility holding company.

*Performance History:* $1000 invested on 12/31/92 was worth $2150 on 12/31/97, a 115 percent increase in five years.

*Plan Specifics:*

- Initial shares can be purchased directly from the company ($250 minimum or automatic monthly investments of at least $25). There is a one-time enrollment fee of $10.
- Partial dividend reinvestment is available.
- No discount.
- OCP: $25 to $150,000 per year.
- Stock is purchased at least weekly with OCPs.
- No purchasing fees.
- Selling costs are $5 plus 12 cents per share.
- Automatic investment services are available.
- IRA option is available ($35 annual fee).
- Safekeeping services are available.
- Gift share transfers are available.
- Direct deposit of dividends is available.
- Dividends are paid March, June, September, and December.

*Performance Rating:* *****

**American Express Co. (NYSE:AXP)**
**200 Vessey St., 49th Floor**
**New York, NY 10285**
**(800) 842-7629, (800) 463-5911, (212) 640-2000**
www.americanexpress.com

*Business Profile:* Provides travel related, financial advisory, and international banking services worldwide.

*Performance History:* $1000 invested on 12/31/92 was worth $4617 on 12/31/97, a 362 percent increase in five years.

*Plan Specifics:*

- Initial shares can be purchased directly from the company ($1000 minimum). There is a one-time enrollment fee of $6 plus six cents per share.
- Partial dividend reinvestment is not available.
- No discount.
- OCP: $50 to $10,000 per month.
- Stock is purchased monthly with OCPs.
- Purchasing costs are $5 plus six cents per share.
- Selling costs are $10 plus 12 cents per share.
- Dividend reinvestment fee: 10 percent of amount invested (75 cents maximum) plus six cents per share.
- Automatic investment services are available ($3 plus six cents per share).
- Safekeeping services are available.
- Gift share transfers are available.
- Direct deposit of dividends is available.
- Dividends are paid February, May, August, and November.

*Performance Rating:* *****

**Ameritech Corp. (NYSE:AIT)**
30 S. Wacker Dr.
Chicago, IL 60606
(800) 774-4117, (888) 752-6248, (800) 233-1342, (800) 257-0902
www.ameritech.com

*Business Profile:* Major telephone holding company for upper-midwestern states.

*Performance History:* $1000 invested on 12/31/92 was worth $2813 on 12/31/97, a 181 percent increase in five years.

*Plan Specifics:*

■ Initial shares can be purchased directly from the company ($1000 minimum or automatic monthly investments of at least $100). There is a one-time enrollment fee of $10 ($6 for shares purchased via auto-invest) plus 10 cents per share.

■ Partial dividend reinvestment is available.

■ No discount.

■ OCP: $100 to $150,000 per year.

■ Stock is purchased weekly with OCPs.

■ Purchasing costs are $5 plus 10 cents per share.

■ Selling costs are $10 plus 12 cents per share.

■ Dividend reinvestment fee: five percent of amount invested ($1 minimum; $3 maximum per quarter)

■ Automatic investment services are available ($1 plus 10 cents per share).

■ IRA option is available.

■ Safekeeping services are available.

■ Gift share transfers are available.

■ A stockholder can borrow against holdings in the plan.

■ Direct deposit of dividends is available.

■ Dividends are paid February, May, August, and November.

*Performance Rating:* \*\*\*\*\*


**Amoco Corp. (NYSE:AN)**
200 E. Randolph Dr.
Chicago, IL 60601
(800) 774-4117, (800) 446-2617, (800) 826-6261, (312) 856-6111
www.amoco.com

*Business Profile:* Largest holder of natural-gas reserves in North America. Refines, markets, and transports crude oil and natural gas worldwide.

*Performance History:* $1000 invested on 12/31/92 was worth $2097 on 12/31/97, a 110 percent increase in five years.

*Plan Specifics:*

■ Initial shares can be purchased directly from the company ($450 minimum). There is a one-time enrollment fee of $8.50.

■ Partial dividend reinvestment is not available.

■ No discount.

■ OCP: $50 to $150,000 per year.

- Stock is purchased weekly with OCPs.
- Purchasing costs are five percent of amount invested ($3 maximum) plus seven cents per share.
- Selling costs are $10 plus 12 cents per share.
- Automatic investment services are available ($1 transaction fee).
- Shares can be sold via the telephone.
- Safekeeping services are available.
- Gift share transfers are available.
- Direct deposit of dividends is available.
- Dividends are paid March, June, September, and December.

*Performance Rating: *****

**Arrow Financial Corp. (NASDAQ: AROW)**
**250 Glen St.**
**Glen Falls, NY 12801**
**(518) 745-1000, (518) 793-4121**

*Business Profile:* Regional banking company with offices in New York and Vermont.

*Performance History:* $1000 invested on 12/31/92 was worth $5296 on 12/31/97, a 430 percent increase in five years.

*Plan Specifics:*

- Initial shares can be purchased directly from the company ($300 minimum).
- Partial dividend reinvestment is not available.
- No discount.
- OCP: $50 to $10,000 per quarter.
- Stock is purchased weekly with OCPs.
- Selling costs are brokerage fees.
- Dividends are paid March, June, September, and December.

*Performance Rating: ****

**Ascent Entertainment Group, Inc. (NASDAQ:GOAL)**
**Church St. Station**
**PO Box 11258**
**New York, NY 10286**
**(800) 727-7033**

*Business Profile:* Operates entertainment and other media businesses.

*Performance History:* Not available.

*Plan Specifics:*

- Initial shares can be purchased directly from the company ($100 minimum). There is a one-time enrollment fee of $7.50.
- Partial dividend reinvestment is available.
- No discount.
- OCP: $20 to $25,000 per year.
- Stock is purchased at least weekly with OCPs.
- Purchasing costs are $2 plus seven cents per share.

- Selling costs are $5 plus 10 cents per share.
- Dividend reinvestment fee: five percent of amount invested ($2 maximum) plus 10 cents per share.
- Automatic investment services are available ($2 plus seven cents per share).
- Safekeeping services are available.
- Gift share transfers are available.
- The company is not currently paying a dividend.

*Performance Rating:* **

**Atmos Energy Corp. (NYSE:ATO)**
**PO Box 650205**
**Dallas, TX 75265-0205**
**(800) 774-4117, (800) 382-8667, (800) 543-3038, (972) 934-9227**
www.atmosenergy.com

*Business Profile:* Supplies natural gas to residential, industrial, agricultural, and commercial users in parts of Kentucky, Louisiana, Texas, Colorado, Kansas, and Missouri.

*Performance History:* $1000 invested on 12/31/92 was worth $2399 on 12/31/97, a 140 percent increase in five years.

*Plan Specifics:*

- Initial shares can be purchased directly from the company ($200 minimum).
- Partial dividend reinvestment is available.
- There is a three percent discount on reinvested dividends.
- OCP: $25 to $100,000 per year.
- Stock is purchased weekly with OCPs.
- Selling costs are $5 plus brokerage fees.
- Automatic investment services are available.
- IRA option is available.
- Safekeeping services are available.
- Dividends are paid March, June, September, and December.

*Performance Rating:* ****

**Bank of New York Co., Inc. (NYSE:BK)**
**48 Wall St.**
**New York, NY 10286**
**(800) 727-7033, (800) 524-4458, (212) 495-1784**
www.bankofny.com

*Business Profile:*

*Performance History:* $1000 invested on 12/31/92 was worth $5005 on 12/31/97, a 400 percent increase in five years.

*Plan Specifics:*

- Initial shares can be purchased directly from the company ($1000 minimum).
- Partial dividend reinvestment is available.
- No discount.
- OCP: $50 to $150,000 per year.
- Stock is purchased monthly with OCPs.

- Selling costs are $2.50 plus brokerage fees.
- Dividends are paid February, May, August, and November.

*Performance Rating:* ****

**Bard (C.R.), Inc. (NYSE:BCR)**
**730 Central Ave.**
**Murray Hill, NJ 07974**
**(800) 828-1639, (908) 277-8000**

*Business Profile:* Supplies medical, diagnostic, and surgical products and is the largest manufacturer of urological products.

*Performance History:* $1000 invested on 12/31/92 was worth $1051 on 12/31/97, a five percent increase in five years.

*Plan Specifics:*

- Initial shares can be purchased directly from the company ($250 minimum). There is a one-time enrollment fee of $15 plus brokerage fees.
- Partial dividend reinvestment is available.
- No discount.
- OCP: $25 minimum; no maximum.
- Stock is purchased weekly with OCPs.
- Purchasing costs are five percent of investment ($10 maximum) plus brokerage fees.
- Selling costs are $15 plus brokerage fees.
- Dividends are paid February, May, August, and November.

*Performance Rating:* ****

**Becton, Dickinson and Company (NYSE:BDX)**
**One Becton Dr.**
**Franklin Lake, NJ 07417**
**(800) 955-4743, (201) 847-6800**

*Business Profile:* Producer of medical supplies and diagnostic equipment.

*Performance History:* $1000 invested on 12/31/92 was worth $2737 on 12/31/97, a 174 percent increase in five years.

*Plan Specifics:*

- Initial shares can be purchased directly from the company ($250 minimum or automatic monthly investment of at least $50).
- Partial dividend reinvestment is available.
- No discount.
- OCP: $50 minimum; no maximum.
- Stock is purchased at least weekly with OCPs.
- Purchasing costs are three cents per share.
- Selling costs are $15 plus 15 cents per share.
- Automatic investment services are available.
- Shares can be sold via the telephone.
- Dividends are paid March, June, September, and December.

*Performance Rating:* *****

**Bedford Property Investors, Inc. (NYSE:BED)**
**270 Lafayette Circle**
**Lafayette, CA 94549**
**(800) 774-5476, (800) 842-7629, (510) 283-8910**
www.bedfordproperty.com

*Business Profile:* Self-administered REIT with investments in industrial and suburban office properties concentrated in the western U.S.

*Performance History:* $1000 invested on 12/31/92 was worth $4607 on 12/31/97, a 361 percent increase in five years.

*Plan Specifics:*

- Initial shares can be purchased directly from the company ($1000 minimum).
- Partial dividend reinvestment is available.
- Up to three percent discount on reinvested dividends and OCPs.
- OCP: $100 to $5000 per month.
- Stock is purchased weekly with OCPs.
- Selling costs are $15 plus 12 cents per share.
- Automatic investment services are available.
- Safekeeping services are available.
- Gift share transfers are available.
- Dividends are paid January, April, July, and October.

*Performance Rating:* \*\*\*


**Bell Atlantic Corp. (NYSE:BEL)**
**1095 Avenue of the Americas**
**New York, NY 10036**
**(800) 266-6778, (212) 395-2121**
www.bellatlantic.com

*Business Profile:* Telephone holding company supplying exchange telephone service to Mid-Atlantic States.

*Performance History:* $1000 invested on 12/31/92 was worth $2205 on 12/31/97, a 121 percent increase in five years.

*Plan Specifics:*

- Initial shares may be purchased directly from the company ($1000 minimum). There is a one-time enrollment fee of $5.
- Partial dividend reinvestment is available.
- No discount.
- OCP: $50 to $200,000 per year.
- Stock is purchased weekly with OCPs.
- Purchasing costs are $2.50 plus three cents per share.
- Selling costs are $10 plus eight cents per share.
- Dividend reinvestment fee: five percent of amount invested ($1 minimum; $2 maximum per quarter).
- Automatic investment services are available ($1 transaction fee).
- IRA option is available ($35 annual fee).

■ Safekeeping services are available.

■ Dividends are paid February, May, August, and November.

*Performance Rating:* \*\*\*\*\*


**BellSouth Corp. (NYSE:BLS)**
**1155 Peachtree St. NE**
**Atlanta, GA 30309**
**(888) 887-2965, (800) 631-6001, (404) 249-2000**
www.bellsouth.com

*Business Profile:* Second-largest telephone holding company providing local exchange service to southeastern states.

*Performance History:* $1000 invested on 12/31/92 was worth $2707 on 12/31/97, a 171 percent increase in five years.

*Plan Specifics:*

■ Initial shares can be purchased directly from the company ($500 minimum) with a one-time enrollment fee of $10.

■ Partial dividend reinvestment is available.

■ No discount.

■ OCP: $50 to $100,000 per year.

■ Stock is purchased weekly with OCPs.

■ Selling costs include brokerage fees, a termination fee, and any transfer taxes.

■ Automatic investment services are available.

■ Safekeeping services are available.

■ Gift share transfers are available.

■ Direct deposit of dividends is available.

■ Dividends are paid February, May, August, and November.

*Performance Rating:* \*\*\*\*\*


**Bob Evans Farms, Inc. (NASDAQ:BOBE)**
**Stock Transfer Dept.**
**PO Box 07863**
**3776 S. High St.**
**Columbus, OH 43207**
**(800) 272-7675, (614) 491-2225**

*Business Profile:* Owns and operates over 300 Bob Evans Restaurants. Also produces fresh and fully cooked sausage products and deli-style salads.

*Performance History:* $1000 invested on 12/31/92 was worth $1089 on 12/31/97, a nine percent increase in five years.

*Plan Specifics:*

■ Initial shares can be purchased directly from the company by residents in 32 states ($50 minimum).

■ Partial dividend reinvestment is available.

■ No discount.

■ OCP: $10 to $10,000 per month.

■ Stock is purchased bimonthly with OCPs.

- Purchasing costs may include brokerage fees.
- Selling costs are brokerage fees.
- Automatic investment services are available.
- Dividends are paid March, June, September, and December.

*Performance Rating:* ****

**Borg-Warner Automotive, Inc. (NYSE:BWA)**
**200 S. Michigan Ave.**
**Chicago, IL 60604**
**(800) 774-4117, (800) 851-4229, (312) 322-8524**
www.bwauto.com

*Business Profile:* Global supplier of highly engineered systems and components, primarily for automotive powertrain applications.

*Performance History:* $1000 invested on 12/31/92 was worth $2226 on 12/31/97, a 123 percent increase in five years.

*Plan Specifics:*

- Initial shares can be purchased directly from the company ($500 minimum).
- Partial dividend reinvestment is available.
- No discount.
- OCP: $50 to $120,000 per year.
- Stock is purchased at least weekly OCPs.
- Selling costs are $15 plus 15 cents per share.
- Automatic investment services are available.
- Shares can be sold via the telephone.
- Safekeeping services are available.
- Gift share transfers are available.
- Direct deposit of dividends is available.
- Dividends are paid February, May, August, and November.

*Performance Rating:* ****

**Boston Beer Co., Inc. (NYSE:SAM)**
**75 Arlington St.**
**Boston, MA 02116**
**(888) 266-6780, (888) 877-2890**
www.samadams.com

*Business Profile:* Seventh largest producer of draft beer.

*Performance History:* Not available.

*Plan Specifics:*

- Initial shares can be purchased directly from the company ($500 minimum or automatic monthly investment of at least $50). There is a one-time enrollment fee of $10 plus 12 cents per share.
- Partial dividend reinvestment is not available.
- No discount.
- OCP: $50 to $10,000 per month.
- Stock is purchased weekly with OCPs.

- Purchasing costs are $5 plus 12 cents per share.
- Selling costs are $25 plus 12 cents per share.
- Automatic investment services are available ($3 transaction fee).
- Safekeeping services are available.
- Gift share transfers are available.
- The company is not currently paying a dividend.

*Performance Rating:* **

**Bowne & Co., Inc. (ASE:BNE)**
**345 Hudson St.**
**New York, NY 10014**
**(800) 524-4458, (212) 924-5500**
www.bowne.com

*Business Profile:* Specializes in financial documentation and communications services for corporate compliance and public financing worldwide.

*Performance History:* $1000 invested on 12/31/92 was worth $2617 on 12/31/97, a 162 percent increase in five years.

*Plan Specifics:*

- Initial shares can be purchased directly from the company ($500 minimum).
- Partial dividend reinvestment is available.
- No discount.
- OCP: $50 to $100,000 per year.
- Stock is purchased weekly with OCPs.
- Selling costs are $15 plus 12 cents per share.
- Automatic investment services are available.
- Safekeeping services are available.
- Gift share transfers are available.
- Dividends are paid March, June, September, and December.

*Performance Rating:* ****

**BRE Properties (NYSE:BRE)**
**One Montgomery St.**
**Telesis Tower, Suite 2500**
**San Francisco, CA 94104-5525**
**(800) 774-4117, (800) 368-8392, (415) 445-6530**
www.breproperties.com

*Business Profile:* Real estate investment trust investing mainly in housing.

*Performance History:* $1000 invested on 12/31/92 was worth $2557 on 12/31/97, a 156 percent increase in five years.

*Plan Specifics:*

- Initial shares can be purchased directly from the company ($500 minimum).
- Partial dividend reinvestment is available.
- No discount.
- OCP: $100 to $10,000 per month.
- Stock is purchased weekly with OCPs.

- Selling costs are $15 plus 12 cents per share.
- Waivers can be obtained for investing more than $10,000 per month by calling 415-445-6530.
- Dividends are paid in March, June, September, and December.

*Performance Rating:* \*\*\*

**Capstead Mortgage Corp. (NYSE:CMO)**
**2711 N. Haskell Ave., Suite 900**
**Dallas, TX 75204**
**(800) 468-9716, (800) 527-7844, (214) 874-2323**
www.capstead.com

*Business Profile:* Leader in the acquisition and security of single-family jumbo first mortgage loans.

*Performance History:* $1000 invested on 12/31/92 was worth $1932 on 12/31/97, a 93 percent increase in five years.

*Plan Specifics:*

- Initial shares can be purchased directly from the company ($250 minimum).
- Partial dividend reinvestment is available.
- Two percent discount on reinvested dividends and OCPs.
- OCP: $50 to $10,000 per month.
- Stock is purchased monthly with OCPs.
- Selling costs are $5 plus brokerage fees.
- Automatic investment services are available.
- Safekeeping services are available.
- Gift share transfers are available.
- Dividends are paid March, June, September, and December.

*Performance Rating:* \*\*

**Carpenter Technology Corp. (NYSE:CRS)**
**101 W. Bern St.**
**Reading, PA 19612**
**(800) 822-9828, (800) 446-2617, (610) 208-2000**
www.cartech.com

*Business Profile:* Produces stainless steel, special alloys, and tool steel.

*Performance History:* $1000 invested on 12/31/92 was worth $2239 on 12/31/97, a 124 percent increase in five years.

*Plan Specifics:*

- Initial shares can be purchased directly from the company ($500 minimum). There is a one-time enrollment fee of $10 plus 10 cents per share.
- Partial dividend reinvestment is available.
- No discount.
- OCP: $25 to $120,000 per year.
- Stock is purchased weekly with OCPs.
- Selling costs are $10 plus 12 cents per share.
- Automatic investment services are available ($1 transaction fee).

- Shares can be sold via the telephone.
- Safekeeping services are available.
- Gift share transfers are available.
- Direct deposit of dividends is available.
- Dividends are paid March, June, September, and December.

*Performance Rating:* ****

**Central & South West Corp. (NYSE:CSR)**
**PO Box 660164**
**Dallas, TX 75266-0164**
**(800) 774-4117, (800) 527-5797, (214) 777-1000**
www.csw.com

*Business Profile:* Utility holding company supplying electric and gas services to Texas, Oklahoma, Louisiana, and Arkansas customers.

*Performance History:* $1000 invested on 12/31/92 was worth $1296 on 12/31/97, a 30 percent increase in five years.

*Plan Specifics:*

- Initial shares can be purchased directly from the company ($250 minimum).
- Partial dividend reinvestment is available.
- No discount.
- OCP: $25 to $100,000 per year.
- Stock is purchased weekly with OCPs.
- Purchasing and selling costs are brokerage fees (not to exceed 10 cents per share).
- Automatic investment services are available.
- Safekeeping services are available.
- Dividends are paid February, May, August, and November.

*Performance Rating:* ***

**Central Hudson Gas & Electric Corp. (NYSE:CNH)**
**284 South Ave.**
**Poughkeepsie, NY 12601-4879**
**(888) 280-3848, (800) 428-9578, (914) 452-2000**
www.cenhud.com

*Business Profile:* Distributes electricity and gas to residential, commercial, and industrial customers in the Hudson River Valley region of New York.

*Performance History:* $1000 invested on 12/31/92 was worth $2004 on 12/31/97, a 100 percent increase in five years.

*Plan Specifics:*

- Initial shares can be purchased directly from the company ($100 minimum).
- Partial dividend reinvestment is available.
- No discount.
- OCP: $50 to $150,000 per year.
- Stock is purchased monthly with OCPs.
- Selling costs are brokerage fees.

- Shares can be sold via the telephone.
- Safekeeping services are available.
- Gift share transfers are available.
- Direct deposit of dividends is available.
- Dividends are paid February, May, August, and November.

*Performance Rating:* \*\*\*


**Chevron Corp. (NYSE:CHV)**
**225 Bush St.**
**San Francisco, CA 94104**
**(800) 774-4117, (800) 842-7629, (415) 894-3940**
www.chevron.com

*Business Profile:* Worldwide crude oil and natural-gas company with important involvements in petrochemicals and minerals.

*Performance History:* $1000 invested on 12/31/92 was worth $2675 on 12/31/97, a 168 percent increase in five years.

*Plan Specifics:*

- Initial shares can be purchased directly from the company ($250 minimum). There is a one-time enrollment fee of $5.
- Partial dividend reinvestment is available.
- No discount.
- OCP: $50 to $100,000 per year.
- Stock is purchased weekly with OCPs.
- Purchasing costs are $3 plus eight cents per share.
- Selling costs are $10 plus eight cents per share.
- Dividend reinvestment fee: five percent of amount invested ($2.50 maximum) plus eight cents per share.
- Automatic investment services are available ($1.50 plus eight cents per share).
- Safekeeping services are available.
- Gift share transfers are available.
- Direct deposit of dividends is available.
- Dividends are paid March, June, September, and December.

*Performance Rating:* \*\*\*\*\*


**Chock Full O'Nuts Corp. (NYSE:CHF)**
**370 Lexington Ave.**
**New York, NY 10017**
**(888) 200-3161, (212) 532-0300**
www.chockfullonuts.com

*Business Profile:* Leading processor of regular, instant, decaffeinated, and gourmet coffee. Also markets other food products.

*Performance History:* $1000 invested on 12/31/92 was worth $908 on 12/31/97, a nine percent decrease in five years.

*Plan Specifics:*
- Initial shares can be purchased directly from the company ($100 minimum).
- No discount.
- OCP: $50 to $100,000 per year.
- Stock is purchased weekly with OCPs.
- Purchasing costs are $7.50 plus 10 cents per share.
- Selling costs are $7.50 plus 10 cents per share.
- Automatic investment services are available.
- The company is not currently paying a dividend.

*Performance Rating:* **

**Chrysler Corp. (NYSE:C)**
**1000 Chrysler Dr.**
**CIMS 485 11 51**
**Auburn Hills, MI 48326**
**(800) 649-9896, (248) 576-5741**
www.chrysler.com

*Business Profile:* Major manufacturer of cars, trucks, and related parts and accessories. Manufactures vehicles under the Chrysler, Jeep, Dodge, and Plymouth brand names. Merging with Daimler-Benz.

*Performance History:* $1000 invested on 12/31/92 was worth $2585 on 12/31/97, a 158 percent increase in five years.

*Plan Specifics:*
- Initial shares can be purchased directly from the company ($1000 minimum or automatic monthly investment of at least $100 for 10 consecutive months). There is a one-time enrollment fee of $15.
- Partial dividend reinvestment is available.
- No discount.
- OCP: $50 to $350,000 per year.
- Stock is purchased weekly with OCPs.
- Purchasing costs are $5 plus three cents per share.
- Selling costs are $15 plus 12 cents per share.
- Dividend reinvestment fee: five percent of amount invested ($3 maximum).
- Automatic investment services are available ($2 plus three cents per share).
- Shares can be sold via the telephone.
- IRA option is available ($35 annual fee).
- Safekeeping services are available.
- Gift share transfers are available.
- You can borrow against holdings in the plan.
- Direct deposit of dividends is available.
- Dividends are paid January, April, July, and October.

*Performance Rating:* ***

**CILCORP, Inc. (NYSE:CER)**
**300 Hamilton Blvd., Suite 300**
**Peoria, IL 61602**
**(800) 774-4117, (800) 622-5514, (800) 322-3569, (309) 675-8810**
www.cilco.com

*Business Profile:* Public utility holding company providing electricity and gas to customers in central Illinois. Other businesses provide environmental consulting and analytical services.

*Performance History:* $1000 invested on 12/31/92 was worth $1708 on 12/31/97, a 71 percent increase in five years.

*Plan Specifics:*

■ Initial shares can be purchased directly from the company ($250 minimum).

■ Partial dividend reinvestment is available.

■ No discount.

■ OCP: $25 to $25,000 per quarter.

■ Stock is purchased monthly with OCPs.

■ Selling costs are brokerage fees.

■ Safekeeping services are available.

■ Preferred dividends can be reinvested for additional common shares under the plan. This provision applies to preferred dividends on Central Illinois Light Company preferred stock.

■ Dividends are paid March, June, September, and December.

*Performance Rating:* ***


**CMS Energy Corp. (NYSE:CMS)**
**Investor Service Dept.**
**212 W. Michigan Ave.**
**Jackson, MI 49201**
**(800) 774-4117, (517) 788-1867, (313) 436-9200**
www.cmsenergy.com

*Business Profile:* Principle subsidiary is Consumers Power, Michigan's largest utility.

*Performance History:* $1000 invested on 12/31/92 was worth $2818 on 12/31/97, a 182 percent increase in five years.

*Plan Specifics:*

■ Initial shares can be purchased directly from the company ($500 minimum).

■ Partial dividend reinvestment is available.

■ No discount.

■ OCP: $25 to $120,000 per year.

■ Stock is purchased monthly with OCPs.

■ Selling costs are brokerage fees.

■ Automatic investment services are available.

■ Safekeeping services are available.

■ Gift share transfers are available.

■ Preferred stock is eligible for reinvestment for CMS Energy common shares under the plan.

■ Direct deposit of dividends is available.

■ Dividends are paid February, May, August, and November.

*Performance Rating:* ****

**Coastal Corp. (NYSE:CGP)**
**Nine Greenway Plaza**
**Houston, TX 77046**
**(800) 788-2500, (713) 877-1400**
www.coastalcorp.com

*Business Profile:* Operates one of the largest U.S. natural-gas pipeline systems. Activities also include exploration and production, oil refining, and chemicals.

*Performance History:* $1000 invested on 12/31/92 was worth $2750 on 12/31/97, a 175 percent increase in five years.

*Plan Specifics:*

■ Initial shares can be purchased directly from the company ($250 minimum).

■ Partial dividend reinvestment is available.

■ No discount.

■ OCP: $50 to $120,000 per year.

■ Stock is purchased twice monthly with OCPs.

■ Purchasing costs are five cents per share.

■ Selling costs are five cents per share.

■ Automatic investment services are available.

■ Safekeeping services are available.

■ Gift share transfers are available.

■ Dividends are paid January, April, July, and October.

*Performance Rating:* ***

**Community Bank System, Inc. (NYSE:CBU)**
**5790 Widewaters Parkway**
**DeWitt, NY 13214**
**(800) 842-7629, (315) 445-2282**

*Business Profile:* Holding company for Community Bank, a provider of financial products and services.

*Performance History:* $1000 invested on 12/31/92 was worth $3165 on 12/31/97, a 217 percent increase in five years.

*Plan Specifics:*

■ Initial shares can be purchased directly from the company ($500 minimum). There is a one-time enrollment fee of $10.

■ Partial dividend reinvestment is available.

■ No discount.

■ OCP: $100 to $5000 per month.

■ Stock is purchased weekly with OCPs.

■ Purchasing costs are 12 cents per share.

■ Selling costs are $15 plus 12 cents per share.

■ Automatic investment services are available.

- Safekeeping services are available.
- Dividends are paid January, April, July, and October.

*Performance Rating:* \*\*\*

**Compaq Computer Corp. (NYSE:CPQ)**
**PO Box 692000 MS 110701**
**Houston, TX 77269**
**(888) 218-4373, (281) 370-0670**
www.compaq.com

*Business Profile:* Leading worldwide manufacturer of desktop and portable computers and PC servers. Products are sold in more than 100 countries through some 38,000 marketing locations.

*Performance History:* $1000 invested on 12/31/92 was worth $9178 on 12/31/97, an 818 percent increase in five years.

*Plan Specifics:*

- Initial shares can be purchased directly from the company ($250 minimum). There is a one-time enrollment fee of $10.
- Partial dividend reinvestment is available.
- No discount.
- OCP: $50 to $10,000 per month.
- Stock is purchased weekly with OCPs.
- Purchasing costs are $5 plus four cents per share.
- Selling costs are $10 plus seven cents per share.
- Automatic investment services are available ($2.50 plus four cents per share).
- Safekeeping services are available.
- Gift share transfers are available.
- Shares can be sold via telephone.
- Dividends are paid January, April, July, and October.

*Performance Rating:* \*\*\*\*

**COMSAT Corp. (NYSE:CQ)**
**Shareholder Services**
**6560 Rock Spring Dr.**
**Bethesda, MD 20817**
**(800) 727-7033, (301) 214-3200**
www.comsat.com

*Business Profile:* Provides satellite communications service, consulting service, and video entertainment operations.

*Performance History:* $1000 invested on 12/31/92 was worth $1370 on 12/31/97, a 37 percent increase in five years.

*Plan Specifics:*

- Initial shares can be purchased directly from the company ($250 minimum).
- Partial dividend reinvestment is not available.
- No discount.
- OCP: $50 to $40,000 per year.

- Stock is purchased monthly with OCPs.
- Selling costs are $5 plus six cents per share.
- Dividends are paid March, June, September, and December.

*Performance Rating:* ****

**Conectiv, Inc. (NYSE:CIV)**
**800 King St.**
**Wilmington, DE 19899**
**(800) 365-6495, (302) 429-3114**
www.aenergy.com

*Business Profile:* Public utility holding company with interests in energy-related products and services and telecommunications services.

*Performance History:* Not available.

*Plan Specifics:*

- Initial shares can be purchased directly from the company ($500 minimum). There is a one-time enrollment fee of $7.50.
- Partial dividend reinvestment is available.
- No discount.
- OCP: $50 to $200,000 per year.
- Stock is purchased weekly with OCPs.
- Purchasing costs are three cents per share.
- Selling costs are $5 plus three cents per share.
- Automatic investment services are available.
- Safekeeping services are available.
- Direct deposit of dividends is available.
- Dividends are paid January, April, July, and October.

*Performance Rating:* **

**Consolidated Freightways Corp. (NASDAQ:CFWY)**
**175 Linfield Dr.**
**Menlo Park, CA 94025**
**(800) 727-7033, (800) 524-4458, (415) 326-1700**
www.cfwy.com

*Business Profile:* Provides general freight service across the U.S., Canada, and Mexico.

*Performance History:* $1000 invested on 12/31/92 was worth $1689 on 12/31/97, a 69 percent increase in five years.

*Plan Specifics:*

- Initial shares can be purchased directly from the company ($100 minimum). There is a one-time enrollment fee of $7.50.
- No discount.
- OCP: $25 to $50,000 per year.
- Stock is purchased at least weekly with OCPs.
- Selling costs are $15 plus 12 cents per share.
- Automatic investment services are available.
- Shares can be sold via the telephone.

- Safekeeping services are available.
- The company is not currently paying a dividend.

*Performance Rating:* \*\*\*

**CRIIMI MAE Inc. (NYSE:CMM)**
**11200 Rockville Pike**
**Rockville, MD 20852**
**(888) 266-6785, (800) 266-0535, (301) 816-2300**

*Business Profile:* Self-administered REIT that invests in government-insured and guaranteed mortgages, as well as uninsured mortgage and mortgage-related products.

*Performance History:* $1000 invested on 12/31/92 was worth $2532 on 12/31/97, a 153 percent increase in five years.

*Plan Specifics:*

- Initial shares can be purchased directly from the company ($500 minimum).
- Partial dividend reinvestment is available.
- Two percent discount on reinvested dividends and OCPs.
- OCP: $100 to $10,000 per month.
- Stock is purchased monthly with OCPs.
- Selling costs are $10 plus brokerage fees.
- Automatic investment services are available.
- Safekeeping services are available.
- Gift share transfers are available.
- Dividends are paid March, June, September, and December.

*Performance Rating:* \*\*\*

**Cross Timbers Oil Co. (NYSE:XTO)**
**810 Houston St., Suite 2000**
**Fort Worth, TX 76102**
**(800) 774-4117, (888) 877-2892, (817) 870-2800**
www.crosstimbers.com

*Business Profile:* Operates oil and gas wells in Oklahoma, Texas, New Mexico, and Wyoming.

*Performance History:* $1000 invested on 12/31/92 was worth $2590 on 12/31/97, a 159 percent increase in five years.

*Plan Specifics:*

- Initial shares can be purchased directly from the company ($500 minimum).
- Partial dividend reinvestment is available.
- No discount.
- OCP: $50 to $10,000 per month.
- Stock is purchased weekly with OCPs.
- Purchasing costs are 12 cents per share.
- Selling costs are $15 plus 12 cents per share.
- Safekeeping services are available.

- Gift share transfers are available.
- Direct deposit of dividends is available.
- Dividends are paid January, April, July, and October.

*Performance Rating:* ***


**Crown American Realty Trust (NYSE:CWN)**
**Pasquerilla Plaza**
**Johnstown, PA 15907**
**(800) 774-4117, (814) 536-4441**
www.crownam.com

*Business Profile:* Self-administered REIT that owns, operates, and develops enclosed shopping malls in Pennsylvania and six other states.

*Performance History:* $1000 invested on 12/31/92 was worth $812 on 12/31/97, a 19 percent decrease in five years.

*Plan Specifics:*

- Initial shares can be purchased directly from the company ($100 minimum).
- Partial dividend reinvestment is available.
- No discount.
- OCP: $100 to $5000 per quarter.
- Stock is purchased monthly with OCPs.
- Selling costs are brokerage plus other fees.
- Dividends are paid March, June, September, and December.

*Performance Rating:* **


**CSX Corp. (NYSE:CSX)**
**901 E. Cary St.**
**Richmond, VA 23219-4031**
**(800) 774-4117, (800) 521-5571, (804) 782-1400**
www.csx.com

*Business Profile:* Provides rail, shipping, barge, and logistics services.

*Performance History:* $1000 invested on 12/31/92 was worth $1743 on 12/31/97, a 74 percent increase in five years.

*Plan Specifics:*

- Initial shares can be purchased directly from the company ($500 minimum). There is a one-time enrollment fee of $10.
- Partial dividend reinvestment is available.
- No discount.
- OCP: $50 to $10,000 per month.
- Stock is purchased weekly with OCPs.
- Selling costs are $10 plus 15 cents per share.
- Automatic investment services are available.
- Safekeeping services are available.
- Gift share transfers are available.
- Dividends are paid March, June, September, and December.

*Performance Rating:* ****

**Curtiss-Wright Corp. (NYSE:CW)**
**1200 Wall St. W.**
**Lyndhurst, NJ 07071**
**(888) 266-6793, (800) 416-3743, (201) 896-8400**

*Business Profile:* Manufacturer of components and systems used in the aerospace, industrial, flow-control, and marine industries.

*Performance History:* $1000 invested on 12/31/92 was worth $2545 on 12/31/97, a 154 percent increase in five years.

*Plan Specifics:*

- Initial shares can be purchased directly from the company ($2000 minimum or automatic monthly investment of at least $100).
- Partial dividend reinvestment is available.
- Twenty share minimum for reinvestment of dividends.
- No discount.
- OCP: $100 to $10,000 per month.
- Stock is purchased at least weekly with OCPs.
- Purchasing costs are $5.
- Selling costs are $15 plus 12 cents per share.
- Dividend reinvestment fee: five percent of amount invested ($2.50 maximum).
- Automatic investment services are available.
- Safekeeping services are available.
- Gift share transfers are available.
- Dividends are paid January, April, July, and October.

*Performance Rating:* \*\*\*


**Darden Restaurants, Inc. (NYSE:DRI)**
**5900 Lake Ellenor Dr.**
**Orlando, FL 32809**
**(800) 829-8432, (407) 245-4000**

*Business* Profile: Operates chains of restaurants across the U.S., including 652 Red Lobster's and 461 Olive Garden's.

*Performance History:* Not available.

*Plan Specifics:*

- Initial shares can be purchased directly from the company ($1000 minimum). There is a one-time enrollment fee of $10.
- Partial dividend reinvestment is available.
- 50 share minimum for reinvestment of dividends.
- No discount.
- OCP: $50 to $25,000 per quarter.
- Stock is purchased weekly with OCPs.
- Purchasing costs are $5 plus 10 cents per share.
- Selling costs are $15 plus 10 cents per share.
- Automatic investment services are available ($1.50 transaction fee).
- Dividend reinvestment fee: five percent of amount invested ($1 minimum, $5 maximum).

- Safekeeping services are available.
- Gift share transfers are available.
- Direct deposit of dividends is available.
- Dividends are paid May and November.

*Performance Rating:* ***

**Dayton Hudson Corp. (NYSE:DH)**
**Attn: Investor Relations Dept.**
**777 Nicollet Mall**
**Minneapolis, MN 55402**
**(888) 268-0203, (800) 317-4445, (612) 370-6732**
www.shop-at.com

*Business Profile:* Operator of department and retail stores.

*Performance History:* $1000 invested on 12/31/92 was worth $2951 on 12/31/97, a 195 percent increase in five years.

*Plan Specifics:*

- Initial shares can be purchased directly from the company ($500 minimum or automatic monthly investments of at least $50 for 10 consecutive months). There is a one-time enrollment fee of $10 plus 10 cents per share.
- Partial dividend reinvestment is available.
- No discount.
- OCP: $50 to $100,000 per year.
- Stock is purchased at least weekly with OCPs.
- Purchasing costs are $5 plus 10 cents per share.
- Selling costs are $10 plus 12 cents per share.
- Dividend reinvestment fee: five percent of amount invested ($3 maximum) plus 10 cents per share.
- Automatic investment services are available ($2 plus 10 cents per share).
- Shares can be sold via the telephone.
- Safekeeping services are available.
- Gift share transfers are available.
- Direct deposit of dividends is available.
- Dividends are paid March, June, September, and December.

*Performance Rating:* ****

**Deere and Co. (NYSE:DE)**
**John Deere Road**
**Moline, IL 61265**
**(800) 268-7369, (309) 765-8000**
www.deere.com

*Business Profile:* One of the largest producers of farm equipment. Also produces construction machinery and lawn and garden equipment.

*Performance History:* $1000 invested on 12/31/92 was worth $4567 on 12/31/97, a 357 percent increase in five years.

*Plan Specifics:*

- Initial shares can be purchased directly from the company ($500 minimum). There is a one-time enrollment fee of $7.50 plus three cents per share.
- Partial dividend reinvestment is available.
- No discount.
- OCP: $100 to $10,000 per month.
- Stock is purchased weekly with OCPs.
- Purchasing costs are $3 plus five cents per share.
- Selling costs are $10 plus five cents per share.
- Dividend reinvestment fee: five percent of amount invested ($3 maximum) plus five cents per share.
- Automatic investment services are available ($1 transaction fee).
- Safekeeping services are available.
- Gift share transfers are available.
- Direct deposit of dividends is available.
- Dividends are paid February, May, August, and November.

*Performance Rating:* \*\*\*\*

**Disney (Walt) Co. (NYSE:DIS)**
**PO Box 11447**
**Burbank, CA 91510-1447**
**(800) 948-2222, (818) 553-7200**
www.disney.com

*Business Profile:* Major entertainment company with broadcasting, movie, and theme-park operations.

*Performance History:* $1000 invested on 12/31/92 was worth $2379 on 12/31/97, a 138 percent increase in five years.

*Plan Specifics:*

- Initial shares can be purchased directly from the company ($1000 minimum or automatic monthly investments of at least $100). There is a one-time enrollment fee of $10.
- If you do not make your initial purchase of stock directly, you need at least 10 shares in order to enroll in the plan.
- No discount.
- Partial dividend reinvestment is not available.
- OCP: $100 to $250,000 per year.
- Stock is purchased at least weekly and daily, if practicable, with OCPs.
- Purchasing costs are $5 plus four cents per share.
- Selling costs are $10 plus four cents per share.
- Automatic investment services are available ($1 plus four cents per share).
- You must maintain at least five whole shares of Disney in your plan account. If your account balance falls below five shares, your participation in the plan may be terminated. If you are a new investor who has signed up for automatic

debit, your account will be exempt from this requirement until you accumulate five whole shares in the account.

■ Dividends are paid February, May, August, and November.

*Performance Rating:* *****


**Dominion Resources, Inc. (NYSE:D)**
**PO Box 26532**
**Richmond, VA 23261**
**(800) 552-4034, (804) 775-5700**
www.domres.com

*Business Profile:* Electric utility holding company serving Virginia and North Carolina.

*Performance History:* $1000 invested on 12/31/92 was worth $1491 on 12/31/97, a 49 percent increase in five years.

*Plan Specifics:*

■ Initial shares can be purchased directly from the company ($250 minimum).

■ Partial dividend reinvestment is available.

■ No discount.

■ OCP: $40 up to $100,000 per quarter.

■ Stock is purchased monthly with OCPs.

■ Selling costs are brokerage fees.

■ Automatic investment services are available.

■ Safekeeping services are available.

■ Dividends are paid March, June, September, and December.

*Performance Rating:* ****


**Dow Jones and Company (NYSE:DJ)**
**200 Liberty St.**
**New York, NY 10281**
**(800) 842-7629, (212) 416-2000**
www.dowjones.com

*Business Profile:* Publisher of *The Wall Street Journal* and *Barron's.* Dow Jones provides newswire and news retrieval services.

*Performance History:* $1000 invested on 12/31/92 was worth $2210 on 12/31/97, a 121 percent increase in five years.

*Plan Specifics:*

■ Initial shares can be purchased directly from the company ($1000 minimum). The company will waive the minimum if an investor agrees to automatic monthly investments of at least $100. There is a one-time enrollment fee of $5.

■ Partial dividend reinvestment is available.

■ Ten share minimum for reinvestment of dividends.

■ No discount.

■ OCP: $100 to $10,000 per month.

■ Stock is purchased weekly with OCPs.

■ Purchasing costs are 12 cents per share.

- Selling costs are $15 plus 12 cents per share.
- Automatic investment services are available.
- Safekeeping services are available.
- Gift share transfers are available.
- Dividends are paid February, May, August, and November.

*Performance Rating:* ***


**DQE, Inc. (NYSE:DQE)**
**Dividend Reinvestment**
**PO Box 68**
**Pittsburgh, PA 15230-0068**
**(800) 247-0400, (412) 393-6167**
www.dqe.com

*Business Profile:* The principal subsidiary, Duquesne Light Company, provides electric power to customers in southwestern Pennsylvania.

*Performance History:* $1000 invested on 12/31/92 was worth $2112 on 12/31/97, a 111 percent increase in five years.

*Plan Specifics:*

- Initial shares can be purchased directly from the company (minimum $100). There is a one-time enrollment fee of $5.
- Partial dividend reinvestment is available.
- No discount.
- OCP: $10 to $60,000 per year.
- Stock is purchased monthly with OCPs.
- Purchasing costs are five cents per share.
- Selling costs are seven cents per share.
- Automatic investment services are available.
- Preferred dividends can be reinvested for additional common shares under the plan.
- Dividends are paid January, April, July, and October.

*Performance Rating:* ****


**DTE Energy (NYSE:DTE)**
**PO Box 33380**
**Detroit, MI 48232**
**(800) 774-4117, (800) 551-5009, (313) 235-4000**
www.dteenergy.com

*Business Profile:* Supplies electricity and steam to customers in southeastern Michigan.

*Performance History:* $1000 invested on 12/31/92 was worth $1516 on 12/31/97, a 52 percent increase in five years.

*Plan Specifics:*

- Initial shares can be purchased directly from the company ($100 minimum).
- Partial dividend reinvestment is available.
- No discount.

- OCP: $25 to $100,000 per year.
- Stock is purchased monthly with OCPs.
- Purchasing costs are $1 plus brokerage fees.
- Selling costs are brokerage fees.
- Safekeeping services are available.
- Gift share transfers are available.
- Preferred dividends can be reinvested for additional common shares under the plan.
- Dividends are paid January, April, July, and October.

*Performance Rating:* **

**Duke Realty Investments, Inc. (NYSE:DRE)**
**8888 Keystone Crossing, Suite 1200**
**Indianapolis, IN 46240**
**(800) 774-4117, (800) 278-4353, (317) 574-3531**
www.dukereit.com

*Business Profile:* Real estate investment trust that focuses on warehouses and office buildings.

*Performance History:* $1000 invested on 12/31/92 was worth $4238 on 12/31/97, a 324 percent increase in five years.

*Plan Specifics:*

- Initial shares can be purchased directly from the company ($250 minimum).
- Partial dividend reinvestment is not available.
- Four percent discount on reinvested dividends.
- OCP: $100 to $5000 per month.
- Stock is purchased monthly with OCPs.
- Selling costs are brokerage fees.
- Automatic investment services are available.
- Safekeeping services are available.
- Dividends are paid February, May, August, and November.

*Performance Rating:* ****

**Eastern Company**
**(ASE:EML)**
**112 Bridge St.**
**Naugatuck, CT 06770**
**(800) 633-3455, (203) 729-2255**

*Business Profile:* Maker of security products that serves the industrial, transportation, and underground mining markets.

*Performance History:* $1000 invested on 12/31/92 was worth $2236 on 12/31/97, a 124 percent increase in five years.

*Plan Specifics:*

- Initial shares can be purchased directly from the company ($250 minimum). There is a one-time enrollment fee of $5.
- Partial dividend reinvestment is available.

- No discount.
- OCP: $50 to $150,000 per year.
- Stock is purchased weekly with OCPs.
- Selling costs are a five percent service charge ($1 minimum, $10 maximum) plus 10 cents per share.
- Automatic investment services are available.
- Safekeeping services are available.
- Dividends are paid March, June, September, and December.

*Performance Rating:* ***

**Eastman Kodak Co. (NYSE:EK)**
**343 State St.**
**Rochester, NY 14650**
**(800) 253-6057, (716) 724-4000**
www.kodak.com

*Business Profile:* Largest worldwide manufacturer of photographic products.

*Performance History:* $1000 invested on 12/31/92 was worth $2165 on 12/31/97, a 117 percent increase in five years.

*Plan Specifics:*

- Initial shares can be purchased directly from the company ($150 minimum).
- Partial dividend reinvestment is available.
- No discount.
- OCP: $50 to $120,000 per year.
- Stock is purchased weekly with OCPs.
- Selling costs are $10 plus 10 cents per share.
- Automatic investment services are available.
- Shares can be sold via the telephone.
- Safekeeping services are available.
- Gift share transfers are available.
- Dividends are paid January, April, July, and October.

*Performance Rating:* ****

**EMCEE Broadcast Products, Inc. (NASDAQ:ECIN)**
**PO Box 68**
**Susquehanna St. Extension**
**White Haven, PA 18661**
**(888) 200-3167, (717) 443-9575**
www.emcee-brd.com

*Business Profile:* Producer of television-transmission products, including microwave transmitters for the wireless-cable industry, and low-power television transmitters for the broadcast industry.

*Performance History:* Not available.

*Plan Specifics:*

- Initial shares can be purchased directly from the company ($100 minimum).
- No discount.

- OCP: $50 to $10,000 per transaction ($100,000 per year).
- Stock is purchased weekly with OCPs.
- Purchasing costs are $7.50 plus 10 cents per share.
- Selling costs are $7.50 plus 10 cents per share.
- Dividend reinvestment fee: four percent of amount invested ($4 maximum) plus six cents per share.
- Automatic investment services are available.
- Shares can be sold via the telephone.
- Safekeeping services are available.
- The company is not currently paying a dividend.

*Performance Rating: NR*

**Energen Corp. (NYSE:EGN)**
**2101 Sixth Ave., N.**
**Birmingham, AL 35203**
**(800) 774-4117, (800) 286-9178, (205) 326-2700**
www.energen.com

*Business Profile:* Parent company for Alabama gas utility and oil and gas exploration company.

*Performance History:* $1000 invested on 12/31/92 was worth $2727 on 12/31/97, a 173 percent increase in five years.

*Plan Specifics:*

- Initial shares can be purchased directly from the company ($250 minimum).
- Partial dividend reinvestment is available.
- No discount.
- OCP: $25 to $100,000 per year.
- Stock is purchased monthly with OCPs.
- Selling costs are brokerage fees and transfer taxes.
- Automatic investment services are available.
- Safekeeping services are available.
- Gift share transfers are available.
- Direct deposit of dividends is available.
- Dividends are paid March, June, September, and December.

*Performance Rating: *****

**Enron Corp. (NYSE:ENE)**
**1400 Smith St.**
**Houston, TX 77002**
**(800) 662-7662, (800) 446-2617, (713) 853-6161**
www.enron.com

*Business Profile:* Operates large natural-gas pipeline facility and is involved in oil and gas production.

*Performance History:* $1000 invested on 12/31/92 was worth $2011 on 12/31/97, a 101 percent increase in five years.

*Plan Specifics:*

■ Initial shares can be purchased directly from the company ($250 minimum). There is a one-time enrollment fee of $17 plus brokerage fees.

■ Partial dividend reinvestment is available.

■ No discount.

■ OCP: $25 to $120,000 per year.

■ Stock is purchased weekly with OCPs.

■ Selling costs are $15 plus 12 cents per share.

■ Automatic investment services are available ($1 transaction fee).

■ Shares can be sold via the telephone.

■ Safekeeping services are available.

■ Gift share transfers are available.

■ Direct deposit of dividends is available.

■ Dividends are paid March, June, September, and December.

*Performance Rating:* \*\*\*\*


**Entergy Corp. (NYSE:ETR)**
**639 Loyola Ave.**
**New Orleans, LA 70113**
**(800) 225-1721, (800) 333-4368, (504) 529-5262**
www.entergy.com

*Business Profile:* Utility holding company serving portions of Arkansas, Louisiana, Mississippi, Missouri, and Texas.

*Performance History:* $1000 invested on 12/31/92 was worth $1249 on 12/31/97, a 25 percent increase in five years.

*Plan Specifics:*

■ Initial shares can be purchased directly from the company ($1000 minimum).

■ Partial dividend reinvestment is available.

■ Up to three percent discount on OCPs.

■ OCP: $100 to $3000 per month.

■ Stock is purchased monthly with OCPs.

■ Purchasing costs include brokerage fees.

■ Selling costs include brokerage fees.

■ Dividends are paid March, June, September, and December.

*Performance Rating:* \*\*


**Equifax, Inc. (NYSE:EFX)**
**PO Box 4081**
**1600 Peachtree St. NW**
**Atlanta, GA 30302**
**(888) 887-2971, (800) 568-3476, (404) 885-8000**

*Business Profile:* Provides information services to businesses for insurance claims and credit evaluation purposes.

*Performance History:* $1000 invested on 12/31/92 was worth $4204 on 12/31/97, a 320 percent increase in five years.

*Plan Specifics:*

■ Initial shares can be purchased directly from the company ($500 minimum).

■ Partial dividend reinvestment is not available.

■ No discount.

■ OCP: $50 to $10,000 per month.

■ Stock is purchased weekly with OCPs.

■ Initial and subsequent purchasing costs are $5 plus seven cents per share.

■ Selling costs are $15 plus seven cents per share.

■ Automatic investment services are available.

■ Dividends are paid March, June, September, and December.

*Performance Rating:* *****

**Equitable Companies, Inc. (NYSE:EQ)**
**787 Seventh Ave.**
**New York, NY 10019**
**(800) 437-8736, (212)-554-1234**
www.eqshare.com

*Business Profile:* Financial services organization involved in the sale of individual life insurance and annuities and in asset management and investment banking.

*Performance History:* $1000 invested on 12/31/92 was worth $3704 on 12/31/97, a 270 percent increase in five years.

*Plan Specifics:*

■ Initial shares can be purchased directly from the company ($500 minimum).

■ Partial dividend reinvestment is not available.

■ No discount.

■ OCP: $50 to $50,000 per year.

■ Stock is purchased weekly with OCPs.

■ Selling costs are $10 plus 12 cents per share.

■ Automatic investment services are available.

■ Dividends are paid March, June, September, and December.

*Performance Rating:* ****

**Equity Residential Properties Trust (NYSE:EQR)**
**Two N. Riverside Plaza, Suite 400**
**Chicago, IL 60606**
**(800) 337-5666, (312) 474-1300**
www.eqr.com

*Business Profile:* Self-administered and self-managed equity real estate investment trust.

*Performance History:* $1000 invested on 12/31/92 was worth $2352 on 12/31/97, a 135 percent increase in five years.

*Plan Specifics:*

■ Initial shares can be purchased directly from the company ($250 minimum).

■ Partial dividend reinvestment is available.

■ Up to five percent discount on OCPs.

- OCP: $250 to $5000 per month.
- Stock is purchased monthly with OCPs.
- Selling costs are service charges plus brokerage fees.
- Automatic investment services are available.
- Safekeeping services are available.
- Dividends are paid January, April, July, and October.

*Performance Rating:* \*\*\*


**Essex Property Trust, Inc. (NYSE:ESS)**
**925 E. Meadow Drive**
**Palo Alto, CA 94303**
**(800) 945-8245, (650) 494-3700**

*Business Profile:* Self-administered and self-managed REIT that owns and operates more than 40 multi-family real estate investments and retail properties.

*Performance History:* Not available.

*Plan Specifics:*

- Initial shares can be purchased directly from the company ($100 minimum).
- Partial dividend reinvestment is available.
- No discount.
- OCP: $100 to $20,000 per month.
- Stock is purchased weekly with OCPs.
- Purchasing costs are $5.
- Selling costs are $10 plus 15 cents per share.
- Automatic investment services are available.
- Safekeeping services are available.
- Dividends are paid January, April, July, and October.

*Performance Rating:* \*\*\*


**Exxon Corp. (NYSE:XON)**
**PO Box 160369**
**Irving, TX 75016**
**(800) 252-1800, (972) 444-1000**
www.exxon.com

*Business Profile:* Major factor in worldwide petroleum markets.

*Performance History:* $1000 invested on 12/31/92 was worth $2446 on 12/31/97, a 145 percent increase in five years.

*Plan Specifics:*

- Initial shares can be purchased directly from the company ($250 minimum).
- Partial dividend reinvestment is available.
- No discount.
- OCP: $50 to $200,000 per year.
- Stock is purchased weekly with OCPs.
- Selling costs are $5 plus brokerage fees.
- Automatic investment services are available.

- IRA option is available ($20 annual fee).
- Safekeeping services are available.
- Gift share transfers are available.
- Direct deposit of dividends is available.
- Dividends are paid March, June, September, and December.

*Performance Rating:* *****

**Fannie Mae (NYSE:FNM)**
**3900 Wisconsin Ave. NW**
**Washington, DC 20016**
**(888) 289-3266, (800) 910-8277, (202) 752-7115**

*Business Profile:* Largest secondary buyer of real-estate mortgages in the US.

*Performance History:* $1000 invested on 12/31/92 was worth $3393 on 12/31/97, a 239 percent increase in five years.

*Plan Specifics:*

- Initial shares can be purchased directly from the company ($250 minimum or an automatic monthly investment of at least $25 for 12 consecutive months). For participants in Young Shareholder Account, the minimum is $100, or $12 through automatic monthly investment with a minimum of 12 consecutive purchases. There is a one-time enrollment fee of $15.
- Partial dividend reinvestment is available.
- Thirty-five share minimum for reinvestment of dividends.
- No discount.
- OCP: $25 ($10 for Young Shareholder Accounts) to $250,000 per year.
- Stock is purchased weekly with OCPs.
- Purchasing costs are $5 for investments of $25 to $2500; investments greater than $2500 are $5 plus brokerage fees. For Young Shareholder Accounts, purchasing costs are free for investments of $10 to $100, $5 for investments of $25 to $2500, and $5 plus brokerage fees for investments greater than $2500.
- Selling costs are $15 plus brokerage fees for all accounts.
- Automatic investment services are available.
- Shares can be sold via the telephone.
- IRA option is available ($35 annual fee).
- Safekeeping services are available.
- Gift share transfers are available.
- Direct deposit of dividends is available.
- Dividends are paid February, May, August, and November.

*Performance Rating:* *****

**Fed One Bancorp (NYSE:FOBC)**
**21 Twelfth St.**
**Wheeling, WV 26003**
**(800) 742-7540, (888) 261-6780, (304) 234-1100**
www.fedone.com

*Business Profile:* A holding company for Fed OneBank operating in West Virginia and Ohio.

*Performance History:* $1000 invested on 12/31/92 was worth $5476 on 12/31/97, a 448 percent increase in five years.

*Plan Specifics:*

- Initial shares can be purchased directly from the company ($250 minimum). There is a one-time enrollment fee of $5.
- Partial dividend reinvestment is available.
- No discount.
- OCP: $100 to $10,000 per month.
- Stock is purchased weekly with OCPs.
- Purchasing costs are $5.
- Selling costs are $15 plus 12 cents per share.
- Automatic investment services are available.
- Safekeeping services are available.
- Gift share transfers are available.
- Dividends are paid January, April, July, and October.

*Performance Rating:* ***

**Finova Group, Inc. (NYSE:FNV)**
**1850 N. Central Ave., MS 1159**
**Phoenix, AZ 85004**
**(800) 774-4117, (800) 734-6682 Ext. 2821, (602) 207-2821**
www.finova.com

*Business Profile:* Major finance company specializing in "middle market" deals.

*Performance History:* $1000 invested on 12/31/92 was worth $4617 on 12/31/97, a 362 percent increase in five years.

*Plan Specifics:*

- Initial shares can be purchased directly from the company ($500 minimum).
- Partial dividend reinvestment is available.
- No discount.
- OCP: $50 to $25,000 per quarter.
- Stock is purchased weekly with OCPs.
- Selling costs are $10 plus eight cents per share.
- Automatic investment services are available.
- Safekeeping services are available.
- Gift share transfers are available.
- Direct deposit of dividends is available.
- Dividends are paid January, April, July, and October.

*Performance Rating:* *****

**First Financial Holdings, Inc. (NASDAQ:FFCH)**
**34 Broad St.**
**Charleston, SC 29401**
**(800) 998-9151, (803) 529-5800**

*Business Profile:* Holding company for First Federal Savings and Loan Association, which operates 33 banking offices in eastern South Carolina.

*Performance History:* $1000 invested on 12/31/92 was worth $5930 on 12/31/97, a 493 percent increase in five years.

*Plan Specifics:*

■ Initial shares can be purchased directly from the company ($250 minimum).
■ Partial dividend reinvestment is available.
■ No discount.
■ OCP: $100 to $5000 per month.
■ Stock is purchased daily with OCPs.
■ Selling costs are $3.50 plus brokerage fees.
■ Automatic investment services are available.
■ Safekeeping services are available.
■ Gift share transfers are available.
■ Dividends are paid February, May, August, and November.

*Performance Rating:* ***

**FirstEnergy Corp. (NYSE:FE)**
**76 S. Main St.**
**Akron, OH 44308**
**(800) 736-3402, (330) 384-5100**
www.firstenergycorp.com

*Business Profile:* Provides service to 2.1 million customers in north and central Ohio and western Pennsylvania.

*Performance History:* Not available.

*Plan Specifics:*

■ Initial shares can be purchased directly from the company ($250 minimum).
■ Partial dividend reinvestment is available.
■ No discount.
■ OCP: $25 to $100,000 per year.
■ Stock is purchased bimonthly with OCPs.
■ Purchasing costs are brokerage fees (nine cents per share maximum).
■ Selling costs are brokerage fees (nine cents per share maximum).
■ Safekeeping services are available.
■ Direct deposit of dividends is available.
■ Dividends are paid March, June, September, and December.

*Performance Rating:* **

**Food Lion, Inc. Class A (NASDAQ:FDLNA)**
**PO Box 1330**
**2110 Executive Dr.**
**Salisbury, NC 28145**
**(888) 232-9530, (704) 633-8250**
www.foodlion.com

*Business Profile:* Operates retail food supermarkets primarily in the southeastern U.S.

*Performance History:* $1000 invested on 12/31/92 was worth $1158 on 12/31/97, a 16 percent increase in five years.

*Plan Specifics:*

- Initial shares can be purchased directly from the company ($250 minimum or automatic monthly investment of at least $50 for five consecutive months). There is a one-time enrollment fee of $10.
- Partial dividend reinvestment is available.
- No discount.
- OCP: $50 to $150,000 per year.
- Stock is purchased at least weekly with OCPs.
- Purchasing costs are $5 plus brokerage fees.
- Selling costs are $15 plus brokerage fees.
- Automatic investment services are available ($2 transaction fee).
- Shares can be sold via the telephone.
- Safekeeping services are available.
- Gift share transfers are available.
- Direct deposit of dividends is available.
- Dividends are paid January, April, July, and October.

*Performance Rating:* \*\*\*

**Ford Motor Co. (NYSE:F)**
**The American Road**
**Dearborn, MI 48121**
**(800) 955-4791, (800) 279-1237, (313) 322-3000**
www.ford.com

*Business Profile:* Second largest motor vehicle manufacturer.

*Performance History:* $1000 invested on 12/31/92 was worth $2748 on 12/31/97, a 175 percent increase in five years.

*Plan Specifics:*

- Initial shares can be purchased directly from the company ($1000 minimum or automatic monthly investments of at least $100 for 10 consecutive months). One-time enrollment fee of $10 plus three cents per share.
- Partial dividend reinvestment is available.
- No discount.
- OCP: $50 to $250,000 per year.
- Stock is purchased weekly with OCPs.
- Purchasing costs are $5 plus three cents per share.
- Selling costs are $15 plus 12 cents per share.
- Dividend reinvestment fee: five percent of amount invested ($5 maximum) plus three cents per share.
- Automatic investment services are available ($1 plus three cents per share).
- Shares can be sold via the telephone.
- IRA option is available ($35 annual fee).
- Safekeeping services are available.

■ Gift share transfers are available.

■ You can borrow against holdings in the plan.

■ Dividends are paid March, June, September, and December.

*Performance Rating:* ****

**Frontier Insurance Group, Inc. (NYSE:FTR)**
**195 Lake Louise Marie Road**
**Rock Hill, NY 12775**
**(888) 200-3162, (914) 796-2100**

*Business Profile:* Property and casualty insurer and reinsurer whose principal lines include medical and dental malpractice.

*Performance History:* $1000 invested on 12/31/92 was worth $1899 on 12/31/97, a 90 percent increase in five years.

*Plan Specifics:*

■ Initial shares can be purchased directly from the company ($100 minimum).

■ Partial dividend reinvestment is available.

■ No discount.

■ OCP: $50 to $100,000 per year.

■ Stock is purchased weekly with OCPs.

■ Purchasing costs are $7.50 plus 10 cents per share.

■ Selling costs are $7.50 plus 10 cents per share.

■ Automatic investment services are available.

■ Safekeeping services are available.

■ Dividends are paid January, April, July, and October.

*Performance Rating:* ****

**GenCorp Inc. (NYSE:GY)**
**175 Ghent Road**
**Fairlawn, OH 44333-3300**
**(800) 727-7033, (216) 869-4200, (330) 869-4200**
www.gencorp.com

*Business Profile:* Technology-based company with strong positions in the defense/automotive and polymer products markets.

*Performance History:* $1000 invested on 12/31/92 was worth $2744 on 12/31/97, a 174 percent increase in five years.

*Plan Specifics:*

■ Initial shares can be purchased directly from the company ($500 minimum).

■ Partial dividend reinvestment is available.

■ No discount.

■ OCP: $50 to $120,000 per year.

■ Stock is purchased every 45 days with OCPs.

■ Selling costs are brokerage fees.

■ Dividends are paid February, May, August, and November.

*Performance Rating:* ****

**General Electric Co. (NYSE:GE)**
**Reinvestment Plan Services**
**PO Box 120068**
**Stamford, CT 06912**
**(800) 786-2543, (203) 373-2816**
www.ge.com

*Business Profile:* Operations in aerospace, aircraft engines, major appliances, power systems, broadcasting, and financial services.

*Performance History:* $1000 invested on 12/31/92 was worth $3912 on 12/31/97, a 291 percent increase in five years.

*Plan Specifics:*

- Initial shares can be purchased directly from the company ($250 minimum). There is a one-time enrollment fee of $7.50.
- Partial dividend reinvestment is available.
- No discount.
- OCP: $10 to $10,000 per week.
- Stock is purchased monthly with OCPs.
- Purchasing costs are $3.
- Selling costs are $10 plus 15 cents per share.
- Automatic investment services are available ($1 per transaction).
- Safekeeping services are available.
- Dividends are paid January, April, July, and October.

*Performance Rating:* *****


**General Growth Properties, Inc. (NYSE:GGP)**
**55 W. Monroe, Suite 3100**
**Chicago, IL 60603-5060**
**(800) 774-4117, (888) 291-3713, (312) 551-5000**
www.generalgrowth.com

*Business Profile:* Real estate investment trust that owns, develops, and operates shopping malls.

*Performance History:* $1000 invested on 12/31/92 was worth $2042 on 12/31/97, a 104 percent increase in five years.

*Plan Specifics:*

- Initial shares can be purchased directly from the company ($200 minimum or automatic monthly investments of at least $50). There is a one-time enrollment fee of $15.
- Partial dividend reinvestment is available.
- No discount.
- OCP: $50 to $125,000 per quarter.
- Stock is purchased weekly with OCPs.
- Purchasing costs are $5 plus five cents per share.
- Selling costs are $10 plus 15 cents per share.
- Dividend reinvestment fee: four percent of amount invested ($2.50 maximum).
- Automatic investment services are available ($3 per transaction).

- A $5 fee is assessed for each certificate withdrawal request.
- Gift share transfers are available.
- Dividends are paid January, April, July, and October.

*Performance Rating:* ***

**Gillette Co. (NYSE:G)**
**Prudential Tower Bldg.**
**Suite 4800**
**Boston, MA 02199**
**(800) 730-4001, (800) 643-6989, (617) 421-7000**
www.gillette.com

*Business Profile:* Manufactures razor blades, toiletries, cosmetics, and electric shavers.

*Performance History:* $1000 invested on 12/31/92 was worth $3763 on 12/31/97, a 276 percent increase in five years.

*Plan Specifics:*

- Initial shares can be purchased directly from the company ($1000 minimum). There is a one-time enrollment fee of $10 plus brokerage fees.
- Partial dividend reinvestment is not available.
- No discount.
- OCP: $100 to $120,000 per year.
- Stock is purchased weekly with OCPs.
- Purchasing costs are $5 plus eight cents per share.
- Selling costs are brokerage fees.
- Dividend reinvestment fee: $1.25 plus eight cents per share.
- Automatic investment services are available.
- Dividends are paid March, June, September, and December.

*Performance Rating:* *****

**Glenborough Realty Trust, Inc. (NYSE:GLB)**
**400 S. El Camino Real**
**San Mateo, CA 94402**
**(888) 266-6785, (800) 998-9151, (415) 343-9300**

*Business Profile:* REIT that owns a portfolio of 58 industrial, office, hotel, retail, and multifamily properties.

*Performance History:* Not available.

*Plan Specifics:*

- Initial shares can be purchased directly from the company ($250 minimum).
- Partial dividend reinvestment is not available.
- No discount.
- OCP: $100 to $10,000 per month.
- Stock is purchased daily with OCPs.
- Purchasing costs are $5 plus brokerage fees.

- Selling costs are $7.50 plus brokerage fees.
- Dividend reinvestment fee: brokerage fees.
- Automatic investment services are available (75 cents plus brokerage fees).
- Safekeeping services are available.
- Gift share transfers are available.
- Dividends are paid February, May, August, and November.

*Performance Rating:* \*\*\*

**Goodyear Tire and Rubber Co. (NYSE:GT)**
**1144 E. Market St.**
**Akron, OH 44316**
**(800) 453-2440, (800) 317-4445, (216) 796-2121**
www.goodyear.com

*Business Profile:* Largest U.S. manufacturer of tires and rubber products and operates a petroleum pipeline.

*Performance History:* $1000 invested on 12/31/92 was worth $2055 on 12/31/97, a 105 percent increase in five years.

*Plan Specifics:*

- Initial shares can be purchased directly from the company ($250 minimum or automatic monthly investment of at least $25 for 10 consecutive months). There is a one-time enrollment fee of $10 plus three cents per share.
- Partial dividend reinvestment is available.
- No discount.
- OCP: $25 to $150,000 per year.
- Stock is purchased weekly with OCPs.
- Purchasing costs are three cents per share.
- Selling costs are $15 plus 15 cents per share.
- Dividend reinvestment fee: $1 plus three cents per share.
- Automatic investment services are available.
- Safekeeping services are available.
- Gift share transfers are available.
- Direct deposit of dividends is available.
- Dividends are paid March, June, September, and December.

*Performance Rating:* \*\*\*\*

**GreenPoint Financial Corp. (NYSE:GPT)**
**90 Park Ave.**
**New York, NY 10016**
**(800) 842-7629, (212) 834-1711**
www.greenpoint.com

*Business Profile:* Owns New York state-chartered thrift with branches in the New York metropolitan area.

*Performance History:* $1000 invested on 12/31/92 was worth $4186 on 12/31/97, a 319 percent increase in five years.

*Plan Specifics:*

- Initial shares can be purchased directly from the company ($2000 minimum).
- Partial dividend reinvestment is available.
- 100 share minimum for reinvestment of dividends.
- No discount.
- OCP: $100 to $10,000 per month.
- Purchasing costs are $5 plus 12 cents per share.
- Selling costs are $15 plus 12 cents per share.
- Automatic investment services are available.
- Safekeeping services are available.
- Dividends are paid March, June, September, and December.

*Performance Rating:* ***

**Guidant Corp. (NYSE:GDT)**
**111 Monument Circle, 29th Floor**
**Indianapolis, IN 46204**
**(800) 537-1677, (800) 317-4445, (317) 971-2000**
www.guidant.com

*Business Profile:* Manufacturer of a wide range of products used in cardiac rhythm management and coronary artery disease intervention.

*Performance History:* Not available.

*Plan Specifics:*

- Initial shares can be purchased directly from the company ($250 minimum). There is a one-time enrollment fee of $15 plus three cents per share.
- Partial dividend reinvestment is available.
- No discount.
- OCP: $50 minimum; no maximum.
- Stock is purchased weekly with OCPs.
- Purchasing costs are five percent of the amount invested (maximum $7.50) plus three cents per share.
- Selling costs are $15 plus 12 cents per share.
- Dividend reinvestment fee: up to $3 per reinvestment.
- Automatic investment services are available ($1 transaction fee).
- Shares can be sold via the telephone.
- Safekeeping services are available.
- Gift share transfers are available.
- Direct deposit of dividends is available.
- Dividends are paid March, June, September, and December.

*Performance Rating:* *****

**Harland (John H.) Company (NYSE:JH)**
2939 Miller Rd.
Decatur, GA 30039
(800) 649-2202, (800) 446-2617, (770) 981-9460
www.harland.net

*Business Profile:* Provides products and services to the financial industry.

*Performance History:* $1000 invested on 12/31/92 was worth $953 on 12/31/97, a five percent decrease in five years.

*Plan Specifics:*

- Initial shares can be purchased directly from the company ($500 minimum or automatic monthly investments of at least $100 for five consecutive months). There is a one-time enrollment fee of $15 plus three cents per share.
- Partial dividend reinvestment is available.
- No discount.
- OCP: $50 to $250,000 per year.
- Stock is purchased weekly with OCPs.
- Purchasing costs are $5 plus three cents per share.
- Selling costs are $15 plus 12 cents per share.
- Automatic investment services are available ($2 plus three cents per share).
- Safekeeping services are available.
- Gift share transfers are available.
- Direct deposit of dividends is available.
- Dividends are paid March, June, September, and December.

*Performance Rating:* ***

**Hawaiian Electric Industries, Inc. (NYSE:HE)**
PO Box 730
Honolulu, HI 96808-0730
(808) 543-5662, (808) 532-5841
www.hei.com

*Business Profile:* Hawaii-based electric utility holding company.

*Performance History:* $1000 invested on 12/31/92 was worth $1561 on 12/31/97, a 56 percent increase in five years.

*Plan Specifics:*

- Initial shares can be purchased directly from the company ($250 minimum).
- Partial dividend reinvestment is available.
- No discount.
- OCP: $25 to $120,000 per year.
- Stock is purchased bimonthly with OCPs.
- Selling costs are $10 plus brokerage fees.
- Automatic investment services are available.
- Safekeeping services are available.

- Preferred stock is eligible for reinvestment for common shares under the plan.
- Dividends are paid March, June, September, and December.

*Performance Rating:* **

**Hillenbrand Industries, Inc. (NYSE:HB)**
**700 State Route 46 East**
**Batesville, IN 47006**
**(800) 774-4117, (800) 286-9178, (812) 934-7000**
www.hillenbrand.com

*Business Profile:* Leading provider of burial caskets and hospital beds.

*Performance History:* $1000 invested on 12/31/92 was worth $1555 on 12/31/97, a 56 percent increase in five years.

*Plan Specifics:*

- Initial shares can be purchased directly from the company ($250 minimum).
- Partial dividend reinvestment is available.
- No discount.
- OCP: $100 to $50,000 per year.
- Stock is purchased weekly with OCPs.
- Purchasing costs are $5 plus 10 cents per share.
- Selling costs are $10 plus 10 cents per share.
- Automatic investment services are available.
- Safekeeping services are available.
- Gift share transfers are available.
- Dividends are paid February, May, August, and November.

*Performance Rating:* ****

**Home Depot, Inc. (NYSE:HD)**
**2727 Paces Ferry Road**
**Atlanta, GA 30339**
**(800) 774-4117, (800) 730-4001, (770) 433-8211**
www.homedepot.com

*Business Profile:* Home-improvement retailer operating 580 stores in the U.S. and Canada.

*Performance History:* $1000 invested on 12/31/92 was worth $1777 on 12/31/97, a 78 percent increase in five years.

*Plan Specifics:*

- Initial shares can be purchased directly from the company ($250 minimum). There is a one-time enrollment fee of $5.
- Partial dividend reinvestment is not available.
- No discount.
- OCP: $25 to $100,000 per year.
- Stock is purchased weekly with OCPs.
- Selling costs are $5 plus 15 cents per share.

- Dividend reinvestment fee: five percent of amount invested ($2.50 maximum) plus five cents per share.
- Automatic investment services are available.
- Safekeeping services are available.
- Dividends are paid March, June, September, and December.

*Performance Rating:* *****


**Home Properties of NY, Inc. (NYSE:HME)**
**850 Clinton Square**
**Rochester, NY 14604**
**(800) 774-4117, (800) 937-5449, (716) 546-4900**

*Business Profile:* Real estate investment trust.

*Performance History:* $1000 invested on 12/31/92 was worth $1832 on 12/31/97, an 83 percent increase in five years.

*Plan Specifics:*

- Initial shares can be purchased directly from the company ($2000 minimum).
- Partial dividend reinvestment is available (must reinvest dividends on at least 100 shares.)
- Three percent discount on reinvested dividends and OCPs.
- OCP: $50 to $5000 per month.
- Stock is purchased monthly with OCPs.
- Selling costs are brokerage fees.
- Dividends are paid February, May, August, and November.

*Performance Rating:* ***


**Houston Industries, Inc. (NYSE:HOU)**
**Investor Services Dept.**
**PO Box 4505**
**Houston, TX 77210**
**(800) 774-4117, (800) 231-6406, (713) 207-3000**
www.houind.com

*Business Profile:* Electric utility holding company provides electricity to regions of the Texas Gulf Coast.

*Performance History:* $1000 invested on 12/31/92 was worth $1777 on 12/31/97, a 78 percent increase in five years.

*Plan Specifics:*

- Initial shares can be purchased directly from the company ($250 minimum).
- Partial dividend reinvestment is available.
- No discount.
- OCP: $50 to $120,000 per year.
- Stock is purchased at least weekly with OCPs.
- Selling costs are brokerage fees.
- Automatic investment services are available.

- Shares can be sold via the telephone.
- IRA option is available ($29 annual fee for balances under $10,000).
- Safekeeping services are available.
- Gift share transfers are available.
- Direct deposit of dividends is available.
- Houston Industries debentures, first mortgage bonds, and preferred stock are eligible for reinvestment.
- Dividends are paid March, June, September, and December.

*Performance Rating:* ***

**Illinova Corp. (NYSE:ILN)**
**500 South 27th St.**
**Decatur, IL 62525**
**(800) 750-7011, (800) 800-8220, (217) 424-6600**
www.illinova.com

*Business Profile:* Holding company that owns Illinois Power, an electric and gas utility that serves northern, central, and southern Illinois.

*Performance History:* $1000 invested on 12/31/92 was worth $1416 on 12/31/97, a 42 percent increase in five years.

*Plan Specifics:*

- Initial shares can be purchased directly from the company ($250 minimum).
- Partial dividend reinvestment is available.
- No discount.
- OCP: $25 to $60,000 per year.
- Stock is purchased bimonthly with OCPs.
- Selling costs are brokerage fees.
- Automatic investment services are available.
- Safekeeping services are available.
- Gift share transfers are available.
- Dividends are paid February, May, August, and November.

*Performance Rating:* ***

**Interchange Financial Services Corp. (ASE:ISB)**
**Park 80 West/Plaza Two**
**Saddle Brook, NJ 07662**
**(201) 703-2265**

*Business Profile:* Holding company operating commercial banking offices in Bergen and Passaic counties, New Jersey.

*Performance History:* $1000 invested on 12/31/92 was worth $4066 on 12/31/97, a 307 percent increase in five years.

*Plan Specifics:*

- Initial shares can be purchased directly from the company ($100 minimum).
- Partial dividend reinvestment is not available.
- No discount.
- OCP: $25 per month to no maximum (in multiples of $10).

- Stock is purchased monthly with OCPs.
- Purchasing costs are brokerage fees.
- Selling costs are brokerage fees.
- Dividends are paid January, April, July, and October.

*Performance Rating:* \*\*\*

**International Business Machines Corp. (NYSE:IBM)**
**One New Orchard Rd.**
**Armonk, NY 10504**
**(888) 421-8860, (800) 446-2617, (914) 765-1900**
www.ibm.com

*Business Profile:* Largest producer of mainframe, small business, and personal computers.

*Performance History:* $1000 invested on 12/31/92 was worth $4487 on 12/31/97, a 349 percent increase in five years.

*Plan Specifics:*

- Initial shares can be purchased directly from the company ($500 minimum or automatic monthly investments of at least $50 for 10 consecutive months). There is a one-time enrollment fee of $15.
- Partial dividend reinvestment is available.
- No discount.
- OCP: $50 to $250,000 per year.
- Stock is purchased weekly with OCPs.
- Purchasing costs are $5.
- Selling costs are $15 plus 10 cents per share.
- Dividend reinvestment fee: two percent of amount invested ($3 maximum).
- Automatic investment services are available ($1 transaction fee).
- Safekeeping services are available.
- Gift share transfers are available.
- Direct deposit of dividends is available.
- Dividends are paid March, June, September, and December.

*Performance Rating:* \*\*\*\*\*

**Interstate Energy Corp. (NYSE:LNT)**
**PO Box 2568**
**Madison, WI 53701-2568**
**(800) 356-5343, (608) 252-3311**

*Business Profile:* Provides electric energy, natural gas, and water in parts of Iowa, Minnesota, Illinois, and Wisconsin.

*Performance History:* Not available.

*Plan Specifics:*

- Initial shares can be purchased directly from the company ($250 minimum or automatic monthly investments of at least $25).
- Partial dividend reinvestment is available.
- No discount.

- OCP: $25 to $120,000 per year.
- Stock is purchased monthly with OCPs.
- Selling costs are brokerage fees.
- Automatic investment services are available.
- Safekeeping services are available.
- Gift share transfers are available.
- Direct deposit of dividends is available.
- Dividends are paid February, May, August, and November.

*Performance Rating:* ****

**Investors Financial Services Corp. (NASDAQ:IFIN)**
**89 South St.**
**Boston, MA 02111**
**(888) 333-5336, (617) 330-6700**
www.investorsbnk.com

*Business Profile:* Provides asset administration services for the financial service industry.

*Performance History:* $1000 invested on 12/31/92 was worth $2467 on 12/31/97, a 147 percent increase in five years.

*Plan Specifics:*

- Initial shares can be purchased directly from the company ($250 minimum). There is a one-time enrollment fee of $10 plus 10 cents per share.
- Partial dividend reinvestment is not available.
- No discount.
- OCP: $100; no maximum.
- Stock is purchased weekly with OCPs.
- Purchasing costs are $5 plus 10 cents per share.
- Selling costs are $15 plus 12 cents per share.
- Automatic investment services are available ($2 plus 10 cents per share).
- Safekeeping services are available.
- Gift share transfers are available.
- Direct deposit of dividends is available.
- Dividends are paid February, May, August, and November.

*Performance Rating:* ****

**IPALCO Enterprises, Inc. (NYSE:IPL)**
**25 Monument Circle**
**PO Box 1595**
**Indianapolis, IN 46206-1595**
**(800) 774-4117, (800) 877-0153, (317) 261-8394**
www.ipalco.com

*Business Profile:* Holding company for electric utility serving Indianapolis.

*Performance History:* $1000 invested on 12/31/92 was worth $2330 on 12/31/97, a 133 percent increase in five years.

*Plan Specifics:*

■ Initial shares can be purchased directly from the company ($250 minimum).

■ Partial dividend reinvestment is available.

■ No discount.

■ OCP: $25 to $100,000 per year.

■ Stock is purchased bimonthly with OCPs.

■ Purchasing and selling costs are brokerage fees.

■ Automatic investment services are available.

■ Safekeeping services are available.

■ Gift share transfers are available.

■ Direct deposit of dividends is available.

■ Dividends are paid January, April, July, and October.

*Performance Rating:* \*\*\*\*\*

**Johnson Controls, Inc. (NYSE:JCI)**
**Shareholder Services**
**PO Box 591**
**Milwaukee, WI 53201-0591**
**(800) 524-6220, (414) 228-1200**
www.jci.com

*Business Profile:* Major producer of automated building controls, batteries, automotive seating, and plastics.

*Performance History:* $1000 invested on 12/31/92 was worth $2411 on 12/31/97, a 141 percent increase in five years.

*Plan Specifics:*

■ Initial shares can be purchased directly from the company ($50 minimum).

■ A partial dividend reinvestment is available.

■ No discount.

■ OCP: $50 to $15,000 per quarter.

■ Stock is purchased monthly with OCPs.

■ Selling costs are $5 plus brokerage fees.

■ Direct deposit of dividends is available.

■ Dividends are paid March, June, September, and December.

*Performance Rating:* \*\*\*\*

**Justin Industries, Inc. (NASDAQ:JSTN)**
**2821 W. 7th St.**
**Fort Worth, TX 76107**
**(800) 727-7033, (817) 336-5125**
www.justinind.com

*Business Profile:* Produces western-style footwear, face brick, concrete blocks, and other building materials.

*Performance History:* $1000 invested on 12/31/92 was worth $1498 on 12/31/97, a 50 percent increase in five years.

*Plan Specifics:*

■ Initial shares can be purchased directly from the company ($500 minimum). There is a one-time enrollment fee of $7.50 plus 10 cents per share.

■ Partial dividend reinvestment is available.

■ No discount.

■ Maximum single optional investment: $5000

■ OCP: $25 to $100,000 per year.

■ Stock is purchased at least weekly with OCPs.

■ Purchasing costs are 10 cents per share.

■ Selling costs are 10 cents per share.

■ Automatic investment services are available.

■ Safekeeping services are available.

■ Dividends are paid January, April, July, and October.

*Performance Rating:* ***

**Kaman Corp. (NASDAQ: KAMNA)**
**PO Box 1**
**Bloomfield, CT 06002**
**(800) 842-7629, (860) 243-7100**
www.kaman.com

*Business Profile:* Provides products and services for defense markets and distributes industrial and commercial products.

*Performance History:* $1000 invested on 12/31/92 was worth $1992 on 12/31/97, a 99 percent increase in five years.

*Plan Specifics:*

■ Initial shares can be purchased directly from the company ($250 minimum).

■ Partial dividend reinvestment is not available.

■ Ten share minimum for reinvestment of dividends.

■ No discount.

■ OCP: $50 to $60,000 per year.

■ Stock is purchased monthly with OCPs.

■ Purchasing costs are $5 plus 12 cents per share.

■ Selling costs are $15 plus 12 cents per share.

■ Automatic investment services are available ($3 plus 12 cents per share).

■ Safekeeping services are available.

■ Dividends are paid January, April, July, and October.

*Performance Rating:* ***

**Kellwood Company (NYSE:KWD)**
**600 Kellwood Parkway**
**Chesterfield, MO 63017**
**(314) 576-3100**

*Business Profile:* Manufacturer and marketer of value-oriented apparel and recreational camping products.

*Performance History:* $1000 invested on 12/31/92 was worth $1917 on 12/31/97, a 92 percent increase in five years.

*Plan Specifics:*

■ Initial shares can be purchased directly from the company ($100 minimum).

■ Partial dividend reinvestment is available.

■ No discount.

■ OCP: $25 to $3000 per month.

■ Stock is purchased monthly with OCPs.

■ Selling costs are $5 plus brokerage fees.

■ Dividends are paid March, June, September, and December.

*Performance Rating:* ***

**Kerr-McGee Corp. (NYSE:KMG)**
**Kerr-McGee Center**
**Oklahoma City, OK 73102**
**(800) 395-2662, (800) 786-2556, (405) 270-1313**

*Business Profile:* Produces oil and natural gas, industrial chemicals and coal.

*Performance History:* $1000 invested on 12/31/92 was worth $1628 on 12/31/97, a 63 percent increase in five years.

*Plan Specifics:*

■ Initial shares can be purchased directly from the company ($750 minimum).

■ Partial dividend reinvestment is not available.

■ No discount.

■ OCP: $10 to $3000 per quarter.

■ Stock is purchased monthly with OCPs.

■ No purchasing or selling costs.

■ Dividends are paid January, April, July, and October.

*Performance Rating:* ****

**Lear Corp. (NYSE:LEA)**
**21557 Telegraph Rd.**
**Southfield, MI 48086-5008**
**(800) 524-4458, (248) 746-1500**
www.lear.com

*Business Profile:* Largest independent manufacturer of automotive interior systems.

*Performance History:* $1000 invested on 12/31/92 was worth $2583 on 12/31/97, a 158 percent increase in five years.

*Plan Specifics:*

■ Initial shares can be purchased directly from the company ($250 minimum).

■ Partial dividend reinvestment is not available.

■ No discount.

■ OCP: $50 to $150,000 per year.

■ Stock is purchased monthly with OCPs.

- Purchasing costs are $2 plus seven cents per share.
- Selling costs are $5 plus seven cents per share.
- Safekeeping services are available.
- The company is not currently paying a dividend.

*Performance Rating:* \*\*\*

**Libbey, Inc. (NYSE:LBY)**
**300 Madison Ave.**
**PO Box 10060**
**Toledo, OH 43604**
**(800) 727-7033, (419) 325-2100**

*Business Profile:* Leading producer of glass tableware.

*Performance History:* $1000 invested on 12/31/92 was worth $3046 on 12/31/97, a 205 percent increase in five years.

*Plan Specifics:*

- Initial shares can be purchased directly from the company ($100 minimum). There is a one-time enrollment fee of $7.50 plus seven cents per share.
- Partial dividend reinvestment is available.
- No discount.
- OCP: $20 to $25,000 per year.
- Stock is purchased weekly with OCPs.
- Purchasing costs are seven cents per share.
- Selling costs are $5 plus seven cents per share.
- Automatic investment services are available.
- Safekeeping services are available.
- Dividends are paid March, June, September, and December.

*Performance Rating:* \*\*\*

**Liberty Property Trust (NYSE:LRY)**
**65 Valley Stream Parkway, Suite 100**
**Malvern, PA 19355**
**(800) 944-2214, (610) 648-1700**
www.libertyproperty.com

*Business Profile:* Self-administered REIT that owns and manages one of the largest portfolios of suburban industrial and office properties in the United States.

*Performance History:* Not available.

*Plan Specifics:*

- Initial shares can be purchased directly from the company ($1000 minimum).
- Partial dividend reinvestment is available.
- Three percent discount on reinvested dividends.
- OCP: $250 to $7500 per month.
- Selling costs are $10 plus brokerage fees.
- Automatic investment services are available.

- Safekeeping services are available.
- Dividends are paid January, April, July, and October.

*Performance Rating:* \*\*\*


**Lilly (Eli) & Co. (NYSE:LLY)**
**Shareholder Services**
**Lilly Corporate Center**
**Indianapolis, IN 46285**
**(800) 451-2134, (317) 276-3219**
www.elililly.com

*Business Profile:* Leading supplier of prescription drugs including antibiotics.

*Performance History:* $1000 invested on 12/31/92 was worth $5397 on 12/31/97, a 440 percent increase in five years.

*Plan Specifics:*

- Initial shares can be purchased directly from the company (minimum $1000). There is a one-time enrollment fee of $15.
- Partial dividend reinvestment is not available.
- No discount.
- OCP: $50 to $150,000 per year.
- Stock is purchased weekly with OCPs.
- Purchasing costs are $5 plus three cents per share.
- Selling costs are $10 plus 12 cents per share.
- Dividend reinvestment fee: three percent of amount invested ($3 maximum) plus 13 cents per share.
- Automatic investment services are available ($2 plus three cents per share).
- Safekeeping services are available.
- Shares can be sold via telephone.
- Gift share transfers are available.
- Direct deposit of dividends is available.
- Dividends are paid March, June, September, and December.

*Performance Rating:* \*\*\*\*\*


**Longs Drug Stores Co. (NYSE:LDG)**
**141 North Civic Dr.**
**Walnut Creek, CA 94596**
**(888) 213-0886, (510) 937-1170**
www.longs.com

*Business Profile:* Operates a drugstore chain with 345 stores in the western United States.

*Performance History:* $1000 invested on 12/31/92 was worth $2064 on 12/31/97, a 106 percent increase in five years.

*Plan Specifics:*

- Initial shares can be purchased directly from the company ($500 minimum).
- Partial dividend reinvestment is available.

- No discount.
- OCP: $25 to $5000 per quarter.
- Stock is purchased weekly with OCPs.
- Initial and subsequent purchasing costs are $5 plus 12 cents per share.
- Selling costs are $15 plus 12 cents per share.
- Dividend reinvestment fee: five percent of amount invested (minimum 50 cents, maximum $10).
- Automatic investment services are available.
- Safekeeping services are available.
- Gift share transfers are available.
- Dividends are paid January, April, July, and October.

*Performance Rating: ****

**Lucent Technologies, Inc. (NYSE:LU)**
**600 Mountain Ave.**
**Murray Hill, NJ 07974**
**(800) 774-4117, (888) 582-3686, (908) 582-8500**
www.lucent.com

*Business Profile:* One of the world's largest providers of telecommunication equipment.

*Performance History:* Not available.

*Plan Specifics:*

- Initial shares can be purchased directly from the company ($1000 minimum or automatic monthly investments of at least $100). There is a one-time enrollment fee of $7.50.
- Partial dividend reinvestment is available.
- No discount.
- OCP: $100 to $50,000 per year.
- Stock is purchased at least weekly with OCPs.
- Purchasing costs are 10 percent ($2 maximum) of amount invested plus 10 cents per share.
- Selling costs are $10 plus 10 cents per share.
- Dividend reinvestment fee: 10 percent of amount invested ($2 maximum per quarter) plus 10 cents per share.
- Automatic investment services are available.
- Shares can be sold via the telephone.
- IRA option is available ($35 annual fee).
- Safekeeping services are available.
- Gift share transfers are available.
- Dividends are paid March, June, September, and December.

*Performance Rating: *****

**Macerich Co. (NYSE:MAC)**
**233 Wilshire Blvd.**
**Santa Monica, CA 90401**
**(800) 567-0169, (310) 394-6911**
www.macerich.com

*Business Profile:* Acquires, owns, redevelops, manages, and leases regional shopping centers. Currently owns 24 shopping centers throughout the U.S.

*Performance History:* $1000 invested on 12/31/92 was worth $1884 on 12/31/97, an 88 percent increase in five years.

*Plan Specifics:*

■ Initial shares can be purchased directly from the company ($250 minimum or automatic monthly investments of at least $50 for five consecutive months).

■ Partial dividend reinvestment is available.

■ No discount.

■ OCP: $50 to $250,000 per year.

■ Stock is purchased weekly with OCPs.

■ Selling costs are $10 plus 12 cents per share.

■ Automatic investment services are available.

■ Shares can be sold via the telephone.

■ Safekeeping services are available.

■ Gift share transfers are available.

■ Direct deposit of dividends is available.

■ Dividends are paid March, June, September, and December.

*Performance Rating:* ***


**Madison Gas & Electric Co. (NASDAQ:MDSN)**
**PO Box 1231**
**133 S. Blair St.**
**Madison, WI 53701-1231**
**(800) 356-6423, (608) 252-7923**
www.mge.com

*Business Profile:* Wisconsin-based electric and gas utility.

*Performance History:* $1000 invested on 12/31/92 was worth $1412 on 12/31/97, a 41 percent increase in five years.

*Plan Specifics:*

■ Initial shares can be purchased directly from the company ($50 minimum).

■ Partial dividend reinvestment is available.

■ No discount.

■ OCP: $25 to $25,000 per quarter.

■ Stock is purchased monthly with OCPs.

■ Purchasing costs are brokerage fees.

■ Selling costs are brokerage fees.

- Automatic investment services are available.
- Safekeeping services are available.
- Gift share transfers are available.
- Direct deposit of dividends is available.
- Dividends are paid March, June, September, and December.

*Performance Rating:* \*\*\*\*

**Mattel, Inc. (NYSE:MAT)**
**333 Continental Blvd.**
**El Segundo, CA 90245**
**(888) 909-9922, (310) 252-2000**
www.hotwheels.com

*Business Profile:* World's largest toy company.

*Performance History:* $1000 invested on 12/31/92 was worth $3003 on 12/31/97, a 200 percent increase in five years.

*Plan Specifics:*

- Initial shares can be purchased directly from the company ($500 minimum). There is a one-time enrollment fee of $10.
- Partial dividend reinvestment is not available.
- No discount.
- OCP: $100 to $100,000 per year.
- Stock is purchased weekly with OCPs.
- Purchasing costs are $5 plus eight cents per share.
- Selling costs are $10 plus 15 cents per share.
- Automatic investment services are available ($2.50 transaction fee).
- Dividends are paid January, April, July, and October.

*Performance Rating:* \*\*\*\*

**McDonald's Corp. (NYSE:MCD)**
**McDonald's Plaza**
**Oak Brook, IL 60521**
**(800) 774-4117, (800) 228-9623, (800) 621-7825, (630) 623-3000**
www.mcdonalds.com

*Business Profile:* Worldwide leader in the fast-food industry.

*Performance History:* $1000 invested on 12/31/92 was worth $2031 on 12/31/97, a 103 percent increase in five years.

*Plan Specifics:*

- Initial shares can be purchased directly from the company ($1000 minimum or automatic monthly investments of at least $100). There is a one-time enrollment fee of $5 plus an annual account fee of $3.
- Partial dividend reinvestment is not available.
- No discount.
- OCP: $100 to $250,000 per year.
- Stock is purchased weekly with OCPs.

- Purchasing costs are $5 plus 10 cents per share ($5 maximum).
- Selling costs are $10 plus 10 cents per share ($5 maximum).
- Automatic investment services are available ($1 plus 10 cents per share ($5 maximum)).
- IRA option is available ($35 annual fee).
- Safekeeping services are available.
- Shares can be sold via telephone.
- Gift share transfers are available.
- Dividends are paid March, June, September, and December.

*Performance Rating:* \*\*\*\*\*

**MCN Energy Group, Inc. (NYSE:MCN)**
**500 Griswold St.**
**Detroit, MI 48226**
**(800) 955-4793, (313) 256-5500**
www.mcnenergy.com

*Business Profile:* Distributes, transmits, and stores natural gas in Michigan.

*Performance History:* $1000 invested on 12/31/92 was worth $3151 on 12/31/97, a 215 percent increase in five years.

*Plan Specifics:*

- Initial shares can be purchased directly from the company ($250 minimum or automatic monthly investment of at least $25). There is a one-time processing fee of $10.
- Partial dividend reinvestment is available.
- No discount.
- OCP: $25 to $150,000 per year.
- Stock is purchased weekly with OCPs.
- Purchasing costs are three cents per share.
- Selling costs are $15 plus 15 cents per share.
- Automatic investment services are available.
- Shares can be sold via the telephone.
- IRA option is available.
- Safekeeping services are available.
- Gift share transfers are available.
- Direct deposit of dividends is available.
- Dividends are paid February, May, August, and November.

*Performance Rating:* \*\*\*\*\*

**Meadowbrook Insurance Group, Inc. (NYSE:MIG)**
**26600 Telegraph Road**
**Southfield, MI 48034**
**(800) 649-2579, (800) 519-3111, (248) 358-1100**

*Business Profile:* Provider of risk-management programs.

*Performance History:* Not available.

*Plan Specifics:*

■ Initial shares can be purchased directly from the company ($250 minimum or automatic monthly investments of at least $50 for five consecutive months).

■ Partial dividend reinvestment is available.

■ No discount.

■ OCP: $25 to $50,000 per year.

■ Stock is purchased weekly with OCPs.

■ Selling costs include a service charge plus brokerage fee.

■ Automatic investment services are available.

■ Shares can be sold via the telephone.

■ Safekeeping services are available.

■ Dividends are paid January, April, July, and October.

*Performance Rating:* ***

**Mellon Bank Corp. (NYSE:MEL)**
**One Mellon Bank Center**
**Pittsburgh, PA 15258**
**(800) 842-7629, (412) 234-5000**
www.mellon.com

*Business Profile:* Holding company for bank subsidiaries that operate 420 banking offices and supermarket branches in Delaware, Maryland, New Jersey, Pennsylvania, and Canada.

*Performance History:* $1000 invested on 12/31/92 was worth $4130 on 12/31/97, a 313 percent increase in five years.

*Plan Specifics:*

■ Initial shares can be purchased directly from the company ($500 minimum). There is a one-time enrollment fee of $6 plus 12 cents per share.

■ Partial dividend reinvestment is available.

■ Five share minimum for reinvestment of dividends.

■ No discount.

■ OCP: $100 to $100,000 per month.

■ Stock is purchased weekly with OCPs.

■ Selling costs are $15 plus 12 cents per share.

■ Automatic investment services are available.

■ Shares can be sold via the telephone.

■ Safekeeping services are available.

■ Gift share transfers are available.

■ Direct deposit of dividends is available.

■ Dividends are paid February, May, August, and November.

*Performance Rating:* ***

**Mercantile Bancorporation, Inc. (NYSE:MTL)**
**311 W. Monroe St.**
**PO Box A-3309**
**Chicago, IL 60690-3309**
**(800) 774-4117, (800) 720-0417, (314) 425-2525**
www.mercantile.com

*Business Profile:* Registered bank holding company headquartered in St. Louis, Missouri.

*Performance History:* $1000 invested on 12/31/92 was worth $3265 on 12/31/97, a 227 percent increase in five years.

*Plan Specifics:*

- Initial shares can be purchased directly from the company ($500 minimum or automatic monthly investments of at least $100).
- Partial dividend reinvestment is available.
- No discount.
- OCP: $100 to $120,000 per year.
- Stock is purchased weekly with OCPs.
- Purchasing costs are $3 plus five cents per share.
- Selling costs are $10 plus five cents per share.
- Automatic investment services are available ($1.50 plus five cents per share).
- Safekeeping services are available.
- Gift share transfers are available.
- Direct deposit of dividends is available.
- Dividends are paid January, April, July, and October.

*Performance Rating:* ***


**Merck & Co., Inc. (NYSE:MRK)**
**PO Box 100**
**Whitehouse Sta., NJ 08889-0100**
**(800) 774-4117, (800) 613-2104, (908) 423-6627**
www.merc.com

*Business Profile:* Leading producer of human and animal pharmaceuticals and specialty chemicals.

*Performance History:* $1000 invested on 12/31/92 was worth $2825 on 12/31/97, a 183 percent increase in five years.

*Plan Specifics:*

- Initial shares can be purchased directly from the company ($350 minimum or automatic monthly investments of at least $50). There is a one-time enrollment fee of $5.
- Partial dividend reinvestment is available.
- No discount.
- OCP: $50 to $50,000 per year.

- Stock is purchased weekly with OCPs.
- Purchasing costs are $5 plus one cent per share.
- Selling costs are $5 plus one cent per share.
- Dividend reinvestment fee: four percent of amount invested ($2 maximum) plus one cent per share.
- Automatic monthly investments are available ($2 plus one cent per share).
- Shares can be sold via the telephone.
- Safekeeping services are available.
- Dividends are paid January, April, July, and October.

*Performance Rating:* *****

**Meritor Automotive, Inc. (NYSE:MRA)**
**2135 W. Maple Rd.**
**Troy, MI 48084**
**(800) 483-2277, (248) 435-1000**

*Business Profile:* Producer of automotive systems and components.

*Performance History:* Not available.

*Plan Specifics:*

- Initial shares can be purchased directly from the company ($500 minimum or automatic monthly investments of at least $50 for 10 consecutive months). There is a one-time enrollment fee of 10 plus 10 cents per share.
- Partial dividend reinvestment is available.
- No discount.
- OCP: $50 to $100,000 per year.
- Stock is purchased weekly with OCPs.
- Purchasing costs are $5 plus 10 cents per share.
- Selling costs are $10 plus 12 cents per share.
- Automatic investment services are available ($2 plus 10 cents per share).
- Dividend reinvestment fee: five percent of amount invested ($3 maximum) plus 10 cents per share.
- Shares can be sold via the telephone.
- Safekeeping services are available.
- Gift share transfers are available.
- Dividends are paid March, June, September, and December.

*Performance Rating:* ***

**Michaels Stores, Inc. (NASDAQ:MIKE)**
**8000 Bent Branch Dr.**
**PO Box 619566**
**Irving, TX 75063**
**(800) 577-4676, (972) 409-1300**
www.michaels.com

*Business Profile:* Retailer of arts, crafts, framing, floral, decorative wall décor, and seasonal merchandise for the hobbyist and do-it-yourself home decorator.

*Performance History:* $1000 invested on 12/31/92 was worth $849 on 12/31/97, a 15 percent decrease in five years.

*Plan Specifics:*

■ Initial shares can be purchased directly from the company ($500 minimum).

■ Partial dividend reinvestment is available.

■ Up to five percent discount on OCPs.

■ OCP: $100 to $2500 per month.

■ Stock is purchased monthly with OCPs.

■ Selling costs are $10 plus 12 cents per share.

■ Automatic investment services are available.

■ Safekeeping services are available.

■ Gift share transfers are available.

■ The company is not currently paying a dividend.

*Performance Rating:* ***


**MidAmerican Energy Co. (NYSE: MEC)**
**666 Grand Ave.**
**PO Box 9244**
**Des Moines, IA 50306-9244**
**(800) 247-5211, (515) 242-4300**
www.midamerican.com

*Business Profile:* Electric utility holding company.

*Performance History:* $1000 invested on 12/31/92 was worth $1954 on 12/31/97, a 95 percent increase in five years.

*Plan Specifics:*

■ Initial shares can be purchased directly from the company ($250 minimum).

■ Partial dividend reinvestment is available.

■ No discount.

■ OCP: $25 to $10,000 per month.

■ Stock is purchased monthly with OCPs.

■ Purchasing costs include a service charge plus brokerage fee.

■ Selling costs include a service charge plus brokerage fee.

■ Safekeeping services are available.

■ Direct deposit of dividends is available.

■ Dividends are paid March, June, September, and December.

*Performance Rating:* ***


**MidSouth Bancorp Inc. (ASE:MSL)**
**102 Versailles Blvd.**
**Lafayette, LA 70501**
**(800) 842-7629, (318) 237-8343**
www.midsouthbank.com

*Business Profile:* Holding company for MidSouth National Bank, which operates 13 banking offices in southern Louisiana.

*Performance History:* Not available.

*Plan Specifics:*

- Initial shares can be purchased directly from the company ($1000 minimum or automatic monthly investment of at least $100).
- Partial dividend reinvestment is available.
- Twenty-five share minimum for reinvestment of dividends.
- No discount.
- OCP: $100 to $10,000 per month.
- Stock is purchased weekly with OCPs.
- Selling costs are $15 plus 12 cents per share.
- Automatic investment services are available.
- Shares can be sold via the telephone.
- IRA option is available ($29 annual fee).
- Safekeeping services are available.
- Dividends are paid January, April, July, and October.

*Performance Rating:* \*\*\*

**Minnesota Power & Light Co.  (NYSE:MPL)**
**30 W. Superior St.**
**Duluth, MN 55802-2093**
**(800) 774-4117, (800) 535-3056, (218) 723-3974**
www.mnpower.com

*Business Profile:* Provides electric services in a 26,000-square mile area of upper Minnesota and northwestern Wisconsin. Provides water services in Wisconsin, Florida, North Carolina, and South Carolina.

*Performance History:* $1000 invested on 12/31/92 was worth $1801 on 12/31/97, an 80 percent increase in five years.

*Plan Specifics:*

- Initial shares can be purchased directly from the company ($250 minimum).
- Partial dividend reinvestment is available.
- No discount.
- OCP: $10 to $100,000 per year.
- Stock is purchased monthly with OCPs.
- Minnesota Power & Light will sell up to 99.99 shares in one transaction per year; otherwise, you must go through your own broker to sell shares.
- Safekeeping services are available.
- Preferred dividends are eligible for reinvestment for additional common shares under the plan.
- Dividends are paid March, June, September, and December.

*Performance Rating:* \*\*\*

**Mobil Corp. (NYSE:MOB)**
**3225 Gallows Rd.**
**Fairfax, VA 22037-0001**
**(800) 648-9291, (703) 849-3000**
www.mobil.com

*Business Profile:* Leading worldwide integrated oil company.

*Performance History:* $1000 invested on 12/31/92 was worth $2766 on 12/31/97, a 177 percent increase in five years.

*Plan Specifics:*

- Initial shares can be purchased directly from the company ($250 minimum).
- Partial dividend reinvestment is not available.
- No discount.
- OCP: $10 to $7500 per month.
- Stock is purchased weekly with OCPs.
- Selling costs are $5 plus 10 cents per share.
- Automatic investment services are available.
- IRA option is available ($20 annual fee).
- Safekeeping services are available.
- Gift share transfers are available.
- Dividends are paid March, June, September, and December.

*Performance Rating:* ****


**Morgan Stanley Dean Witter (NYSE:MWD)**
**Exchange Pl.**
**PO Box 989**
**Jersey City, NJ 07311**
**(800) 228-0829, (800) 622-2393, (212) 761-4000**
www.deanwitterdiscover.com

*Business Profile:* Company is involved in credit services and securities operations.

*Performance History:* $1000 invested on 12/31/92 was worth $4038 on 12/31/97, a 304 percent increase in five years.

*Plan Specifics:*

- Initial shares can be purchased directly from the company ($1000 minimum).
- Partial dividend reinvestment is available.
- No discount.
- OCP: $100 to $40,000 per year.
- Stock is purchased bimonthly with OCPs.
- Selling costs are $5 plus brokerage fees.
- Dividends are paid January, April, July, and October.

*Performance Rating:* ****

**Morton International, Inc. (NYSE:MII)**
**100 N. Riverside Plaza**
**Chicago, IL 60606-1596**
**(800) 774-4117, (800) 990-1010, (312) 807-2000**
www.mortonintl.com

*Business Profile:* Diversified company with interests in specialty chemicals and salt.

*Performance History:* $1000 invested on 12/31/92 was worth $1793 on 12/31/97, a 79 percent increase in five years.

*Plan Specifics:*

■ Initial shares can be purchased directly from the company ($1000 minimum). There is a one-time enrollment fee of $10 plus 12 cents per share.

■ Partial dividend reinvestment is available.

■ No discount.

■ OCP: $50 to $60,000 per year.

■ Stock is purchased weekly with OCPs.

■ Purchasing costs are five percent of the amount invested ($10 maximum) plus 12 cents per share.

■ Selling costs are $15 plus 12 cents per share.

■ Dividend reinvestment fee: three percent of amount invested ($2.50 maximum) plus 12 cents per share.

■ Automatic investment services are available ($25 minimum).

■ Shares can be sold via the telephone.

■ IRA option is available.

■ Safekeeping services are available.

■ Gift share transfers are available.

■ Direct deposit of dividends is available.

■ Dividends are paid March, June, September, and December.

*Performance Rating:* ****

**Mycogen Corp. (NASDAQ:MYCO)**
**5501 Oberlin Dr.**
**San Diego, CA 92121**
**(800) 477-6506, (619) 453-8030**
www.mycogen.com

*Business Profile:* Producer of biotechnology-based pesticides and pest-resistant crop varieties.

*Performance History:* $1000 invested on 12/31/92 was worth $1339 on 12/31/97, a 34 percent increase in five years.

*Plan Specifics:*

■ Initial shares can be purchased directly from the company ($250 minimum). There is a one-time enrollment fee of $10.

■ No discount.

■ OCP: $100 to $100,000 per year.

■ Stock is purchased weekly with OCPs.

- Purchasing costs are $5 plus eight cents per share.
- Selling costs are $10 plus 15 cents per share.
- Automatic investment services are available ($2.50 plus eight cents per share).
- The company is not currently paying a dividend.

*Performance Rating:* \*\*\*

**NationsBank Corp. (NYSE:NB)**
**NationsBank Corporate Center**
**Charlotte, NC 28255**
**(800) 642-9855, (704) 386-5000**
www.nationsbank.com

*Business Profile:* Financial-services holding company that provides commercial, retail, and foreign banking services; originates home-mortgage loans; and operates full-service and discount-securities businesses.

*Performance History:* $1000 invested on 12/31/92 was worth $2767 on 12/31/97, a 177 percent increase in five years.

*Plan Specifics:*

- Initial shares can be purchased directly from the company ($1000 minimum). There is a one-time enrollment fee of $10.
- Partial dividend reinvestment is available.
- No discount.
- OCP: $50 to $120,000 per year.
- Stock is purchased weekly with OCPs.
- Selling costs are $15 plus eight cents per share.
- Automatic investment services are available.
- Safekeeping services are available.
- Gift share transfers are available.
- Direct deposit of dividends is available.
- Dividends are paid March, June, September, and December.

*Performance Rating:* \*\*\*\*

**Nationwide Financial Services (NYSE:NFS)**
**PO Box 2598**
**Jersey City, NJ 07303**
**(800) 409-7514  (800) 519-3111**

*Business Profile:* The firm is a provider of long-term savings and retirement products.

*Performance History:* Not available.

*Plan Specifics:*

- Initial shares can be purchased directly from the company ($500 minimum). There is a one-time enrollment fee of $15.
- Partial dividend reinvestment is available.
- No discount.
- OCP: $100 to $120,000 per year.
- Stock is purchased weekly with OCPs.

- Purchasing costs are $5 plus brokerage fees.
- Selling costs are $15 plus brokerage fees.
- Dividend reinvestment fee: five percent of amount invested ($3 maximum) plus brokerage fees.
- Automatic investment services are available ($2 plus brokerage fees).
- Safekeeping services are available.
- Gift share transfers are available.
- Direct deposit of dividends is available.
- Dividends are paid January, April, July, and October.

*Performance Rating:* ***

**New England Business Services, Inc. (NYSE:NEB)**
**500 Main St.**
**Groton, MA 01471**
**(800) 736-3001**

*Business Profile:* Supplies standardized business forms, software, and related printed products, selling primarily by mail order to small businesses throughout the U.S., Canada, and U.K.

*Performance History:* $1000 invested on 12/31/92 was worth $2277 on 12/31/97, a 128 percent increase in five years.

*Plan Specifics:*

- Initial shares can be purchased directly from the company ($250 minimum).
- Partial dividend reinvestment is available.
- No discount.
- OCP: $50 to $100,000 per year.
- Stock is purchased weekly with OCPs.
- Purchasing costs are $5 plus eight cents per share.
- Selling costs are $10 plus 15 cents per share.
- Automatic investment services are available ($2.50 plus eight cents per share).
- Dividend reinvestment fee: $1.25.
- Shares can be sold via the telephone.
- Direct deposit of dividends is available.
- Dividends are paid February, May, August, and November.

*Performance Rating:* ***

**Newport Corp. (NASDAQ:NEWP)**
**1791 Deere Ave.**
**Irvine, CA 92606**
**(888) 200-3169, (800) 222-6440**
www.newport.com

*Business Profile:* Produces a line of instruments, components, and accessories for the laser and electro-optical market, which includes industrial, governmental, and educational customers.

*Performance History:* $1000 invested on 12/31/92 was worth $2520 on 12/31/97, a 152 percent increase in five years.

*Plan Specifics:*

■ Initial shares can be purchased directly from the company ($100 minimum).
■ Partial dividend reinvestment is not available.
■ No discount.
■ OCP: $50 to $100,000 per year.
■ Stock is purchased weekly with OCPs.
■ Purchasing costs are $7.50 plus 10 cents per share.
■ Selling costs are $7.50 plus 10 cents per share.
■ Automatic investment services are available.
■ Safekeeping services are available.
■ Direct deposit of dividends is available.
■ Dividends are paid January and July.

*Performance Rating:* ****

**Newport News Shipbuilding, Inc. (NYSE:NNS)**
**4101 Washington Ave.**
**Newport News, VA 23607**
**(800) 649-1861, (800) 446-2617, (757) 380-2000**
www.nns.com

*Business Profile:* Designs, manufactures, repairs, overhauls, and refuels nuclear-pow-
ered aircraft carriers and submarines for the U.S. Navy.

*Performance History:* $1000 invested on 12/31/92 was worth $1621 on 12/31/97, a 62
percent increase in five years.

*Plan Specifics:*

■ Initial shares can be purchased directly from the company ($500 minimum).
There is a one-time enrollment fee of $10 plus 10 cents per share brokerage
fees.
■ Partial dividend reinvestment is available.
■ No discount.
■ OCP: $50 to $250,000 per year.
■ Stock is purchased weekly with OCPs.
■ Purchasing costs are $5 plus 10 cents per share.
■ Selling costs are $15 plus 12 cents per share.
■ Dividend reinvestment fee: five percent of amount invested ($3 maximum)
plus 10 cents per share.
■ Automatic investment services are available ($2 plus 10 cents per share).
■ Safekeeping services are available.
■ Dividends are paid January, April, July, and October.

*Performance Rating:* ***

**Norwest Corp. (NYSE:NOB)**
**6th and Marquette**
**Minneapolis, MN 55479**
**(800) 774-4117, (888) 291-3713, (612) 667-1234**
www.norwest.com

*Business Profile:* Delaware-based diversified financial services company. Through its subsidiaries and affiliates, Norwest provides retail, commercial, and corporate banking services, as well as a variety of other financial services. They plan to merge with Wells Fargo.

*Performance History:* $1000 invested on 12/31/92 was worth $4070 on 12/31/97, a 307 percent increase in five years.

*Plan Specifics:*

- Initial shares can be purchased directly from the company ($250 minimum or automatic monthly investments of at least $25). There is a one-time enrollment fee of $10.
- Partial dividend reinvestment is available.
- No discount.
- OCP: $25 to $10,000 per month.
- Stock is purchased weekly with OCPs.
- Purchasing costs are $3 plus three cents per share.
- Selling costs are $10 plus three cents per share.
- Dividend reinvestment fee: four percent of amount invested (maximum $4) plus six cents per share.
- Automatic investment services are available ($1 plus three cents per share).
- Shares can be sold via the telephone.
- Safekeeping services are available.
- Gift share transfers are available.
- Direct deposit of dividends is available.
- Dividends are paid March, June, September, and December.

*Performance Rating:* ****

**OGE Energy Corp. (NYSE:OGE)**
**PO Box 321**
**Oklahoma City, OK 73101-0321**
**(800) 774-4117, (800) 395-2662, Ext. 6711, (405) 553-3000**
www.oge.com

*Business Profile:* Provides electricity to customers in Oklahoma and portions of Arkansas.

*Performance History:* $1000 invested on 12/31/92 was worth $2263 on 12/31/97, a 126 percent increase in five years.

*Plan Specifics:*

- Initial shares can be purchased directly from the company ($250 minimum). There is a one-time enrollment fee of $3.
- Partial dividend reinvestment is available.
- No discount.
- OCP: $25 to $100,000 per year.

- Stock is purchased bimonthly with OCPs.
- Selling costs are $10 plus 12 cents per share.
- Automatic investment services are available.
- IRA option is available.
- Safekeeping services are available.
- Direct deposit of dividends is available.
- Preferred dividends are eligible for reinvestment in additional common shares under the plan.
- Dividends are paid January, April, July, and October.

*Performance Rating:* ****


**Old National Bancorp (NASDAQ:OLDB)**
**420 Main St.**
**Evansville, IN 47708**
**(800) 774-4117, (800) 677-1749, (812) 464-1434**
www.oldnational.com

*Business Profile:* Indiana-based holding company for banks in Indiana, Kentucky, and Illinois.

*Performance History:* $1000 invested on 12/31/92 was worth $1864 on 12/31/97, an 86 percent increase in five years.

*Plan Specifics:*

- Initial shares can be purchased directly from the company ($500 minimum). There is a one-time enrollment fee of $5.
- Partial dividend reinvestment is available.
- Three percent discount on reinvested dividends.
- OCP: $50 to $50,000 per year.
- Stock is purchased monthly with OCPs.
- Selling costs are $10. Limit 100 shares sold per month.
- Automatic investment services are available.
- Safekeeping services are available.
- Gift share transfers are available.
- Dividends are paid March, June, September, and December.

*Performance Rating:* ****


**Oneok, Inc. (NYSE:OKE)**
**PO Box 871**
**Tulsa, OK 74102-0871**
**(800) 653-8083, (918) 588-7158**
www.oneok.com

*Business Profile:* Natural-gas utility in Oklahoma with interests in gas and oil exploration and production.

*Performance History:* $1000 invested on 12/31/92 was worth $2756 on 12/31/97, a 176 percent increase in five years.

*Plan Specifics:*

■ Initial shares can be purchased directly from the company ($100 minimum).

■ Partial dividend reinvestment is available.

■ No discount.

■ OCP: $25 to $100,000 per year.

■ Stock is purchased bimonthly with OCPs.

■ Selling costs are brokerage fees.

■ Automatic investment services are available.

■ IRA option is available.

■ Safekeeping services are available.

■ Gift share transfers are available.

■ Direct deposit of dividends is available.

■ Preferred dividends are eligible for reinvestment of additional common shares under the plan.

■ Dividends are paid February, May, August, and November.

*Performance Rating:* ****

**Owens-Corning (NSYE:OWC)**
**One Owens Corning Parkway**
**Toledo, OH 43659**
**(800) 472-2210, (800) 438-7465, (419) 248-8000**
www.owens-corning.com

*Business Profile:* Developer of fiberglass filaments for use in the construction, transportation, marine, aerospace, energy, appliance, packaging, and electronics industries.

*Performance History:* $1000 invested on 12/31/92 was worth $960 on 12/31/97, a four percent decrease in five years.

*Plan Specifics:*

■ Initial shares can be purchased directly from the company ($1000 minimum or automatic monthly investment of at least $100).

■ Partial dividend reinvestment is available.

■ Twenty-five share minimum for reinvestment of dividends.

■ No discount.

■ OCP: $100 to $120,000 per year.

■ Stock is purchased weekly with OCPs.

■ Selling costs are $15 plus 12 cents per share.

■ Automatic investment services are available.

■ Safekeeping services are available.

■ Gift share transfers are available.

■ Dividends are paid January, April, July, and October.

*Performance Rating:* ***

**Penney (J.C.) Co., Inc. (NYSE:JCP)**
**PO Box 10001**
**Dallas, TX 75301**
**(800) 565-2576, (800) 842-9470, (972) 431-1000**
www.jcpenney.com

*Business Profile:* Major retailer with outlets in all 50 states.

*Performance History:* $1000 invested on 12/31/92 was worth $1875 on 12/31/97, an 87 percent increase in five years.

*Plan Specifics:*

- Initial shares can be purchased directly from the company ($250 minimum). There is a one-time enrollment fee of $10.
- Partial dividend reinvestment is available.
- No discount.
- OCP: $25 to $10,000 per month.
- Stock is purchased weekly with OCPs.
- Purchasing costs are $1.50 plus six cents per share.
- Selling costs are $15 plus six cents per share.
- Automatic investment services are available.
- Dividends are paid February, May, August, and November.

*Performance Rating:* \*\*\*\*

**Peoples Energy Corp. (NYSE:PGL)**
**130 E. Randolph Dr.**
**PO Box 2000**
**Chicago, IL 60690-2000**
**(800) 774-4117, (800) 228-6888, (800) 901-8878, (312) 240-4292**
www.pecorp.com

*Business Profile:* A holding company for two natural gas utilities that serve nearly one million customers in Chicago and communities in northeastern Illinois.

*Performance History:* $1000 invested on 12/31/92 was worth $1759 on 12/31/97, a 76 percent increase in five years.

*Plan Specifics:*

- Initial shares can be purchased directly from the company ($250 minimum).
- Partial dividend reinvestment is available.
- No discount.
- OCP: $25 to $100,000 per year.
- Stock is purchased twice a month with OCPs.
- Selling costs are brokerage fees.
- Automatic investment services are available.
- Direct deposit of dividends is available.
- Dividends are paid January, April, July, and October.

*Performance Rating:* \*\*\*

**Pharmacia & Upjohn, Inc. (NYSE:PNU)**
**7000 Portage Road**
**Kalamazoo, MI 49001**
**(800) 774-4117, (800) 323-1849**
www.pharmacia.se

*Business Profile:* Ninth largest pharmaceutical company in the world.

*Performance History:* $1000 invested on 12/31/92 was worth $1091 on 12/31/97, a nine percent increase in five years.

*Plan Specifics:*

- Initial shares can be purchased directly from the company ($250 minimum).
- Partial dividend reinvestment is available.
- No discount.
- OCP: $50 to $100,000 per year.
- Stock is purchased weekly with OCPs.
- Purchasing costs are $3 plus eight cents per share.
- Selling costs are $10 plus eight cents per share.
- Dividend reinvestment fee: five percent of amount invested ($2.50 maximum) plus eight cents per share.
- Automatic investment services are available ($1.50 plus eight cents per share).
- Gift share transfers are available.
- Dividends are paid February, May, August, and November.

*Performance Rating:* \*\*\*

**Philadelphia Suburban Corp. (NYSE:PSC)**
**762 W. Lancaster Ave.**
**Bryn Mawr, PA 19010**
**(800) 774-4117, (800) 205-8314, (800) 842-7629, (610) 527-8000**
www.suburbanwater.com

*Business Profile:* Philadelphia-based water utility holding company.

*Performance History:* $1000 invested on 12/31/92 was worth $3720 on 12/31/97, a 272 percent increase in five years.

*Plan Specifics:*

- Initial shares can be purchased directly from the company ($500 minimum).
- Partial dividend reinvestment is available.
- Five percent discount on reinvested dividends.
- OCP: $50 to $30,000 per year.
- Stock is purchased weekly with OCPs.
- Selling costs are $15 plus 12 cents per share.
- Must be a shareholder of record 15 days prior to record date to participate in the plan.
- Automatic investment services are available.
- Shares can be sold via the telephone.
- IRA option is available.
- Safekeeping services are available.

- Gift share transfers are available.
- Direct deposit of dividends is available.
- Dividends are paid March, June, September, and December.

*Performance Rating:* \*\*\*\*

**Phillips Petroleum Co. (NYSE:P)**
**Phillips Building**
**Bartlesville, OK 74004**
**(888) 887-2968, (918) 661-6600**
www.phillips66.com

*Business Profile:* Integrated oil and gas company. Also produces plastics and petrochemicals and is the largest U.S. producer of natural gas liquids.

*Performance History:* $1000 invested on 12/31/92 was worth $2265 on 12/31/97, a 127 percent increase in five years.

*Plan Specifics:*

- Initial shares can be purchased directly from the company ($500 minimum). There is a one-time enrollment fee of $10.
- Partial dividend reinvestment is available.
- No discount.
- OCP: $50 to $10,000 per month.
- Selling costs are $15 plus five cents per share.
- Automatic investment services are available.
- Dividends are paid March, June, September, and December.

*Performance Rating:* \*\*\*

**Piedmont Natural Gas Co. (NYSE:PNY)**
**PO Box 33068**
**Charlotte, NC 28233**
**(800) 774-4117, (800) 438-8410, (800) 633-4236, (704) 364-3120**
www.piedmontng.com

*Business Profile:* Provides natural gas to Piedmont region of North and South Carolina and metropolitan Nashville, Tennessee.

*Performance History:* $1000 invested on 12/31/92 was worth $2280 on 12/31/97, a 128 percent increase in five years.

*Plan Specifics:*

- Initial shares can be purchased directly from the company ($250 minimum).
- Partial dividend reinvestment is available.
- Five percent discount on reinvested dividends.
- OCP: $25 to $3000 per month.
- Stock is purchased monthly with OCPs.
- Selling costs are brokerage fees and any transfer tax.
- Automatic investment services are available.
- Safekeeping services are available.
- Dividends are paid January, April, July, and October.

*Performance Rating:* \*\*\*\*

**Pinnacle West Capital Corp. (NYSE:PNW)**
PO Box 52133
Phoenix, AZ 85072-2133
(800) 774-4117, (800) 457-2983, (602) 379-2500
www.pinnaclewest.com

*Business Profile:* Electric utility holding company providing services to portions of Arizona.

*Performance History:* $1000 invested on 12/31/92 was worth $2410 on 12/31/97, a 141 percent increase in five years.

*Plan Specifics:*

■ Initial shares can be purchased directly from the company ($50 minimum).

■ Partial dividend reinvestment is available.

■ No discount.

■ OCP: $50 to $60,000 per year.

■ Stock is purchased monthly with OCPs.

■ Purchasing and selling costs are brokerage fees and related service charges.

■ Automatic investment services are available.

■ Safekeeping services are available.

■ Preferred dividends can be reinvested in common stock.

■ Dividends are paid March, June, September, and December.

*Performance Rating:* **

**Procter & Gamble Co. (NYSE:PG)**
One Procter & Gamble Plaza
PO Box 599
Cincinnati, OH 45201
(800) 764-7483, (513) 983-1100
www.pg.com

*Business Profile:* Markets household items, personal-care products, and consumer foods.

*Performance History:* $1000 invested on 12/31/92 was worth $3342 on 12/31/97, a 234 percent increase in five years.

*Plan Specifics:*

■ Initial shares can be purchased directly from the company (minimum $250). There is a one-time enrollment fee of $5.

■ Partial dividend reinvestment is available.

■ No discount.

■ OCP: $100 to $120,000 per year.

■ Stock is purchased weekly with OCPs.

■ Purchasing and selling fees are $2.50 plus nominal brokerage fees. The firm also charges up to $1 per reinvested dividends.

■ Automatic investment services are available.

■ Dividends are paid February, May, August, and November.

*Performance Rating:* *****

**Providian Financial Corp. (NYSE:PVN)**
**201 Mission St.**
**28th Floor**
**San Francisco, CA 94105**
**(800) 482-8690, (800) 317-4445, (415) 543-0404**
www.providian.com

*Business Profile:* Provides secured VISA and MasterCard credit cards. Also offers home-equity loans, revolving lines of credit, and insurance premium finance.

*Performance History:* $1000 invested on 12/31/92 was worth $2978 on 12/31/97, a 198 percent increase in five years.

*Plan Specifics:*

- Initial shares can be purchased directly from the company ($500 minimum or automatic monthly investment of at least $50 for 10 consecutive months). There is a one-time enrollment fee of $15.
- Partial dividend reinvestment is available.
- No discount.
- OCP: $50 to $250,000 per year.
- Stock is purchased weekly with OCPs.
- Purchasing costs are $5 plus three cents per share.
- Selling costs are $15 plus 12 cents per share.
- Dividend reinvestment fee: five percent of amount invested ($3 maximum).
- Automatic investment services are available ($2 plus three cents per share).
- Shares can be sold via the telephone.
- Safekeeping services are available.
- Gift share transfers are available.
- Dividends are paid March, June, September, and December.

*Performance Rating:* \*\*\*


**Public Service Co. of North Carolina (NYSE:PGS)**
**Shareholder Service**
**PO Box 1398**
**Gastonia, NC 28053-1398**
**(800) 774-4117, (800) 784-6443, (704) 864-6731**

*Business Profile:* Provides natural gas to clients in 26 counties in North Carolina.

*Performance History:* $1000 invested on 12/31/92 was worth $1583 on 12/31/97, a 58 percent increase in five years.

*Plan Specifics:*

- Initial shares can be purchased directly from the company ($250 minimum).
- Partial dividend reinvestment is available.
- Five percent discount on reinvested dividends.
- OCP: $25 to $15,000 per quarter.
- Stock is purchased monthly with OCPs.
- Selling costs are nominal.
- Automatic investment services are available.

- Safekeeping services are available.
- Dividends are paid January, April, July, and October.

*Performance Rating:* ***

### Public Service Enterprise Group, Inc. (NYSE:PEG)
PO Box 1171
Newark, NJ 07101-1171
(800) 242-0813, (201) 430-7000
www.pseg.com

*Business Profile:* New Jersey-based public utility holding company.

*Performance History:* $1000 invested on 12/31/92 was worth $1507 on 12/31/97, a 51 percent increase in five years.

*Plan Specifics:*

- Initial shares can be purchased directly from the company ($250 minimum or automatic monthly investments of at least $50). There is a one-time enrollment fee of $10.
- Partial dividend reinvestment is available.
- No discount.
- OCP: $50 to $125,000 per year.
- Stock is purchased monthly with OCPs.
- Selling costs are brokerage fees.
- Dividends are paid March, June, September, and December.

*Performance Rating:* **

### Public Service of New Mexico (NYSE:PNM)
PO Box 1047
Albuquerque, NM 87103-9937
(800) 545-4425, (505) 241-2700
www.pnm.com

*Business Profile:* Provides gas and electricity in north central New Mexico.

*Performance History:* $1000 invested on 12/31/92 was worth $2010 on 12/31/97, a 101 percent increase in five years.

*Plan Specifics:*

- Initial shares can be purchased directly from the company ($50 minimum).
- Partial dividend reinvestment is available.
- No discount.
- OCP: $50 to $60,000 per year.
- Stock is purchased monthly with OCPs.
- Purchasing costs are service charges plus brokerage fees.
- Selling costs are service charges plus brokerage fees.
- Safekeeping services are available.
- Gift share transfers are available.
- Dividends are paid February, May, August, and November.

*Performance Rating:* ***

**Quaker Oats Co. (NYSE:OAT)**
**321 North Clark St.**
**Chicago, IL 60610**
**(800) 774-4117, (800) 344-1198, (800) 286-9178, (312) 222-7111**
www.quakeroats.com

*Business Profile:* Major producer of branded food products.

*Performance History:* $1000 invested on 12/31/92 was worth $1893 on 12/31/97, an 89 percent increase in five years.

*Plan Specifics:*

- Initial shares can be purchased directly from the company ($500 minimum). There is a one-time enrollment fee of $10.
- Partial dividend reinvestment is available.
- No discount.
- OCP: $50 to $120,000 per year.
- Stock is purchased weekly with OCPs.
- Purchasing costs are $5 plus 10 cents per share.
- Selling costs are $10 plus 10 cents per share.
- Dividend reinvestment fee: 75 cents transaction fee.
- Automatic investment services are available ($1.50 transaction fee plus 10 cents per share).
- Safekeeping services are available.
- Gift share transfers are available.
- Dividends are paid January, April, July, and October.

*Performance Rating:* ****


**Questar Corp. (NYSE:STR)**
**PO Box 45433**
**Salt Lake City, UT 84145-0433**
**(800) 729-6788, (801) 534-5885, (801) 324-5000**
www.questarcorp.com

*Business Profile:* Energy-based holding company engaged in retail distribution, interstate transmission, exploration, and storage of natural gas. The firm is also involved in microwave communications and commercial real estate.

*Performance History:* $1000 invested on 12/31/92 was worth $1994 on 12/31/97, a 99 percent increase in five years.

*Plan Specifics:*

- Initial shares can be purchased directly from the company ($250 minimum). There is a one-time enrollment fee of $10. Not available in Florida, Kansas, Vermont, North Carolina, and North Dakota.
- Partial dividend reinvestment is available.
- No discount.
- OCP: $50 to $100,000 per year.
- Stock is purchased monthly with OCPs.
- Purchasing costs may include brokerage fees.

- Safekeeping services are available.
- Dividends are paid March, June, September, and December.

*Performance Rating:* *****

**Reader's Digest Association, Inc. (NYSE:RDA)"**
**c/o Chemical Bank**
**450 W. 33rd St., 15th Floor**
**New York, NY 10001**
**(800) 242-4653, (914) 238-1000**
www.readersdigest.com

*Business Profile:* Leading marketer of magazines, books, and home-entertainment products.

*Performance History:* $1000 invested on 12/31/92 was worth $527 on 12/31/97, a 47 percent decrease in five years.

*Plan Specifics:*

- Initial shares can be purchased directly from the company ($1000 minimum).
- Partial dividend reinvestment is available.
- Investors must have at least 10 shares in plan in order to reinvest dividends.
- No discount.
- OCP: $100 to $10,000 per month.
- Stock is purchased weekly with OCPs.
- Purchasing costs are $5 plus 12 cents per share.
- Selling costs are $15 plus 12 cents per share.
- Automatic investment services are available.
- Dividends are paid February, May, August, and November.

*Performance Rating:* ***

**Redwood Trust, Inc. (NYSE:RWT)**
**591 Redwood Highway, Suite 3100**
**Mill Valley, California 94941**
**(800) 774-4117, (800) 526-0801, (415) 389-7373**
www.redwoodtrust.com

*Business Profile:* Real estate investment trust.

*Performance History:* $1000 invested on 12/31/92 was worth $1309 on 12/31/97, a 31 percent increase in five years.

*Plan Specifics:*

- Initial shares can be purchased directly from the company ($500 minimum).
- Two percent discount on reinvested dividends, 0 to 2 percent on OCPs.
- Partial dividend reinvestment is available.
- OCP: $500 to $5000 per month.
- Stock is purchased monthly with OCPs.
- Selling costs are service charges plus brokerage fees.
- Automatic investment services are available.

- Safekeeping services are available.
- Dividends are paid January, April, July, and October.

*Performance Rating:* \*\*\*

**Regions Financial Corp. (NASDAQ:RGBK)**
**417 N. 20th St.**
**Birmingham, AL 35202-0247**
**(800) 922-3468, (800) 446-2617, (205) 326-7100**
www.regionsbank.com

*Business Profile:* Multibank holding company serving primarily Alabama and north-western Florida.

*Performance History:* $1000 invested on 12/31/92 was worth $2739 on 12/31/97, a 174 percent increase in five years.

*Plan Specifics:*

- Initial shares can be purchased directly from the company ($500 minimum).
- Partial dividend reinvestment is not available.
- No discount.
- OCP: $25 to $120,000 per year.
- Stock is purchased monthly with OCPs.
- Selling costs are brokerage fees plus a $50 charge if account is closed within six months of its opening.
- Automatic investment services are available ($1 transaction fee).
- Shares can be sold via the telephone.
- Safekeeping services are available.
- Dividends are paid January, April, July, and October.

*Performance Rating:* \*\*\*\*\*

**Roadway Express, Inc. (NASDAQ:ROAD)**
**PO Box A3309**
**Chicago, IL 60690**
**(800) 774-4117, (800) 991-8947, (330) 384-1717**
www.roadway.com

*Business Profile:* One of the largest U.S. motor carriers of less-than-truckload freight.

*Performance History:* Not available.

*Plan Specifics:*

- Initial shares can be purchased directly from the company ($250 minimum). There is a one-time enrollment fee of $10.
- Partial dividend reinvestment is available.
- No discount.
- OCP: $50 to $100,000 per year.
- Stock is purchased weekly with OCPs.
- Purchasing costs are $5 plus 10 cents per share.
- Selling costs are $10 plus 10 cents per share.
- Automatic investment services are available ($1.50 plus 10 cents per share).

- Safekeeping services are available.
- Gift share transfers are available.
- Dividends are paid March, June, September, and December.

*Performance Rating:* ***

**Robbins & Myers, Inc. (NYSE:RBN)**
**1400 Kettering Tower**
**Dayton, OH 45423**
**(800) 622-6757, (937) 222-2610**
www.moyno.com

*Business Profile:* Designs, manufactures, and markets fluid-management products for process industries on a global basis.

*Performance History:* $1000 invested on 12/31/92 was worth $4668 on 12/31/97, a 367 percent increase in five years.

*Plan Specifics:*

- Initial shares can be purchased directly from the company ($500 minimum).
- Partial dividend reinvestment is available.
- No discount.
- OCP: $50 to $5000 per quarter.
- Stock is purchased monthly with OCPs.
- Selling costs are five percent of amount invested ($5 maximum) plus brokerage fees.
- Automatic investment services are available.
- Dividends are paid January, April, July, and October.

*Performance Rating:* ***

**Rockwell International Corp. (NYSE:ROK)**
**600 Anton Blvd.**
**Costa Mesa, CA 92626-7147**
**(800) 842-7629, (800) 204-7800, (412) 565-4090**
www.rockwell.com

*Business Profile:* Manufacturer of components and systems for use in electronic, communication, and aviation applications.

*Performance History:* $1000 invested on 12/31/92 was worth $2320 on 12/31/97, a 132 percent increase in five years.

*Plan Specifics:*

- Initial shares can be purchased directly from the company ($1000 minimum). There is a one-time enrollment fee of $5.
- Partial dividend reinvestment is available.
- No discount.
- OCP: $100 to $100,000 per year.
- Stock is purchased weekly with OCPs.
- Purchasing costs are $5 plus 10 cents per share.
- Selling costs are $15 plus 12 cents per share.
- Automatic investment services are available.

■ Safekeeping services are available.

■ Gift share transfers are available.

■ Dividends are paid March, June, September, and December.

*Performance Rating:* ****


**SBC Communications, Inc. (NYSE:SBC)**
**175 East Houston**
**Houston, TX 78205-2233**
**(888) 836-5062, (800) 351-7221, (210) 821-4105**
www.sbc.com

*Business Profile:* Telephone holding company with investments in cellular telephone service, cable television, and international ventures.

*Performance History:* $1000 invested on 12/31/92 was worth $2418 on 12/31/97, a 142 percent increase in five years.

*Plan Specifics:*

■ Initial shares can be purchased directly from the company ($500 minimum). There is a one-time enrollment fee of $10.

■ Partial dividend reinvestment is available.

■ No discount.

■ OCP: $50 to $120,000 per year.

■ Stock is purchased weekly with OCPs.

■ Selling costs are $10 plus five cents per share.

■ Automatic investment services are available.

■ Shares can be sold via the telephone.

■ IRA option is available ($35 annual fee).

■ Safekeeping services are available.

■ Gift share transfers are available.

■ Dividends are paid February, May, August, and November.

*Performance Rating:* *****


**SCANA Corp. (NYSE:SCG)**
**Shareholder Services 054**
**Columbia, SC 29218**
**(800) 763-5891, (800) 774-4117, (803) 733-6817**
www.scana.com

*Business Profile:* Public utility holding company supplying electric power and gas service to South Carolina residents.

*Performance History:* $1000 invested on 12/31/92 was worth $1501 on 12/31/97, a 50 percent increase in five years.

*Plan Specifics:*

■ Initial shares can be purchased directly from the company ($250 minimum).

■ Partial dividend reinvestment is available.

■ No discount.

■ OCP: $25 to $100,000 per year.

■ Stock is purchased bimonthly with OCPs.

- Selling costs are brokerage fees and any transfer tax.
- Safekeeping services are available.
- Gift share transfers are available.
- Direct deposit of dividends is available.
- Dividends are paid January, April, July, and October.

*Performance Rating:* *\*\*\*\*\**

**Schnitzer Steel Industries, Inc. (NASDAQ:SCHN)**
**3200 NW Yeon Ave.**
**Portland, OR 97210**
**(800) 727-7033, (503) 224-9900**

*Business Profile:* The firm is an integrated recycler of steel products.

*Performance History:* $1000 invested on 12/31/92 was worth $1520 on 12/31/97, a 52 percent increase in five years.

*Plan Specifics:*

- Initial shares can be purchased directly from the company ($500 minimum).
- Partial dividend reinvestment is available.
- No discount.
- OCP: $50 to $100,000 per year.
- Automatic investment services are available.
- Dividends are paid February, May, August, and November.

*Performance Rating:* *\*\*\**

**Sears, Roebuck & Co. (NYSE:S)**
**3333 Beverly Rd.**
**Hoffman Estates, IL 60179**
**(800) 732-7780, (888) 732-7788, (847) 286-2500**
www.sears.com

*Business Profile:* Manages general merchandise stores nationwide.

*Performance History:* $1000 invested on 12/31/92 was worth $3168 on 12/31/97, a 217 percent increase in five years.

*Plan Specifics:*

- Initial shares can be purchased directly from the company ($500 minimum or automatic monthly investments of at least $100). There is a one-time enrollment fee of $10 plus three cents per share.
- Partial dividend reinvestment is available.
- No discount.
- OCP: $50 to $150,000 per year.
- Stock is purchased weekly with OCPs.
- Purchasing costs are five percent of total amount invested ($7.50 maximum) plus three cents per share.
- Selling costs are $15 plus 12 cents per share.
- Dividend reinvestment fee: five percent of amount invested ($3 maximum) plus three cents per share.
- Automatic investment services are available ($1 plus three cents per share).

- IRA option is available ($35 annual fee).
- Safekeeping services are available.
- Share can be sold via telephone.
- Gift share transfers are available.
- Dividends are paid January, April, July, and October.

*Performance Rating:* ****

**Security Capital Pacific Trust (NYSE:PTR)**
**7670 South Chester St.**
**Englewood, CO 80112**
**(800) 842-7629, (800) 851-9677, (303) 708-5959**

*Business Profile:* Focuses on the acquisition, development, operation, and long-term ownership of multifamily properties in the western U.S.

*Performance History:* $1000 invested on 12/31/92 was worth $2368 on 12/31/97, a 137 percent increase in five years.

*Plan Specifics:*

- Initial shares can be purchased directly from the company ($200 minimum).
- Partial dividend reinvestment is available.
- Up to five percent discount on reinvested dividends and OCPs.
- OCP: $200 to $5000 per month.
- Stock is purchased daily with OCPs.
- Automatic investment services are available.
- Purchase fees are 12 cents per share.
- Safekeeping services are available.
- Dividends are paid February, May, August, and November.

*Performance Rating:* ***

**SEMCO Energy, Inc. (NASDAQ:SMGS)**
**405 Water St.**
**PO Box 5026**
**Port Huron, MI 48061-5026**
**(800) 649-1856, (800) 255-7647, (810) 987-2200**

*Business Profile:* Supplier of natural gas to parts of Michigan.

*Performance History:* $1000 invested on 12/31/92 was worth $1196 on 12/31/97, a 20 percent increase in five years.

*Plan Specifics:*

- Initial shares can be purchased directly from the company ($250 minimum).
- Partial dividend reinvestment is available.
- No discount.
- OCP: $25 to $100,000 per year.
- Stock is purchased monthly with OCPs.
- Must go through own broker to sell 100 or more shares.

- Purchasing costs are 10 cents per share.
- Dividends are paid February, May, August, and November.

*Performance Rating:* \*\*\*


**Sempra Energy (NYSE: SRE)**
**101 Ash St.**
**San Diego, CA 92101**
**(800) 307-7343, (800) 826-5942, (619) 239-7700**
www.enova.com

*Business Profile:* Provides electric and gas services to customers in southern California.

*Performance History:* $1000 invested on 12/31/92 was worth $1599 on 12/31/97, a 60 percent increase in five years.

*Plan Specifics:*

- Initial shares can be purchased directly from the company ($500 minimum or automatic monthly investments of at least $25 for 10 consecutive months). There is a one-time enrollment fee of $15.
- Partial dividend reinvestment is available.
- No discount.
- OCP: $25 to $150,000 per year.
- Stock is purchased at least weekly with OCPs.
- Selling costs are $10 plus three cents per share.
- Automatic investment services are available (50 cent transaction fee).
- Shares can be sold via the telephone.
- Safekeeping services are available.
- Gift share transfers are available.
- You can borrow against holdings in the plan.
- Direct deposit of dividends is available.
- Dividends are paid January, April, July, and October.

*Performance Rating:* \*\*\*\*


**SIS Bancorp Inc. (NASDAQ:SISB)**
**1441 Main St.**
**Springfield, MA 01102**
**(888) 877-2891**

*Business Profile:* Holding company for Springfield Institution for Savings, which operates in Western Massachusetts and Connecticut.

*Performance History:* $1000 invested on 12/31/92 was worth $4212 on 12/31/97, a 321 percent increase in five years.

*Plan Specifics:*

- Initial shares can be purchased directly from the company ($1000 minimum).
- Partial dividend reinvestment is not available.
- 25 share minimum for reinvestment of dividends.
- No discount.
- OCP: $100 to $10,000 per month.

- Stock is purchased weekly with OCPs.
- Purchasing costs are $5 plus 12 cents per share.
- Selling costs are $15 plus 12 cents per share.
- Automatic investment services are available ($3 plus 12 cents per share).
- Safekeeping services are available.
- Gift share transfers are available.
- Dividends are paid February, May, August, and November.

*Performance Rating:* \*\*\*

**Snap-On, Inc. (NYSE:SNA)**
**2801 80th St.**
**PO Box 1410**
**Kenosha, WI 53141**
**(800) 501-9474, (414) 656-5200**
www.snapon.com

*Business Profile:* Manufacturer and distributor of hand tools, power tools, tool storage products, and diagnostic and shop equipment.

*Performance History:* $1000 invested on 12/31/92 was worth $2310 on 12/31/97, a 131 percent increase in five years.

*Plan Specifics:*

- Initial shares can be purchased directly from the company ($500 minimum or automatic monthly investments of at least $100 for five consecutive months).
- Partial dividend reinvestment is available.
- No discount.
- OCP: $100 to $150,000 per year.
- Stock is purchased weekly with OCPs.
- Purchasing costs are $2.
- Selling costs are $15 plus 15 cents per share.
- Automatic investment services are available.
- Shares can be sold via the telephone.
- Safekeeping services are available.
- Dividends are paid March, June, September, and December.

*Performance Rating:* \*\*\*\*

**Southern Company (NYSE:SO)**
**Stockholder Services**
**PO Box 54250**
**Atlanta, GA 30308-0250**
**(800) 774-4117, (800) 554-7626**
www.southernco.com

*Business Profile:* Domestic and international producer of electricity, particularly focused in southeastern U.S.

*Performance History:* $1000 invested on 12/31/92 was worth $1792 on 12/31/97, a 79 percent increase in five years.

*Plan Specifics:*

■ Initial shares can be purchased directly from the company ($250 minimum). There is a one-time enrollment fee of $10.

■ Partial dividend reinvestment is available.

■ No discount.

■ OCP: $25 to $150,000 per year.

■ Stock is purchased bimonthly with OCPs.

■ Selling costs are six cents per share.

■ Automatic investment services are available.

■ Safekeeping services are available.

■ Gift share transfers are available.

■ Direct deposit of dividends is available.

■ Dividends are paid March, June, September, and December.

*Performance Rating:* *****

**Southern Union (NYSE:SUG)**
**504 Lavaca St., 8th Floor**
**Austin, TX 78701**
**(800) 793-8938, (800) 736-3001, (512) 477-5852**

*Business Profile:* Electric utility holding company serving much of the Southeast.

*Performance History:* $1000 invested on 12/31/92 was worth $3741 on 12/31/97, a 274 percent increase in five years.

*Plan Specifics:*

■ Initial shares can be purchased directly from the company ($250 minimum). There is a one-time enrollment fee of $5.

■ Partial dividend reinvestment is not available.

■ No discount.

■ OCP: $50 to $100,000 per year.

■ Stock is purchased bimonthly with OCPs.

■ Purchasing costs are five percent of investment amount ($1 minimum, $2.50 maximum) plus brokerage fees.

■ Selling costs are $10 plus brokerage fees.

■ Automatic investment services are available.

■ Safekeeping services are available.

■ Gift share transfers are available.

■ Dividend is paid in December.

*Performance Rating:* ***

**Sunstone Hotel Investors, Inc. (NYSE:SSI)**
**115 Calle de Industries, Suite 201**
**San Clemente, CA 92672**
**(800) 774-4117, (888) 261-6776, (714) 361-3900**

*Business Profile:* Real estate investment trust that owns mid-priced and upscale hotels in the western United States.

*Performance History:* $1000 invested on 12/31/92 was worth $2223 on 12/31/97, a 122 percent increase in five years.

*Plan Specifics:*

- Initial shares can be purchased directly from the company ($1000 minimum).
- Partial dividend reinvestment is available.
- Up to five percent discount on reinvested dividends and OCPs.
- OCP: $100 to $3000 per month.
- Stock is purchased monthly with OCPs.
- Purchasing and selling costs may include brokerage fees.
- Safekeeping services are available.
- OCP of more than $3000 is available with a waiver from Sunstone.
- Dividends are paid February, May, August, and November.

*Performance Rating:* ***


**Synovus Financial Corp. (NYSE:SNV)**
**901 Front Ave., Suite 301**
**Columbus, GA 31901**
**(800) 337-0896, (706) 649-4818**

*Business Profile:* Southeast interstate bank holding company also involved in credit-card processing.

*Performance History:* $1000 invested on 12/31/92 was worth $5302 on 12/31/97, a 430 percent increase in five years.

*Plan Specifics:*

- Initial shares can be purchased directly from the company ($250 minimum). There is a one-time enrollment fee of $10.
- Partial dividend reinvestment is available.
- Ten share minimum for reinvestment of dividends.
- No discount.
- OCP: $50 to $250,000 per year.
- Stock is purchased weekly with OCPs.
- Purchasing costs are $2.50 plus eight cents per share.
- Selling costs are $10 plus 15 cents per share.
- Automatic investment services are available.
- Safekeeping services are available.
- Gift share transfers are available.
- Direct deposit of dividends is available.
- Dividends are paid January, April, July, and October.

*Performance Rating:* ****

**Tandy Corp. (NYSE:TAN)**
**1800 One Tandy Center**
**Fort Worth, TX 76102**
**(888) 218-4374, (817) 390-3700**
www.tandy.com

*Business Profile:* Retailer of consumer electronics.

*Performance History:* $1000 invested on 12/31/92 was worth $2764 on 12/31/97, a 176 percent increase in five years.

*Plan Specifics:*

- Initial shares can be purchased directly from the company ($250 minimum). There is a one-time enrollment fee of $10.
- Partial dividend reinvestment is available.
- No discount.
- OCP: $50 to $150,000 per year.
- Stock is purchased weekly with OCPs.
- Purchasing costs are $5 plus four cents per share.
- Selling costs are $15 plus seven cents per share.
- Automatic investment services are available ($2.50 plus four cents per share).
- Shares can be sold via the telephone.
- Safekeeping services are available.
- Gift share transfers are available.
- Dividends are paid January, April, July, and October.

*Performance Rating:* ***

**Taubman Centers, Inc. (NYSE:TCO)**
**200 East Long Lake Road**
**Bloomfield Hills, MI 48304**
**(800) 774-4117, (248) 258-6800**
www.taubman.com

*Business Profile:* The REIT general partner of The Taubman Realty Group LP that owns, operates, and develops regional shopping centers throughout the U.S.

*Performance History:* $1000 invested on 12/31/92 was worth $1708 on 12/31/97, a 71 percent increase in five years.

*Plan Specifics:*

- Initial shares can be purchased directly from the company ($250 minimum).
- Partial dividend reinvestment is available.
- No discount.
- OCP: $25 to $25,000 per month.
- Purchasing costs are $5 plus 12 cents per share.
- Selling costs are $15 plus 12 cents per share.
- Automatic investment services are available.
- Dividends are paid January, April, July, and October.

*Performance Rating:* **

**Tektronix, Inc. (NYSE:TEK)**
**2660 SW Pkwy.**
**Wilsonville, OR 97070**
**(800) 842-7629, (503) 627-7111**
www.tek.com

*Business Profile:* Leading manufacturer of oscilloscopes. Also produces printers, X terminals, and television systems.

*Performance History:* $1000 invested on 12/31/92 was worth $3215 on 12/31/97, a 221 percent increase in five years.

*Plan Specifics:*

- Initial shares can be purchased directly from the company ($500 minimum). There is a one-time enrollment fee of $5 plus 12 cents per share.
- Partial dividend reinvestment is available.
- No discount.
- OCP: $100 to $10,000 per month.
- Stock is purchased weekly with OCPs.
- Purchasing costs are $5 plus 12 cents per share.
- Selling costs are $15 plus 12 cents per share.
- Automatic investment services are available.
- Dividend reinvestment fee: five percent of amount invested ($0.50 minimum, $10 maximum).
- Shares can be sold via the telephone.
- Safekeeping services are available.
- Gift share transfers are available.
- Direct deposit of dividends is available.
- Dividends are paid January, April, July, and October.

*Performance Rating:* ***


**Tenneco, Inc. (NYSE:TEN)**
**1275 King St.**
**Greenwich, CT 06831**
**(800) 519-3111, (800) 446-2617, (203) 863-1000**
www.tenneco.com

*Business Profile:* Holding company with interests in natural-gas pipelines, construction, and farm equipment.

*Performance History:* $1000 invested on 12/31/92 was worth $1160 on 12/31/97, a 16 percent increase in five years.

*Plan Specifics:*

- Initial shares can be purchased directly from the company ($500 minimum).
- Partial dividend reinvestment is available.
- No discount.
- OCP: $50 to $60,000 per year.
- Stock is purchased weekly with OCPs.
- Purchasing costs are five percent of amount invested ($3 maximum) plus brokerage fees.

- Selling costs are service charges plus brokerage fees.
- Automatic investment services are available.
- Shares can be sold via the telephone.
- Safekeeping services are available.
- Preferred dividends are eligible for reinvestment in additional common shares under the plan.
- Dividends are paid March, June, September, and December.

*Performance Rating:* ***

**Texaco, Inc. (NYSE:TX)**
**2000 Westchester Ave.**
**White Plains, NY 10650**
**(800) 283-9785, (914) 253-4000**
www.texaco.com

*Business Profile:* Fully integrated oil company.

*Performance History:* $1000 invested on 12/31/92 was worth $2228 on 12/31/97, a 123 percent increase in five years.

*Plan Specifics:*

- Initial shares can be purchased directly from the company ($250 minimum).
- Partial dividend reinvestment is not available.
- No discount.
- OCP: $50 to $120,000 per year.
- Stock is purchased at least bimonthly with OCPs.
- Purchasing and selling costs are approximately four cents per share.
- Automatic investment services are available.
- Safekeeping services are available.
- Gift share transfers are available.
- Direct deposit of dividends is available.
- Dividends are paid March, June, September, and December.

*Performance Rating:* ****

**Thornburg Mortgage Asset Corp. (NYSE:TMA)**
**119 East Marcy St.**
**Santa Fe, New Mexico 87501**
**(800) 509-5586, (505) 989-1900**
www.thornburgmortgage.com

*Business Profile:* Mortgage REIT investing mainly in adjustable-rate mortgage-backed securities financed with equity and short-term borrowed funds.

*Performance History:* $1000 invested on 12/31/92 was worth $1602 on 12/31/97, a 60 percent increase in five years.

*Plan Specifics:*

- Initial shares can be purchased directly from the company ($500 minimum).
- Partial dividend reinvestment is available.
- Up to five percent discount on dividend reinvestments and OCPs.
- OCP: $100 to $5000 per month.

- Stock is purchased monthly with OCPs.
- Automatic investment services are available.
- Safekeeping services are available.
- Gift share transfers are available.
- Dividends are paid January, April, July, and October.

*Performance Rating:* \*\*


**Timken Co. (NYSE:TKR)**
**1835 Dueber Ave. S.W.**
**Canton, OH 44706**
**(888) 347-2453, (330) 438-3000**
www.timken.com

*Business Profile:* The leading manufacturer of bearings and alloy steels for the auto, machinery, railroad, aerospace, and agricultural industries.

*Performance History:* $1000 invested on 12/31/92 was worth $2970 on 12/31/97, a 197 percent increase in five years.

*Plan Specifics:*

- Initial shares can be purchased directly from the company ($1000 minimum). The firm will waive the minimum if an investor agrees to an automatic monthly investment of $100. There is a one-time enrollment fee of $10 plus brokerage fees.
- Partial dividend reinvestment is available.
- No discount.
- OCP: $100 to $250,000 per year.
- Stock is purchased weekly with OCPs.
- Purchasing costs are $3 plus 10 cents per share.
- Selling costs are $15 plus 12 cents per share.
- Automatic investment services are available.
- Direct deposit of dividends is available.
- Shares can be sold via telephone.
- Dividends are paid March, June, September, and December.

*Performance Rating:* \*\*\*


**TNP Enterprises, Inc. (NYSE:TNP)**
**4100 International Plaza**
**PO Box 2943**
**Fort Worth, TX 76113**
**(800) 774-4117, (800) 727-7033, (817) 731-0099**
www.tnpe.com

*Business Profile:* A holding company engaged in generating, purchasing, transmitting, and distributing electricity in Texas and New Mexico.

*Performance History:* $1000 invested on 12/31/92 was worth $2360 on 12/31/97, a 136 percent increase in five years.

*Plan Specifics:*

- Initial shares can be purchased directly from the company ($100 minimum). There is a one-time enrollment fee of $5.
- Partial dividend reinvestment is not available.
- No discount.
- OCP: $25 to $100,000 per year.
- Stock is purchased at least monthly with OCPs.
- Selling costs are $5 plus brokerage fees.
- Automatic investment services are available.
- Shares can be sold via the telephone.
- Safekeeping services are available.
- Gift share transfers are available.
- Dividends are paid March, June, September, and December.

*Performance Rating:* **

**Transocean Offshore, Inc. (NYSE:RIG)**
**4 Greenway Plaza (77046)**
**PO Box 2765**
**Houston, TX 77252-2765**
**(800) 727-7033, (800) 524-4458, (713) 871-7500**

*Business Profile:* Engages in contract drilling of oil and gas wells in offshore areas.

*Performance History:* $1000 invested on 12/31/92 was worth $4500 on 12/31/97, a 350 percent increase in five years.

*Plan Specifics:*

- Initial shares can be purchased directly from the company ($500 minimum).
- Partial dividend reinvestment is available.
- No discount.
- OCP: $25 to $100,000 per year.
- Stock is purchased at least weekly with OCPs.
- Selling costs are $10 plus 10 cents per share.
- Automatic investment services are available.
- Safekeeping services are available.
- Gift share transfers are available.
- Dividends are paid March, June, September, and December.

*Performance Rating:* ***

**Tribune Company (NYSE:TRB)**
**435 N. Michigan Ave.**
**Chicago, IL 60611**
**(800) 924-1490, (800) 446-2617, (312) 222-9100**
www.tribune.com

*Business Profile:* Communications company involved in newspaper publishing, broadcasting, and entertainment.

*Performance History:* $1000 invested on 12/31/92 was worth $2758 on 12/31/97, a 176 percent increase in five years.

*Plan Specifics:*

■ Initial shares can be purchased directly from the company ($500 minimum or automatic monthly investments of at least $50 for 10 consecutive months). Initial purchase fee is $10 plus 10 cents per share.

■ Partial dividend reinvestment is available.

■ No discount.

■ OCP: $50 to $120,000 per year.

■ Stock is purchased weekly with OCPs.

■ Purchase fees are $5 ($2 if made via automatic monthly debit) plus 10 cents per share.

■ The firm charges a maximum $3 to reinvest dividends.

■ Selling costs are $10 plus 12 cents per share.

■ Shares can be sold via the telephone.

■ Dividends are paid March, June, September, and December.

*Performance Rating:* *\*\*\*\*\**

**Tyson Foods, Inc. (NYSE:TSN)**
**2210 W. Oaklawn Dr.**
**Springdale, AR 72762**
**(800) 822-7096, (800) 446-2617**
www.tyson.com

*Business Profile:* World's largest producer and marketer of poultry-based products.

*Performance History:* $1000 invested on 12/31/92 was worth $1308 on 12/31/97, a 31 percent increase in five years.

*Plan Specifics:*

■ Initial shares can be purchased directly from the company ($250 minimum). There is a one-time enrollment fee of $7.50 plus three cents per share.

■ Partial dividend reinvestment is not available.

■ No discount.

■ OCP: $50; no maximum.

■ Stock is purchased weekly with OCPs.

■ Selling costs are $15 plus 10 cents per share.

■ Automatic investment services are available ($1 transaction fee).

■ Safekeeping services are available.

■ Gift share transfers are available.

■ Dividends are paid March, June, September, and December.

*Performance Rating:* *\*\*\**

**United Wisconsin Services, Inc. (NYSE:UWZ)**
**401 W. Michigan St.**
**Milwaukee, WI 53202**
**(414) 276-3737, (414) 226-6900**

*Business Profile:* Provider of managed-care services and employee-benefit products in the U.S.

*Performance History:* $1000 invested on 12/31/92 was worth $911 on 12/31/97, a nine percent decrease in five years.

*Plan Specifics:*

■ Initial shares can be purchased directly from the company ($100 minimum).

■ Partial dividend reinvestment is available.

■ No discount.

■ OCP: $100 per quarter to $100,000 per year.

■ Stock is purchased monthly with OCPs.

■ Selling costs are brokerage fees.

■ Safekeeping services are available.

■ Dividends are paid March, June, September, and December.

*Performance Rating:* ***

**U.S. West Communications Group (NYSE:USW)**
**7800 East Orchard Road**
**Englewood, CO 80111**
**(800) 537-0222, (303) 793-6500**
www.uswest.com

*Business Profile:* Telecommunications company serving the Great Plains, Rocky Mountain, and Pacific Northwest states.

*Performance History:* $1000 invested on 12/31/92 was worth $2631 on 12/31/97, a 163 percent increase in five years.

*Plan Specifics:*

■ Initial shares can be purchased directly from the company ($300 minimum).

■ Need four shares to participate in the plan.

■ Partial dividend reinvestment is available.

■ No discount.

■ OCP: $25 to $100,000 per year.

■ Stock is purchased weekly with OCPs.

■ DRIP administrative fees are $4 per year.

■ Selling costs are approximately six cents per share.

■ Participants can reinvest dividends to purchase shares of either U.S. West Communications or U.S. West Media Group.

■ Automatic investment services are available.

■ Dividends are paid February, May, August, and November.

*Performance Rating:* ****

**Urban Shopping Centers, Inc. (NYSE:URB)**
**900 N. Michigan Ave.**
**Chicago, IL 60611**
**(800) 774-4117, (800) 992-4566**

*Business Profile:* Real estate investment trust specializing in regional shopping malls.

*Performance History:* $1000 invested on 12/31/92 was worth $2037 on 12/31/97, a 104 percent increase in five years.

*Plan Specifics:*

■ Initial shares can be purchased directly from the company ($500 minimum). There is a one-time enrollment fee of $7.50 plus brokerage fees.

■ Partial dividend reinvestment is available.

■ No discount.

■ OCP: $50; no maximum

■ Stock is purchased weekly with OCPs.

■ Purchasing costs are five percent of investment ($3 maximum) plus brokerage fees.

■ Selling costs are $10 plus brokerage fees.

■ Shares can be sold via the telephone.

■ Automatic investment services are available ($1 transaction fee).

■ Safekeeping services are available.

■ Gift share transfers are available.

■ Dividends are paid March, June, September, and December.

*Performance Rating:* ***

**UtiliCorp United, Inc. (NYSE:UCU)**
**Shareholder Relations**
**PO Box 13287**
**Kansas City, MO 64199-3287**
**(800) 647-2789, (800) 487-6661, (816) 421-6600**
www.utilicorp.com

*Business Profile:* Provides electric power and natural gas to eight states and a Canadian province.

*Performance History:* $1000 invested on 12/31/92 was worth $1899 on 12/31/97, a 90 percent increase in five years.

*Plan Specifics:*

■ Initial shares can be purchased directly from the company for residents in all but Louisiana, Illinois, and Montana ($250 minimum).

■ Partial dividend reinvestment is available.

■ Five percent discount on reinvested dividends.

■ OCP: $50 to $10,000 per month.

■ Stock is purchased monthly with OCPs.

■ Selling costs are brokerage fees.

■ IRA option is available.

■ Automatic investment services are available.

■ Safekeeping services are available.

■ Gift share transfers are available.

■ Dividends are paid March, June, September, and December.

*Performance Rating:* ***

**Valspar Corp. (NYSE:VAL)**
**1101 Third St. South**
**Minneapolis, MN 55415**
**(800) 842-7629, (612) 332-7371**
www.valspar.com

*Business Profile:* Manufacturer of paint and coatings used in consumer, packaging, industrial, and specialty applications.

*Performance History:* $1000 invested on 12/31/92 was worth $2586 on 12/31/97, a 159 percent increase in five years.

*Plan Specifics:*

- Initial shares can be purchased directly from the company ($1000 minimum).
- Partial dividend reinvestment is available.
- Twenty-five share minimum for reinvestment of dividends.
- No discount.
- OCP: $100 to $10,000 per month.
- Stock is purchased weekly with OCPs.
- Purchasing costs are $5 plus 12 cents per share.
- Selling costs are $15 plus 12 cents per share.
- Automatic investment services are available ($3 plus 12 cents per share).
- Shares can be sold via the telephone.
- Dividends are paid January, April, July, and October.

*Performance Rating:* ****

**Wal-Mart Stores, Inc. (NYSE:WMT)**
**702 Southwest 8th St.**
**PO Box 116**
**Bentonville, AR 72716**
**(800) 438-6278, (501) 273-4000**
www.wal-mart.com

*Business Profile:* Largest retailer in the U.S.

*Performance History:* $1000 invested on 12/31/92 was worth $1275 on 12/31/97, a 27 percent increase in five years.

*Plan Specifics:*

- Initial shares can be purchased directly from the company ($250 minimum or automatic monthly investments of at least $25). There is a one-time enrollment fee of $20 plus 10 cents per share.
- Partial dividend reinvestment is available for holders of more than 200 shares.
- No discount.
- OCP: $50 to $150,000 per year.
- Stock is purchased at least weekly with OCPs.
- Purchasing costs are $5 plus 10 cents per share.
- Selling costs are $20 plus 10 cents per share.
- Automatic investment services are available ($2 plus 10 cents per share).
- Shares can be sold via the telephone.
- An IRA option is available.

- Safekeeping services are available.
- Gift share transfers are available.
- Dividends are paid January, April, July, and October.

*Performance Rating:* *****


**Walgreen Co. (NYSE:WAG)**
**200 Wilmot Rd.**
**Deerfield, IL 60015**
**(800) 774-4117, (800) 286-9178, (847) 940-2500**
www.walgreens.com

*Business Profile:* Leading drugstore chain.

*Performance History:* $1000 invested on 12/31/92 was worth $3049 on 12/31/97, a 205 percent increase in five years.

*Plan Specifics:*

- Initial shares can be purchased directly from the company ($50 minimum). There is a one-time enrollment fee of $10.
- No discount.
- OCP: $50 to $60,000 per year.
- Stock is purchased at least weekly with OCPs.
- Purchasing fees are $5 plus 10 cents per share.
- Selling costs are $10 plus 10 cents per share.
- Automatic investment services are available ($1.50 plus 10 cents per share).
- Dividends are paid March, June, September, and December.

*Performance Rating:* *****


**Warner-Lambert Co. (NYSE:WLA)**
**201 Tabor Road**
**Morris Plains, NJ 07950**
**(888) 767-7166, (800) 446-2617, (973) 540-2000**
www.warner-lambert.com

*Business Profile:* Manufactures prescription pharmaceuticals and OTC medications with interests in gums, mints, and other consumer products.

*Performance History:* $1000 invested on 12/31/92 was worth $4132 on 12/31/97, a 313 percent increase in five years.

*Plan Specifics:*

- Initial shares can be purchased directly from the company ($250 minimum or automatic monthly investment of at least $50 for five consecutive months). There is a one-time enrollment fee of $15 plus three cents per share.
- Partial dividend reinvestment is available.
- No discount.
- OCP: $50 minimum; no maximum.
- Stock is purchased weekly with OCPs.
- Purchasing costs are $5 plus three cents per share.
- Selling costs are $15 plus 12 cents per share.

- Dividend reinvestment fee: five percent of amount invested ($3 maximum) plus three cents per share.
- Automatic investment services are available ($2 plus 13 cents per share).
- Shares can be sold via the telephone.
- Safekeeping services are available.
- Dividends are paid March, June, September, and December.

*Performance Rating:* *****

**Weingarten Realty Investors (NYSE:WRI)**
**2600 Citadel Plaza Dr.**
**Houston, TX 77008**
**(888) 887-2966, (713) 866-6000**
www.weingarten.com

*Business Profile:* Real estate investment trust developing shopping centers primarily in southern states.

*Performance History:* $1000 invested on 12/31/92 was worth $1664 on 12/31/97, a 66 percent increase in five years.

*Plan Specifics:*

- Initial shares can be purchased directly from the company ($500 minimum).
- Partial dividend reinvestment is available.
- No discount.
- OCP: $100 to $25,000 per month.
- Stock is purchased at least quarterly with OCPs.
- Purchasing costs are five percent of amount invested ($3 maximum) plus brokerage fees.
- Selling costs are $5 plus brokerage fees.
- $5 termination fee.
- Dividends are paid March, June, September, and December.

*Performance Rating:* ***

**Western Resources, Inc. (NYSE:WR)**
**818 Kansas Ave.**
**PO Box 889**
**Topeka, KS 66601-0889**
**(800) 774-4117, (800) 527-2495, (785) 575-6300**
www.wstnres.com

*Business Profile:* Natural gas and electric utility serving customers in Kansas and Oklahoma.

*Performance History:* $1000 invested on 12/31/92 was worth $1857 on 12/31/97, an 86 percent increase in five years.

*Plan Specifics:*

- Initial shares can be purchased directly from the company ($250 minimum).
- Partial dividend reinvestment is available.
- No discount.
- OCP: $50 to $120,000 per year.

- Stock is purchased bimonthly with OCPs.
- Purchasing costs are brokerage fees and any other fees.
- Selling costs are brokerage fees and any transfer tax.
- Automatic investment services are available.
- Safekeeping services are available.
- Dividends are paid January, April, July, and October.

*Performance Rating:* \*\*\*

**Whitman Corp. (NYSE:WH)**
**3501 Algonquin Rd.**
**Rolling Meadows, IL 60008**
**(800) 660-4187, (847) 818-5000**
www.whitmancorp.com

*Business Profile:* Consumer goods and beverage company.

*Performance History:* $1000 invested on 12/31/92 was worth $1946 on 12/31/97, a 95 percent increase in five years.

*Plan Specifics:*

- Initial shares can be purchased directly from the company ($250 minimum). There is a one-time enrollment fee of $10 plus three cents per share.
- Partial dividend reinvestment is available.
- No discount.
- OCP: $50 to $120,000 per year.
- Stock is purchased weekly with OCPs.
- Purchasing costs are five percent of the total amount invested ($7.50 maximum) plus three cents per share.
- Selling costs are $15 plus 12 cents per share.
- Dividend reinvestment fee: five percent of amount invested ($3 maximum) plus three cents per share.
- Automatic investment services are available ($2 plus three cents per share).
- Shares can be sold via the telephone.
- Safekeeping services are available.
- Gift share transfers are available.
- Dividends are paid January, April, July, and October.

*Performance Rating:* \*\*\*

**WICOR, Inc. (NYSE:WIC)**
**PO Box 334**
**Milwaukee, WI 53201**
**(800) 236-3453, (414) 291-6550, (414) 291-7026**
www.wicor.com

*Business Profile:* Natural gas utility holding company serving customers in Wisconsin.

*Performance History:* $1000 invested on 12/31/92 was worth $2228 on 12/31/97, a 123 percent increase in five years.

*Plan Specifics:*
- Initial shares can be purchased directly from the company ($500 minimum).
- Partial dividend reinvestment is available.
- No discount.
- OCP: $100 to $10,000 per month.
- Stock is purchased weekly with OCPs.
- Selling costs are $15 plus 12 cents per share.
- Automatic investment services are available.
- Safekeeping services are available.
- Gift share transfers are available.
- Direct deposit of dividends is available.
- Dividends are paid February, May, August, and November.

*Performance Rating:* ****

**Wisconsin Energy Corp. (NYSE:WEC)**
**PO Box 2949**
**231 W. Michigan St.**
**Milwaukee, WI 53201**
**(800) 558-9663, (414) 221-2345**
www.wisenergy.com

*Business Profile:* Provides electric power, gas, and steam to portions of Wisconsin and Michigan.

*Performance History:* $1000 invested on 12/31/92 was worth $1409 on 12/31/97, a 41 percent increase in five years.

*Plan Specifics:*
- Initial shares can be purchased directly from the company ($50 minimum).
- Partial dividend reinvestment is available.
- No discount.
- OCP: $25 to $50,000 per quarter.
- Stock is purchased bimonthly with OCPs.
- Selling costs may include brokerage fees.
- Automatic investment services are available.
- Shares can be sold via the telephone.
- Preferred dividends are eligible for reinvestment for additional common shares under the plan.
- Direct deposit of dividends is available.
- Dividends are paid March, June, September, and December.

*Performance Rating:* ****

**WPS Resources Corp. (NYSE:WPS)**
700 N. Adams St.
PO Box 19001
Green Bay, WI 54307
(800) 236-1551
www.wpsr.com

*Business Profile:* Utility company supplying electricity and natural gas to customers in northern Wisconsin and an adjacent part of Michigan.

*Performance History:* $1000 invested on 12/31/92 was worth $1447 on 12/31/97, a 45 percent increase in five years.

*Plan Specifics:*

- Initial shares can be purchased directly from the company ($100 minimum).
- Partial dividend reinvestment is available.
- No discount.
- OCP: $25 to $100,000 per year.
- Stock is purchased monthly with OCPs.
- Selling costs are brokerage fees.
- Safekeeping services are available.
- Dividends are paid March, June, September, and December.

*Performance Rating:* ****

**XXSYS Technologies, Inc. (NASDAQ:XSYS)**
4619 Viewridge Ave.
San Diego, CA 92123
(888) 200-3166, (619) 974-8200
www.xxsys.com

*Business Profile:* Develops composite technologies from defense industries to replace metals in high-volume markets such as infrastructure and seismic retrofit.

*Performance History:* Not available.

*Plan Specifics:*

- Initial shares can be purchased directly from the company ($100 minimum).
- No discount.
- OCP: $50 to $10,000 per transaction ($100,000 per year).
- Stock is purchased weekly with OCPs.
- Purchasing costs are $7.50 plus 10 cents per share.
- Selling costs are $7.50 plus 10 cents per share.
- Dividend reinvestment fee: four percent of amount invested ($4 maximum) plus six cents per share.
- Automatic investment services are available.
- Shares can be sold via the telephone.
- Safekeeping services are available.
- The company is not currently paying a dividend.

*Performance Rating:* *

**York International Corp. (NYSE:YRK)**
c/o Chemical Bank
450 W. 33rd St., 15th Floor
New York, NY 10001
(800) 774-4117, (800) 437-6726
www.york.com

*Business Profile:* Global manufacturer of heating, ventilating, air conditioning, and refrigeration products.

*Performance History:* $1000 invested on 12/31/92 was worth $1249 on 12/31/97, a 25 percent increase in five years.

*Plan Specifics:*

- Initial shares can be purchased directly from the company ($1000 minimum or automatic monthly investments of at least $100).
- Partial dividend reinvestment is available.
- No discount.
- Investors need to have at least 100 shares in the plan in order to reinvest dividends.
- OCP: $100 to $10,000 per month.
- Stock is purchased weekly with OCPs.
- Selling costs are $15 plus 12 cents per share.
- Automatic investment services are available.
- Dividends are paid March, June, September, and December.

*Performance Rating:* ****

# NATIONAL INVESTMENT CLUBS

I f you know you need to get in the investment game but are concerned about going it alone, joining an investment club that's part of the National Association of Investors Corporation (NAIC) may be the way to get off square one. This appendix lists the NAIC regional contacts and telephone numbers for all of these "armies of the revolution." If you are interested in attending an upcoming NAIC investor fair or educational seminar (which are excellent places to hook up with others interested in starting an investment club), call the NAIC regional contact nearest you. If you and other like-minded individuals are thinking of starting your own investment club, the NAIC provides extremely useful information to its members. Call the NAIC for membership information at (248) 583-6242.

## NAIC Regional Contacts

**ALABAMA**

    Shelley S. Billingsley (205) 539-3435

    Robert H. Lewis (334) 682-5291

**Emerald Coast (South Alabama)**

    Maurice Johnson (334) 986-8170

**ARIZONA**

**Phoenix**

    Voice Messaging (602) 249-7656

**Southern Arizona**

    Joan Eddy (520) 825-8630

**CALIFORNIA**

**Central California**

    Dean Beeman (209) 431-1785

    Voice Mail (209) 439-NAIC

**Channel Islands**

    Voice Mail (805) 482-4600

    Will Chandler (805) 373-0877

**Loma Priela**

    Jeanie (805) 773-3033

    Verla (805) 543-5979

**Los Angeles**

Message Center (818) 772-NAIC

**Orange County**

Joyce McClain (714) 996-5615

**Sacramento Valley**

Announcement Line (916) 853-1235

Jennefer Peele (702) 831-4561

**San Diego**

Voice Mail (760) 741-4137

**San Francisco**

Mary Lynn Pelican (510) 656-2521

**Shasta Buttes**

Robert Boisselle (916) 243-1637

Beulah Wilkinson (916) 343-3793
(days M-F)

**Silicon Valley**

Russell Malley (408) 225-2527

**COLORADO**

**Denver**

Lou Methner (303) 333-8160

Voice Messaging (303) 382-6927

**Pikes Peak**

Bruce Hodgkins (719) 495-1003

Linda Prall (719) 495-9695

**CONNECTICUT**

**Yankee Council**

Don Kerski (860) 257-6337

**DELAWARE**

**Delaware Blue Hen**

Doug Clarke (302) 994-8384

**DISTRICT OF COLUMBIA**

**Metro-Washington**

Voice Mail (202) 387-1950

Juan Lacey (202) 387-1950
(option 7)

**FLORIDA**

**Big Bend**

D. E. Campbell (850) 894-0642

Stephanie Kirby (850) 877-6671

**Jacksonville-St. Augustine**

Marty Geiser (904) 471-7272

**Southeast Florida**

Mary Beck (954) 763-2866

**Palm Beach-North County**

Carolyn Northcutt (561) 575-5697

**Palm Beach-South County**

Marilynn Bever (561) 575-5697

**Northwest Florida**

Frank Wilson (904) 623-5341

**Miami**

Pat Miller (305) 274-8648

**South West Florida**

Melba Congleton (941) 995-6505

Rebecca Freas (941) 498-3308

**Space Coast (Brevard)**

Ken Peters (407) 777-0502

**Daytona Area**

Merle Harris (904) 441-0671

**Deltona Area**

Donna Kearns (407) 574-4309

**Gainesville**

Mike Rollo (352) 375-0143

**Orlando**

Bruce Phillips (407) 281-8866

**Tampa Bay-Bradenton/Sarasota Area**

Nathan Mann (941) 927-7243

**Tampa Bay Area**

Barbara Murphy (813) 933-5936

**GEORGIA**

**Atlanta**

Billy Williams (770) 210-3085

**HAWAII**

**Aloha Hawaii**

Ryan Muraoka (808) 523-0033

Voice Mail (808) 521-1799

**IDAHO**

**Snake River**

TBA

**Southwest Idaho**

Greg Byrd (208) 376-9194

**ILLINOIS**

**Chicago**

Program Info./Voice Mail (773) 736-4444

**Central Illinois**

Kaye Beschomer (309) 444-8841

Betty Sinnock (309) 543-3361 (days)

**NW Illinois Investors**

James E. Walsh (815) 232-3186

Larry Scoggins (815) 233-0114

**INDIANA**

**Central Indiana**

Kenn Kern (317) 357-4903

Sam Hiatt (317) 359-8102

**Evansville Tri-State**

Norman Campbell (812) 465-4174

**IOWA**

**Central Iowa**

Jim Vogel (515) 276-5377

**KANSAS**

**Kansas City**

Janice Stonestreet (913) 451-0620

**KENTUCKY**

**Bluegrass**

Bea Gaunder (606) 224-2362

Mary Cordray (606) 272-1663

**Derby City (Louisville)**

Peggy Gorbandt (502) 491-6215

Diane Young (502) 426-2641

**LOUISIANA**

**ArkLaTex**

Debra Byers (318) 686-5984

**Southwest Louisiana**

Linda Matthews (318) 856-0136

**LOUISIANA-MISSISSIPPI**

**LA/MS**

Charmaine DeMouy (504) 241-7609

Ann Eugene (504) 241-5558

**MAINE**

Howard Clark (207) 761-1636

**MARYLAND**

Voice Mail (410) 235-7070

JoAnn Linck (410) 750-1992

**MASSACHUSETTS**

**Boston/New England**

Walter Steeves, Jr. (781) 449-2742

**MICHIGAN**

**Capitol Area (Lansing)**

Tresa Ransburg (517) 694-8619

Shirley Foster (517) 485-4447

**Mid-Michigan**

Ken Kavula (810) 640-2231

**Southeastern Michigan**

Joyce Manby (248) 626-7041

John Nye (313) 274-8995

Diane Amendt (313) 478-9866 or 837-3634

**Western Michigan-Grand Rapids**

Beth Hamm (616) 949-6979

Madge Gehling (616) 949-7869

**St. Joseph/Kalamazoo**

Jerry Duck (616) 663-2097

**Northwest Region**

Ginger Carrick (616) 941-9514

**MINNESOTA**

**Minneapolis/St. Paul**

Voice Mail (612) 932-9686

**MISSOURI**

**Kansas City**

See Kansas City, Kansas

**Ozarks**

Ing Stevenson (417) 883-6669

**MONTANA**

**Yellowstone**

Joyce Schmidt (307) 672-2396

Gary Wirrell (406) 245-2177

**NEBRASKA**

**Omaha-Heartland**

Tom Hauptman (402) 393-4962

**NEVADA**

**Southern Nevada**

Jennefer Peele (702) 831-4561

Molly Johnson (702) 727-4531

**NEW HAMPSHIRE**

**Granite State**

Dick Connor (603) 886-3232
(9 am–6 pm only)

Paula Krolikoski (603) 778-1462

**NEW JERSEY**

Joe Smith (201) 568-4456

Phil Crocker (732) 382-3051

**NEW MEXICO**

Alan Ruger (505) 822-9322

Bob Blailock (505) 864-1679

**NEW YORK**

**Long Island**

Jack Rodolico (516) 593-6454

**New York City**

Answerline (718) 856-8462

Phyllis Pawlovsky (212) 744-0249

Louis Schoell (212) 263-6888

**Staten Island**

Joe Fischer (718) 948-5048

**Westchester**

Linda Smalheiser (914) 693-8845

**Upstate New York**

Suzanne Ayer (518) 766-7031

**Western New York**

Bob Zelin (716) 741-3446

**NORTH CAROLINA**

**Central North Carolina**

Saundra Williams (919) 250-9837

**Greater Piedmont-Council**

Voice Mail (704) 563-5345

**North Carolina Triad**

Louise Sechter (336) 945-0530

Neal Sheffield, Jr. (336) 373-0510

**Western North Carolina**

Bill Crum (704) 891-2686

Joan Reinhardt (704) 697-2165

**OHIO**

**Central Ohio**

LaVonne Raney (614) 451-8448

Esther Curtis (614) 459-1029

Beth Gilbert (614) 451-6831

**Northeast Ohio—Cleveland**

Gayle Matlock (216) 461-2358
(evenings)

Gerhard Moskal (216) 333-6526
(evenings)

Information Line (216) 556-3014

**Akron**

Lee Barnes (330) 644-1196

**Northwest Buckeye**

Sue Wiseman (419) 726-8112

Fred Dickenson (419) 352-0192

**OKI Tri-State Cincinnati**

Paul Fohl (513) 662-2212

**Dayton**

Malvina Anderson (513) 832-2942

**OKLAHOMA**

**Greater Tulsa Area**

Bill Smith (918) 689-3289
Cathy Grosenick
(918) 581-1808

**Oklahoma City**

Robert T. Shipe (405) 672-1268

**OREGON**

**Portland**

Voice Mail (503) 242-0801
Joyce Clawson (503) 241-6471

**State of Jefferson**

Alyse Dodd (541) 488-4091

Carol Stark (541) 799-3002

**PENNSYLVANIA**

**Central Pennsylvania**

Chuck Reinbrecht (717) 691-5725

**Delaware Valley**

Helen Meussner (215) 428-3720

Ralph Cioffi (609) 767-1325

**Pittsburgh**

Don Franty (412) 279-8176

**RHODE ISLAND**

**Yankee**

Ralph Solmonese (401) 884-1882

**SOUTH CAROLINA**

**South Carolina-Upstate**

W. L. King (803) 484-5482
(days)/(803) 484-6657 (evenings)

Pearl Black (864) 288-9872

Lynn Wiser (864) 232-7815

**Midland**

JoAnn Sheler (803) 536-9646

Susan Segroves (803) 798-8008

**SOUTH DAKOTA**

**Sioux Empire**

Leonard Johnson (605) 332-0147

**TENNESSEE**

**East Tennessee**

Cathy Brake (423) 694-3910

Dee Bumpers (423) 982-9157

**Greater Memphis**

Pat Broadhead (901) 388-0782

**Volunteer State-Nashville**

Charlotte (Sissy) Miller
(615) 370-3717

**TEXAS**

**Costal Bend**

Michael Sysell (512) 991-7810

**Dallas/Fort Worth**

Council Hotline (214) 890-2885

Hall Martin (972) 385-1216

**Heart of Texas**

Bernice Schnerr (512) 926-8483

**Houston**

Council Hotline (713) 599-2491 or
phone/fax (281) 336-7163

**South Texas**

Gene Weaver (210) 658-5800

**West Texas-Amarillo**

Jim Clemmer (806) 381-9442

**Floydada**

Janet Lloyd (806) 983-3450

**UTAH**

**Wasatch**

Cathy Howick (801) 538-3817 or
(801) 364-8628

**VERMONT**

Fran Kirchner (802) 464-8036

**VIRGINIA**

**Central Virginia**

Voice Mail (804) 756-8084

Charles B. Beverage, Jr.
(804) 270-3776

**Hampton Roads**

Ed Hardin (757) 424-2575

Voice Mail (757) 498-2749

**WASHINGTON**

**Inland Empire-Spokane**

Bill Fautch (509) 226-3269

Leonard Salladay (509) 328-5672

**Puget Sound**

Lois Nordwall/Council Hotline
(206) 236-7270

**WEST VIRGINIA**

**WV/OH**

Don Falkner (740) 374-9405

**WISCONSIN**

**Fox Valley**

Jack Smith (920) 725-7426

**Milwaukee**

Vern Prigge (414) 476-4519

Ruth Segal (414) 544-5964

**South Central Wisconsin**

Robert Wynn (608) 273-8308

# APPENDIX C

# AMERICAN DEPOSITORY RECEIPTS

The following American Depository Receipts (ADRs) are part of the J.P. Morgan Shareholder Services Plan and the Global BuyDIRECT program that is offered by the Bank of New York. Each ADR listing includes the country in which the company is headquartered, the stock symbol and stock exchange on which the ADR trades (NYSE—New York Stock Exchange; ASE—American Stock Exchange; NASDAQ—Nasdaq market), and a brief corporate profile. I also provide, when available, the company's Web site address. This is an excellent source of additional information on the company. As I did with U.S. direct-purchase plans (refer to the Directory of U.S. direct-purchase plans in Appendix A), I provide a similar performance rating for each ADR. The performance ratings range from the highest (*****) to the lowest (*). These ratings take into account the companies's earnings and dividend growth records, financial positions, industry growth prospects, and the overall suitability for investment. I've also provided, when possible, a performance history of the ADR. The performance data shows what a $1000 investment at the end of 1994 would have become three years later. Investors who are interested in enrollment information and other financial data on these ADRs should contact Morgan at (800) 749-1687, (800) 428-4237, or (800) 774-4117.

# J.P. Morgan Shareholder Services Plan

### ABN Amro Holding N.V. (NYSE:AAN)
**Amsterdam, Netherlands**
www.abnamro.com
*Business Profile:* ABN AMRO provides a wide range of banking services both domestically and internationally. Through subsidiaries, the company conducts business through more than 1000 branches in the Netherlands and 706 branches in 69 other countries.

*Three-Year Performance History:* Not available.

*Performance Rating:* ****

### Adecco S.A. (NASDAQ:ADECY)
**Lausanne, Switzerland**
www.adecco.com
*Business Profile:* Adecco is a worldwide provider of personnel services. The company operates in North America through its wholly owned subsidiary, Adia Services.

*Three-Year Performance History:* Not available.

*Performance Rating:* ****

### Akzo Nobel N.V. (NASDAQ:AKZOY)
**Arnhem, Netherlands**
www.akzonobel.com
*Business Profile:* Akzo Nobel provides customers throughout the world with healthcare products, coatings, chemicals, and fibers.

*Three-Year Performance History:* $1000 invested on 12/31/94 was worth $1550 on 12/31/97, a 55 percent increase in three years.

*Performance Rating:* ****

### Amcor Ltd. (NASDAQ:AMCRY)
**South Melbourne Victoria, Australia**
*Business Profile:* Amcor is a leading container, packaging, and paper concern.

*Three-Year Performance History:* $1000 invested on 12/31/94 was worth $628 on 12/31/97, a 37 percent decrease in three years.

*Performance Rating:* **

### Amway Japan Ltd. (NYSE:AJL)
**Meguro-Ku, Tokyo, Japan**
www.amway.co.jp
*Business Profile:* A direct-selling company, Amway Japan distributes approximately 160 consumer products in four core product lines: personal care, housewares, nutrition, and home care. Products are distributed through a nationwide network of independent distributors.

*Three-Year Performance History:* Not available.

*Performance Rating:* ***

### Aracruz Celulose S.A. (NYSE:ARA)
**Rio de Janeiro, Brazil**
www.aracruz.com.br
*Business Profile:* Aracruz Celulose is a producer of bleached eucalyptus kraft market pulp, the raw material used for making tissue, printing, writing, and specialty papers in addition to liquid packaging board.

*Three-Year Performance History:* $1000 invested on 12/31/94 was worth $3118 on 12/31/97, a 212 percent increase in three years.

*Performance Rating:* \*\*\*

**Asia Satellite Telecommunications Holdings Ltd. (NYSE:SAT)**
**Hong Kong**
www.asiasat.com
*Business Profile:* Asia Satellite operates two satellites. The firm provides satellite transponder capacity to the broadcasting and telecommunications markets.

Three-Year Performance History: Not available.

*Performance Rating:* \*\*\*

**Baan Company N.V. (NASDAQ:BAANF)**
**Patten, Netherlands**
www.baan.com
*Business Profile:* Baan Company provides open system client/server-based enterprise software. This software helps integrate various corporate functions such as distribution, finance, inventory, manufacturing, and sales.

*Three-Year Performance History:* Not available.

*Performance Rating:* \*\*\*\*

**Banco de Santander S.A. (NYSE:STD)**
**Madrid, Spain**
www.bsantander.com
*Business Profile:* Through subsidiaries and associated companies, Banco de Santander conducts commercial and retail banking activities, investment management, mortgage finance, credit life insurance, underwriting leasing, factoring, and pension fund consulting.

*Three-Year Performance History:* $1000 invested on 12/31/94 was worth $2879 on 12/31/97, a 188 percent increase in three years.

*Performance Rating:* \*\*\*\*

**Banco Santiago (NYSE:SAN)**
**Santiago, Chile**
www.bsantiag.cl
*Business Profile:* Banco Santiago operates a general commercial and consumer banking business.

*Three-Year Performance History:* Not available.

*Performance Rating:* \*\*\*

**Banco Wiese Limitado (NYSE:BWP)**
**Lima, Peru**
*Business Profile:* Banco Wiese, the second-largest commercial bank in Peru, provides general banking services to companies and individuals. The company is also engaged in investment management and securities trading.

*Three-Year Performance History:* Not available.

*Performance Rating:* \*\*

**Barclays plc (NYSE:BCS)**
**London, England**
www.barclays.co.uk
*Business Profile:* Barclays is involved in the banking and investment banking businesses.

*Three-Year Performance History:* $1000 invested on 12/31/94 was worth $3090 on 12/31/97, a 209 percent increase in three years.

*Performance Rating:* ***

**Benetton Group S.p.A. (NYSE:BNG)**
**Ponzano Veneto, Italy**
www.benetton.com
*Business Profile:* Through subsidiaries, Benetton Group designs, manufactures, and markets distinctive casual apparel for men, women, and children under the brand name United Colors of Benetton.

*Three-Year Performance History:* $1000 invested on 12/31/94 was worth $1517 on 12/31/97, a 52 percent increase in three years.

*Performance Rating:* ***

**The BOC Group plc (NYSE:BOX)**
**Surrey, England**
www.boc.com
*Business Profile:* The BOC Group consists of four main businesses: gases, health care, vacuum technology, and distribution services.

*Three-Year Performance History:* Not available.

*Performance Rating:* ***

**British Airways plc (NYSE:BAB)**
**Middlesex, England**
www.british-airways.com
*Business Profile:* British Airways operates international and domestic scheduled and charter air services for passengers and cargo.

*Three-Year Performance History:* $1000 invested on 12/31/94 was worth $1828 on 12/31/97, an 83 percent increase in three years.

*Performance Rating:* ****

**British Petroleum Co., plc (NYSE:BP)**
**London, England**
www.bp.com
*Business Profile:*

British Petroleum, a diversified petroleum and petrochemical company, produces, transports, refines, and markets crude oil and natural gas. They also produce polymers and olefins.

*Three-Year Performance History:* $1000 invested on 12/31/94 was worth $2227 on 12/31/97, a 123 percent increase in three years.

*Performance Rating:* ****

**British Telecommunications plc (NYSE:BTY)**
**London, England**
www.bt.com
*Business Profile:* A provider of local and long-distance telephone service, British Telecommunications is also involved in mobile communication services, line connections, video conferencing, and closed-circuit television.

*Three-Year Performance History:* $1000 invested on 12/31/94 was worth $1806 on 12/31/97, an 81 percent increase in three years.

*Performance Rating:* \*\*\*\*

**Cadbury Schweppes plc (NYSE:CSG)**
**London, England**
www.cadburyschwepps.com
*Business Profile:* Cadbury Schweppes produces, markets, and distributes branded confectioneries and beverages.

*Three-Year Performance History:* $1000 invested on 12/31/94 was worth $1652 on 12/31/97, a 65 percent increase in three years.

*Performance Rating:* \*\*\*\*

**Canon, Inc. (NASDAQ:CANNY)**
**Tokyo, Japan**
www.canon.com
*Business Profile:* Canon manufactures a wide range of copy machines, computer peripherals, business systems, cameras, camcorders, and optical-related products.

*Three-Year Performance History:* $1000 invested on 12/31/94 was worth $1392 on 12/31/97, a 39 percent increase in three years.

*Performance Rating:* \*\*\*\*

**Carlton Communications plc (NASDAQ:CCTVY)**
**London, England**
www.carltonplc.co.uk
*Business Profile:* Carlton Communications owns the largest commercial television enterprise in the U.K. In addition, the company produces prerecorded videocassettes and provides feature film processing, print duplication services, and production and post-production facilities. The firm also designs, makes, and sells digital and analog products.

*Three-Year Performance History:* $1000 invested on 12/31/94 was worth $1421 on 12/31/97, a 42 percent increase in three years.

*Performance Rating:* \*\*\*\*

**Compania Cervecerias Unidas S.A. (NASDAQ:CCUUY)**
**Santiago, Chile**
www.ccu-sa.com
*Business Profile:* Compania Cervecerias Unidas is a producer, bottler, and distributor of beer, carbonated and non-carbonated soft drinks, and wine in Chile and Argentina.

*Three-Year Performance History:* $1000 invested on 12/31/94 was worth $1186 on 12/31/97, a 19 percent increase in three years.

*Performance Rating:* NR

**Consorcio G Grupo Dina, S.A. de C.V. (NYSE:DIN)**
**Col. Del Valle, Mexico**
www.motorcoach.ca
*Business Profile:* Consorcio G Grupo Dina is a manufacturer of medium- and heavy-duty trucks and intercity buses. The company makes and distributes replacement parts and plastic components for trucks, buses, and other vehicles.

*Three-Year Performance History:* $1000 invested on 12/31/94 was worth $628 on 12/31/97, a 37 percent decrease in three years.

*Performance Rating:* **

**Corporacion Bancaria de Espana S.A. (NYSE:AGR)**
**Madrid, Spain**
*Business Profile:* Through subsidiaries, Corporacion Bancaria de Espana provides corporate banking, mortgage financing, institutional banking, retail banking, international banking, foreign currency, government securities, money-market trading, investment banking, fund management, and insurance services.

*Three-Year Performance History:* $1000 invested on 12/31/94 was worth $1946 on 12/31/97, a 95 percent increase in three years.

*Performance Rating:* ***

**CSR Ltd. (NASDAQ:CSRLY)**
**Sydney, Australia**
*Business Profile:* CSR, a building and construction-materials company, operates through six business groups: construction materials, building materials, construction and building materials, timber products, sugar, and aluminum.

*Three-Year Performance History:* $1000 invested on 12/31/94 was worth $1470 on 12/31/97, a 47 percent increase in three years.

*Performance Rating:* **

**Dassault Systemes S.A. (NASDAQ:DASTY)**
**Suresnes Cedex, France**
www.dsweb.com
*Business Profile:* Dassault Systemes focuses on five industrial sectors: automotive and transportation, aerospace, consumer goods, fabrication and assembly, and plant design and shipbuilding. The company's software products offer a full range of design, analysis, manufacturing, and post-production support application.

*Three-Year Performance History:* Not available.

*Performance Rating:* ****

**Electrolux AB (NASDAQ:ELUXY)**
**Stockholm, Sweden**
www.electrolux.se
*Business Profile:* Electrolux manufactures indoor and outdoor household appliances, floor-care products, sewing machines, and commercial appliances sold in over 60 countries.

*Three-Year Performance History:* $1000 invested on 12/31/94 was worth $1381 on 12/31/97, a 38 percent increase in three years.

*Performance Rating:* ***

**Endesa S.A. (NYSE:ELE)**
**Madrid, Spain**
*Business Profile:* Endesa is the largest producer of electricity in Spain.

*Three-Year Performance History:* $1000 invested on 12/31/94 was worth $1974 on 12/31/97, a 97 percent increase in three years.

*Performance Rating:* \*\*\*

**Fiat S.p.A. (NYSE:FIA)**
**Turin, Italy**
www.fiat.com
*Business Profile:* Fiat is involved in automobiles, commercial vehicles, and agricultural and construction equipment. Other operations include aviation engines and related parts, railroad systems, chemical products, man-made fibers, industrial components, metallurgical products, and batteries.

*Three-Year Performance History:* $1000 invested on 12/31/94 was worth $899 on 12/31/97, a 10 percent decrease in three years.

*Performance Rating:* \*\*\*

**Fresenius Medical Care AG (NYSE:FMS)**
**Oberursel, Germany**
*Business Profile:* Fresenius Medical Care develops, manufactures, and supplies dialysis products. The company is a provider of integrated home health-care services, offering nursing and support services.

*Three-Year Performance History:* Not available.

*Performance Rating:* \*\*\*\*

**Grupo Casa Autrey (NYSE:ATY)**
**Mexico City, Mexico**
www.autrey.com
*Business Profile:* Grupo Casa Autrey is a distributor of pharmaceutical and consumer products. The company also distributes a number of periodicals, weekly magazines, and children's books.

*Three-Year Performance History:* $1000 invested on 12/31/94 was worth $978 on 12/31/97, a two percent decrease in three years.

*Performance Rating:* \*\*\*

**Guangshen Railway Co., Ltd. (NYSE:GSH)**
**Shenzhen, China**
*Business Profile:* Guangshen Railway provides railroad passenger and freight transportation and is the sole railroad between Guangzhou and Shenzhen.

*Three-Year Performance History:* Not available.

*Performance Rating:* \*\*\*

**Imperial Chemical Industries plc (NYSE:ICI)**
**London, England**
www.ici.com
*Business Profile:* Imperial Chemical's business operations consist of paints, materials, and specialty chemicals. The firm purchased the specialty chemicals businesses from Unilever in 1997.

*Three-Year Performance History:* $1000 invested on 12/1/94 was worth $1593 on 12/31/97, a 59 percent increase in three years.

*Performance Rating:* \*\*\*\*

**ING Groep NV (NYSE:ING)**
**Amsterdam, Netherlands**
www.inggroup.com
*Business Profile:* Offering a comprehensive range of life and non-life insurance, commercial and investment banking, asset management, and related products.

*Three-Year Performance History:* Not available.

*Performance Rating:* ****

**Istituto Mobilaire Italiano S.p.A. (NYSE:IMI)**
**Rome, Italy**
www.imisigeco.it
*Business Profile:* Istituto Mobilaire Italiano pursues banking activities including brokerage, market making, underwriting, and syndication of Eurobonds and equities, foreign exchange, and money market trading.

*Three-Year Performance History:* $1000 invested on 12/31/94 was worth $2112 on 12/31/97, a 111 percent increase in three years.

*Performance Rating:* ***

**LucasVarity plc (NYSE:LVA)**
**London, England**
www.lucasvarity.co.uk
*Business Profile:* LucasVarity, a global supplier of automotive, diesel engine, aftermarket, and aerospace products and systems, makes vehicle braking, diesel fuel injection, flight control, engine control, and cargo handling systems.

*Three-Year Performance History:* Not available.

*Performance Rating:* ***

**Matsushita Electric Industrial Co., Ltd. (NYSE:MC)**
**Osaka, Japan**
www.panasonic.co.jp
*Business Profile:* Matsushita Electric manufactures video and audio equipment, home appliances, communication and industrial equipment, batteries, kitchen-related products, electronic components, and other products.

*Three-Year Performance History:* $1000 invested on 12/31/94 was worth $948 on 12/31/97, a five percent decrease in three years.

*Performance Rating:* ***

**National Westminster Bank plc (NYSE:NW)**
**London, England**
www.natwestgroup.com
*Business Profile:* National Westminster Bank provides banking and financial-related activities in the United Kingdom. These activities include life and investment services, insurance services, card services, mortgage services, and risk management and investment services.

*Three-Year Performance History:* $1000 invested on 12/31/94 was worth $2335 on 12/31/97, a 134 percent increase in three years.

*Performance Rating:* ****

**New Holland NV (NYSE:NH)**
**Amsteveen, Netherlands**
www.newholland.com
*Business Profile:* Formed through the 1991 merger of the agricultural and construction equipment divisions of Fiat and Ford, the company consists of two groups, agricultural equipment and construction equipment. Farm machinery, harvesters, balers, and loaders make up the agricultural group. The construction segment includes excavators, loaders, and self-propelled graders. Fiat owns roughly 69 percent of the company.
*Three-Year Performance History:* Not available.
*Performance Rating:* ****

**Nippon Telegraph & Telephone Corp. (NYSE:NTT)**
**Tokyo, Japan**
www.ntt.co.jp
*Business Profile:* Nippon Telegraph & Telephone, the largest telecommunications company in Japan, provides local and long-distance nationwide and domestic telephone services. The company also sells terminal equipment and leases telephone and telegraph lines, telex equipment, and facilities. The company is to be broken into three companies sometime in fiscal year 1999, two regional companies and a long-distance provider.
*Three-Year Performance History:* $1000 invested on 12/31/94 was worth $999 on 12/31/97, a 0 percent increase in three years.
*Performance Rating:* ***

**Norsk Hydro AS (NYSE:NHY)**
**Oslo, Norway**
www.hydro.com
*Business Profile:* Norsk Hydro's operations consist of agriculturals, oil and gas, petrochemicals, and light metals. The agricultural segment produces ammonia and fertilizer products, engages in the trade of grains and feedstuff blends, and sells industrial chemicals and gases for explosives production and nitrogen chemicals. The oil and gas group explores for and produces oil and gas in the Norwegian sector of the North Sea. Production of polyvinyl chloride, ethylene, propylene, vinyl chloride monomer, chlorine, and caustic soda makes up the petrochemicals division. Light metals is comprised of the aluminum, energy, and magnesium divisions. The company conducts farming of Atlantic salmon.
*Three-Year Performance History:* $1000 invested on 12/31/94 was worth $1393 on 12/31/97, a 39 percent increase in three years.
*Performance Rating:* ****

**Novo-Nordisk A/S (NYSE:NVO)**
**Bagsvaerd, Denmark**
www.novo.dk
*Business Profile:* Novo-Nordisk produces pharmaceuticals including insulin, industrial enzymes, products for gynecological use, growth hormones, and hematology products. The company has over 40 percent of the world market for insulin.
*Three-Year Performance History:* $1000 invested on 12/31/94 was worth $3166 on 12/31/97, a 217 percent increase in three years.
*Performance Rating:* *****

**Oce NV (NASDAQ:OCENY)**
**Venlo, Netherlands**
www.oce.com
*Business Profile:* Oce designs, makes, markets, and services copying equipment, plotter systems and materials, photosensitive materials and graphic films, and laser printing systems.
*Three-Year Performance History:* Not available.
*Performance Rating:* ****

**Pacific Dunlop Ltd. (NASDAQ:PDLPY)**
**Melbourne Victoria, Australia**
www.pacdun.com
*Business Profile:* Pacific Dunlop has several business groups. The firm's South Pacific Tyres segment makes and retails vehicular and aircraft tires under the Dunlop, Goodyear, and Olympic brand names. Ansell International consists of the making and marketing of latex-dipped products. The production and marketing of aluminum, copper, and optical fiber cables makes up the Cables and Industrial Products segment. And, the distribution of cable and a wide range of electrical products to the industrial and contractor markets make up the Pacific Distribution group.
*Three-Year Performance History:* $1000 invested on 12/31/94 was worth $848 on 12/31/97, a 15 percent decrease in three years.
*Performance Rating:* **

**The Rank Group plc (NASDAQ:RANKY)**
**London, England**
www.rank.com
*Business Profile:* A supplier to the film and television industries, Rank Group owns holiday and hotel businesses (such as the Hard Rock Café)and operates organized recreation and leisure facilities. Aside from film studios, film laboratories, and cinema exhibition, the company owns a 50 percent stake in Universal Studios Florida. Other business ventures include a 49 percent voting interest in Rank Xerox, Ltd., which makes and markets xerographic copiers and duplicators.
*Three-Year Performance History:* $1000 invested on 12/31/94 was worth $928 on 12/31/97, a seven percent decrease in three years.
*Performance Rating:* ***

**Reuters Group plc (NASDAQ:RTRSY)**
**London, England**
www.reuters.com
*Business Profile:* Reuters Group collects and distributes financial and historical data in many of the world's markets. The company designs, installs, and maintains digital and video information management systems and offers an equity trading service.
*Three-Year Performance History:* $1000 invested on 12/31/94 was worth $1567 on 12/31/97, a 57 percent increase in three years.
*Performance Rating:* ****

**Royal Dutch Petroleum Co. (NYSE:RD)**
**The Hague, Netherlands**
www.shell.com
*Business Profile:* Through subsidiaries, Royal Dutch Petroleum produces crude oil, natural gas, chemicals, coal, and metals. It also provides integrated petroleum services in the U.S.

*Three-Year Performance History:* $1000 invested on 12/31/94 was worth $2203 on 12/31/97, a 120 percent increase in three years.

*Performance Rating:* *****

**Santos Ltd. (NASDAQ:STOSY)**
**Adelaide, Australia**
*Business Profile:* Santos is involved in the exploration and production of petroleum products. The company produces one-third of the natural gas consumed in Australia. The company also has an interest in the Bowen Basin, one of the world's coal-producing regions.

*Three-Year Performance History:* Not available.

*Performance Rating:* **

**Sony Corp. (NYSE:SNE)**
**Tokyo, Japan**
www.sony.com
*Business Profile:* Sony operates its business in three segments: electronics, entertainment, and insurance and financing. The electronics group consists of video equipment, audio equipment, televisions, and other electronic-related equipment. The entertainment segment produces and markets compact discs, records, and prerecorded audio and videocassettes. It also produces and distributes motion pictures through television programming, theatrical exhibition, and home video. The insurance and financing division consists mainly of the individual life insurance business operated in Japan.

*Three-Year Performance History:* $1000 invested on 12/31/94 was worth $1658 on 12/31/97, a 66 percent increase in three years.

*Performance Rating:* ****

**TAG Heuer International S.A. (NYSE:THW)**
**Dicks, Luxembourg**
www.tag-heuer.ch
*Business Profile:* TAG Heuer designs, makes, and sells sport watches and chronographs. The company sells its products to independent distributors and directly to retailers in more than 100 countries.

*Three-Year Performance History:* Not available.

*Performance Rating:* **

**TDK Corp. (NYSE:TDK)**
**Tokyo, Japan**
www.tdk.com
*Business Profile:* TDK produces magnetic products, ceramic and assembled components, recording devices, semiconductors, and a variety of recording media. Ceramic and assembled components include capacitors, inductors, filters, high-frequency modules, and switching power supplies. Recording devices are made up of magnetic heads and spindle motors for hard-disk drives, and thermal heads for video decks and floppy-disk drives. Recording media includes magnetic recording tapes for audio and video equipment, floppy disks, and optical disks.

*Three-Year Performance History:* $1000 invested on 12/31/94 was worth $1556 on 12/31/97, a 56 percent increase in three years.

*Performance Rating:* ****

**Telecom Argentina STET-France Telecom S.A. (NYSE:TEO)**
**Buenos Aires, Argentina**
www.telecom.com.ar/english/index.html
*Business Profile:* Telecom Argentina STET-France provides public telecommunications and basic telephone services in the northern region of Argentina.

*Three-Year Performance History:* Not available.

*Performance Rating:* \*\*\*

**Telefonica del Peru S.A. (NYSE:TDP)**
**Lima, Peru**
www.unired.net.pe
*Business Profile:* Telefonica del Peru offers local, domestic, and international long-distance telephone services. Other services include cellular telephone and paging services, business communications, and cable television.

*Three-Year Performance History:* Not available.

*Performance Rating:* \*\*\*

**Telefonos de Mexico S.A. (NYSE:TMX)**
**Col. Cuauhtemoc, Mexico**
www.telmex.com.mx
*Business Profile:* Through subsidiaries, Telefonos de Mexico provides domestic and international long-distance and local telephone services. The company also provides voice, data, and cellular services.

*Three-Year Performance History:* $1000 invested on 12/31/94 was worth $1634 on 12/31/97, a 63 percent increase in three years.

*Performance Rating:* \*\*\*

**Tubos de Acero de Mexico, S.A. (ASE:TAM)**
**Mexico City, Mexico**
*Business Profile:* Tubos de Acero de Mexico produces seamless steel pipes, including casing, tubing, and drill pipe. The company also produces and markets line pipes, mechanical pipes, and cold-drawn pipes.

*Three-Year Performance History:* $1000 invested on 12/31/94 was worth $4613 on 12/31/97, a 361 percent increase in three years.

*Performance Rating:* \*\*\*

**Unilever NV (NYSE:UN)**
**Rotterdam, Netherlands**
www.unilever.com
*Business Profile:* Unilever produces foods, detergents, and personal hygiene products. The company's food division focuses on six main areas including margarine, tea, ice cream, culinary products, frozen foods, and bakery products. The hygiene products include toiletries, cosmetics, and fragrances.

*Three-Year Performance History:* $1000 invested on 12/31/94 was worth $2300 on 12/31/97, a 130 percent increase in three years.

*Performance Rating:* \*\*\*\*\*

**Unilever plc (NYSE:UL)**
**London, England**
www.unilever.com
*Business Profile:* Unilever produces foods, detergents, and personal hygiene products. The company's food division focuses on six main areas including margarine, tea,

ice cream, culinary products, frozen foods, and bakery products. The hygiene products include toiletries, cosmetics, and fragrances. Unilever plc and Unilever NV constitute a diversified international group of businesses operating as a single entity.

*Three-Year Performance History:* $1000 invested on 12/31/94 was worth $2072 on 12/31/97, a 107 percent increase in three years.

*Performance Rating:* *****

### Westpac Banking Corp., Ltd. (NYSE:WBK)
**Sydney, Australia**
www.westpac.com.au

*Business Profile:* Operating through a network of over 1500 branches worldwide, Westpac Banking is one of four major banking groups in Australia. The company is engaged in retail, commercial, and institutional banking activities. In addition, the company finances company activities, manages investments, and handles insurance and mortgage processing.

*Three-Year Performance History:* $1000 invested on 12/31/94 was worth $2219 on 12/31/97, a 122 percent increase in three years.

*Performance Rating:* ****

### Zeneca Group plc (NYSE:ZEN)
**London, England**
www.zeneca.com

*Business Profile:* Zeneca researches, develops, and makes ethical pharmaceuticals, agricultural chemicals, specialty chemicals, and seeds. The firm owns Salick Health Care, which operates cancer treatment and diagnosis centers in the US. Pharmaceuticals consist of cardiovascular, respiratory, anticancer, and anti-infectives. Agrochemicals include herbicides, insecticides, fungicides, and seeds. Organic chemicals, bioproducts, and coatings make up the specialty-chemical segment.

*Three-Year Performance History:* $1000 invested on 12/31/94 was worth $2862 on 12/31/97, a 186 percent increase in three years.

*Performance Rating:* ****

# Bank of New York's Global BuyDIRECT Plan

The following ADRs participate in the Global BuyDIRECT program. Investors interested in obtaining enrollment information for these companies should call Bank of New York at 800-345-1612, 800-943-9715, or 800-774-4117.

### Administradora de Fondos de Pensiones Provida (NYSE:PVD)
**Santiago, Chile**
www.proida.cl

*Business Profile:* AFP Provida offers various pension-related services, including the collection of affiliated worker contributions, management of affiliated workers's accounts, investments of contributions, and payments of pension, life, and disability benefits.

*Three-Year Performance History:* Not available.

*Performance Rating:* ***

**Ahold N.V. (NYSE: AHO)**
**Zaandam, Netherlands**
www.ahold.nl
*Business Profile:* Through subsidiaries, Ahold operates supermarkets and non-food retail stores in the Netherlands, U.S., Czech Republic, Portugal, Poland, Spain, and five Asian countries.

*Three-Year Performance History:* $1000 invested on 12/31/94 was worth $2617 on 12/31/97, a 162 percent increase in three years.

*Performance Rating:* ****

**Arcadis N.V. (NASDAQ:ARCAF)**
**Arnhem, Netherlands**
www.arcadis.nl
*Business Profile:* Arcadis provides environmental and other specialized consulting/engineering, contracting, hydrocarbon, and remediation services worldwide. Its environmental services include contamination investigation, remedial engineering, air quality services, waste mineralization, toxicology, and risk assessment. The company also provides consulting services with regards to infrastructure planning and design, and building and project management.

*Three-Year Performance History:* $1000 invested on 12/31/94 was worth $1258 on 12/31/97, a 26 percent increase in three years.

*Performance Rating:* ***

**Asia Pulp & Paper Company Ltd. (NYSE:PAP)**
**Singapore**
www.asiapulppaper.com
*Business Profile:* Asia Pulp & Paper is one of the largest vertically integrated producers of pulp and paper. Products include printing and writing paper, converted and value-added products, tissue paper, containerboard, and boxboard.

*Three-Year Performance History:* Not available.

*Performance Rating:* ***

**Astra AB (NYSE:A)**
**Sodertalje, Sweden**
www.astra.com
*Business Profile:* Astra AB researches, develops, and produces a wide variety of pharmaceuticals for gastrointestinal disorders, respiratory and cardiovascular disease, the central nervous system, infection, and pain control. The company also produces medical devices mainly used for surgery, radiology, urotherapy, and odontology.

*Three-Year Performance History:* Not available.

*Performance Rating:* ****

**Atlas Pacific Ltd. (NASDAQ:APCFY)**
**Western Australia, Australia**
www.atlaspacific.com.au
*Business Profile:* Atlas Pacific is a producer of South Sea pearls. Its Indonesian pearling interests are the main operations of the company.

*Three-Year Performance History:* Not available.

*Performance Rating:* *

**Banco Bilbao Vizcaya, S.A. (NYSE:BBV)**
**Bilbao, Spain**
www.bbv.es
*Business Profile:* Through subsidiaries, Banco Bilbao Vizcaya conducts retail, whole-sale, private, and investment banking, as well as brokerage services.

*Three-Year Performance History:* $1000 invested on 12/31/94 was worth $4315 on 12/31/97, a 332 percent increase in three years.

*Performance Rating:* \*\*\*\*

**Banco de Galicia (NASDAQ:BGALY)**
**Buenos Aires, Argentina**
www.bancogalicia.com.ar
*Business Profile:* Banco de Galicia is a full-range provider of financial services to individuals and corporate customers in the commercial and investment banking areas.

*Three-Year Performance History:* $1000 invested on 12/31/94 was worth $2253 on 12/31/97, a 125 percent increase in three years.

*Performance Rating:* \*\*\*

**Banco Ganadero S.A. (NYSE:BGA)**
**Santafe de Bogota, Colombia**
*Business Profile:* Banco Ganadero is a leading commercial bank in Colombia. Through subsidiaries and affiliates, the company also offers a variety of financial-related services.

*Three-Year Performance History:* Not available.

*Performance Rating:* \*\*\*

**Banco Rio de la Plata S.A. (NYSE:BRS)**
**Buenos Aires, Argentina**
www.bancorio.com.ar
*Business Profile:* Banco Rio, one of the largest private sector commercial banks in Argentina, conducts general and commercial investment banking. In addition, the company develops and sells mutual funds, sells insurance products, provides for-eign trade financing, and conducts an international banking business.

*Three-Year Performance History:* Not available.

*Performance Rating:* \*\*\*

**BanColombiano S.A. (NYSE:CIB)**
**Medellin, Colombia**
www.bic.com.co
*Business Profile:* BanColombiano provides general banking products and services, as well as dollar-denominated products, to upper-income individuals and middle cor-porate markets.

*Three-Year Performance History:* Not available.

*Performance Rating:* \*\*

**Bank of Ireland Group (NYSE:IRE)**
**Dublin, Ireland**
www.bank-of-ireland.co.uk
*Business Profile:* Bank of Ireland provides a broad range of banking and other finan-cial-related services. The company's main divisions include retail banking, corporate

and treasury, and other group activities that consist of trust and securities services, fund management, stock brokerage, corporate finance, and life insurance.

*Three-Year Performance History:* Not available.

*Performance Rating:* \*\*\*\*

### Bank of Tokyo-Mitsubishi Ltd. (NYSE:MBK)
**Tokyo, Japan**
www.btm.co.jp/index_e.htm

*Business Profile:* Through subsidiaries, Bank of Tokyo conducts a full range of domestic and international banking services through offices in Japan and around the world.

*Three-Year Performance History:* $1000 invested on 12/31/94 was worth $602 on 12/31/97, a 40 percent decrease in three years.

*Performance Rating:* \*\*\*

### Biora AB (NASDAQ:BIORY)
**Malmo, Sweden**
www.biora.se

*Business Profile:* Biora manufactures dental products. The company's principle product is Emdogain, which promotes tooth-supporting tissue regrowth and aids in tooth reattachment. The company is also developing other products based on Emdogain technology.

*Three-Year Performance History:* Not available.

*Performance Rating:* \*\*\*

### Blue Square-Israel Ltd. (NYSE:BSI)
**Givatayim, Israel**
www.coop.co.il

*Business Profile:* Blue Square offers a broad range of consumer products through its supermarkets, department stores, and specialty stores. The company is one of the largest retailers in Israel.

*Three-Year Performance History:* Not available.

*Performance Rating:* \*\*\*

### Boral Ltd. (NASDAQ:BORAY)
**Sydney, New South Wales Australia**
www.boral.com.au

*Business Profile:* Boral operates two core businesses—building and construction materials and energy. The energy segment is the only major integrated explorer, producer, and distributor of gas in Australia and is primarily engaged in the distribution of natural gas and liquefied petroleum gas.

*Three-Year Performance History:* $1000 invested on 12/31/94 was worth $1021 on 12/31/97, a two percent increase in three years.

*Performance Rating:* \*\*

### Bufete Industrial, S.A. (NYSE:GBI)
**Mexico City, Mexico**
www.bufete.com

*Business Profile:* Through subsidiaries, Bufete Industrial designs, constructs, modernizes, and expands industrial plants and infrastructure projects.

*Three-Year Performance History:* $1000 invested on 12/31/94 was worth $340 on 12/31/97, a 66 percent decrease in three years.

*Performance Rating:* **

### Cantab Pharmaceuticals plc (NASDAQ:CNTBY)
**Cambridge, England**

*Business Profile:* Cantab Pharmaceuticals researches and develops proprietary bio-pharmaceuticals for the treatment of infectious and inflammatory diseases.

*Three-Year Performance History*: $1000 invested on 12/31/94 was worth $2500 on 12/31/97, a 150 percent increase in three years.

*Performance Rating:* **

### CBT Group plc (NASDAQ:CBTSY)
**Clonskeagh, Ireland**
www.cbtsys.com

*Business Profile:* CBT Group develops, publishes, and markets client/server, Internet, and corporate intranet software and technologies.

*Three-Year Performance History:* Not available.

*Performance Rating:* ****

### Coca-Cola FEMSA S.A. de C.V. (NYSE:KOF)
**Cuauhtemoc, Mexico**
www.femsa.com/cocacola.html

*Business Profile:* Coca-Cola FEMSA produces, markets, and distributes the soft drink products of Coca-Cola Company, as well as other products in Mexico and Argentina.

*Three-Year Performance History*: $1000 invested on 12/31/94 was worth $2751 on 12/31/97, a 175 percent increase in three years.

*Performance Rating:* ***

### Cresud S.A.C.I.F. y A. (NASDAQ:CRESY)
**Buenos Aires, Argentina**

*Business Profile:* Cresud produces agricultural products such as crops, beef cattle, and milk. The company is also involved in forest-related production activities.

*Three-Year Performance History:* Not available.

*Performance Rating:* ***

### De Rigo S.p.A. (NYSE:DER)
**Longarone, Italy**
www.derigo.com

*Business Profile:* De Rigo manufactures premium-priced sunglasses worldwide.

*Three-Year Performance History:* Not available.

*Performance Rating:* **

### Diageo plc (NYSE:DEO)
**London, England**
www.diageo.com

*Business Profile:* Diageo, created by the merger of Grand Metropolitan and Guinness, produces and sells food, liquor, and other consumer goods. The food segment is comprised of two principal segments—Pillsbury and Burger King. The drinks sector is comprised of United Distillers and Vintners, a major international organization of wine and spirits producers, distillers, importers, exporters, distributors, and retailers.

*Three-Year Performance History:* Not available.

*Performance Rating:* \*\*\*\*

**Doncasters plc (NYSE:DCS)**
**Derbyshire, England**
www.doncasters.com
*Business Profile:* Doncasters manufactures highly engineered components for tolerance-critical applications in the aerospace, industrial gas, and steam turbine industries. It also produces specialized components in metals and alloys.

*Three-Year Performance History:* Not available.

*Performance Rating:* \*\*\*\*

**ECSoft Group plc (NASDAQ:ECSGY)**
**Hertfordshire, United Kingdom**
www.ecsoft-group.com
*Business Profile:* ECSoft is a provider of information technology consulting, applications development, and systems integration services. It serves customers in telecommunications, financial services, retailing, transportation, and energy services, as well as public sector agencies. The company's services are provided to customers migrating from mainframe computer environments to open client/server distributed computing environments.

*Three-Year Performance History:* Not available.

*Performance Rating:* \*\*\*\*

**Elan plc (NYSE:ELN)**
**County Westmeath, Ireland**
www.elan.ie
*Business Profile:* Through license arrangements with major pharmaceutical firms, Elan develops and licenses drug delivery systems formulated to improve absorption and utilization.

*Three-Year Performance History:* $1000 invested on 12/31/94 was worth $2874 on 12/31/97, a 187 percent increase in three years.

*Performance Rating:* \*\*\*\*\*

**Empresas ICA Sociedad Controladora S.A. (NYSE:ICA)**
**Mexico City, Mexico**
www.ica.com.mx/index.html
*Business Profile:* Empresas ICA Sociedad Controladora operates in three main sectors: heavy construction, industrial construction, and urban and housing construction. In addition, the company manufactures and markets industrial goods and markets construction aggregates such as limestone.

*Three-Year Performance History:* $1000 invested on 12/31/94 was worth $1220 on 12/31/97, a 22 percent increase in three years.

*Performance Rating:* \*\*

**Empresas La Moderna, S.A. de C.V. (NYSE:ELM)**
**Monterrey N.L., Mexico**
*Business Profile:* Empresas La Moderna has shifted its focus away from cigarettes to agrobiotechnology and packaging products.

*Three-Year Performance History:* Not available.

*Performance Rating:* \*\*\*

**Empresas Telex-Chile S.A. (NYSE:TL)**
**Santiago, Chile**
www.chilesat.net/telexcl.htm
*Business Profile:* Empresas Telex-Chile is a diversified telecommunications company that provides long-distance and related services directly to corporate customers and to the general public.

*Three-Year Performance History:* Not available.

*Performance Rating:* \*\*

**Esprit Telecom Group plc (NASDAQ:ESPRY)**
**Reading, United Kingdom**
www.esprittele.com/esprit.htm
*Business Profile:* Esprit Telecom provides international and national long-distance telecommunications services. The company has developed an integrated digital telecommunications network of leased fiber-optic lines, microwave transmission facilities, and digital switching technology directly linking 14 European cities, as well as Washington, D.C. and New York.

*Three-Year Performance History:* Not available.

*Performance Rating:* \*\*\*

**FAI Insurances Group Ltd. (NYSE:FAI)**
**New South Wales, Australia**
www.fai.com.au
*Business Profile:* FAI Insurance, one of the most integrated financial-services groups in Australia, provides general and life insurance, home loan, personal financing, financial planning, property management, and aged care services. Through its wholly owned subsidiary, Oceanic Coal Australia Ltd., the company is also a major exporter of coal.

*Three-Year Performance History:* $1000 invested on 12/31/94 was worth $700 on 12/31/97, a 30 percent decrease in three years.

*Performance Rating:* \*\*

**Fila Holding S.p.A. (NYSE:FLH)**
**Biella (Vercelli), Italy**
www.fila.com
*Business Profile:* Fila is a producer of athletic footwear and sportswear and has centered its product development and marketing efforts in the U.S.

*Three-Year Performance History:* $1000 invested on 12/31/94 was worth $1029 on 12/31/97, a three percent increase in three years.

*Performance Rating:* \*\*\*

**Flamel Technologies S.A. (NASDAQ:FLMLY)**
**Venissieux Cedex, France**
www.flamel-technologies.fr
*Business Profile:* Flamel Technologies is a pharmaceutical and medical-device company. The company develops drug delivery systems that optimize the absorption of drugs and improve effectiveness.

*Three-Year Performance History:* Not available.

*Performance Rating:* \*\*

**Freepages Group plc (NASDAQ:FREEY)**
**Oxford, England**
*Business Profile:* Through its proprietary database software and generic interactive response mechanisms, Freepages provides classified directory information by telephone or over the Internet.

*Three-Year Performance History:* Not available.

*Performance Rating:* **

**Gallaher Group plc (NYSE:GLH)**
**Surrey, England**
*Business Profile:* Gallaher, the UK-based spin-off of American Brands, manufactures and markets cigarettes, cigars, pipe tobacco, and hand-rolling tobacco.

*Three-Year Performance History:* Not available.

*Performance Rating:* ****

**General Cable plc (NASDAQ:GCN)**
**London, England**
www.generalcable.co.uk
*Business Profile:* Through three main subsidiaries, General Cable offers business and residential telecommunications as well as cable-television services. The company builds and operates owned and leased integrated broadband communications networks. These networks are constructed using fiber-optic broadband technology, providing high transmission capacity for the delivery of voice, data, video, and entertainment services.

*Three-Year Performance History:* Not available.

*Performance Rating:* ****

**Great Central Mines Ltd. (NASDAQ:GTCMY)**
**Melbourne, Victoria Australia**
www.ausgold.com/gcm
*Business Profile:* Great Central Mines, a major Australian gold producer and exploration company, wholly owns and operates two gold mines.

*Three-Year Performance History:* $1000 invested on 12/31/94 was worth $533 on 12/31/97, a 47 percent decrease in three years.

*Performance Rating:* **

**Groupe AB (NYSE:ABG)**
**Saint Denis, France**
abweb.com/abid/index.html
*Business Profile:* Groupe AB creates, develops, produces, and acquires television programming in France. The company's focus is on youth- and family-oriented programming.

*Three-Year Performance History:* Not available.

*Performance Rating:* **

**Grupo Elektra S.A. de C.V. (NYSE:EKT)**
**Mexico City, Mexico**
www.elektra.com.mx
*Business Profile:* Targeting the low- and middle-income segments of the Mexican population, Grupo Elektra specializes in the sale of brand-name electronics, major appliances, and household furniture. In addition, the company is engaged in mer-

chandising basic clothing and also has an indirect interest in TV Azteca, a Mexican broadcast television station.

*Three-Year Performance History:* Not available.

*Performance Rating:* \*\*\*\*

### Grupo Imsa S.A. de C.V. (NYSE:IMY)
**Garza Garcia NL, Mexico**
www.grupoimsa.com
*Business Profile:* Grupo Imsa, a diversified industrial company, processes steel, produces automotive and industrial batteries, and makes construction-related products.

*Three-Year Performance History:* Not available.

*Performance Rating:* \*\*\*

### Grupo Industrial Durango S.A. de C.V. (NYSE:GID)
**Durango, Mexico**
*Business Profile:* Grupo Industrial Durango, a diversified packaging company, produces corrugated containers, containerboard, industrial paper, molded pulp egg cartons, multi-wall bags and sacks, and packaging for consumer goods.

*Three-Year Performance History*: $1000 invested on 12/31/94 was worth $1000 on 12/31/97, a 0 percent increase in three years.

*Performance Rating:* \*\*\*

### Grupo Iusacell S.A. de C.V. (NYSE:CEL)
**Lomas de Chapultepec, Mexico**
*Business Profile:* Grupo Iusacell provides non-wireline cellular telephone services to subscribers and has agreements with over 60 U.S. and other foreign operators to provide its subscribers with international roaming. Bell Atlantic owns more than 40 percent of the company.

*Three-Year Performance History:* Not available.

*Performance Rating:* \*\*\*

### Grupo Tribasa S.A. de C.V. (NYSE:GTR)
**Mexico City, Mexico**
*Business Profile:* Through subsidiaries, Grupo Tribasa develops, constructs, and operates highways, and constructs large-scale infrastructures. The company also makes and sells construction aggregates, asphalt, concrete, prefabricated concrete components, and other construction materials.

*Three-Year Performance History:* $1000 invested on 12/31/94 was worth $393 on 12/31/97, a 61 percent decrease in three years.

*Performance Rating:* \*\*

### Harmony Gold Mining Co., Ltd. (NASDAQ:HGMCY)
**Johannesburg, South Africa**

*Business Profile:* Harmony Gold operates gold mines, treats surface reserves, and performs other related activities including extraction, processing, and smelting.

*Three-Year Performance History:* Not available.

*Performance Rating:* \*

**Huntingdon Life Sciences Group plc (NYSE:HTD)**
**Cambridgeshire, England**
*Business Profile:* Serving the pharmaceutical and industrial-chemical industries, Huntingdon Life Sciences provides worldwide biological safety-testing and research services. The company's biological safety evaluations identify risks to humans, animals, or the environment resulting from the process of manufacturing or the use of a wide range of compounds.

*Three-Year Performance History*: $1000 invested on 12/31/94 was worth $1381 on 12/31/97, a 38 percent increase in three years.

*Performance Rating:* **

**Industrie Natuzzi S.p.A. (NYSE:NTZ)**
**Santeramo, Italy**
www.natuzzi.com
*Business Profile:* Industrie Natuzzi designs, makes, and sells contemporary and traditional leather and fabric upholstered furniture. It also sells a line of leather upholstered motion furniture.

*Three-Year Performance History*: $1000 invested on 12/31/94 was worth $1233 on 12/31/97, a 23 percent increase in three years.

*Performance Rating:* ***

**IRSA Inversiones y Representaciones S.A. (NYSE:IRS)**
**Buenos Aires, Argentina**
www.irsa.com.ar
*Business Profile:* IRSA acquires and develops rental properties in the office and retail sectors of Argentina and Brazil. The company also acquires property for development and resale in the residential real estate sector. Financier George Soros owns a 25 percent stake.

*Three-Year Performance History:* Not available.

*Performance Rating:* ***

**Ispat International N.V. (NYSE:IST)**
**Rotterdam, Netherlands**
www.ispatinternational.com
*Business Profile:* Ispat, one of the fastest-growing steel companies worldwide, produces a diverse range of high-quality semi-finished and finished steel products utilizing the integrated mini-mill process. Products sold include direct reduced iron, semifinished and finished flat products, and semifinished and flat finished long products. The company is buying Inland Steel.

*Three-Year Performance History:* Not available.

*Performance Rating:* ***

**Israel Land Development Co., Ltd. (NASDAQ:ILDCY)**
**Tel Aviv, Israel**
www.ildc.co.il
*Business Profile:* Israel Land develops real estate; owns and manages media businesses, hotels, income properties, and an insurance company; and also owns an emergency medical care service.

*Three-Year Performance History*: $1000 invested on 12/31/94 was worth $1488 on 12/31/97, a 49 percent increase in three years.

*Performance Rating:* **

**Istituto Nazionale delle Assicurazioni S.p.A. (NYSE:INZ)**
**Rome, Italy**
www.ina.it
*Business Profile:* INA, one of the largest life insurers in Italy, offers a broad range of individual life insurance and commercial non-life insurance products. The company also has one of the largest portfolios of investment real estate, consisting of a mix of commercial and residential properties primarily located in the Rome and Milan metropolitan areas.

*Three-Year Performance History:* Not available.

*Performance Rating:* ***

**Koor Industries Ltd. (NYSE:KOR)**
**Tel Aviv, Israel**
www.koor.co.il
*Business Profile:* Koor's main operations consist of telecommunications and electronics, chemicals, food, energy, and building and infrastructure materials. The company is also involved in real estate, artillery weapons, metal products, industrial, agricultural, and consumer products. The firm also provides financial and waste management services.

*Three-Year Performance History:* Not available.

*Performance Rating:* ***

**London International Group plc (NASDAQ:LONDY)**
**London, England**
www.lig.com
*Business Profile:* London International produces and markets a broad range of latex products including barrier contraceptives and surgical, household, and industrial gloves. The company is also involved in health and beauty aids and baby implements.

*Three-Year Performance History:* $1000 invested on 12/31/94 was worth $1993 on 12/31/97, a 99 percent increase in three years.

*Performance Rating:* ***

**Luxottica Group S.p.A. (NYSE:LUX)**
**Agordo (Belluno), Italy**
www.luxottica.it
*Business Profile:* Luxottica designs, manufactures, and markets high-quality eyeglass frames and sunglasses.

*Three-Year Performance History:* $1000 invested on 12/31/94 was worth $1865 on 12/31/97, an 86 percent increase in three years.

*Performance Rating:* ***

**Maderas y Sinteticos S.A. (NYSE:MYS)**
**Santiago, Chile**
www.masisa.com
*Business Profile:* Maderas y Sinteticos produces raw melamine-laminated and wood-veneered particleboard, medium-density fiberboard, and other lumber-related products.

*Three-Year Performance History:* $1000 invested on 12/31/94 was worth $395 on 12/31/97, a 61 percent decrease in three years.

*Performance Rating:* **

**Makita Corp. (NASDAQ:MKTAY)**
**Aichi, Japan**
www.makita.co.jp
*Business Profile:* Makita manufactures and services a wide range of electric power tools, such as portable woodworking and general purpose tools, stationary woodworking machines, and related accessories and parts.

*Three-Year Performance History*: $1000 invested on 12/31/94 was worth $532 on 12/31/97, a 47 percent decrease in three years.

*Performance Rating:* **

**Matav-Cable Systems Media Ltd. (NASDAQ:MATVY)**
**Netanya, Israel**
www.matav.co.il
*Business Profile:* Matav-Cable Systems Media provides broadband CATV and related telecommunications services. The company, having exclusive licenses in four operating areas, is also preparing to turn its cable infrastructure into a platform for sound, data, multimedia interactive TV, and the Internet.

*Three-Year Performance History:* Not available.

*Performance Rating:* ***

**Mavesa, S.A. (NYSE:MAV)**
**Caracas, Venezuela**
*Business Profile:* Mavesa manufactures, markets, and distributes branded consumer processed food and cleaning products. Principle products include mayonnaise, laundry soaps, and soap by-products. The company also provides technical and financial services to the agricultural sector.

*Three-Year Performance History:* Not available.

*Performance Rating:* ***

**Medeva plc (NYSE:MDV)**
**London, England**
www.medeva.co.uk
*Business Profile:* Medeva, through subsidiaries, develops and sells branded pharmaceuticals and generic products. The company also produces central nervous system and respiratory products, vaccines, and hospital products, which are sold directly to pharmacists and pharmaceutical wholesalers.

*Three-Year Performance History:* $1000 invested on 12/31/94 was worth $1134 on 12/31/97, a 13 percent increase in three years.

*Performance Rating:* ***

**Micro Focus Group plc (NASDAQ:MIFGY)**
**Newbury, Berkshire United Kingdom**
www.mfltd.co.uk
*Business Profile:* Micro Focus designs and develops programming tools and technology. It allows developers to manage and extend their enterprise applications for client/server computing, legacy maintenance and development, and Year 2000 assessment and implementation. The company also offers support and consulting services.

*Three-Year Performance History:* $1000 invested on 12/31/94 was worth $3296 on 12/31/97, a 230 percent increase in three years.

*Performance Rating:* ***

**NEC Corp. (NASDAQ:NIPNY)**
**Tokyo, Japan**
www.nec.co.jp
*Business Profile:* NEC is an international supplier of electronic products. These products are primarily comprised of communications systems and equipment, semiconductors, computers and industrial electronic systems, and electronic devices.

*Three-Year Performance History:* $1000 invested on 12/31/94 was worth $945 on 12/31/97, a six percent decrease in three years.

*Performance Rating:* ***

**Nera ASA (NASDAQ:NERAY)**
**Bergen, Norway**
www.nera.no
*Business Profile:* Nera is a supplier of telecommunications systems and equipment. The firm is the world's largest supplier of mobile satellite communications equipment.

*Three-Year Performance History:* Not available.

*Performance Rating:* **

**NetCom Systems AB (NASDAQ:NECSY)**
**Stockholm, Sweden**
www.netcom-systems.se
*Business Profile:* Through subsidiaries, NetCom provides mobile telecommunications services, international and national public telephony, Internet and data communications, and cable television.

*Three-Year Performance History:* Not available.

*Performance Rating:* ***

**NFC plc (ASE:NFC)**
**London, England**
*Business Profile:* NFC offers a wide range of logistics and transport services. Subsidiaries include Allied Van Lines. The company also offers full service leasing of commercial vehicles, truck rental, engineering services, and the full service leasing and fleet management of cars and other car service products.

*Three-Year Performance History*: $1000 invested on 12/31/94 was worth $875 on 12/31/97, a 13 percent decrease in three years.

*Performance Rating:* ***

**NICE Systems Ltd. (NASDAQ:NICEY)**
**Tel Aviv, Israel**
www.nice.com
*Business Profile:* NICE Systems designs, manufactures, and markets digital recording and retrieval systems, known as voice logging systems, that simultaneously record and monitor communications from multiple channels and provide advanced data archiving and retrieval features. These products are based on an open architecture and incorporate enhanced digital networking and voice processing technologies.

*Three-Year Performance History:* Not available.

*Performance Rating:* ***

**OLS Asia Holdings Ltd. (NASDAQ:OLSAY)**
**Wanchai, Hong Kong**
www.olsasia.com
*Business Profile:* Through subsidiaries, OLS Asia Holdings provides construction contracting, turnkey projects, and project management. The company specializes in large-scale building renovations, alterations and additions, interior design, fit-outs, commercial and retail podiums, luxury apartments, and housing estates.
*Three-Year Performance History:* Not available.
*Performance Rating:* *

**OzEmail Ltd. (NASDAQ:OZEMY)**
**Sydney, Australia**
www.ozemail.com
*Business Profile:* OzEmail provides Internet services and support. Its services range from low-cost dial-up to high-performance continuous access services integrating the company's ISDN capabilities and its consulting expertise.
*Three-Year Performance History:* Not available.
*Performance Rating:* ***

**P.T. Pasifik Satelit Nusantara (NASDAQ:PSNRY)**
**Jakarta, Indonesia**
*Business Profile:* P.T. Pasifik Satelit, expected to launch its first geosynchronous satellite in late 1998, provides communications services and is developing a satellite-based, hand-held digital mobile telecommunications systems to provide telephone and data services to subscribers in the Asia-Pacific region.
*Three-Year Performance History:* Not available.
*Performance Rating:* **

**Portugal Telecom S.A. (NYSE:PT)**
**Lisboa Codex, Portugal**
www.telecom.pt
*Business Profile:* Portugal Telecom provides domestic long distance and international telephone services. The company also offers a wide range of other telecommunications services including mobile telephone, paging, data communications, and cable television.
*Three-Year Performance History:* Not available.
*Performance Rating:* ***

**Repsol, S.A. (NYSE:REP)**
**Madrid, Spain**
www.repsol.com
*Business Profile:* Repsol, through plants, refineries, and other facilities throughout Spain, explores, develops, produces, and markets crude oil and natural gas; transports petroleum products, liquefied petroleum gas, and natural gas; and produces refined petroleum products and petrochemicals.
*Three-Year Performance History:* $1000 invested on 12/31/94 was worth $2528 on 12/31/97, a 153 percent increase in three years.
*Performance Rating:* ***

**Saville Systems plc (NASDAQ:SAVLY)**
**Galway, Ireland**
www.savillesys.com
*Business Profile:* Serving the telecommunications industry, Saville Systems creates customized customer care and billing solutions for service providers.
*Three-Year Performance History:* Not available.
*Performance Rating:* \*\*\*\*

**Select Appointments (Holdings) plc (NASDAQ:SELAY)**
**Hertsfordshire, England**
www.selectgroup.com
*Business Profile:* Select Appointments provides temporary and contract staffing services to a wide variety of businesses, professional, service organizations, and governmental agencies, as well as permanent placement, outsourcing, and training.
*Three-Year Performance History:* Not available.
*Performance Rating:* \*\*\*\*

**SELECT Software Tools plc (NASDAQ:SLCTY)**
**Gloucestershire, England**
www.selectst.com
*Business Profile:* SELECT Software develops, markets, and supports component-based modeling tools that enable users to develop high-end client/server software applications.
*Three-Year Performance History:* Not available.
*Performance Rating:* \*\*

**Senetek plc (NASDAQ:SNTKY)**
**London, England**
www.senetekplc.com
*Business Profile:* Senetek, a science-driven biotechnology company, develops technologies to provide better solutions for a broad array of aging-related health problems around the world.
*Three-Year Performance History:* Not available.
*Performance Rating:* \*\*

**SGS-THOMSON Microelectronics N.V. (NYSE:STM)**
**St. Genis Pouilly, France**
www.st.com
*Business Profile:* SGS-THOMSON, a global independent semiconductor company, designs, develops, and markets a broad range of semiconductor integrated circuits and discrete devices used in a variety of micro-electronic applications.
*Three-Year Performance History:* Not available.
*Performance Rating:* \*\*\*

**SmithKline Beecham plc (NYSE:SBH)**
**Middlesex, England**
www.sb.com
*Business Profile:* SmithKline Beecham develops and markets human pharmaceuticals, over-the-counter medicines, consumer healthcare products, and clinical laboratory testing services.

*Three-Year Performance History:* $1000 invested on 12/31/94 was worth $3087 on 12/31/97, a 209 percent increase in three years.

*Performance Rating:* ****

**Supermercados Unimarc S.A. (NYSE:UNR)**
**Santiago, Chile**
www.unimarc.cl
*Business Profile:* Supermercados Unimarc, an operator of supermarkets in Chile and Buenos Aires, offers fresh foods, specialty service departments, and a wide selection of recognized brand name and private label goods.

*Three-Year Performance History:* Not available.

*Performance Rating:* ***

**Telecomunicacoes Brasileiras S.A. (NYSE:TBR)**
**Brasilia, Brazil**
www.telebras.com.br
*Business Profile:* Telebras is the primary supplier of public telecommunications services in Brazil. The company has plans to split into 13 distinct business entities.

*Three-Year Performance History:* Not available.

*Performance Rating:* ****

**TV Azteca S.A. de C.V. (NYSE:TZA)**
**Fuentes Del Pedregal, Mexico**
www.tvazteca.com.mx
*Business Profile:* TV Azteca, the second-largest television broadcasting company in Mexico, owns and operates two national television networks in Mexico City and numerous other stations throughout Mexico.

*Three-Year Performance History:* Not available.

*Performance Rating:* ***

**Valmet Corp. (NYSE:VA)**
**Helsinki, Finland**
www.valmet.com
*Business Profile:* Valmet is a leading international manufacturer of paper and board machines, paper finishing systems, and air systems. The company also produces automation equipment, power transmissions, and automobiles.

*Three-Year Performance History:* Not available.

*Performance Rating:* ***

**Vimpel Communications (NYSE:VIP)**
**Moscow, Russia**
*Business Profile:* VimpelCom is the largest provider of cellular telecommunications services in Russia.

*Three-Year Performance History:* Not available.

*Performance Rating:* ****

**Vodafone Group plc (NYSE:VOD)**
**Berkshire, England**
*Business Profile:* Vodafone's principle business is the operation of the analog and digital cellular radio networks in the United Kingdom.

*Three-Year Performance History*: $1000 invested on 12/31/94 was worth $2358 on 12/31/97, a 136 percent increase in three years.

*Performance Rating:* ****

**WMC Ltd. (NYSE:WMC)**
**Victoria, Australia**
www.wmc.com.au

*Business Profile:* WMC's main business is the discovery, development, production, processing, and marketing of minerals, metals, petroleum, and fertilizers. Its overseas interests include mineral exploration in North and South America, the Philippines, and Eastern and Western Africa.

*Three-Year Performance History*: $1000 invested on 12/31/94 was worth $631 on 12/31/97, a 37 percent decrease in three years.

*Performance Rating:* ***

**Xeikon N.V. (NASDAQ:XEIKY)**
**Mortsel, Belgium**

*Business Profile:* Xeikon produces and sells a digital color printing system and related consumables, including toners, developers, and usage parts.

*Three-Year Performance History:* Not available.

*Performance Rating:* ***

**YPF S.A. (NYSE:YPF)**
**Buenos Aires, Argentina**
www.ypf.com

*Business Profile:* YPF, Argentina's largest company, explores, develops, and produces oil and natural gas. It also refines, markets, transports, and distributes oil and a broad range of petroleum products, petroleum derivatives, petrochemicals, and liquid petroleum gas.

*Three-Year Performance History:* $1000 invested on 12/31/94 was worth $1842 on 12/31/97, an 84 percent increase in three years.

*Performance Rating:* ***

# REFERENCES

*AAII Computerized Investing*

*AAII Journal*

*The Bank of New York ADR Index*, The Bank of New York

*Barron's*

*Bloomberg Personal*

*Business Week*

*Buyside*

*Charles Schwab Mutual Fund Select Focus*

*Currency*

*Direct*

*DM News*

*The Dow Jones Averages*, edited by Phyllis S. Pierce

*The Dow Theory*

*Dow Theory Forecasts*

*The Dow Theory: William Peter Hamilton's Track Record Re-Considered*, Steven J. Brown, William N. Goetzmann, and Alok Kumar

*DRIP Investor*

*Fidelity Focus*

*Financial Analysts Journal* (Association for Investment Management and Research)

*Financial World*

*Forbes*

*Fortune*

*Four Ways to Diversify a U.S. Stock Portfolio* by Elizabeth Bennett

*Index of Economic Freedom Rankings* by Bryan T. Johnson, Kim R. Holmes, and Melanie Kirkpatrick

*Individual Investor*

*International Herald Tribune*

*Investment News*

*Investor's Business Daily*

*Investors Chronicle*

*Journal of Accountancy*

*Kiplinger's Personal Finance Magazine*

*Los Angeles Times*

*Money*

*Morningstar Mutual Funds*

*The New York Times*

*No-Load Stock Insider*

*The Orange County Register*

Quarterly and annual reports from various companies

*Securities Industry News*

*SmartMoney*

*Sound Mind Investing*

*Standard & Poor's Stock Reports*

*Standard & Poor's Research Reports*

*USA Today*

*Value Line Investment Survey*

*The Wall Street Journal Book of International Investing* by John A. Prestbo and Douglas R. Sease

*The Wall Street Journal*

*Wall Street & Technology*

*The Whole Internet User's Guide & Catalog* by Ed Krol

*Working Woman*

*Worth*

# INDEX

# ABOUT THE AUTHOR

**Charles B. Carlson** is the individual investor's best ally. He frequently appears in the media and is a sought-after expert for interviews in *Money*, *BusinessWeek*, *The Wall Street Journal*, and other publications. Publisher of his own *DRIP Investor* newsletter and co-manager of the Strong Dow 30 Value Fund, Carlson is the author of several McGraw-Hill bestsellers that virtually triggered the individual investor revolution: *Buying Stocks Without a Broker*, *No-Load Stocks*, *Free Lunch on Wall Street*, and *Chuck Carlson's 60-Second Investor*. Carlson is a Chartered Financial Analyst (CFA) and holds an MBA from the University of Chicago.

**Chuck Carlson, author of the *Individual Investor Revolution*, invites you to receive a charter rate subscription to the *DRIP Investor*.**

Chuck's widely acclaimed, authoritative monthly service is devoted to the exploding fields of No-Load Stocks™ and dividend reinvestment plans (DRIPs).

### As a DRIP Investor subscriber ...

➤ Discover the latest breakthroughs in No-Load stock investing.

➤ Find out what companies offer dividend reinvestment plans—and how to contact them.

➤ Learn how to effectively manage your portfolio—and maximize profits.

This service is a "must-have" for anyone participating or wanting to participate, in this revolutionary method of investing.

> *"I am enjoying every copy of* DRIP Investor, *and it is just what I need. Every stock I purchase must have a DRIP. Why—because I just can't see paying a broker the fee for placing my order when there is a better way of ordering the stock. You are doing a fine job each month on* DRIP Investor. *I pick up a number of useful items from each issue. Keep up the good work!"*
>
> R.D., Redmond, OR

> *"If you want to get seriously involved in acquiring shares through DRIPs, you should ... subscribe to Charles Carlson's monthly newsletter,* DRIP Investor.*"*
>
> Terry Savage, *"New Money Strategies for the 90s."*

**See Charter Rate Coupon on next page ▌▌▌➡**

As an *Individual Investor Revolution* reader, you are entitled to receive the Charter Rate of only $59 for a full year—a savings of over 25%.

With your subscription you will also receive:

- DRIP Investor custom 3-ring storage binder, plus ...

- DRIP Starter Kit, a 32-page step-by-step blueprint for success in No-Load Stocks and DRIPs.

To take advantage of this generous offer, cut out this coupon and mail it today ... or call toll-free

# 1-800-233-5922

Money-back guarantee.
You may cancel at any time for a pro rata refund.

# CHARTER RATE

❑YES, start my subscription to *DRIP Investor* immediately at the Charter Rate of only $59 for one year, a $20 savings. Send me the FREE storage binder and 32-page DRIP Starter Kit. I understand I may cancel anytime for a pro rata refund.

_____
Name                          (Please Print)

_____
Address

_____
City                          State              Zip

Phone: (     )  _____        98XB1II8
    Area Code              Number

**Payment Method**  ❑ check or money order enclosed.

Please Charge:   ❑ VISA   ❑ MasterCard   ❑ DISCOVER   ❑ AMERICAN EXPRESS

_ _ _ _ - _ _ _ _ - _ _ _ _ - _ _ _ _
Credit Card Number

_____
Expiration Date        Signature required for credit card orders
*Not valid until accepted by:*
    **DRIP Investor • 7412 Calumet Ave. • Hammond, IN 46324-2692**
    www.dripinvestor.com    *Published by Horizon Publishing Company*

**The author of the *Individual Investor Revolution* invites you to receive Dow Theory Forecasts—at an incredibly low price.**

Start a special three-month introductory "mini subscription" to the widely read *Dow Theory Forecasts* weekly investment service for just $29.50, and receive an Individual Stock Report at no extra charge!

As a *Dow Theory Forecasts* subscriber, you will have access to . . .

➤ No nonsense recommendations in quality stocks with a solid financial future
➤ An authoritative research source—we do the "digging" for you.
➤ Crisp, concise writing style. Designed for easy, fast reading to fit your busy schedule.

**Take advantage of this special introductory offer, clip the coupon below and mail it today . . . or, for fastest service,**

**call 1-800-233-5922**

**100% Satisfaction Guaranteed. If you are not completely satisfied with your subscription, you may cancel at anytime for a pro rata refund.**

# THE LOW PRICED STOCK SURVEY

Dear Investor . . . Over the years, my BIPP stock picking system has uncovered untold numbers of stocks with built-in profit potential months (sometimes years) before their hidden value becomes public knowledge. Take advantage of this unique stock picking system by subscribing to *The Low Priced Stock Survey*. You will receive my FREE Special Report, *Finding the Stock Market Superstars of Tomorrow*. In it I'll give you the complete story about nine different kinds of stocks with built-in profit potential. Your satisfaction is guaranteed.

*Randy Roeing*

### Finding the Stock Market Superstars of Tomorrow

This $25 value Special Report explains my unique BIPP Stock Picking System in detail, including:

✔ The various kinds of Built-In Profit Potential that allow selected stocks to realize triple-digit investment gains
✔ 11 keys to determining a product's impact on share price
✔ Five things to look for when sizing up management and how each can send share prices soaring . . . and more.

> *"I have subscribed to at least two dozen newsletters over the years. The Low Priced Stock Survey is by far the best. I have made a lot of money over the years with your recommendations."* –
> Robert J. Enos

**Take advantage of this offer by mailing the coupon below or call toll-free 1-800-233-5922**

**100% Satisfaction Guaranteed. If you are not completely satisfied with your subscription, you may cancel at anytime for a pro rata refund.**

- - - - - - - - - - - - - - - - - - - - - - - -

❑ **YES,** I want to take advantage of Randy Roeing's unique stock picking system. Enclosed is my payment of $97 for a one year subscription (26 issues). I understand I will also receive FREE, Randy's Special Report, *Finding the Stock Market Superstars of Tomorrow.*

Name _____ (Please Print) _____

Address _____

City _____ State _____ Zip _____

Phone: ( ____ ) _____
   Area Code   Number

98XB1II8

**Payment Method:** ❑ check or money order enclosed.

Please charge:  ❑ VISA  ❑ MasterCard  ❑ DISCOVER  ❑ AMERICAN EXPRESS

____ ____ ____ ____ - ____ ____ ____ ____ - ____ ____ ____ ____ - ____ ____ ____ ____
Credit Card Number

_____   _____
Expiration Date   Signature required for credit card orders

*Not valid until accepted by:*

**The Survey • 7412 Calumet Ave. • Hammond, IN 46324-2692**
*Published by Horizon Publishing Company*

# Today's *Value* Investor

### Your Guide to Wall Street's Best Bargains

**Discover the Sane Alternative to an Insane Market.** Timothy Vick, financial analyst, author of *Lessons for the Individual Investor*, and editor of *Today's Value Investor*, brings you his back-to-basics approach to investing. *Today's Value Investor* is a unique newsletter devoted to finding the best undervalued stocks on Wall Street.

*Learn and profit from the investment method that produced fortunes for America's most successful investors.*

**Take advantage of this special introductory offer:**
## 6 months for only $39
*— Subscribe Now —*

**Return the coupon below, or call**
## 1-800-233-5922

**100% Satisfaction Guaranteed. If you are not completely satisfied with your subscription, you may cancel at anytime for a pro rata refund.**

---

❑ **YES**, I want to take advantage of this special introductory offer. Start my subscription immediately. Enclosed is my payment of just $39 for a six month subscription.

Name _____ (Please Print)

Address _____

City _____ State _____ Zip _____

Phone: ( ) _____
    Area Code   Number                98XB1II8

**Payment Method**  ❑ check or money order enclosed.

Please charge:   ❑ *VISA*  ❑ MasterCard  ❑ DISCOVER  ❑ AMERICAN EXPRESS

_ _ _ _ - _ _ _ _ - _ _ _ _ - _ _ _ _

Credit Card Number

_____

Expiration Date      Signature required for credit card orders

*Not valid until accepted by*

**Today's Value Investor • 7412 Calumet Ave. • Hammond, IN 46324-2692**
***Published by Horizon Publishing Company***